MACEDONIA

MACEDONIA

FROM PHILIP II TO THE ROMAN CONQUEST

René Ginouvès
General editor
Ioannis Akamatis, Manolis Andronicos, Aikaterini Despinis,
Stella Drougou, Anne-Marie Guimier-Sorbets,
Lilly Kahil, Georgia Karamitrou-Mentessidi,
Kalliopi D. Lazaridou, Dimitris Pandermalis,
Olivier Picard, Michael Sakellariou

Miltiades B. Hatzopoulos
Editor of the English edition

Princeton University Press

*To the memory
of Manolis Andronicos*

Illustrations on the first pages:

*1. Vergina, Tomb of Eurydice, about 340
BC. The burial chamber. This tomb, the
last excavated by Manolis Andronicos,
has revealed some notable aspects of
Hellenistic architecture, with its false
interior façade (the doors and windows
are simply painted) enhanced by vivid
colours, and provides an early example
of 'easel painting', with the back of the
throne treated almost as a 'picture.'*

*2. Dionysiac group in ivory. Vergina,
Tomb of the Prince, end of the fourth
century BC. The young Pan, playing the
flute, goes before a bearded man with a
jovial appearance, who could be ·
Dionysos, holding a thyrsos in his right
hand, and supported by a Maenad
(unless this is Ariadne). The modelling is
of exceptionally high quality, especially
for an object of such small dimensions.*

*3. Pella, mosaic of the Stag Hunt, central
panel, end of the fourth century BC. This
scene signed by Gnosis consists of a
pyramidal composition depicting two
confronted hunters preparing, one with a
double axe and the other with a sword,
to strike a stag which is being bitten in
the flank by a dog. The violence of their
movements causes the chlamydes to fly
up, and one of the hunters has lost his
petasos. The use of foreshortening and
shadows to render the third dimension
shows that the mosaicist has attempted
to achieve pictorial effects.*

Copyright © 1994
by Princeton University Press
Published by Princeton University Press
41 William Street
Princeton, New Jersey 08540
In the United Kingdom:
Princeton University Press
Chichester, West Sussex

Princeton University Press books are
printed on acid-free paper and meet the
guidelines for permanence and durability
of the Committee on Production
Guidelines for Book Longevity of the
Council on Library Resources

This book has been composed in Times

Printed in Greece

Translated from the original French
edition by David Hardy

LC number 93-38156

Art Director: Richard Medioni

CONTENTS

ΓΝΛΛΕΙΣΕΓΟΗ

PREFACE

It is a pleasant duty to have to thank those who have entrusted to me the conception of this work, and those who have agreed so readily to participate in its realisation. First of all, M. Goèry Delacôte, then Director of Scientific and Technical Information at CNRS. He it was who, as early as June 1989, conceived the idea of a book dealing with Greece that would meet a whole range of conditions: it would interest enthusiasts of unusual archaeological discoveries and devotees of history; it would please lovers of fine books and fine pictures and would be of use to teachers and to students; it would offer an accessible synthesis to curious readers and make available to researchers as much factual and bibliographical information as possible, particularly with regard to recent discoveries.

The subject that matched these varied and occasionally almost contradictory imperatives was at once found. Macedonia in fact has provided for about the last fifteen years, and increasingly with each passing year, an astonishing wealth of archaeological discoveries, some of which have revised our view of artistic creation in ancient Greece, and a profusion of studies in the ancient history of Macedonia. Within this vast field, I soon selected the period from the fourth century BC to the Roman conquest since, at the present time, there is no comprehensive treatment of this, even though historical research in recent years has led to all kinds of changes — illuminating in particular an artistic life of exceptionally high quality.

Once the organisation of the book had been established, and once the chronological boundaries of the enterprise had been fixed, there remained one obstacle of some size: the geographical boundaries of Macedonia changed continually, even within the relatively short span of the period chosen and, without even taking account of the exceptional phenomenon represented by the Empire of Alexander, it was decided to take into account only those sites that were part of Macedonia during the period under consideration — a simple rule, though its application nonetheless raised certain difficulties. One should not expect to find here (as sometimes in works dealing with ancient Macedonia) the art of Thasos in the Archaic period; and, of the creations of the Hellenistic period, we shall be concerned only with those of the Macedonian kingdom, even though the rulers of other Hellenistic kingdoms were also Macedonians. By contrast, space had to be found for the monuments erected by the kings of Macedonia outside their kingdom, despite the uncertainties connected with them. Finally, we have presented the history of events as it relates to the history of cultural systems, to social and economic history, and to the history of religious and artistic life, without over-fragmenting what was a unified phenomenon in a state of continuous evolution.

Despite our efforts to keep as close as possible to the current state of research and excavation, we are aware of certain weaknesses in the work: there are still too many objects, of all kinds, including even masterpieces, that have not yet been published long years after their discovery. Happily, this situation is resolving itself, and the bibliography will give the specialist a good idea of the proliferation of studies that has been a feature of recent years. Sometimes, investigation is not advanced enough for a synthesis to be presented and some selection was in any case inevitable. It was impossible, in view of the material, to study all the sites, all the monuments, all the objects — to give, for example an exhaustive list of all the 'Macedonian tombs', the conventional name given to a type of tomb that will frequently be encountered below, with a comprehensive bibliography for each.

If we feel that we have not failed in our efforts, this is thanks to the quality of the experts who have agreed to be associated with this difficult enterprise. Of the archaeologists, I shall first mention Professor Manolis Andronicos, of the University of Thessalonike, famous for the results of his excavations at Vergina; just before his death in 1991, he wrote the major chapter on the 'Macedonian tombs'. Professor Dimitris Pandermalis, of the University of Thessalonike, and director of the investigation of Dion, agreed to set forth the Hellenistic phase on his site. Professor Ioannis Akamatis, of the University of Thessalonike, has produced the section relating to his excavation at Pella; Mrs. Aikaterini Despinis has done the same for the tombs at Sindos; Professor Stella Drougou for the Hellenistic pottery; Mrs. Georgia Karamitrou-Mendessidi for the site of Aiane; Mrs. Kalliopi D. Lazaridou, who is carrying on the work of her father at Amphipolis, presents this city in the Hellenistic period. The Greek involvement in the work, however, also called widely upon historians of repute. First of all, Professor Michael Sakellariou, Fellow of the Academy of Athens, composed the fundamental chapters on Alexander, the Diadochi, and the struggle with Rome, setting events of baffling complexity in the particular perspective of Macedonia. Dr. Miltiades Hatzopoulos, historian and epigraphist, has dealt with the history of Macedonia before Philip and has prepared a whole series of valuable contributions shedding light on the institutions, the language and the sanctuaries. As for the French involvement, I shall mention, in alphabetical order, that of Professor Anne-Marie Guimier-Sorbets, whose work on the study of the Greek mosaic is well known; she has here written the valuable syntheses on Macedonian mosaic and on parietal decoration; the contribution of Professor Lilly Kahil, director of research at CNRS, on mythology, for which she was so well qualified by her role as general secretary of the *Lexicon Iconographicum Mythologiae Classicae;* finally, Professor Olivier Picard, former Director of the French School at Athens, historian and numismatist, has written the chapter on the Macedonia of Philip II, and two notes on the coinage; Professor Picard has also contributed in other ways to this work, however, in particular in discussing its conception with me. For my part, I have composed the chapter on Macedonian dedications outside Macedonia, the sections relating to the palaces of Vergina and Pella, and some pages of connecting text. It was our desire that the work should appear as though written by a single hand, even though some chapters are a combination of sections written by five or six people. But the contribution made by each one is made clear in the list of authors at the end of the book. Editorial demands have occasionally obliged us to reduce the length of the texts — I have always done so with regret. It is a pleasure to thank those colleagues who have agreed to read all or part of the manuscript and to give me the benefit of their advice. Professor G. Roux, especially, helped to clarify the section on the dedications of the Macedonian kings outside Macedonia.

RENÉ GINOUVÈS

4. *Macedonian helmet, Lefkadia, wall-painting from the Tomb of Lyson and Kallikles. The helmet is equipped with cheek-pieces, and the importance of the warrior is shown by the central plume and the two feathers at the sides.*

INTRODUCTION

5. Figure of Victory on a bronze cheek-piece found at Tymphaia, fourth century BC. Winged Nike, her spear in her right hand, advances vigorously, raising her shield very high in a movement that causes the drapery of her clothes to balloon out.

Only a few decades ago we were accustomed to look at Macedonia through the eyes of the Athenians. Hellenists preserved the echo of the passionate orations of Demosthenes against this people that he refused to accept in the Greek world. Our classical education had taught us to place the heart of Greece in southern Greece, and even then not in Boiotia, nor in Sparta, but in Athens, whose role in the development of philosophical thought, in the establishment of a certain kind of democracy, and in the creation of unrivalled artistic masterpieces, led us to judge Greek affairs, more or less consciously, as Athenians — especially since our written sources were largely Athenian.

It was also true that since the end of last century, archaeological excavations had been concentrated mainly in southern Greece, with well-known results, whereas until 1912 Macedonia had remained under the occupation of the Turks, who were not overly concerned with the development of archaeology.

Since about thirty years ago, and above all since the discovery by Manolis Andronicos of the royal tombs at Vergina from 1977 onwards, a change of perspective has taken place in favour of Macedonia. In a rather curious way, political events have assisted this movement by bringing to the head of the Greek state a personality from Macedonia, who very quickly appreciated the significance of extensive excavations in 'redressing the balance' of the archaeological geography of Greece. The whole world now knows what experts in linguistics, ethnology and history have been explaining for a long time: ancient Macedonia was fundamentally a Greek land, populated by individuals speaking a variety of Greek, and living since very early times in contact with the centres of civilisation of southern Greece, even though other influences and special conditions kept in existence ways of living that the rest of Greece was progressively abandoning. In this way, we have learned to look at Greek history also from the point of view of Macedonia — and it is

essentially from this perspective that the present volume sets out the events and the creations of the fourth, third and second centuries BC.

But this change of viewpoint is also explained and justified by the great interest attaching to the questions raised by Macedonian history, and the paradoxes it raises. The most obvious lies in the following observation: in 360 BC, when Philip II was proclaimed king of Macedonia, his country was considered barbarian by the Athenians and by many others, and had just endured a half-century of convulsions and defeats. Thirty-three years later, on the death of Alexander, Macedonia had conquered the greatest empire the West had ever known. Scholars have spoken of a 'Greek miracle'. Was not this a kind of 'Macedonian miracle'? It is in any case an astonishing sequence of events, the explanation for which we may seek in certain conditions, and by scrutinising the remarkable personalities of two men, Philip II and Alexander the Great..

Finally, another paradox, the history of Macedonia after Alexander is a succession of battles in which defeats largely outnumber victories. Every time that the kingdom was on the point of recovering real power, alliances were formed to destroy it, and this story ended soon enough in the death, at the hands of the Romans, of the kingdom of Macedonia, the first of the Hellenistic monarchies to collapse. However, these centuries of instability and misfortunes at the same time saw an astonishing flowering inside Macedonia itself and in the Macedonian kingdoms that transported the influence of Greece to the ends of the known world. And when the Macedonian kingdom disappeared, its spirit lived on in the Roman empire, which became heir to its legacy. Here too, the explanation of this paradox is to be sought in the astonishing vitality of the Macedonian achievement: it had successfully fused the diverse traditions of Greece with other riches borrowed from the conquered lands, to make of them a possession of universal value.

The rediscovery
of Macedonia

After the collapse of the ancient world, in the course of the seventh century AD, the name of Macedonia, at least in its original geographical sense[1], vanished from current usage. Only learned books and popular legends preserved the memory of it, associated with the exploits of Alexander the Great and his father Philip. It was not until nine centuries later that a first wave of lovers of antiquity began to establish a connection between the glorious tales of Macedonian history and the remains they encountered on their journeyings. Ever since that time, naturalists, missionaries, doctors, diplomatic agents, or agents of other sort, have scoured the country in order to accomplish their particular task, to be sure, but also to bend over the ancient remains.

In the forefront of these lovers of antiquity, who are usually called 'travellers', stand two eminent persons: Esprit-Marie Cousinéry, Chancellor, Vice-consul, and then Consul of France in Thessalonike, and Lieutenant-colonel W.M. Leake, secret agent of His Britannic Majesty. They have left very full descriptions of the ancient remains and the state of Macedonia at the beginning of the nineteenth century. At about the same period, the work of J.G. Droysen and other German scholars made ancient Macedonia an object of study for learned specialists.

But it was not until the opening of the archaeological schools in Athens, beginning in the middle of the nineteenth century — the French school the first of them — that a happy synthesis was achieved of these two traditions, that of the explorers in the field and that of the scholars in the study. We owe to this synthesis the first archaeological excavation on Macedonian soil, at Palatitsa, the site of the ancient capital of the kingdom, as well as that masterpiece of nineteenth-century archaeological literature, the *Mission de Macedoine* by L. Heuzey. The end of that century and the beginning of the following were marked by the massive contribution of German *Altertumswissenschaft.* Macedonia occupied a special place in theses and monographs, while profound and original historical syntheses — like that of K.J. Beloch — followed one upon the other. And, above all, systematic collections of the non-literary sources appeared.

The Great War saw the resumption of investigation on Macedonian territory, thanks to the huge presence on the Balkan front of archaeologists — professional and amateur, French and English — serving in the allied army on the Eastern Front. But even before the conflagration, the Balkan Wars, which had made it possible to detach the territories of ancient Macedonia from the Ottoman yoke and attach them almost entirely to the Greek kingdom, were to bring an end to the quasi-monopoly in archaeology exercised by the major western nations. Greek excavations were commenced very quickly on the main sites of the country: Pella, Dion, Edessa and Palatitsa-Vergina, ultimately to be identified as ancient Aigeai. Meanwhile, the Americans had brought to light Olynthos in Chalkidike, and the French, Philippoi in east Macedonia, while the Berlin Academy entrusted the editing of the corpus of inscriptions from Macedonia to the American Ch. Edson and the Scot J.M.R. Cormack. These enterprises were interrupted by the Second World War and the Greek Civil War, which raged in Macedonia until 1949.

It was only in the fifties that the abandoned sites began to be reopened. New ones were soon added to them, either by conscious decision, as at Amphipolis, or as a result of chance discoveries made during construction work in the urban centres or during deep ploughing. The uncovering of the royal tombs at Vergina by Manolis Andronicos, at the beginning of 1977, was to crown the efforts of the Greek scholars in spectacular fashion. The wealth of archaeological material had made it necessary to build a large archaeological museum in Thessalonike and several smaller museums in centres of less importance.

Two eminent scholars, the Englishman N.G.L. Hammond, who had criss-crossed Macedonia with the Greek Resistance during the German occupation, and Fanoula Papazoglou, a Yugoslav of Greek descent, succeeded in combining the known data in two monumental syntheses on the history and historical geography of ancient Macedonia.

Today, alongside the new excavations, there remains an equally enormous, and much more urgent task. The task, first, of conserving the sites and antiquities that are threatened by a process of urban development as rapid as it is unplanned, which presupposes the systematic exploration of this huge, largely unknown country.

Second, the task of study and publication of an incessantly increasing quantity of material, of which we shall soon not know the circumstances under which it was discovered. A number of collective projects, launched by the Minster of Culture with the assistance of the

6

6. *Scenery of Mount Olympos. The forest, a major source of Macedonia's economic wealth, became an instrument in her political game.*

local Ephorates of Antiquities, the University of Thessalonike and the Research Centre for Greek and Roman Antiquity, are attempting to respond to the most pressing needs: establishment of archives, site surveys, inventories of objects, publication of corpora. The systematic collection of the epigraphic material, for example, one third of which is completely unpublished, in the course of computerisation by the Research Centre for Greek and Roman Antiquity of the National Hellenic Research Foundation is renewing our knowledge of the institutions, the society and the speech of Macedonia. Did not a veteran of Greek archaeology observe, quite rightly, that 'the best excavations take place in museums'? Happily, Macedonia is also benefitting, at present, from admirably conducted excavations in the field.

1

THE EMERGENCE OF MACEDONIA

7. The excavation of
Aiane: acropolis, upper
terraces. The recent
investigation of this and
neighbouring sites has
revised our view of the
civilisation of Upper
Macedonia, which was
much more developed
and penetrated by
southern influences
than had been hitherto
suspected.

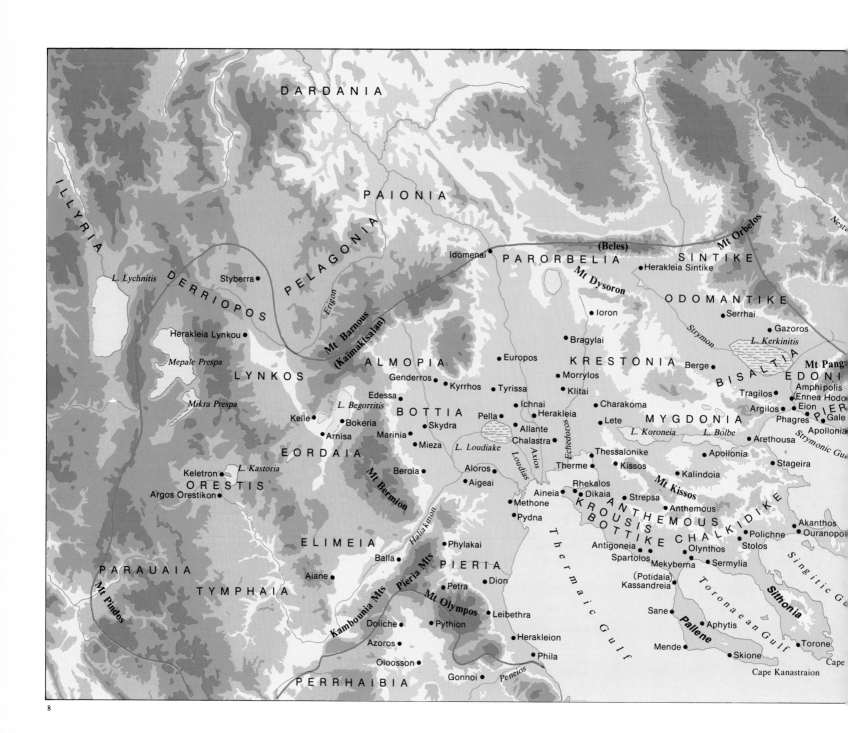

DARDANIA

PAIONIA

ILLYRIA

PELAGONIA

DERRIOPOS

L. Lychnitis Styberra •

Erigon

Idomenai • PARORBELIA (Beles) SINTIKE *Mt Orbelos* *Nest*

Hentes • Herakleia Sintike

Mt Dysoron ODOMANTIKE

Mt Barnous • Ioron *Strymon* • Serrhai

Herakleia Lynkou • (Kaïmaktsalan) • Bragylai KRESTONIA Berge • *L. Kerkinitis* • Gazoros

Mepale Prespa ALMOPIA • Europos • Morrylos BISALTIA EDONI Mt Pang

LYNKOS Genderros • • Kyrrhos • Tyrissa • Klitai Tragilos • Amphipolis (Ennea Hodo

Mikra Prespa Edessa • • Charakoma MYGDONIA Argilos • • Eion PIER

L. Begorritis BOTTIA • Ichnai • Lete *L. Koroneia* *L. Bolbe* Phagres • • Gale

Kelle • • Bokeria • Skydra Pella • Herakleia Apollonia Arethousa • Apollonia

EORDAIA • Arnisa Marinia • • Allante • Kissos • Kalindoia • Stageira

Keletron • *L. Kastoria* • Mieza *L. Loudiake* Chalastra Therme • Thessalonike • Apollonia •

ORESTIS • Beroia Aloros • Rhekalos • Mt Kissos

Argos Orestikon • Mt Bermion Aigeai • Aineia • Dikaia • Strepsa • • Anthemous

ELIMEIA Methone • KROUSIS ANTHEMOUS Akanthos

PARAUAIA Pydna • BOTTIKE CHALKIDIKE • Ouranopo

• Phylakai Antigoneia • • Polichne

Balla • *Thermaic Gulf* Spartolos • Olynthos • Stolos •

Haliakmon PIERIA Mekyberna • • Sermylia

Aiane • Petra • • Dion (Potidaia) Sithonia

TYMPHAIA Kassandreia

Kambounia Mts *Pieria Mts* Mt Olympos Leibethra • Sane • *Toronaean Gulf* *Singitic Gu*

Mt Pindos Doliche • Pythion • Aphytis •

Azoros • • Herakleion Mende • Pallene • Torone

Oloosson • • Phila • Skione Cape

Gonnoi • *Peneios*

PERRHAIBIA Cape Kanastraion

8

---

8. Physical map of Macedonia. The heart of Macedonia in the historical period, the great central plain of Bottiaia, can be seen, watered by the rivers Haliakmon, Loudias, Axios (the Vardar of the Slavs) and Gallikos, the alluvial deposits of which have significantly changed the coastline since Antiquity; and, to the south, the small plain of Pieria. Both are surrounded and protected by mountain massifs. The area covered by the dried-up lakes is indicated by horizontal blue lines; the boundary of Macedonia before the Roman conquest by a red line.

The Natural and Human Resources

The lands

There are peoples who owe their identity to a country, and countries that owe their identity to a people. If the Americans are the product of America, Macedonia, by contrast, is nothing more than the country of the Makedones. Hence the difficulty in defining it precisely in geographical terms. Throughout history, the boundaries of the country have followed the expansion of the Macedonian people, from the Pindos range in the west to the plain of Philippoi in the east, and from Mount Olympos in the south to the Axios gorge between mounts Barnous (Kaïmaktsalan) and Orbelos (Beles) in the north. We shall speak here of the country in the form it had achieved at the end of the Hellenistic period and before the Roman domination, as a result of conquest, the colonisation of lands, and the expulsion and assimilation of the 'indigenous' peoples.

Almost ninety percent of this 'historical' Macedonia falls within the present borders of Greece, of which it is the most northerly province[1] (fig. 8). It is bo unded on the south by Mount Olympos and the Cambounian mountains, on the west by the Pindos range and Lake Prespa, and on the north by Mounts Barnous and Orbelos; to the east, Macedonia proper did not extend beyond the Strymon valley down to the reign of Philip V. It is possible, though not certain, that in the very last years of Macedonian independence, the frontier extended as far as Mount Lekani, to include the plain of Philippoi. The historical process by which the geographical unit that we call Macedonia emerged thus accounts for the country's lack of unity.

The cradle of Macedonian power consisted of the large alluvial plain formed by the rivers Haliakmon, Loudias and Axios, and the smaller plain of Pieria (Katerini), along with the foothills of the mountains surrounding them: Olympos, the Pierian mountains, and Bermion and Barnous. The centre of the large plain, which was called Bottiaia or Emathia in antiquity, was occupied until the beginning of the present century by swamps and a lake (Lake Loudiake), which was connected with the sea by the river Loudias. To the west of these two plains stretched Upper Macedonia, a series of mountain massifs, each forming an independent kingdom: Elimeia on the middle Haliakmon, Orestis on the upper Haliakmon and around Lake Kastoria, and Lynkos in the present plain of Florina. With the exception of Eordaia, in the basin of lakes Begorritis and Petres, these kingdoms were only annexed by the Temenid kingdom during the course of the fourth century. Further to the west, Tymphaia-Parauaia. and Atintania, straddling the Pindos range, acted as the boundary of Macedonia, and also formed the transition between Macedonia and Epirus.

The new territories to the east of the Axios, the conquest of which was begun by Alexander I and brought to completion by Philip II, exhibit greater variety: in the centre was Mygdonia, the strip of land between lakes Koroneia and Bolbe, to the north the continental plain of Krestonia, to the south the inland regions of Anthemous, Bottike and Chalkidike, the last thrusting its three fingers deeply into the Aegean sea, and to the east of Mount Dysoron, along the river Strymon, Sintike, Bisaltia, Odomantike and Edonis.

Two major communication routes — which were to become Roman roads — lent a certain unity to this vast country. The first linked the Danube basin, via the Morava and Axios valleys, with the Thermaic gulf, and beyond it with southern Greece; the second — the famous *Via Egnatia* of the Romans — made it possible to traverse the Balkan peninsula from west to east, from the ports on the Illyrian coast, Apollonia and Dyrrachium, to Sestos or Byzantium at the gates of Asia. These two axes were royal roads, laid and measured in stades by the Macedonian administration.

To the Greeks of the south, Macedonia was an exotic country. The traveller who penetrates the Vale of Tempe to enter Pieria discovers a land the scale, if not the nature, of which is completely different. He is greeted by the permanent snows of Mount Olympos, the highest

9

10

9. *The Haliakmon near
its mouth; it flows
slowly in numerous
meanders towards the
flat coast of the
Thermaic Gulf.*

10. *The site of Edessa,
once famous for its
waterfalls, which used
to be identified with
Aigeai, the ancient
capital of the kingdom;
it dominates a plain
rich in vineyards
producing wines famous
in Antiquity, as also at
the present day.*

mountain in Greece (2917 m). Straight roads, bordered by tall poplars, lead him across vast grass-lands, watered by perennial rivers (fig. 9), whose banks are grazed not only by goats and sheep, but also by cows and — not so long ago — buffalo. Except for a strip along the coast he does not see any olive trees. As he ascends once more to the high plateaux, he encounters forests of oak, beech and even birch. Although the lion and the wild ox, once the favourite trophies of royal hunts[2], no longer frequent the hills and valleys, the deer, the lynx, the wolf and the bear still resist the attacks of hunters. Over the vast stretches of lakes Prespa and Begorritis (fig. 11) fly swans, storks and pelicans, while in their depths swarm freshwater fish.

This picture of Macedonia — which 'progress' is in the process of changing, at least in part — is probably not very different from that which met the eyes of the traveller in Classical antiquity, and we may suppose that the reactions of a modern Athenian discovering this country for the first time are not very different from those of a Demosthenes or an Aeschines.

The people

According to legend, the three brothers who founded the Macedonian kingdom were breeders of animals: the first grazed horses, the second cows, and the youngest smaller animals, sheep and goats. It was under the guidance of these last, according to other legends, that the youngest brother, who became the first Macedonian king, was to occupy the site of Aigeai, the future capital of the kingdom. These founding legends, together with parallels drawn from observation of the pastoral peoples of the modern Balkans, suggest that the first Macedonians were a group of Greek-speaking transhumant shepherds, closely related to the Thessalian Magnetes. Having, over the centuries, moved around the pastures of Mount Olympos and the Pierian mountains and the winter pastures in the plains of Pieria and Emathia, they took possession of the strategic site of Aigeai towards 700 BC and settled there.

Literary texts, inscriptions and coins all confirm that transhumant pasturing of goats and sheep, together with the breeding of cows and horses in the plains watered by the great rivers, continued to be one of the main activities of the Macedonians until the end of antiquity and beyond. Transhumance requires discipline and courage to control the movement of the animals and deal with the dangers involved. Encounters with wild beasts and hostile humans cannot have been unusual during the

11

11. A Macedonian lake. It allows us to imagine the appearance in the Hellenistic period of the lake, connected with the sea, that covered a large area of Bottiaia.

migrations across the mountain wildernesses. It was accordingly an excellent school for a nation of hunters and warriors. According to our sources, a young Macedonian was not integrated into adult society until he had killed a wild boar in the hunt and an enemy in combat.

Nevertheless, on the rich alluvial land in Pieria and Bottiaia, the Macedonians who devoted themselves to more sedentary occupations cultivated cereals, vegetables and all kinds of fruit trees. If the climate was not favourable to the olive, except in Chalkidike, the foothills in the large Emathian plain already in antiquity produced some of the best wines in the Greek peninsula (fig. 10). The rise of Macedonian agriculture is inseparable from the mastery of the natural environment. The great works designed to drain marshes by regulating watercourses, and the land-reclamation schemes undertaken by Philip II, which so impressed Theophrastus, were undoubtedly not confined to the plain of Philippoi of which he speaks. Although malaria seems to have continued to be endemic on the edge of Lake Loudiake, the

vigorous health of the Macedonian armies demonstrates that the extent of this scourge was by no means comparable with that discovered by the authorities of the French army of the East at the beginning of the present century.

The Macedonian land was not merely a source of agricultural wealth. It concealed mineral treasures, too: copper, iron and, in the eastern part, gold and silver in exceptionally large quantities for the Greek world. From the beginning of the fifth century, under Alexander I, the equivalent of one talent of silver a day was extracted from the mines of Bisaltia, while those in the territory of Philippoi brought Philip II, in the middle of the following century, the fabulous sum of over one thousand talents a year. The working of the mines, which was exclusively a royal prerogative, and the exploitation of the forests, also in the hands of the state, constituted the two foundations of the material strength of the monarchy. The importance of the forests, not only in economic, but also in political and even diplomatic terms, is revealed by the ancient authors and also by a series of inscriptions. In order to establish their hegemony, it was imperative that the Greek cities be able to secure supplies of raw materials. If Athens was dependent on the materials needed to build her navy, the Macedonian monarchs were at the same time concerned to ensure that their country retained control of this much-coveted natural wealth.

The exploitation of the mines and forests was accompanied by the development of activities related to converting and marketing the raw materials. Consequently, from its entrance into history at the beginning of the fifth century, Macedonia gives the appearance not only of a rural, but also of a partly urbanised society. Already in the reign of Alexander I the ancient authors refer to a number of urban settlements, for which they use the term *polis.* The Macedonian expansion to the east and the annexation of an ever-increasing number of colonies founded by the southern Greeks were to accelerate this movement. But if this contributed to the development of the country, it at the same time exposed the cohesion of the people and the state to serious threats.

The Macedonians were not the first inhabitants of the country to which they gave their name. The ancient authors refer to the Pieres in Pieria, the Brygoi, ancestors of the Phrygians, the mysterious Bottiaians, who allegedly came from Crete, and the inevitable Pelasgians in Emathia, the Almopi in Almopia, the Eordoi in Eordaia, the Mygdonians, the Edonians, the Bisaltai and the Krestones in the eastern part of the future kingdom. Our ignorance of the languages spoken by these groups — with the exception, in part, of the Brygoi-Phrygians — reduces them to mere names, and it is only the collection and study of the onomastic material revealed by the inscriptions that is beginning to make it possible approximately to locate and identify them.

The origin of the Macedonians themselves has, for more than a century, been the object of a lively debate, in which scientific considerations are occasionally inextricably intermingled with ulterior motives of a political nature. For a long time we lacked conclusive epigraphic evidence: the known documents were at once rare and late, inscribed at a period when the adoption of the Attic *koine*[3] had obliterated the ancestral speech of the Macedonian people. We therefore had to rely on the contradictory evidence of the ancient authors, who sometimes draw a distinction between the Macedonians and the Greeks, and sometimes insist on the common origins and common language shared by the Macedonians and the other Greeks. As for the collections of glosses, that is the rare words attributed by the ancient grammarians to the Macedonians, their marginal nature and the uncertainty of the manuscript tradition deprives them of a large measure of their credibility.

Today, the discovery, collection and publication of a large number of inscriptions, often of an early date, permits us to study proper names and technical terms that preserve phonetic and morphological features of the ancestral language. Equally, we now possess a systematic account of the differences of this language from the norms of the *koine.* It is thus possible for the first time to form a fairly precise idea of the Macedonian speech. It was a Greek dialect, intermediate between Thessalian and the northwest dialects, whose phonology had been influenced to a limited extent by the languages of the conquered peoples, in which the distinction between voiced and unvoiced consonants tended to be blurred.

Although it is true that Philip succeeded in fusing the different populations within his kingdom into a single people, the study of the onomasticon reveal that, until the conquest of Macedonia by the Romans, the military élite, and therefore the ruling strata of society, were drawn from the descendants of the conquering Greeks. In Upper Macedonia the *ethnos* (which is incorrectly translated as 'tribe', but which in reality consisted of a group established on a territory subdivided into villages) continued to be the basic political unit until the Roman period. In Lower Macedonia, in contrast, land occupation and territorial organisation was based, ever since the entrance of the country onto the stage of History at the beginning of the Classical period, on units consisting of urban centres and their surrounding territory, for which the authors use the term *polis*, with varying degrees of reservation. Although modern historians readily speak of Macedonian 'barons', feudalism is as foreign as tribalism to the social organisation of ancient Macedonia. It would similarly be improper to speak of a hereditary nobility; what we see is an aristocracy of merit, naturally inclined to reproduce itself, in the manner of any ruling class, and which might receive from the king not fiefs but land with full ownership, in recompense for services rendered.

The Rise of Macedonia

The early periods

Human occupation in Macedonia goes back to the Palaeolithic period[4]. Remains of very early phases are rare, but at least two sites have been identified, in Upper Macedonia (Palaiokastron) and especially in Chalkidike (Petralona), that attest to a human presence at least fifty thousand years old. It is from 6000 BC onwards, however, that traces of human establishments begin to multiply. The early Neolithic inhabitants of Macedonia[5] were engaged in stock-raising, mainly of goats and sheep, and practised an elementary agriculture. The excavations at Nea Nikomedia, near Beroia, the best-studied site from this period, reveal a material and spiritual culture of some sophistication (fig. 12).

The site of Servia in Upper Macedonia occupied for the Middle Neolithic period (5000-4000 BC) a position comparable to that held by Nea Nikomedia for the preceding period. The rearing of pigs and bovines seems to have overtaken that of goats and sheep. The pottery and the clay figurines attest to close contacts with the regions further south, especially with Thessaly — connections which continued and intensified in the Late Neolithic. By contrast, the sites identified in East Macedonia (Sitagroi, Dikili Tash) reveal marked affinities with the Thracian regions, during both the Middle and Late Neolithic.

The transition from the Late Neolithic to the Early Bronze Age[6] is obscure and controversial, with the dates proposed ranging from 3000 to 2400 BC. Both the organisation of the environment and the pottery confirm once again the close relations between Macedonia (or at least Central and West Macedonia) and Thessaly. The spread of this new culture may correspond with the arrival in the region of the first pre-Hellenic peoples of Indo-European origins, known mainly by the name 'Pelasgians'.

The Middle Bronze Age is very poorly known, but with the transition to the Late Bronze Age, remains become abundant in the central part of the country, between the rivers Strymon and Axios. The turn of the third to the

12. Female figurine from Nea Nikomedia, clay, Early Neolithic period, about 6000 BC. The figurine combines a series of geometric volumes with a special emphasis on the fullness of the haunches, promising fertility; it was found, with others like it, in a building interpreted as a shrine.

12

second millennium saw the arrival of groups who spoke an Indo-European dialect that would later become Greek. These were the future creators of the Mycenaean civilisation.

The Late Bronze Age raises a major problem: the question of the northern frontier of the Mycenaean world. Mycenaean pottery reached the coastal regions of central Macedonia in significant quantities, even penetrated the interior of the land along the main rivers and was soon imitated by the local workshops. All indications are, however, that the Thermaic gulf and its hinterland never formed part of an 'Achaean' kingdom. Until very recently, Thessaly was regarded as the outer limit of the Mycenaean world to the north. The discovery in recent years of Mycenaean installations in Pieria (Hagios Demetrios) and Elimeia (Aiane) is in the process of rapidly changing this picture (figs 13, 14). It is not completely out of the question that the traditional concept of a Mycenaean world cut off from Macedonia by the massif of Mount Olympos will soon have to be revised, and the northern borders of that world pushed back to the basin of the river Haliakmon.

With the transition to the Iron Age[7], about 1000 BC, the question of the relations between ethnic groups and between different types of material culture becomes an acute one. The most mysterious and exciting remains are the

13. Amphora in 'Mycenaean' style from Ano Komi, near Aiane. The discovery of an object like this in the heart of Upper Macedonia, and also the one in figure 14, demonstrates that the Mycenaean sphere of influence extended further north than had been supposed until quite recently.

14. Head of a 'Mycenaean' figurine in terracotta, also from Ano Komi. The facial details, with the wide-open eyes and expressive features, are rendered in dark brown, as is the hair.

13

hundreds of funerary tumuli in the large cemetery at Vergina, the earliest of which go back to 900 BC. Can these already be associated with the Macedonians? According to tradition, which no doubt carries a kernel of historical truth, it was the capture of the Brygian ('Brygoi' is the name given to the Phrygians of Europe) citadel of Edessa by a Temenid king, who is sometimes called Perdikkas and sometimes Karanos (*Caranus cum magna multitudine Graecorum* — Justin, following Theopompus), and his Greek followers, and the conversion of his people from transhumant shepherds into settled farmers, that constituted the act by which the Macedonian kingdom was founded. According to this same tradition, which the historian Theopompus had probably gathered from the Macedonians themselves, the first acts reckoned to have been taken by the conquerors included the substitution of the Greek name Aigeai for the Brygian name Edessa and the selection of a burial place for the members of the dynasty. As the excavations of recent years have demonstrated, this burial place was none other than the cemetery at Vergina.

From the Archaic period to the middle of the fifth century BC

Over the long centuries, the history of Macedonia amounts to a series of mythical stories concerning the kings. The small kingdom was surrounded by peoples either even more primitive (Illyrians, Paionians, Thracians, and other 'barbarians' to the north and east), or scarcely more advanced than the Macedonians themselves (Epirotes, Thessalians and other Greek *ethne* to the west and south).

Contact was made with the enterprising and dangerous Greeks of the cities only through the colony of Methone, established by the Eretrians of Euboia at the mouth of the river Haliakmon in the seventh century. From their harbour, located about two kilometres away from the fortified town, they exported high-quality timber from the Macedonian forests, a material sadly lacking in southern Greece. It was this same timber, and possibly precious metals, even at this early date, that attracted Peisistratos during his years in exile (556-546 BC) at Rhaikalos near Anthemous.

The Persian expansion in Europe, which began with the expedition of Darius against the Scythians in 512 BC, overturned the traditional balances and pitched Macedonia into the whirlwind of power politics (fig. 15). Herodotus recounts how, in 510 BC, the Persians sent an ambassador to the Macedonian court, no doubt at Aigeai, to demand submission from the aged King Amyntas I, but the heir to the throne, the young Alexander, had the insolent barbarians put to death. It was perhaps after this incident, the truth and authenticity of which have been disputed, that Alexander took part in the Olympic games, after first establishing his Greek origins before the Hellanodikai, who were encountering a Macedonian for the first time. Amyntas died in 495 BC leaving the impetuous but wily young prince on the throne. When, in 492 BC, Darius sent his general Mardonios to Europe to prepare for the campaign against the Greeks who had participated in the Ionian revolt, Alexander pretended to submit. Ultimately, however, the Persian expedition, which ended in the defeat at Marathon in 490 BC, was a naval one and thus did not pass through Macedonia.

It is possible that the attitude adopted by Alexander I towards the Persians enabled him to extend his kingdom to the Axios and impose his suzerainty on the small kingdoms of Upper Macedonia. In any event, it did not prevent him from exporting to Athens the timber which was used to build the fleet that defeated the Persians at Salamis. In recognition for his services, Athens honoured Alexander with the titles of *proxenos* and *euergetes*. This marked the beginning of a long and tumultuous relationship, compounded of attraction and distrust, between the city of Athens and the Macedonian kings.

In 480 BC, the countless troops of Xerxes' expeditionary force invaded Macedonia, drinking dry its rivers as they passed, according to Herodotus. The Macedonians, like all the peoples of northern Greece, had no alternative but to submit to the orders of the Great King. Throughout the war, however, Alexander maintained secret contacts with the Greeks. He forewarned them that their positions in the pass of Tempe risked being encircled, protected Boiotia from Persian exactions, and helped Athens to bring pressure to bear on the Spartans in order to oblige them to send an expeditionary force to mainland Greece. Finally, Herodotus reports that on the eve of the battle of Plataea, Alexander rode alone at night to the Greek camp to disclose the Persian plans and put his fellow-countrymen on their guard. What is certain is that after the victory of the Greek allies, he resolutely changed camp and harassed the Persians in retreat, inflicting heavy losses on them, no doubt at Ennea Hodoi at the

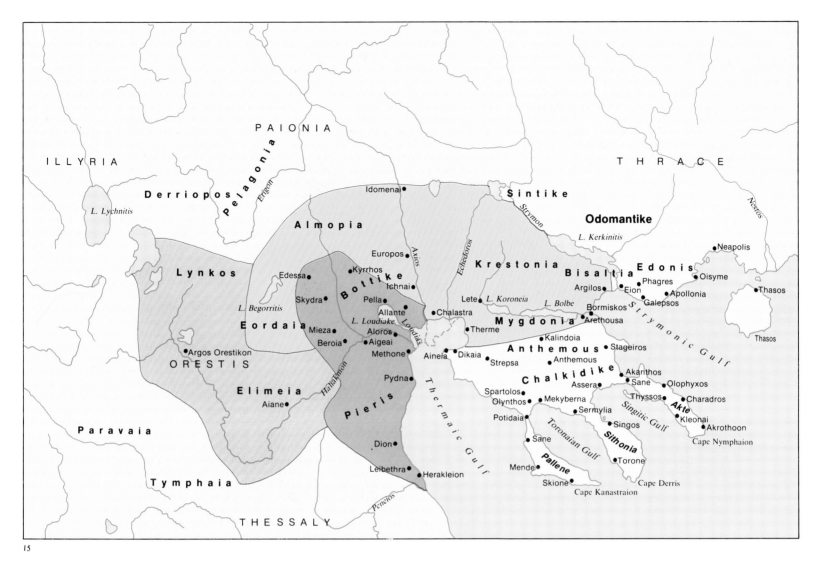

ILLYRIA

PAIONIA

THRACE

Derriopos

P e l a g o n i a

Erigon

L. Lychnitis

Idomenai

S i n t i k e

Strymon

Odomantike

L. Kerkinitis

A l m o p i a

Europos

Neapolis

K r e s t o n i a   B i s a l t i a   E d o n i s

Kyrrhos

Echedoros

Phagres

Oisyme

L y n k o s

Edessa

B o t t i k e

Ichnai

Argilos   Eion

Apollonia

Thasos

Skydra

Pella

Lete   *L. Koroneia*

Galepsos

L. Begorritis

Allante

L. Bolbe

Bormiskos

S t r y m o n i c

E o r d a i a

Mieza

L. Loudiake

Chalastra

Arethousa

M y g d o n i a

G u l f

Aloros

Thasos

Argos Orestikon

Beroia

Aigeai

Therme

Kalindoia

O R E S T I S

Methone

Aineia   Dikaia

A n t h e m o u s   Stageiros

Haliakmon

Strepsa

Anthemous

E l i m e i a

Loudias

Pydna

C h a l k i d i k e

Akanthos

Aiane

Spartolos

Assera

Sane   Olophyxos

P i e r i s

Olynthos

Mekyberna

Thyssos   **Akte**

P a r a v a i a

T h e r m a i c

Potidaia

Sermylia

Singitic Gulf

Charadros

Kleonai

Dion

G u l f

Sane

Toronaian Gulf

Singos

Akrothoon

Leibethra

Mende

Pallene

S i t h o n i a

Cape Nymphaion

T y m p h a i a

Herakleion

Skione

Torone

Peneios

Cape Kanastraion

Cape Derris

THESSALY

15

15. *The Argead*
kingdom towards the
end of the sixth century
BC (dark beige), with
the acquisitions of
Alexander I (mid-beige)
and the kingdoms that
recognised the
suzerainty of this king
(light beige).

crossing of the river Strymon. With the spoils
he erected two gold statues in the pan-Hellenic
sanctuaries at Olympia and Delphi.

The ambiguities in the policy of Alexander I
foreshadowed the line of conduct that the Macedonian kings, caught in a vice between stronger
powers, would be obliged to follow throughout
the fifth century. Alexander was undoubtedly
at one with the Greeks and desired at all costs
to have the Macedonians admitted on an equal
footing to the concert of Greek cities and
peoples. This desire is attested by his participation in the Olympic games, by his dedications at
the pan-Hellenic sanctuaries, and by his inviting
to Macedonia the most brilliant Greek minds
of his time, amongst them the poets Pindar
and Bacchylides, and the historians Herodotus
and Hellanikos.

The Persian retreat allowed Alexander to
fill the vacuum left by them and annex Mygdonia, Krestonia, Anthemous and Bisaltia, thereby advancing the eastern frontier of his kingdom to the Strymon (fig. 15). However, Athenian ambitions ran counter to his expansionist
designs in the valley of this river, so rich in
timber for the construction of ships and in precious metals. Despite this relative set-back,

however, the reign of Alexander I paved the
way for the future greatness of Macedonia.
Alexander succeeded in doubling the area of his
kingdom, modernised it by attracting entire
populations from southern Greece, and endowed it for the first time with an abundant
coinage of good quality. His fine octadrachms,
perhaps depicting the king himself, on horseback, in hunting dress and followed by his dog,
form the most eloquent testimony to his success
(fig. 18).

Coinage

The mountains between the Axios and the
Nestos were one of the major silver-bearing regions in Antiquity; this is attested by the reputation for fabulous wealth of the deposits of
Pangaion, which began to be exploited at a very
early date, particularly to make jewellery like
that found in the Macedonian necropolis at
Sindos[8]. And West Macedonia had an abundant coinage from the last quarter of the sixth
century. Money made its appearance there later
than in Asia Minor or Athens — other areas
with mines that served as models — since the
striking of coins presupposes not only a supply

of metal, but also a political organisation to impose their use. In this sphere the Macedonian and Thracian tribes, who borrowed from the cities of Ionia their system of subdivisions based on the stater divided into three *trites*, demonstrated their originality: instead of adopting coinage systems that were independent of each other, like the Greek cities, they struck a series of issues (figs 16, 17) that were distinguished by different designs (Centaur carrying off a Maenad, herdsman leading a pair of oxen, horseman taming his horse, etc.). Most of the pieces are anonymous, but some bear the names of different tribes. Although one cannot speak of a federal coinage, there was certainly a regional coinage system, connected with some of the Greek coastal cities such as Thasos, and no doubt also with the Persian empire, which was master of the region between 512 and 478 BC.

These issues ceased in the years following the second Persian War, but the system was resumed by Alexander I, who inaugurated the royal series by placing on the reverse of his coins a number of the ancient types. The silver coinage dwindled in the second half of the fifth century, but it was never abandoned and it should be stressed that, in terms of the use of coins, Macedonia was more advanced than many of the Greek cities.

In the same way, the Macedonian kings adopted bronze coinage well in advance of the others. This was known in the Black Sea area and in Italy and Sicily in the form of very heavy pieces. But a true bronze coinage with pieces of low value (which has the double advantage of relieving the strain on public finances by utilising a non-precious metal, and of facilitating the small-scale exchanges of everyday life) did not appear before the end of the fifth century.

Artistic life

From the point of view of artistic life, the Archaic and Classical periods in Macedonia seem to have been marked by a real disparity between the regions in contact with the outside world, whether the world of the East or southern Greece, and the remote areas, where influences could only penetrate with difficulty. To arrive at a properly balanced judgement, however, account must be taken also of the scanty nature of our documentation, especially in the sphere of architecture[9], though it is slowly being enriched by isolated finds and recent excavations.

We may now assume for religious architecture the existence of large-scale buildings,

16. 17. 18

16. Coin: Thraco-Macedonian stater. About 500-480 BC. The subject shows the importance of the Dionysiac myths in northern Greece.

17. Silver Thraco-Macedonian octodrachm, about 500-480 BC. Some have connected it with Aigeai, on account of the goat, the Greek word for which is at the root of the name of the city and recalls its foundation legends.

18. Silver octodrachm of Alexander I, known as the Philhellene, 495-442 BC. A horseman can be seen armed with two lances, possibly the king himself; beneath the horse is a small dog.

probably in Ionic style, as suggested by two temples whose remains have been discovered in northern Greece, not far from what was then Macedonia. The first, of which notable remains have been discovered on the site of the future Thessalonike[10], dates from the turn of the sixth to the fifth century. It must have been a structure of considerable dimensions and have had very rich decoration; the capital has volutes with no 'eye' and with a slightly convex 'canal' between them, the bottom edge of which has a curve of a slightly dry elegance. Further to the east again, the large Ionic temple at Neapolis-Kavalla[11], which is of equally high quality, probably also reflects the splendour of the Aegean and the coast of Asia Minor. A metope found at Aidonochori, near Serres, dating from the end of the century[12] and depicting a duel between hoplites, attests to an accomplished art, despite its poor state of preservation. It undoubtedly came from the decoration of another large temple, this time Doric, and its very existence reminds us that we are still far from knowing the architectural achievements that would have marked the sixth and fifth centuries in this part of northern Greece, and probably in Macedonia. The site of Aiane, as we shall see, furnishes further proof of this, and it is at the end of the sixth century that the two ancient temples of Demeter seem to have been built at Dion[13].

The temple at Thessalonike also had sculp-

tural decoration, in particular a frieze of which a charming Ionic head survives[14]. There is also evidence of sculpture in the round for this period. The most famous piece is the Kilkis *kouros*[15] from the end of the sixth century, a local representative of that long series of statues of young men that one finds throughout Greece with the faint 'Ionic' smile on their lips. It has been compared with statues from Thasos, and it certainly constitutes further evidence for an opening of northern Greece to the world of Ionia and the islands opposite. A torso of a *kouros* and a head of a *kore* have recently been discovered, this time in Macedonia proper, and even in Upper Macedonia, at Aiane.

There remains a sphere in which the vitality and the richness of Macedonian architecture before the middle of the fifth century manifested themselves. We shall have occasion to return at length to the 'Macedonian tombs' of the Hellenistic period. The tombs of the Archaic and Classical periods already attest to the importance attached to life after death and to funerary ritual. Evidence for this is supplied in particular by the cemetery at Aiane, that of Sindos, and a number of discoveries of recent years at Vergina.

Aiane

The site of Aiane, about twenty kilometres to the south of modern Kozani and just to the

19. Ionic capital found at Aiane. It reveals the transposition on this remote site in Upper Macedonia of a freely interpreted Ionic model (the egg and dart motif is replaced by rectangles).

20

north of the river Haliakmon, is located in the ancient kingdom of Elimeia, which was part of Upper Macedonia. Systematic excavations conducted since 1983 have yielded valuable evidence for a period stretching from the Neolithic to the first century before the Christian era[16]. Towards the top of the hill, on stepped terraces (fig. 7), buildings of significant dimensions were erected from the sixth century, the material from which was unfortunately reused over the centuries in the walls of the neighbouring villages. An L-shaped portico, the arms of which, built of dressed stones, measured 20 and 25 m in length, seems certainly to have formed part of an agora complex. A bronze female statue from the middle of the fifth century has come to light, as well as some column drums, Doric capitals and an Ionic capital (fig. 19), notable for the presence between the semi-palmettes of the corner-stone of four vertical rectangles, replacing the 'eggs' of the echinus.

On a slightly lower terrace, a structure 1.70 m thick and over 20 m long was probably the back wall of a colonnade (fig. 21), of which the bases of five supports have been found. The polygonal masonry was accompanied by sherds dating from the first half of the fifth century.

Amongst the finds, we may also note the presence of two inscriptions, which are amongst the earliest in the whole of Macedonia a potsherd bearing two names and two numerical signs, and the base of a vase inscribed with a name.

The organisation of this acropolis, with its terraces connected by steps cut into the natural rock and enlarged by means of retaining walls, is evidence for conscious and deliberate urban planning. The question arises whether there were any fortifications: perhaps they were amongst the first structures to be destroyed for their material, or did they perhaps coincide with the outer walls of the houses on the periphery of the settlement? Whatever the case, we are here truly in the heart of Upper Macedonia, in a genuine town with a planned urban structure and brilliant architecture — and this in the Archaic period and certainly in the first half of the fifth century, that is to say, one century before the unification of Macedonia by Philip II to which historians have hitherto attributed the foundation of the first urban centres in this part of the country.

At the foot of the hill, an Archaic and Classical cemetery has produced a whole series of tombs which, as elsewhere in Macedonia, are evidence for the importance attached to the cult of the dead. Some of them, constructed of large-scale masonry, were genuinely monu-

20. Terracotta head found at Aiane. Black lines delineate the eyebrows and the contour of the eye, and also the circular patterns on the neck; the red highlights on the cheekbones and the thick lips give the figure an Archaic charm.

21

21. Aiane, acropolis. The terrace with the stoa: The dimensions of this building and the quality of its construction indicate that there was already organised urban life on this site in the fifth century BC.

22

mental (fig. 22). This is true of one tomb, the *peribolos* of which, a square with a side of 10.50 m, enclosed a chamber with a side of 4 m. The architectural remains found nearby suggest that it was surmounted by a structure in the form of a temple. Another, slightly smaller with a *peribolos* 8 m square, has been dated to the fifth century. These tombs, together with a number of others, including some pit graves found intact and dating from the sixth century, form a quite exceptional group.

Amongst the rich grave offerings some equally notable pieces of statuary have been unearthed: a head of a *kore*, a torso of a *kouros*, and a lion. Black- and red-figure pottery indicates the importance of relations with southern Greece (fig. 20), and the economic prosperity is attested by the richness of the jewellery, especially that in female tombs: gold plaques, designed to cover the mouth of the dead, in the form of a lozenge with repoussé decoration, earrings, necklaces, gold pins, silver

bracelets, and also bronze bowls, vases, statuettes, relief terracotta plaques dated to the sixth century or the first half of the fifth, amber beads and miniature iron models of carts, like those yielded by the tombs at Sindos. Here, too, inscriptions underline the fact that the site belonged to the common culture of Greece.

The site is thus of exceptional importance for our knowledge of both history and the history of art. It enables us to dispense with the idea that Upper Macedonia was culturally isolated, and casts light on the dynamism of the economy and the vigour of the political institutions that were capable of organising the space of the dead in the same way as that of the living. Without doubt, these monumental tombs should be attributed to a royal house — the ancient texts preserve some information relating to the fifth century in this sphere — and the town on the acropolis should be considered as Aiane, the capital of the kingdom of the Elimiotes.

22. Aiane, cemetery. At the foot of the acropolis, excavation has uncovered tombs of the sixth and fifth centuries BC, some of which, judging from the size of the burial chamber, may have been royal tombs.

The tombs of Sindos

This ancient cemetery was discovered by chance near the modern village of Sindos, about twenty kilometres to the west of Thessalonike, and was excavated between 1980 and 1982. The excavations have yielded valuable information on the funerary customs of the Archaic and the beginning of the Classical period in this region[17].

The tombs, one hundred and twenty-one in number, are cist graves covered with stone slabs, or simple rectangular pits dug into the clay earth of a low hill, and were used for only one burial each. Even though only about half of them were unplundered, the wealth of their contents was impressive: objects made of terracotta, gold, silver, bronze and a few rare iron objects. A large number of these were designed specially as grave offerings, such as the miniature iron models of furniture or genuine tools, which are amongst the most interesting finds: two- or four-wheeled agricultural carts (fig. 23), three-legged tables, seats, and spits with their supports. These finds come from tombs of men, women and children alike.

Pieces of gold sheet that adorned the garments of men and women, swords, caskets, diadems, and even lozenge-shaped plaques of gold to cover the mouth of the dead, were also part of the funerary equipment (fig. 24). In five tombs — three of women and two of men — the face was covered by a gold mask, and in one case a silver mask. Elsewhere, the mask was replaced by one or more separate plaques.

The tombs of men yielded their share of military equipment: a bronze helmet (fig. 25), at least one iron sword, two spears, an iron knife, and, in four cases, a circular bronze shield. Double pins, placed in the area of the abdomen, probably fastened the himation. Quite often the dead man wore a ring, and in one case the inscription ΔΩPON ('gift') was engraved on the ellipsoidal bezel.

The female tombs of women were rich in jewellery: a pair of large shoulder pins to fasten clothing, bow fibulae to attach necklaces, small chains and other ornaments for the breast. The necklaces are made of gold elements in the form of a double axe or an inverted pyramid, of a pomegranate or a conical or biconical vase, worked in gold sheet with granulation and filigree decoration. In two tombs these necklaces were composed of amber beads. Earrings, which were a common ornament, are here of two types: one the common type, of silver in the form of the Greek letter omega, and the other the Macedonian type, consisting of a band with

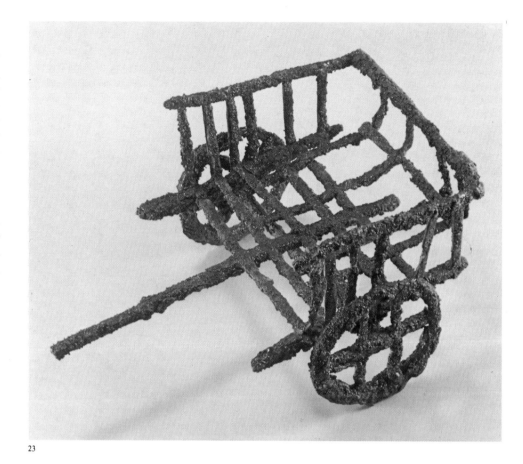

23

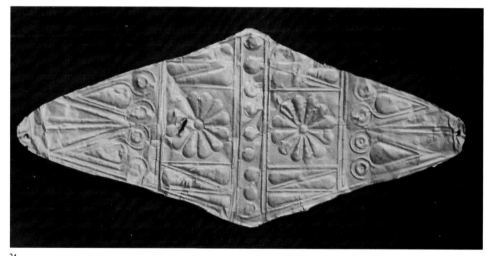

24

23. Miniature iron cart, found in a tomb at Sindos. The object reminds us of the importance of agricultural life in Macedonia.

24. Plaque in the shape of a lozenge, designed to cover the mouth of the deceased, found in a tomb at Sindos, about 540 BC. A string was passed through the hole at either end to keep the object in position.

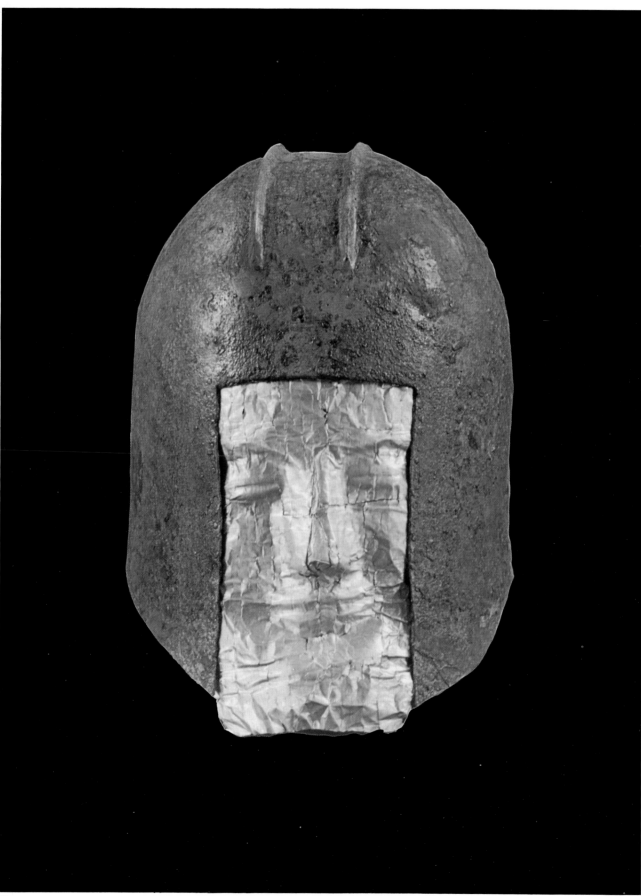

25. Gold funerary mask and bronze helmet, about 520 BC, found in a tomb at Sindos. The mask is made from a trapezium-shaped sheet of gold with repoussé decoration, to which was attached the nose-piece, modelled from a separate sheet of gold; the helmet is of Illyrian type.

an appliqué flower. The jewellery found in two female tombs is particularly impressive, made of rolled gold that encircled the head at the temples.

Bronze vases, terracotta figurines and large numbers of vases, also of terracotta, complete the offerings. With a few rare exceptions they were imported from Attic, Corinthian and Ionian workshops, attesting to the close commercial ties between the inhabitants of the region and the most important artistic centres of the period. In contrast with the pottery, however, where the local production was limited in extent, the working of precious metals was done almost without exception by local artists.

The objects recovered are not merely a mine of information on culture and art. Like those found at Aiane, they are evidence for the flourishing economy of the settlement to which the cemetery was attached, which is known by the name of 'Toumba of Nea Anchialos'. A whole series of finds from a variety of periods attests to the importance of the site, which is perhaps to be identified with ancient Chalastra.

Tombs at Vergina

Only two of the six tombs excavated to date in the Archaic and Classical cemetery at Vergina — an exceptional site, as we shall see below — were unplundered, but all of them yielded valuable information[18].

The earliest (540-530 BC) contained a large quantity of terracotta figurines (clothed *kouroi* and *korai*, and animals), Attic and Corinthian pottery, bronze vases, and gold and silver jewellery.

The second tomb (500-490 BC) was very rich. The deceased woman had been buried with her entire collection of jewellery (figs 27-31): a gold diadem, gold plaques for the hems of her garments, gold jewellery in the form of

26. Silver sandal-soles, Vergina, fourth Archaic tomb, about 480 BC. The richness of the material reflects a sumptuous life-style.

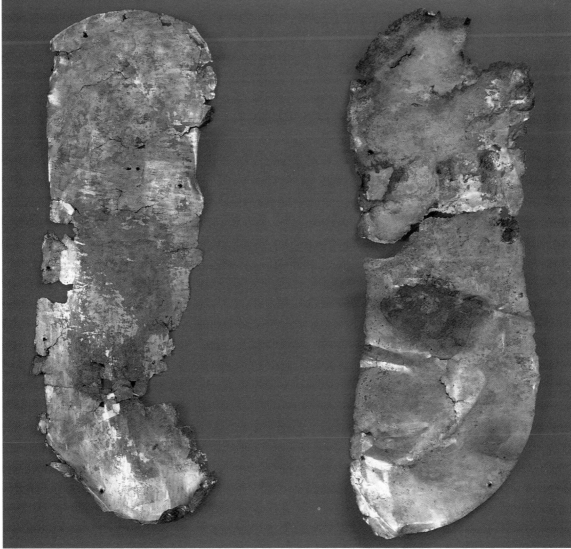

26

27

28

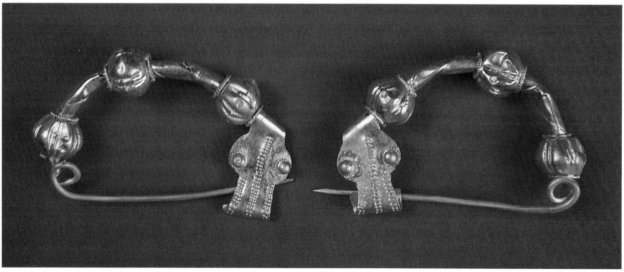

29

27. Gold earrings,
Vergina, second
Archaic tomb, about
500-490 BC. Both
filigree and granulation
techniques were used in
making them.

28. Gold pin-heads,
Vergina, same
provenance. The end of
the heads form a kind
of eight-petalled flower.
These pins were used to
fasten the dress at the
shoulder.

29. Gold fibulae,
Vergina, same
provenance. The
principle is that of the
modern 'safety pin', on
a larger scale and with
a very sophisticated
design.

30. Gold necklace,
Vergina, same
provenance.

spirals, for wearing on the head, gold clasps and pins, gold pendants and earrings, a large quantity of jewellery adorning the breast, and gilded silver sandals. At her feet were placed a bronze hydria and a silver bowl, and eleven bronze bowls surrounded the body, with six terracotta female busts. The tomb also contained an ointment-vase, an iron miniature cart and a glass *unguentarium* of Phoenician type.

The offerings contained in the third tomb (470-460 BC) must have been just as valuable, judging by the gold sandal soles, a number of bronze bowls and a few amber necklace beads that escaped the pillaging.

By contrast, almost nothing has survived from the fourth tomb (towards 480 BC), with the exception of silver soles (fig. 26) and twenty-five terracotta heads (life size), discovered in the fill covering the pit. These images (two male and two female — figs 32-35) probably depicted chthonic deities.

Of the offerings from the fifth tomb (possibly about 450 BC), all that survives is a large number of small gold roundels and two gold conical objects that are difficult to identify, which suggest the existence of other, very precious objects.

Finally, all the metal objects from the sixth tomb, which is of a later date (420-410 BC) had been stolen. Ten white-ground lekythoi were found in it, however, along with a panathenaic amphora, some marble vases, a few others in bronze, an alabastron and two ostrich eggs. The content of these tombs thus demonstrates that in the second half of the sixth and the fifth century, the tombs of the Macedonian capital, or at least the richest of them, contained offerings in great quantities and of astonishing quality, testifying to great piety towards the dead and a firm believe in life after death, and also to the existence of a social class possessed of considerable wealth.

31. Head of a woman, Vergina, second Archaic tomb, about 480 BC. This painted terracotta figure accompanied the dead woman in the tomb, as a promise of life after death.

32. Female terracotta head, Vergina, fourth Archaic tomb, about 480 BC. This figure, and those in the three following illustrations, belonged to a group found on the surface of the tomb, and which must have stood upright, in a strange evocation of the power of death.

33. Female terracotta head, Vergina, same provenance. The hair is here covered by a flat hat, the polos.

34. Male terracotta head, Vergina, same provenance. The face appears to be that of a real person and might be described as realistic, had the artist not striven above all for expressiveness.

35. Male terracotta head, Vergina, same provenance. This very evocative figure is astonishing for the period at which it was produced; it may be a representation of a menacing deity, rather than a portrait.

31

32

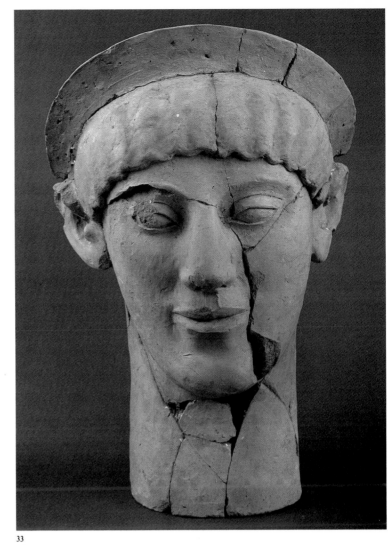

33

34

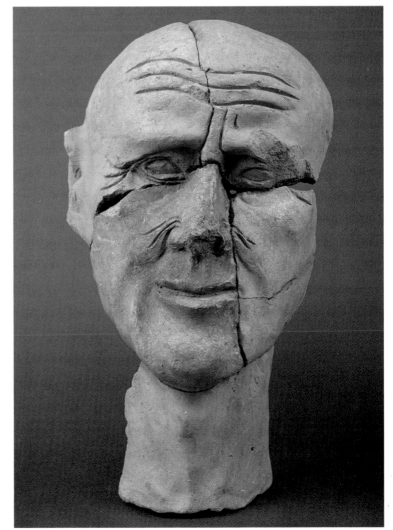

35

From the middle of the fifth century to Philip II

Alexander I died about 442 BC, leaving at least five sons. It seems, however, that it was only at the beginning of 435 BC that one of them, Perdikkas II, was able to consolidate his position at the head of the State, and then at the price of nominating his brother Philip as lieutenant general of the eastern provinces of the kingdom.

Macedonia emerged impoverished and weakened from these dynastic troubles. The kingdoms of Upper Macedonia took advantage of them to contest the Temenid suzerainty that had been imposed on them by Alexander. Athens extended her empire from the coasts of Thrace and Chalkidike to the frontiers of Macedonia. Not content with annexing the Greek cities, and even the 'indigenous' cities of the hinterland that already existed, she reinforced her presence by the founding of colonies, the most important of which, Amphipolis, rose in 437/6 BC at the mouth of the Strymon.

In response to the attempts of Perdikkas to counter this, the Athenians exhorted his brother Philip to rebel, and also the kings of the Elimiotes and the Lynkestai in Upper Macedonia. One of the immediate causes of the Peloponnesian War was to be the revolt against Athens by the cities in Chalkidike, at the instigation of the Macedonian king, who attempted in this way to loosen the vice in which his enemies, the Athenians, were trying to enclose him. Throughout the war, Perdikkas tried to perform a political balancing act, sometimes allying with the Spartans to resist the Athenians, and sometimes re-entering into alliance with the latter, when Sparta proved herself incapable of defending him. These tergiversations were to win for Perdikkas a reputation for inconstancy. Unjustly, for his sole aim was to preserve by any means possible the independence and territorial integrity of his kingdom.

Perdikkas II was succeeded on the throne by his elder son Archelaos, in 413 BC, at the very moment when the Athenian disaster in Sicily was about to smash the naval power of Athens for a long time. The principal danger that the Macedonian kings had had to face for half a century was thus removed. Archelaos could afford to be generous, furnishing the Athenians with the timber they required to reconstruct their fleet. In recognition of this, the Athenians accorded to him and to his children the titles of *proxenos* and *euergetes* of the people.

The respite on the naval front allowed Archelaos to suppress the revolt of his fine city of Pydna, turn his attention to the problems of Upper Macedonia, and intervene in Thessaly to support his friends the Aleuadai of Larisa, who also claimed to be descendants of Herakles. However, the name of Archelaos is associated not so much with these successes in the area of foreign policy as with the internal reforms of Macedonia. He endowed his country once more with an abundant coinage of good quality, and his financial resources enabled him to undertake a number of major works to construct fortresses and military roads, thereby increasing the defensive capability of the country. Finally, he improved the organisation of the cavalry and above all of the hoplite infantry, the weak point of the Macedonian armed forces.

Archelaos was not only a skilled diplomat and an innovative military commander, but also a great lover of arts and letters. His father Perdikkas had already been host to the dithyrambic poet Melanippides, and to Hippokrates of Kos. Archelaos invited to his court Zeuxis, the most celebrated painter of his time who, for an enormous fee, agreed to redecorate his palace, not at Pella, as is often stated, but at Aigeai, where the capital was still located.

The king reorganised the festival of the Olympia, held in the month of October at Dion in honour of Zeus and the nine Muses. The greatest athletes and also the finest artists of Greece came to participate in the gymnastic and musical contests, at which Euripides presented his tragedies *Archelaos* and, probably, the *Bacchae*. The king rewarded him sumptuously, made him his *hetairos*, his companion, and kept him in Macedonia until his death. Centuries later, the Macedonians were still proud of the fact that they had not returned Euripides' remains to Athens, and that they could point to his tomb in their country. Euripides was not the only poet to accept the royal hospitality: so did the great tragedian Agathon, the epic poet Choirilos, the musician Timotheos of Miletus, and perhaps the historian Thucydides. It is to the last named that the king owes his finest epitaph: 'Archelaos' he writes, 'did more for his country than all his predecessors taken together.'

The king died in 399 BC, victim either of a conspiracy or of a hunting accident, leaving as heir his son Orestes, a minor, the guardianship of whom was assumed by one Aeropos, probably a half-brother of the dead king, acting as regent. Two years later, in 398/7 BC, Aeropos removed the young king and assumed the royal title himself, remaining on the throne until his

36. 37

36. Silver diobol of Archelaos I (413-399 BC). Head of Herakles wearing the skin of the Nemean lion; on the reverse, not shown here, the forepart of a wolf devouring his prey. We shall frequently encounter references to Herakles, the legendary ancestor of the Macedonian dynasty, as, for example, in the following illustration.

37. Silver tetradrachm of Amyntas III (394/3-370 BC). Head of Herakles with the Nemean lion; on the reverse, a horse to the right. Images of horsemen and horses evoke one of the features of aristocratic life in Macedonia.

death of illness in 395/4 BC. He was followed not by his son, Pausanias, but by Amyntas II, known as 'The Little', son of Menelaos, who was a brother of Perdikkas II. Amyntas II was assassinated in the very year of his accession, and the crown reverted to Pausanias, the son of Aeropos, who was in turn assassinated in the same year, 394/3 BC, by another Amyntas (III), son of Arrhidaios and grand-son of Amyntas, another brother of Perdikkas II. All these dynastic quarrels seriously enfeebled the kingdom in the space of a few years, bringing to naught all the progress achieved during the reign of Archelaos.

From the beginning of his reign, Amyntas III (fig. 37) had to deal with the attacks of the Illyrians who, under their new chief Bardylis, began to make regular inroads into the western and northern provinces of Macedonia. At a time when the major powers of southern Greece were mobilised for the conflict known as the Corinthian War, the Macedonians could only turn for support to their traditional friends, the Chalkidian League, the foundation of which had been sponsored by Perdikkas II, and the Aleuadai of Larisa, whom Archelaos had assisted a few years earlier.

The rapprochement with the Chalkidians, however, for which the Macedonians paid with all kinds of humiliating concessions, was not enough to save Amyntas from invasion by the Illyrians. This reverse led to his deposition by the Macedonians, who elected in his place one Argaios, probably a son of Archelaos. Argaios did not remain long on the throne, however, for Amyntas was restored in 391 BC, thanks to assistance from the Thessalians. Amyntas succeeded in consolidating the north-west frontier of his kingdom, for the time being at least, by taking as his second wife Eurydice, heir to the royal house of Lynkos.

He was not at the end of his tribulations, however. In fact, the Chalkidians not only refused to return to him the border regions that he had entrusted to them temporarily at the time of the Illyrian invasions, but began to incite the cities of Macedonia to revolt against the royal power. Within a short time, the movement for independence had won a good part of the kingdom, including Pella, where Amyntas had transferred his regular residence. The king of Macedonia was finally saved by the intervention in 382 BC of the Spartans, whose assistance had been sought by other states in the region, apprehensive at the progress made by the Chalkidian League. After three years of warfare, Olynthos capitulated, the Chalkidian League was dissolved for a time, and Macedonia recovered its eastern borderlands, at least in part.

The lull, albeit temporary, on the Illyrian and Chalkidian fronts gave Amyntas the leisure to turn his attention to the south. He entered into alliance with Jason of Pherai, the new and ambitious *tagos*, leader, of the Thessalians, and acquired enough influence to arbitrate in a territorial dispute between the Elimiotes and the Perrhaiboi. Realising that the rapid decline of Sparta was making the Second Athenian Confederacy one of the main powers in southern Greece, Amyntas was reconciled with the Athenians and in this way secured for himself a place in the concert of Greek states. At the pan-Hellenic congress held at Sparta in 371 BC, a representative of the king recognised the rights of the Athenians over Amphipolis, which had become independent of its old mother city in 424 BC.

Amyntas died at an advanced age in 370 BC. In addition to the children of a first marriage, he left three sons born of his union with Eurydice: Alexander, Perdikkas and Philip. The eldest of these, who immediately ascended the throne, had already attained his majority, but his extreme youth encouraged the enemies of the dynasty to resume the war. Alexander had to face simultaneously an Illyrian invasion to the north-west and the advance in the east of the pretender Pausanias, without doubt another son of Archelaos, installed in Kalindoia with the support of the Chalkidians. Pausanias captured Anthemous, Strepsa and Therme in quick succession, and threatened the queen mother, who was shut up with her young sons in the palace at Pella. The situation was saved in the end thanks to the intervention of the Athenian general Iphikrates, who was cruising along the Macedonian coast to prepare for the recapture of Amphipolis.

Alexander took advantage of this respite to intervene in Thessaly, which was prey to civil war, in favour of the Aleuadai. His success provoked a hostile reaction from the Thebans, who had acquired a dominating position in Greek affairs after their victory over the Spartans at Leuctra in 370 BC. The Theban general Pelopidas drove the Macedonian garrisons out of Thessaly, neutralised Alexander by favouring the ambitions of his brother-in-law Ptolemy of Aloros, and obliged the young king to abandon the Athenian alliance and conclude a treaty of alliance with Thebes, and hand over his younger brother Philip as hostage.

Alexander, diminished in stature and under the thumb of the Thebans, did not remain long on the throne. He was assassinated at the insti-gation of Ptolemy, who succeeded him, acting as regent and protector of the young Perdikkas III, still a minor. These dynastic quarrels gave the Thebans, who had discovered the importance of the timber and precious metals in the region, the opportunity to invade Macedonia again and reduce Ptolemy to the role of submissive satellite of Thebes. Two years later, in 365 BC, Perdikkas achieved his majority. Ptolemy, in no hurry to relinquish power, was eliminated. The young king, reverting to the policy of his brother and his father, detached himself from the Thebans and was reconciled with the Athenians, whose general Timotheos was operating in the region at this time against Amphipolis and the Chalkidians.

Perdikkas, however, was not slow to realise that the strengthening of Athens on the north coast of the Aegean sea was not in the interests of Macedonia. The annexation of Pydna and Methone by Timotheos was proof enough of this. In 363 BC he changed camp yet again, turned against the Athenians and introduced a Macedonian garrison into Amphipolis to strengthen the defences of the city. These political tergiversations did not prevent the king from entertaining excellent relations with the most famous Athenians of his day, notably the followers of Plato, one of whom, Euphraios, stayed at Pella and exercised a great influence on the king and his entourage. The Athenian politician Kallistratos, who had fled Athens to escape death, also stayed in Macedonia and reorganised the king's customs duties.

On the whole, Perdikkas III succeeded well enough in preserving the territorial integrity and independence of Macedonia in particularly dangerous circumstances. He was to be surprised by the invasion of Upper Macedonia by the Illyrians of Bardylis, during the summer of 360 BC. The young king concentrated his forces sufficiently to confront the enemy, but the decisive meeting ended in disaster: four thousand Macedonians, including the king himself, remained on the battle field. The country was at the mercy of the barbarians, who turned to devastating the towns and plains of Upper Macedonia.

Artistic life

The period that comprises the second half of the fifth century and the first half of the fourth is marked by an increase in artistic production, which seems, at least in the present state of our knowledge, distinctly richer than in the preceding period.

It is particularly true of the city. The perfect

model of a new city is furnished by Olynthos in Chalkidike, whose history coincides with the period with which we are concerned since, founded in 432 BC, it was destroyed by Philip in 348[19]. Although it is true that Olynthos can be thought of as related to Macedonia only indirectly, even though it was created at the instigation of Perdikkas, it nevertheless supplies us with information about the level of architecture in northern Greece at this period[20].

The city is constructed on the plan known as 'Hippodamean', after the name of the architect Hippodamos of Miletus[21] — that is, with streets spaced out equally in either direction and intersecting at right angles. On the main hill, five longitudinal avenues ran from north to south, intersected by a large number of narrower streets. Each of the rectangles enclosed by two avenues and two of the narrower streets, 300 feet long and 120 wide, is itself subdivided into two longitudinally by an alley, the main purpose of which was ventilation and drainage, with a row of five houses on either side.

These houses, almost square and of roughly equal dimensions, were, in their turn, organised in the same manner: a courtyard in the southern part, bordered on the north by a portico called a *pastas,* behind which were located the private rooms, surmounted by an upper storey. Near the entrance, the *andron,* a reception room for male banquets, had a raised floor for the couches along the walls (we meet this device again in the palaces of the Hellenistic period)[22]. A shop (or a workshop) might open onto the street. Other rooms served specific purposes, one group being formed by the kitchen and the bathroom, the latter frequently equipped with a flat-bottomed tub for bathing. In this way the rooms that needed a water-supply, drainage of waste water, and the use of a hearth were all grouped together. We thus encounter, for the first time in a systematic from, a concern to differentiate and organise the rooms according to their function. Very few sculptures have been discovered at the site, but the *andron* was frequently decorated with pebble mosaics of a type that was to become widespread in Macedonia[23].

It was at this period, too, that the capital of Macedonia was transferred from Aigeai to Pella — according to some scholars, by Archelaos towards the end of the fifth century, but more probably by Amyntas III at the beginning of the fourth[24]. We shall rediscover this site in its Hellenistic condition[25], but we may note here that it had a Hippodamian plan apparently just as rigorous in conception as that of Olynthos. Other sites evolved elsewhere in the country, amongst them Dion (probably also built to a Hippodamian plan) and Amphipolis[26], the form of which we shall study later, during the Hellenistic period.

This period is also marked by a great flowering in the sphere of sculpture, as might be expected. True centres of artistic production could not emerge in ancient Macedonia[27] (any more than in other Greek regions such as Arkadia or Akarnania) as long as the economy was still essentially based on agriculture, and while the social structures were still archaic. On a grave stele found at Nea Kallikrateia in Chalkidike[28], dating from about 440 BC, a young girl, standing, her head slightly inclined, and holding a dove in her left hand, tugs with her right hand at the edge of her garment, in an attitude of noble, melancholy tenderness. This work raises a problem that applies to the whole of northern Greece: it is attributed to a Parian, but would it not rather have been executed locally?

In fact, a whole series of sculptures, throughout the second half of the fifth century, attest to Ionian influence, though they cannot be assigned to any Ionian workshop. We may therefore suppose that the tradition was borrowed and developed in northern Greece, where it assumed its own particular characteristics[29]. One recalls in particular a stele from Dion[30] in Pieria, also about 440 BC, in which the head of the young girl combines the Classicism of the rather heavy profile with traces of affectation in the hair; or again, from the end of the century this time, a grave stele from Pella, preserved in the Istanbul Museum[31]: a warrior, helmeted and carrying a spear and sword, supports himself with his right hand on his round shield, and turns to the left, which is rather unusual. On another stele from Pella[32], still from the end of the century, a child, also facing left, holds a dove, towards which a dog is raising its muzzle. The work is attributed to a local master influenced by the art of Paros. It is, rather, the mark of Attic Classicism that can be seen in a piece found at Dion, dating from the end of the fifth century and depicting a galloping horseman[33].

These creations, like those of the coin engravers, are notable from an artistic point of view but they also attest to the existence of sculpture workshops well acquainted with contemporary art, and of a clientele capable of appreciating and buying them.

2

THE MACEDONIA OF PHILIP II

38. The Lion of Chaironeia. This marble statue protected the mass tomb of the Theban soldiers who fell at the battle of Chaironeia, a decisive episode in the history of Philip II and of Greece.

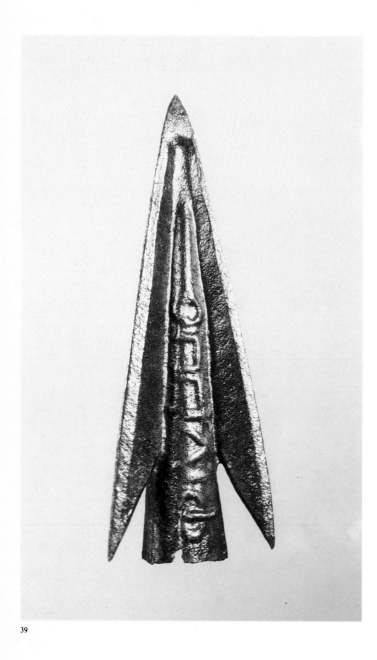

Philip II is the architect of the great kingdom of Macedonia, the man whose political achievements in Greece were to open the way for the conquest of Persia[1]. The study of this personality (fig. 40), to whom an entire historiographical tradition has, quite wrongly, attributed the crime of having assassinated the Greek city, puts the historian in a paradoxical situation: the king is scarcely known to us save through his enemies, and particularly through Demosthenes, whose diatribes have propagated the image of a barbarian (and even a bestial being) intoxicated with blood and wine, who owed his success only to the misfortune, weakness, cowardice or treason of his adversaries. In the works of Aristotle, to whom he entrusted the education of his son, and who counselled him on the settlement of Greek affairs, there are no personal indications. A single passage of the *Politics* speaks of the Macedonian royalty as a system apart, distinct both from the *basileiai* (which were hardly more than one magistracy amongst all the others) and from the Persian autocracy.

The king had several historians, amongst them Theopompus of Chios, who wrote a long series of *Philippica.* Only a few fragments of this survive, however, and we therefore have to be satisfied with the account in the *Universal History* of Diodorus Siculus, an account that is full of gaps and occasionally errors, compiled for readers who lived under Augustus. To the unusual nature of the literary tradition emanating from, or at best focussed on Athens, must be added the difficulties due to the lacunae usually associated with ancient history. However rich it may be, the contribution made by inscriptions (found mainly in southern Greece), coins and the archaeological data is by its very nature incapable of providing us with enough material to sketch the personality of the king, analyse his motives, and understand the true state of the forces in play or the level of the economy.

Accession and reorganisation of the army

It was as a result of a national disaster that the young Philip, at the age of twenty-two, was to become king of the Macedonians: in the summer of 360 BC, his elder brother Perdikkas III was killed and his army massacred by the Illyrians[2]. Macedonia was in danger of being engulfed by the evils which, since the brilliant reign of Alexander I at the time of the Persian Wars, had kept it in a weakened condition —

40. Portrait of Philip: ivory, 3.2 cm high that adorned the wooden couch in the tomb of Philip II. It almost certainly represented the king, identifiable in particular by the wound to his right eye: the ironical smile does not soften his implacable power and will.

39. Arrow-head with the name of Philip, bronze. Found at Olynthos, it calls to mind the capture of the city by the Macedonians in 348 BC: weapons marked with the name of the king in this way were probably made in a state workshop.

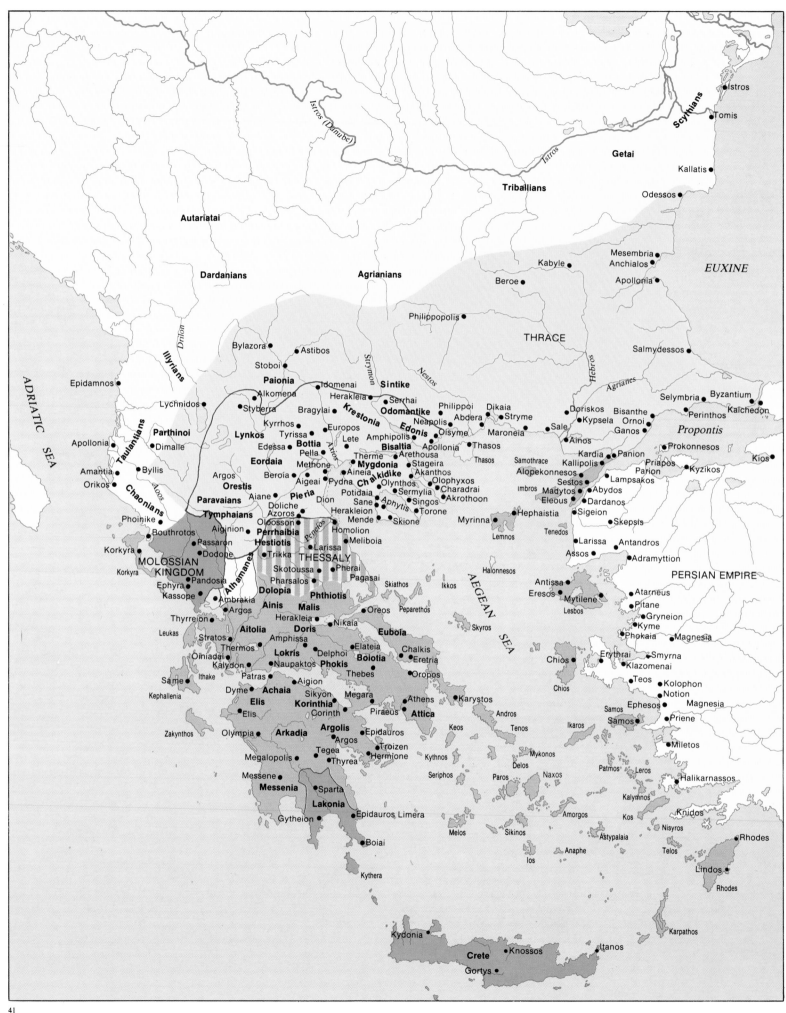

ADRIATIC SEA

EUXINE

AEGEAN SEA

PERSIAN EMPIRE

Propontis

THRACE

THESSALY

MOLOSSIAN KINGDOM

Crete

Scythians

Getai

Triballians

Autariatai

Dardanians

Agrianians

Illyrians

Taulantians

Parthinoi

Chaonians

Orestis

Paravaians

Tymphaians

Perrhaibia

Hestiotis

Dolopia

Ainis

Malis

Phthiotis

Doris

Aitolia

Lokris

Phokis

Boiotia

Euboia

Attica

Achaia

Elis

Korinthia

Argolis

Arkadia

Messenia

Lakonia

Paionia

Sintike

Krestonia

Odomantike

Edonis

Lynkos

Bottia

Eordaia

Bisaltia

Mygdonia

Chalkidike

Pieria

Athamanes

Istros (Danube)

Istros

Istros

Drilon

Strymon

Nestos

Hebros

Agrianes

Axios

Aoos

Peneios

Istros
Tomis
Kallatis
Odessos
Mesembria
Anchialos
Apollonia
Kabyle
Beroe
Philippopolis
Salmydessos
Selymbria
Byzantium
Bisanthe
Perinthos
Kalchedon
Kypsela
Ornoi
Ganos
Doriskos
Ainos
Sale
Kardia
Panion
Prokonnesos
Kios
Kallipolis
Priapos
Parion
Kyzikos
Sestos
Lampsakos
Madytos
Abydos
Eleous
Dardanos
Sigeion
Skepsis
Hephaistia
Myrinna
Antandros
Larissa
Assos
Adramyttion
Atarneus
Pitane
Gryneion
Kyme
Phokaia
Magnesia
Smyrna
Erythrai
Klazomenai
Teos
Kolophon
Notion
Magnesia
Ephesos
Priene
Samos
Miletos
Halikarnassos
Knidos
Rhodes
Lindos
Rhodes
Karpathos
Itanos
Knossos
Kydonia
Gortys
Boiai
Kythera
Epidauros Limera
Gytheion
Sparta
Messene
Megalopolis
Tegea
Thyrea
Hermione
Troizen
Epidauros
Argos
Olympia
Elis
Dyme
Sikyon
Megara
Corinth
Piraeus
Athens
Karystos
Oropos
Thebes
Aigion
Naupaktos
Patras
Kalydon
Oiniadai
Delphoi
Elateia
Chalkis
Eretria
Amphissa
Thermos
Stratos
Thyrreion
Herakleia
Nikaia
Oreos
Pherai
Pagasai
Skiathos
Peparethos
Ikkos
Halonnesos
Skyros
Antissa
Eresos
Mytilene
Chios
Andros
Tenos
Mykonos
Delos
Paros
Naxos
Keos
Kythnos
Seriphos
Siphnos
Sikinos
Ios
Anaphe
Telos
Astypalaia
Amorgos
Patmos
Leros
Kalymnos
Kos
Nisyros
Lemnos
Imbros
Samothrace
Thasos
Thasos
Ikaros
Samos
Melos
Pharsalos
Skotoussa
Trikka
Larissa
Homolion
Meliboia
Mende
Sane
Herakleion
Azoros
Oloosson
Doliche
Aiane
Dion
Pydna
Methone
Beroia
Aigeai
Argos
Edessa
Pella
Aineia
Therme
Potidaia
Olynthos
Sermylia
Aphytis
Singos
Torone
Skione
Akrothoon
Charadrai
Olophyxos
Akanthos
Stageira
Arethousa
Apollonia
Amphipolis
Lete
Europos
Kyrrhos
Tyrissa
Bragylai
Styberra
Herakleia
Serrhai
Idomenai
Alkomena
Stoboi
Astibos
Bylazora
Lychnidos
Epidamnos
Apollonia
Dimalle
Amantia
Byllis
Orikos
Phoinike
Bouthrotos
Korkyra
Korkyra
Dodone
Passaron
Pandosia
Ephyra
Kassope
Ambrakia
Argos
Aiginion
Leukas
Same
Ithake
Zakynthos
Kephallenia
Philippoi
Neapolis
Abdera
Dikaia
Stryme
Maroneia
Oisyme
Samothrace
Alopekonnesos
Tenedos
Thermaios

41

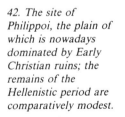

41. Macedonia and Greece at the death of Philip II. The kingdom of Macedonia and its dependencies are shown in beige; Thessaly, which was linked directly with the person of Philip, in beige with green lines; the kingdom of the Molossians, Philip's allies, in dark beige; the Greek states that were members of the Greek Confederacy in green; the neutral Greek states in pink. The boundaries of Macedonia proper before the Roman conquest are indicated by a dark grey line.

42. The site of Philippoi, the plain of which is nowadays dominated by Early Christian ruins; the remains of the Hellenistic period are comparatively modest.

the greed of the barbarian kings who surrounded the country, Illyrians to the northwest, Paionians to the north and Thracians to the east, and the rivalry of the various pretenders, descendants of earlier sovereigns, whose ambitions were sustained by these kings, by the Greek cities of the coast, and even by Athens.

Philip began by gaining time, buying the withdrawal of one party or the neutrality of another, but from 359 BC he took his revenge on Bardylis and crushed the Illyrians in his turn.

An about-turn of this nature cannot of course be attributed to chance, nor even to the king's tactical qualities alone. We should undoubtedly see here the first fruits of the military reorganisation that was to make the Macedonian army the finest in the world (fig. 39). Philip inherited an army whose main force was the cavalry of *hetairoi,* 'companions', a kind of warrior and hunting aristocracy of rich landowners closely associated with the king.

During the sole episode of his youth of which we have knowledge, his time as hostage in Thebes, whose phalanx of hoplites, or heavily armed infantry, was at that period the best in Greece, Philip was able to see for himself the superiority of these battalions. Each man was protected by his shield and that of his neighbour to the right, while his spear menaced the neck or eye of his opponent. Victory went to the phalanx which, advancing in close order on the battle field, succeeded in breaking through

the enemy front by virtue of its weight; the vanquished, having lost the protection of their neighbours, could only seek safety in flight, during the course of which many were massacred.

If the details and chronology of Philip's military reforms remain unknown, it is certain that his greatest work was the development of a national infantry. His men took the name of *pezetairoi,* 'foot companions', which associated them in a way with the prestige of the aristocracy. These men formed the king's guard, and were his favourite corps, at whose head he often charged while Alexander was fighting with the cavalry, and with whom he shared the dangers that cost him four serious wounds, including the loss of an eye during the siege of Methone.

The fate of the southern Greek colonies in northern Greece

Another problem received its definitive solution: that of the southern Greek colonies which, since at least the eighth century, had formed a belt along the Macedonian coast, organising the trade between the peoples of the interior and the Greek world. They occupied the south of Macedonia, the only area in which the olive could be cultivated along with the vine, and the region in which the richest gold and silver mines were located.

42

Two cities had acquired special importance: Amphipolis, which sealed off the lower Strymon valley and therefore access to the Serres basin and eastern Thrace, and which also controlled the east-west route via the lakes of Mygdonia and Pangaian Pieria; and Olynthos, which had succeeded in grouping the Chalkidians around itself in a powerful federation covering a good part of the rich Chalkidike. In the fifth century, these cities were protected from the hostility of the Macedonians or the Thracians by Athens, whose fleet was able to intervene in force in any place and at any time, and whose diplomacy had made Athenian support valuable to the princes of the interior. The hostility of both cities towards the Athenians, arising out of Athens' imperial past, made their situation much more precarious at the very time that the clumsiness of their interventions in Macedonian politics, particularly the support they gave to various of the pretenders in 360 BC, exposed them to vengeance of Philip. The latter was able skilfully to play the conflicting interests off against each other, giving guarantees to the Chalkidians and scheming with the Athenians to seize Amphipolis in 357 BC, where he had gained followers. In the same way, he annexed Olynthos in 349/8 BC, thanks to information from his supporters inside the city.

Amphipolis continued to exist as a city, and the epigraphic and numismatic evidence, only recently known, reveals that it retained a degree of autonomy, with a restricted bronze coinage, under the authority of one of the king's trusted confidants. It was then gradually 'Macedonised'.

At Olynthos, which had little strategic value, the excavations have attested to the violence of the destruction, confirming the testimony of Demosthenes on the wretched fate of the population, which was massacred or sold into slavery. The archaeological material demonstrates, however, that a small city continued to exist. The territory of Olynthos was divided into estates and distributed to the king's followers. This internal colonisation, many other examples of which are attested, demonstrates Philip's concern to remodel his kingdom by transfers of population and the proper exploitation of the territories acquired.

At a difficult moment, several years later, Alexander, in a rhetorical figure that is certainly not without excess, used this conquest as a an argument in favour of his recognition by his subjects: 'Philip, having found [the Macedonians] wandering and impoverished, most of them dressed in animal skins and grazing skinny flocks on the mountain slope, ... made them come down to the plains ... and made city dwellers [of them].'

A number of other Greek cities were integrated into the kingdom, without losing their identity. The Thasians, for example, also in 357 BC, had attempted to found a new city near their silver mines on the mainland, but this had provoked a reaction from the Thracians. Philip profited from their error to refound the city under the name Philippoi, thereby securing large revenues from the mines and a very strong position in the narrows where the marsh that stretched to the foot of the mountain closed off the Drama basin, though he allowed the city a large degree of autonomy.

Philip in Greece

It was thus a picture of many contrasts that the Greeks were able to form of the king at the point when the state of his forces permitted him to intervene in Greece (fig. 41): a will to domination served by a finely polished and perfectly responsive military instrument; an unbridled brutality (though this is far from describing his essential character) to smash obstacles in the way of his ambition; a lack of scruple in his choice of means, but also a good political sense that led him to spare his conquered foe if the latter could be of service in consolidating the system; a profound knowledge of the country that enabled him to seize every opportunity and profit from the weaknesses of Classical Greece.

His principal advantage lay in the fragmentation of Greece into small areas, and the antagonisms between them. These had easily been stirred up by the Persians, who had successfully worn down various cities by pretending to organise Greece to their advantage — Athens, Sparta, Thebes. Moreover, the evolution of military tactics since the Peloponnesian War had favoured the formation of permanent bands of mercenaries, ready to hire themselves out to the highest bidder. The anarchy implicit in this had reached the point where any tyrant possessed of financial means could lay claim to hegemony.

Thus, in Thessaly, the ambitions of the tyrants of Pherai were only thwarted by assassination. This region, situated immediately to the south of Macedonia, had long enjoyed close contacts with the kingdom[3], and the Thessalian aristocracy, passionately fond of horses and hunting, led a rural life that cannot have been perceptibly different from that of the Macedonian aristocracy. It is significant that the other Thessalians preferred to place themselves

43. Thessalian horseman. Stele from Pelinna, middle of the fourth century BC. This figure, with his cuirass, his helmet and his chlamys, which is flying in the wind as his horse rears, offers a happy picture of the Thessalian aristocracy, whose tastes and life style accorded well with those of the Macedonians.

44-45. *Coin of the Amphictiony after Philip's victory in the Sacred War in 346 BC. On the obverse, head of Demeter crowned with ears of corn, with a veil on the back of her head; on the reverse, Apollo seated on the omphalos: the god, leaning with his right arm on the lyre, holds a laurel branch in his left; in front of him, an oracular tripod.*

under the authority of Philip, rather than submit to the yoke of the local tyrants. They elected him (according to a procedure that is not clearly understood, but which involved the ratification of a choice already made, rather than a democratic election) *archon,* that is to say, military commander for life, whose task was to keep Pherai under control. The task was difficult, and Philip had to shoulder it on two occasions, in 353 and 352 BC, before finally crushing the opposing army, leaving 6000 men in the field and taking 3000 prisoners.

The king-*archon* exercised his authority within the framework of legal institutions. Let us take a single example: although it was long suspected that Philip had forbidden the Thessalian cities to strike coins in order to assert his authority, it has recently become clear that under his rule Larisa struck a large number of issues and did not suspend its coinage until much later. The popular discontent about which Demosthenes speculated repeatedly did not lead to revolt; on the contrary, the Thessalian cavalry played an important role in the king's army.

The Thessalian affair is closely bound up with what is perhaps the most characteristic episode in Greek history during the fourth century: the Sacred War, so-called because, the Phokians having plundered the sanctuary of Apollo at Delphi of its riches, the rest of the Amphictiony, an association of peoples who adminstered the sanctuary, rushed to the assistance of the god.

In fact, this religious screen scarcely concealed the game of local and regional internecine conflicts. The rich, independent city of Delphi aroused the jealousy of the rest of Phokis, but was itself divided between clans, of which some had support amongst the Phokians. The latter chafed at the authority that the Boiotians, their more powerful neighbours to the east, claimed to exercise over them.

The seizure of Delphi enabled Onomarchos, one of the Phokian leaders, in 356 BC to form a band capable of attacking the Boiotians, which *ipso facto* gained him the support — shameful, since it was sacrilegious — of their enemies, Athens and Sparta, and also the tyrant of Pherai. The last named appealed to Onomarchos and his Phokians, while the rest of Thessaly, leagued against him, turned to Philip. The king suffered a painful setback, but took his revenge when he massacred his enemies in the battle of the 'Crocus Field' in 352 BC.

Phalaikos succeeded his brother at the head of the Phokians and a number of mercenaries. The fate of Delphi aroused only lukewarm interest in Greece, and Phalaikos succeeded in waging war against the Thebans, not without success, until 346 BC, when the Macedonian king, victorious over the Thracians and ready to sign a peace with Athens, became convinced that in order to consolidate his position in central Greece he would have to put an end to the crisis. The Phokians responsible were exiled, the survivors were condemned to pay a huge fine, and the reorganised Amphictiony gave Philip and his Thessalians a dominating position in the administration of the sanctuary (figs 44, 45).

In the year 346 BC, the king repeated the gesture made by other aspirants to the hegemony of Greece, such as Jason of Pherai, and went to preside over the Pythian games at the head of an ostentatious delegation, a demonstration of his power designed both to offer thanks to the god and to impress the cities, in which his followers were now numerous.

The final struggle with Athens

Demosthenes now saw that Athens had no alternative but to confront the king. The city had clashed with Philip on all fronts: by supporting an ill-fated pretender, by intervening on behalf of Amphipolis and Olynthos, and in the Thracian Wars, when the king had campaigned south of Thermopylai. And on all fronts her position had been seriously breached.

Demosthenes was undoubtedly right to denounce the lack of consistency and the inadequate scale of the military commitment, and also the mistakes made by those in charge due to their constitutional position. In fact, the city's policy was determined not by an annually elected magistrate, but by an orator enjoying popular confidence, whose authority was accepted by the council and the magistrates. The leader and his principal adversary confronted each other in rhetorical combat during the great political trials. The court of the Heliaia, a popular jury of several hundred citizens which, thanks to an astute system of selection by lot, was perfectly representative of the city, then designated the candidate who was thenceforth invested authority by the majority of the citizens.

This system, gradually refined, conferred on Demosthenes, after his victory over Aeschines, the authority and continuity needed to pursue a resolute policy over a period of years, despite the annual changes of magistrates.

But if the political institutions of Athens were functioning relatively well, the same was not true of her military policy. Athens persisted in pursuing her imperial dream of the fifth century, when her fleet enabled her to control the coasts of the Aegean. As we saw at Amphipolis and Olynthos, these ambitions aroused determined opposition, from which Philip profited. His progress in Thessaly and central Greece was facilitated by the paralysis of Athens, which had to deal with the 'Social War', the revolt of her maritime allies.

The defeat of Athens in 355 BC put an end to any organisational structure in the Aegean and favoured piratical activity, which Philip was accused of supporting. The weakened city nonetheless continued to place all her hopes — and a large part of her resources — in her fleet.

Against a continental power whose strength lay in a quasi-professional army, the fleet had been able to provide valuable support, blocking the pass at Thermopylai for a first time, rendering vain the sieges of Perinthos or Byzantium, and protecting the island of Thasos, which remained to the end an Athenian ally.

It remained a fact, however, that the oarsmen could not change themselves into hoplites to face the Macedonian phalanx, and the fleet was not used during the final battle. There is something pathetic in the sight of the most brilliant, the most innovative city in Greece, prisoner of an old dream, placing most of its trust in an inappropriate military weapon.

This process cannot be attributed to Demosthenes, however. From the time of his interventions in the assembly during the siege of Olynthos, he stressed both the mortal danger represented by Philip, and the need for Athens to change policy: she should form a new kind of pan-Hellenic alliance that would have neither a domineering *hegemon* nor subject allies, and change her strategy by placing herself on the same ground as Philip. His model was Greek conduct at the time of the Persian invasion, and this is why he repeatedly compares Philip to the Barbarian.

One school of historians has reproached him for his systematic hostility and his rejection of the new order which, by putting an end to the hitherto prevailing anarchy, was to open the way, through the conquest of the Persian empire, to a glorious future for Hellenism. But this order implied the humbling of Athens and, involving as it did the triumph of a military aristocracy, the questioning of the values of the city.

In power at the beginning of 343 BC, Demosthenes put his policy into practice. Stemming the attacks of Philip in Thrace thanks to the fleet, he attempted through an unflagging diplomatic effort to set on foot a large land force with the support of the Peloponnesians (though the participation in this of the Arkadians and the Messenians led to the refusal of Sparta), and the other traditional enemy, Thebes. It was only after Philip's decision in 340 BC to enter the war and the arrival of the Macedonian forces in Phokis that Thebes consented to the alliance.

The two armies met at Chaironeia, on the western border of Boiotia, in August 338 BC. Overall, Philip possessed superior resources, in terms of men and of silver, but the outcome was uncertain. The Macedonian army had shown that it was not invincible, and the balance of forces seems to have been fairly equal. On the other hand, the Macedonian command was indisputably superior. We have no precise account of the battle (underlining again the great gaps in our information), but it is agreed that a manoeuvre by Philip, who was in command of the infantry, broke the enemy front; the Theban Sacred Band was massacred by Alexander's cavalry (fig. 38).

The Greeks had no further means of resisting Philip. He showed himself generous towards the Athenians, whose regime was not threatened (but where Demosthenes neverthe-

46

less lost his power), but less so towards the Thebans, who lost their dominating role in the Boiotian confederacy and had to accept a Macedonian garrison. Philip also put troops in Ambrakia, Chalkis and Corinth. His choices demonstrated perfect knowledge of the strategic geography of the country, for the 'fetters of Greece' assured Macedonian domination until the intervention of Rome.

The common peace and the project of a campaign against Persia

Chaironeia might have been no more than one great battle amongst others if Philip had been content to impose a form of Macedonian hegemony that could have been eroded in its turn by chance events — like the assassination of the king — and, above all, by a highly prob-

able behind-the-scenes action on the part of Persia, now conscious, albeit a little late, that the most dangerous foe had changed.

Philip's astuteness lay in deciding to construct a durable system by organising a general peace and proposing to the Greeks a legendary project — the conquest of the Persian empire — to which no one could object and which would rid Greece of the mercenary bands, thereby removing one of the causes of anarchy.

Greece had known other arbitraments in the fourth century, and other projects for a 'general peace', imposed by Persia. They had foundered because the Great King had little desire to interfere directly and contented himself with entrusting the responsibility to the most powerful city of the moment, which immediately became a victim of a coalition of its rivals.

The convening of a pan-Hellenic congress at Corinth (fig. 46) in 338 BC took place, of course, under the shadow of the Macedonian army. But it solemnly proclaimed the liberty, autonomy and territorial integrity of the contracting cities and forbade warfare between Greeks, realising an old dream of Plato. Sparta, having refused to participate, was deprived of the conquests she had made in the Archaic period, but was not otherwise threatened.

The Asian expedition was to be brought to a successful conclusion by Alexander. It was not, moreover, designed merely to flatter Greek national pride, with Philip putting a full stop to the work begun by the generation of the Persian wars —a theme constantly repeated by fourth-century writers — nor to resolve the social crisis. It was an act of political necessity, for no one could doubt that the Persian empire would wage against Philip the same kind of campaign of attrition that had enabled it to reassert its power over the Greeks of Asia Minor by weakening European Greece. Nothing of permanence could be constructed so long as Susa was able to foment trouble.

It would be a mistake, however, to consider these measures a total success. The major cities, Athens, Thebes and Sparta, were reduced to impotence, but they were chafing at the leash. Each in turn attempted vainly to shake off the yoke on the news of the death of Philip, then of Alexander.

The political reverse was, moreover, part of an inevitable economic reverse. Athens had been able to swallow the defeat of 404 BC because she had continued throughout the whole of the fourth century to be the leading Aegean port and the main centre for the redistribution of goods. Now the increase in the wealth of Macedonia, attested by the Macedonian tombs, together with the presence of a strong concentration of troops, made this region the leading consumer centre, and this constituted an inexorable threat to the role of the Piraeus.

The assassination of Philip

The reign of Philip ended, as it had begun, in a bloody tragedy. In 336 BC, the king was assassinated in the theatre at Aigeai by one of his bodyguards, while he was presiding over the unprecedented ceremonies for the marriage of his daughter to the king of the Molossians. The official version spoke of a sordid affair of morals, of 'male friendships', popular rumour of a vast political plot in which Queen Olympias, mother of Alexander, was implicated, and even Alexander himself. The criminal having been slaughtered during the course of his flight, the enigma is complete.

One aspect of the wedding ceremony deserves attention. The procession included statues of the twelve Olympian gods and a thirteenth statue, of Philip himself. This embryonic royal cult, however, which was to develop further in the Hellenistic period, played no role in the murder. On the contrary, it is clear that this elevation of the person of the king made the assassination an act of major importance in the political life of Greece, a phenomenon which was completely incomprehensible at Athens, where public life was dominated by the democratic constitution.

The solidity of the work accomplished in the space of twenty-four years by a man who departed life at the age of forty-six is still remarkable: his son Alexander was recognised as king on the very day after the murder without encountering the slightest difficulty, and two military excursions, against some barbarians and against the revolted Thebans, were enough to confirm his authority on all sides. The new state was no longer a disparate conglomeration of diverse conquests, but truly the heart of the new Greek world, as an analysis of its institutions confirms.

The political institutions

The information contained in the ancient authors about Macedonian institutions plunges modern scholars into the depths of confusion[4]. Was Macedonia a unitary *ethnos* state, or a federation of city-states? Pseudo-Skylax, in the middle of the fourth century, uses the term *ethnos*, 'people' of the Macedonians, but at the same time lists a series of *poleis*, or Macedonian cities, thus employing a term which is elsewhere used to designate, alongside the *ethnos*, the other form of independent state known in Greece. Was Macedonia an absolute monarchy, or a democratic kingship? The same Polybius who denounces the inexperience of the Macedonians in the area of democratic government, elsewhere draws attention to the 'democratic' relations between the king and ordinary Macedonians, who are never described as subjects, but as citizens. The ignorance, prejudice and hostility to which the statements in the ancient authors bear witness have left the field free for subjective modern constructions, some of which admire and others denounce ancient Macedonian institutions, frequently for reasons that have to be sought in the personality of the individual writer. The progress made by archaeology, however, and especially by epigraphy and numismatics, increasingly allows us to form a less subjective opinion, based on authentic documents rather than on personal preferences.

The Macedonian kingdom appears from its

46. Site of Corinth. It was dominated in the time of Philip, as at the present day, by the temple of Apollo, dating from the third quarter of the sixth century BC. Immediately to the south stretched the Agora, the centre of political life, in which the Macedonians would later erect a large stoa.

47

48

47-48. *Gold stater of Philip II. On the obverse, head of Apollo; on the reverse, a four-horse chariot at the gallop, an allusion to a victory of the king at the Olympic games.*

restricted by the obligation imposed on him to govern according to the ancestral custom, or *nomos,* of the Macedonians. This regulated his relations with the *ethnos,* and above all with the other members of the dynasty and his Companions — those few dozens (rather than hundreds) of Macedonians that formed his entourage, without whose support he would have been unable to rule effectively. The common people made only rare appearances during this period, notably as a last resort, punishing a king's failure by dismissing him.

The predominating position of the king was due not only to the fact that he was the political, military and religious leader of the Argeadai Makedones, who founded the kingdom of Aigeai, but that he united in his person two other capacities: he was suzerain, more or less recognised and obeyed, of the kings of Upper Macedonia, and at the same time the master of the conquered cities and territories that had not yet been colonised by the Macedonians and integrated into Macedonia proper.

Furthermore, down to the reign of Philip II, although the cities already existed alongside the central authority as administrative, if not political, units, they were nonetheless completely overshadowed by it. About 360 BC, the sanctuary at Epidauros completely ignored the cities and recognised just a single *thearodokos* for the whole of Macedonia: the king, who had his seat at Pella.

From the beginning of the reign of Alexander the Great, our documents, mainly inscriptions, reveal a radically different picture. The pan-Hellenic sanctuaries came into contact with a number of Macedonian cities. These cities possessed all the organs of the *polis* (assemblies, magistrates etc), functioned in the same way as *poleis* (passed decrees, sent out ambassadors), and seemed to be represented as *poleis* at the great concourses of the *ethnos.*

The kingdom, which henceforth comprised both Upper Macedonia and the new territories to the east as far as the plain of Philippoi, seems to have been subdivided into four administrative and military districts. The king was surrounded by a Council of Companions, friends and army generals, which took political decisions with him. The most important of these decisions were submitted for approval to the Assembly of Macedonian citizen-soldiers, which was also competent to pass judgement on capital offences and to acclaim the new king.

Is this richer institutional life due to major constitutional reforms? Does it simply reflect the exceptional conditions attending the reign of Alexander and the Diadochi? Or is it merely

birth as the state of an *ethnos,* a 'people', though one centred around a *polis*-capital, Aigeai. The expansion of Macedonia led to the inclusion within the kingdom of other groupings which from the end of the sixth century are qualified in the sources by the term *polis.* During the course of the following century, some of these detached themselves from the kingdom, when the opportunity arose, either to join other political formations (the Athenian Confederacy) as autonomous units, or in an attempt to achieve independent status.

This movement was to intensify during the first half of the fourth century, under the impulse of the Chalkidian League. For this period, we have no information, of even embryonic nature, on the civic life of these *poleis.* The sources only allow us to catch a glimpse of examples of the central power. The mainspring of this power seems to be the king (figs 47-50). His freedom of action, however, was apparently

49-50. Silver tetradrachm of Philip II. On the obverse, crowned head of Olympian Zeus, the most important god of Macedonia; the image was inspired by the famous statue of Pheidias at Olympia; on the reverse, a horseman carrying the palm of victory, an allusion here too to a victory of Philip at Olympia; between the legs of the horse, a Dionysiac kantharos.

49

50

the result of the increase in and better quality of our sources? Although one cannot deny the quantitative and qualitative leap in our documentation, the innovation represented by some of the institutions, together with the fact that they made their appearance at this period, leaves no doubt that they were the result of a deliberate reform. This is particularly true of the division of Macedonia proper into civic districts, whether we are speaking of true cities, as in Lower Macedonia, or of small *ethne* (Elimeiotai, Lynkestai, Orestai, Tymphaioi) assimilated to cities in administrative terms in Upper Macedonia; of the creation of four regions made necessary by the quadrupling in the area of the kingdom, or of the extension of participation in the assemblies of the *ethnos* and their systematisation.

Our sources expressly attribute the urban development and civic organisation of Macedonia to Philip II. In contrast, the extension to all Macedonians capable of bearing arms of the right to participate in the civic life of the *ethnos* may have been the work of Alexander the Great, if he is indeed the King Alexander who, according to one statement, extended the title of Companion to all Macedonians, whether they served on horse or foot.

Artistic life

This period of Philip II is also a period that saw the birth of a number of masterpieces of Macedonian art which are at the same time masterpieces of Greek art.

This is true for Macedonia itself, where the architectural structure known as the 'Macedonian tomb' was created. It consists of an underground chamber, accessible through a door in the façade, and vaulted. The earliest examples date from immediately after the middle of the century: the Tomb of Eurydice, discovered in 1977 at Vergina by Manolis Andronicos, dates from about 340 BC[5]. Philip himself was entombed in this type of edifice[6], the astonishing descendants of which will be discussed later[7]. We are not dealing here merely with an architectural creation, however. These tombs were also notable for the presence in them of painted decoration that provide the first examples preserved of monumental painting from Greek antiquity. This is also true of a slightly different type of tomb, the monumental cist tomb, one example of which, at Vergina, known as the Tomb of Persephone and also dating from the middle of the fourth century, preserves a masterpiece of this kind of painting[8]. Finally, these burials contained bronze, silver and gold objects of exquisite workmanship. Another sublime piece also dates from this same period: the famous bronze krater from Derveni[9].

This astonishing flowering of the arts in the reign of Philip was given expression outside Macedonia, too, through prestigious structures designed to attest boldly to the wealth and power of the kingdom. The Temenos was built on Samothrace, a masterpiece of both architecture and sculpture in which it appears that Skopas was directly involved[10]; and the construction of the Philippeion was begun at Olympia, in this case the work of Leochares[11]. The Portico of Philip II was erected at Megalopolis[12], and the portico at the Amphiareion at Oropos, which again dates from the middle of the fourth century, should also perhaps be attributed to Macedonia[13]. Philip's reign seems to have instituted an artistic policy whose brilliant results could not but inaugurate a long series of successes.

3
ALEXANDER AND THE DIADOCHI

*51. The Alexander
sarcophagus, from
Sidon, end of the fourth
century BC. The
traditional name of this
object refers to the
carved decoration, of
which a part is shown
here: at the left,
Alexander, wearing the
lion-skin on his head, is
fighting on horseback
with his cavalry, as was
his custom, against the
Persians, who are
indicated by their
oriental dress. Other
figures in the scene may
depict Demetrios
Poliorketes and
Antigonos
Monophthalmos.*

Alexander

Macedonia becomes part of a personal and multinational empire

The historical importance of the accession of Alexander (336 BC) and his Greek policy, while considerable, is yet less than that of his conquests in Asia, which had consequences with world-wide implications. The time separating these two events, moreover, was in the nature of an interlude, since the end of the preparations for the eastern campaign coincided more or less with the death of Philip, and Alexander was from that time on almost completely occupied with measures intended to protect Macedonia against possible dangers before he departed with the flower of his army.

In order to sketch Alexander's personality when, at the age of twenty, he acceded to the throne, specialists turn both to his past and to his future. On the one hand, they strive to weigh the importance in his formation of heredity, and his family, social, cultural and ideological background, and to assess the influence of Philip, who took care to prepare his son to assume his heritage. They also take into account in their analyses the character traits of Alexander after he became king. The results reflect the nature of these researches: they provide a number of more or less probable ideas, which remain more or less unprovable. Since we cannot set out all the data in the dossier, let us content ourselves with a few essential pieces of evidence.

For Alexander's education, Philip called upon the services of Aristotle; to the teenager of sixteen years he left the seal of the kingdom when he himself went off on campaign; to the young man of eighteen he entrusted the task of leading the Macedonian cavalry at the battle of Chaironeia, a task in which Alexander acquitted himself brilliantly. In the meantime, Alexander had experienced at least one Balkan campaign at the side of his father, who, on the other hand had pushed his son (like other children of the Macedonian aristocracy) into taking an interest in Asia.

The historian Theopompus, who produced an abridged version of the history of Herodotus, spent time at the Macedonian court, and Alexander, for his part, devoted himself occasionally to familarising himself with the narrative of the Father of History. We may therefore suppose that Alexander first came to know Herodotus through Theopompus' abridgement, which would have been commissioned by Philip.

Thus, at Philip's death, Alexander (fig. 52) possessed exceptional personal resources — natural gifts, certainly, but also the experience he had acquired in military affairs, and the prestige he consequently enjoyed with the nobles and the people. He was burning to undertake the campaign in Asia prepared by his father, but he began by settling the most urgent problems.

First of all, he had the people suspected, rightly or wrongly, of complicity in the assassination of Philip executed, disembarrassed himself of potential rivals, surrounded himself with loyal, competent and experienced men like Antipatros and Parmenion, and resumed the training of his army.

He was then able to turn to southern Greece. According to the terms of the treaties imposed by Philip, his successor was to assume after him the functions of president of the Thessalian League, member of the Delphic Amphictyony, and commander-in-chief of the armed forces of the Hellenic League. Alexander established his authority by crushing some slight resistance and leaving garrisons in the places provided for in the treaties concluded by his father.

Next he undertook a long campaign throughout the Balkans, winning victories in frequently difficult conditions, and thereby demonstrating his qualities as military commander to the men he would soon be leading in Asia, and discouraging the Thracians and the Illyrians from taking advantage of his absence. This, however, did not prevent the Thebans from rising against the Macedonian garrison occupying their acropolis when they learned of the death of the king — a false report swiftly belied by Alexander himself. Following an unexpected route by forced marches, he succeeded in occupying Thermopylai before the Thebans were joined by their allies, seized their city and razed it to the ground.

52. Portrait of Alexander. This ivory, 3.4 cm high, adorned the wooden couch in the Tomb of Philip at Vergina; the identification of the person depicted in it as Alexander seems almost certain: the slight turn of the neck, the gaze directed upwards, and the impassioned, dreamy expression, were all to become characteristic elements in the traditional portraiture of the king.

Before leaving for Asia, Alexander entrusted the government and defence of Macedonia and the annexed territories to the aged Antipatros, one of his father's generals. Under his command he left 12,000 infantry of the phalanx and 1,500 cavalry — almost half the effective Macedonian forces — but kept for himself the flower of the youth in the form of 12,000 infantry and 1,500 cavalry. In addition to the Macedonians, the army consisted of 7,000 infantry of the Hellenic League, 5,000 other Greek infantry, some mercenaries, 7,000 Balkan infantry, 1,800 Thessalian cavalry, 600 cavalry of the Hellenic League, 900 Balkan cavalry and 1,000 archers: in all, 32,000 infantry and 4,400 cavalry.

Alexander's expedition takes us far outside the bounds of Macedonian history. It was not dictated by national necessity, but by factors of a personal nature. Decided upon by Philip as a pan-Hellenic project[1], it was essentially Alexander's own work and can only be accounted for by certain aspects of his character and beliefs. It was he who drew his army further and further into the immense depths of Asia. The military exploits achieved by his troops would have been impossible without his exceptional gifts as a tactician and leader of men (fig. 51). Within a few months he took possession of Asia Minor, routed Darius himself (Issos, 333 BC), razed Tyre, was welcomed as a liberator in Egypt, crushed the Great King at Arbela (331 BC), conquered Babylon, Susa and Persepolis, and reached the Indus.

Thenceforth Alexander shook off the appearance of a Macedonian king and began to be seen and to act as an oriental despot, even towards the Macedonians, who showed their disapproval. Worse still, far from annexing the conquered lands to the Macedonian state, he laid the foundations of a personal and multinational empire. His personality, the immensity of the task he accomplished, and the consequences of his conquests for a large part of humanity, all make Alexander a unique historical figure in antiquity (figs 53, 54). The history of Macedonia, however, was itself affected by the Asian expedition, and on more than one count. On the one hand, Alexander, his generals and his soldiers were the main force of the Macedonian nation; on the other, the political initiatives taken by the king transformed the Macedonian constitution and integrated Macedonia into a system that broadly transcended the traditional geographical, national and political boundaries. These changes are a real part of Macedonian history in the years 334-323 BC.

The Macedonian state consisted, as we have

53

54

seen[2], of the king and the 'Macedonians', that is, the men of the Macedonian nation, who were politically active when they were gathered together as the assembly. The campaign in Asia created a new institutional situation.

On the one hand, the 'Macedonians' were now of necessity divided into two groups, since some of them stayed in Macedonia while others went on campaign. On the other hand, since power was exercised wherever the king and the assembly were, it shifted from the capital of the kingdom to the successive military encampments. Finally, Alexander was drawn into taking, without the knowledge of the 'Macedonians' who were following him, and even against their wishes, decisions that modified the institutional *status quo,* strengthening the rights of the crown against those of the 'Macedonians'.

A number of Alexander's initiatives went even further, since they made the sovereign master of an empire whose tendency was to absorb the Macedonian state. After his entry into the country of the Parthians in the autumn of 330 BC, Alexander revealed unambiguously his desire to become an Asiatic king: from this time on he wore state dress, following the Persian royal fashion, though avoiding clothes that the Greeks found strange, and even barbarian. Though he did not wear a tiara, preferring instead a diadem, the etiquette of the Persian court was followed at his audiences, and visitors were encouraged to prostrate themselves (*proskynesis*) before receiving from the king the favour of an embrace. However, Alexander was to proceed by stages. He only appeared in his new dress in private, and desisted for a time from demanding *proskynesis* of his companions, knowing full well that they, like all Greeks, saw in this gesture a homage reserved by free men for the gods alone: if rendered to a king, it would make them slaves honouring a despot. But Alexander had his heart set on this constraint and persisted in his efforts to impose it. Only the resistance of his fellow Macedonians and other Greeks made him abandon it.

By demanding of his soldiers that they honour him as befitted an Asiatic despot, he gave notice that he no longer intended to be just the King of the Macedonians, and that their state would be effectively, if not formally, integrated into the empire he had created. In the same spirit, Alexander restored a number of satraps, as early as 330 BC, to the functions they had carried out under Darius, another measure intended to ensure the effective functioning of the administration. But, in 327 BC, he ordained that 30,000 young Persians should receive Macedonian military training and learn Greek. They were called upon to serve in the army alongside the Macedonians and to form a reserve of future officers, administrators and court dignitaries.

Three years later, the king decreed that they be enlisted to replace the aged or wounded Macedonians who were returning home, a decision that was one of the causes of the mutiny at Opis. However, Alexander's ascendancy over his army was such that his men, overcome with remorse, had to give in. The king seized the opportunity and invited 9,000 guests, Macedonians, Persians and others, to a banquet of reconciliation. Significantly, the Macedonians were seated nearest to their king, and the Iranians were given the next places. The appropriate rites were conducted by Greek priests and Persian magi, and all the guests together poured a libation and sang the victory song. Then Alexander said a prayer for 'all sorts of blessings, and especially for harmony and fellowship in the empire between Macedonians and Persians'. The king undoubtedly desired his empire to be multinational, though organised around the Macedonians and the Persians, and that all the peoples in it should live in harmony. The idea of power-sharing should not be taken literally, however, since all authority ultimately belonged to Alexander. He simply wished to remind them that the Macedonians and the Persians were to enjoy the same rights. Once the principle of equality in political and judicial affairs was established, Alexander turned himself to uniting the élite of the two peoples in bonds of matrimony.

For the empire to be governed, or even securely held, there was need, for obvious strategic and administrative reasons, for a capital occupying a central position that was at the same time close to the greatest concentration of the sources of provisions and finance. Babylon offered every advantage, and the king gave it his preference. The Macedonian capital, Pella, thus lost its prominence, and at the same time Macedonia found itself on the periphery of the empire. The soldiers had no delusions about this, realising that Alexander was in this way deciding to establish the centre of the kingdom in Asia forever.

But in 323 BC, after a few days of agony, Alexander died at Babylon, at less than thirty-three years of age, in circumstances that are not entirely clear. In a little over a dozen years' rule he had changed the face of the world.

The Diadochi

From 323 to 276 BC.
The fate of Macedonia
in the balance

Alexander's empire proceeded from his will alone, and depended on his person alone. His premature death therefore led to the abandonment of both the character and the structure that he had given it. The questions relating to the survival of the State, particularly those of the succession and the regency, were in fact discussed and settled according to traditional Macedonian procedures.

Alexander's empire, at once personal and multinational, thus gave way before a political entity already known: the ancient kingdom of the Macedonians, enlarged by the territories conquered by Alexander. However, the state soon became the stake in the struggle between the pretenders to Alexander's heritage, some of them aspiring to inherit it in its entirety, others seeking merely to carve themselves a part of the spoils.

The fate of the empire was not without consequence for Macedonia. If its unity were preserved, Macedonia might occupy either a central or a peripheral place in it. If, on the other hand, the empire were dismembered, Macedonia might form a large state incorporating other countries, or remain alone, or itself disintegrate and be divided between two or even more states.

The question of the succession to the conqueror divided the army. The generals and the cavalry opted for the child that Roxane, the king's widow, was about to give the world, provided that it was a boy and was called Alexander in advance; the infantry, for their part, proclaimed king as Arrhidaios, a son of Philip II and half-brother of the lost king. Arrhidaios was the only member of the royal family who was an adult male, but he was also a weakling. This paradoxical choice, like the acclamation of the king under the name of Philip, seems to have been the infantry's way of expressing their nostalgia for Philip II, in the same spirit as the protestations by the troops and certain notables against Alexander's infringements of the Mace-

donian tradition. The infantry were in fact recruited from amongst the peasantry, a supremely conservative class. A compromise was found: Arrhidaios-Philip (III) and Alexander (IV) shared the kingship and, Roxane having given birth to a son, there were no grounds for going back on this decision.

As for the effective power, which neither of the kings was capable of exercising, it was decided not to entrust this to a single man. Krateros was therefore designated 'protector of the kings', while Perdikkas was already 'chiliarch'[3]. The division of responsibilities is not clear: perhaps those assigned to Krateros would have made him a regent, with Perdikkas exercising supreme control over the state apparatus, but Krateros was absent from Babylon and did not return there. Next came the nomination of the governors in charge of the provinces. Macedonia and Thessaly, and also the supervision of the cities of the Hellenic League, remained in the hands of Antipatros, who soon had to deal with a coalition of Greek states opposed to Macedonia, which included Athens, Aitolia and Phokis. The 'Lamian War' (323-322 BC) lasted until the arrival of Krateros accompanied by the veterans that he was charged with repatriating. Southern Greece was conquered and lost all independence of Macedonia. Antipatros abolished the Hellenic League and made its members, individually, subject states.

With Krateros absent from Babylon, the centre of the empire, Perdikkas found himself the *de facto* wielder of effective power, and Olympias offered him the hand of her daughter Kleopatra, Alexander's sister and aunt of the infant king. But with Antipatros, Lysimachos, Antigonos and Ptolemy leagued against him, his attempt to enter Egypt miscarried, and he fell victim to a conspiracy. The allies resolved to entrust the guardianship of the kings to Antipatros who, instead of taking up residence at Babylon, returned to Macedonia with his charges. Thus, contrary to what Alexander had decided, the government of the State moved from Babylon to Pella and Alexander IV was to be raised as a Macedonian king, not as the absolute ruler of a multinational empire.

The regency of the aged Antipatros lasted only two years. His death, in 319 BC, unleashed

55-56. Silver tetradrachm of Demetrios Poliorketes, after 306 BC. Victory on the richly decorated prow of a warship, blowing a trumpet and holding a standard; on the reverse, Poseidon, seen from behind, brandishes his trident in his right hand. These images commemorate the naval victory by Demetrios over Ptolemy I of Egypt off Salamis in Cyprus in 306 BC.

55

56

conflicts over the succession which led to the death of the kings and the dismemberment of the state, with Macedonia becoming the main part of a kingdom to which were attached Thessaly and a number of annexed territories. In fact, Polyperchon, chosen by Antipatros to succeed him as guardian of the kings, immediately found himself opposed by Cassander, Antipatros' son, and also by Lysimachos, Antigonos and Ptolemy. From Greece, Cassander attacked Polyperchon, who suffered a number of reverses on land and at sea, and found himself cut off in the Peloponnese. Eurydice, wife of Philip-Arrhidaios, then had Cassander proclaimed regent (317 BC). Olympias, who was still in Epirus, fearing that Eurydice and Cassander would eliminate her grandson Alexander IV, hastened to Macedonia with a force of Epirotes and a number of Macedonian units. The Macedonian soldiers with Eurydice refused to fight against the mother of Alexander the Great, and Philip-Arrhidaios and Eurydice were captured and executed. Olympias then had a brother of Cassander and about a hundred of his friends put to death, but Cassander, returning from the Peloponnese, brought her before his army after the siege of Pydna, which inflicted the death penalty upon her. Alexander IV was now sole king (316 BC). Cassander soon revealed his intentions, however, by marrying Thessalonike, half-sister of Alexander the Great, and isolating the young king and his mother.

Cassander then saw Antigonos turn against him. After conquering most of the Asiatic part of the old empire of Alexander, Antigonos aspired to become the sole master of it. He possessed the military and financial resources to match his ambitions, and his strategic and political talents were not inconsiderable. He had himself proclaimed guardian of Alexander IV by his army, which approved the condemnation of Cassander for both the murder of Olympias and the seizure of the young king. Cassander, Lysimachos and Ptolemy, however, formed an alliance to contain his ambitions, and after a number of reverses on several fronts, Antigonos was obliged to come to terms in 311 BC. A clause in the treaty confirmed Cassander as general in Europe until Alexander IV reached his majority; Cassander then proceeded to have the king and his mother assassinated (310-309 BC).

With the disappearance of the king, the pretenders to the throne were able to give free rein to their ambitions. Antigonos was the first to have himself proclaimed king by his army, along with his son, Demetrios Poliorketes (306

57

57. Head of a Gaul.
Hellenistic art has
produced some striking
images of these 'Galatians',
with their hair in disorder,
who posed a mortal threat
to Greece, particularly
Macedonia, and also the
kingdom of Pergamon,
where the original of
this statue was created
in the last quarter of
the third century BC.

BC). Cassander, Lysimachos, Seleukos and Ptolemy followed suit, not so much in order to lay claim to the whole of Alexander's legacy, like Antigonos himself, as to check his appetite and legitimise their own shares. This was done so effectively that Cassander succeeded in making Macedonia a kingdom that was successor to that of the Temenids, after the imperial interlude of Alexander. Thessaly remained a separate kingdom, and parts of Illyria and Paionia became external possessions.

Antigonos had not abandoned his ambitions in Greece, where his son Demetrios had even reconstituted the Hellenic League (an occasion, it seems, of lavish expenditure), and he once more clashed with the coalition of his foes. His forces were crushed at Ipsos, where he himself was killed (301 BC). Being a realist, Cassander did not take part in the partitioning of Antigonos' enormous kingdom.

After the death of Cassander in 297 BC, dynastic internecine quarrels created a serious crisis of power. Pyrrhos of Epirus profited from this to seize two Macedonian provinces, Tymphaia and Parauaia, and Demetrios Poliorketes to add Macedonia to his possessions on the coasts of the eastern Mediterranean and southern Greece (294 BC). This king (figs 55, 56, 62) dreamed of even greater conquests, and had a new capital, Demetrias, built in the Gulf of Pagasai, thus demonstrating that he was far from considering Macedonia to be the heart of his possessions. Haughty and extravagant, his conception of kingship appeared more oriental than Macedonian, to the point that he seemed a foreigner to the eyes of the Macedonians. Demetrios applied himself to strengthening his hold on southern Greece, containing Pyrrhos, and above all realising the imperial ambitions of his father, Antigonos. The man who had roused the Greeks of the south against Cassander and had relied for support on the democracies, was henceforth to pursue the only policy consistent with the interest of a sovereign ruling in Macedonia and Thessaly — siding with the oligarchs against the democrats. Though he had entered into alliance with the Aitolians to contain Cassander, he would henceforth hold them in check for, as masters of Delphi, they obstructed communications between the states of the north and those of the south. In order to carry through this ambitious policy, he put significant land and naval forces in the field: 98,000 infantry, 12,000 cavalry and 500 warships. His aim was first to attack the possessions of Lysimachos in Asia Minor, but he merely succeeded in ranging Lysimachos, Seleukos, Ptolemy and Pyrrhos against him (288 BC) and quit the stage of history when he fell into the hands of Seleukos.

Lysimachos and Pyrrhos then partitioned Macedonia between them, the latter also occupying Thessaly. This understanding, however, forged by a common danger, was not to last. Lysimachos drove out Pyrrhos and incorporated the whole of Macedonia and Thessaly into his huge multinational kingdom, which stretched as far as the Danube and covered a large part of Asia Minor. He was in turn defeated and killed defending his possessions in Asia Minor, which had been invaded by Seleukos (281 BC). The latter was on the way to occupy his European possessions, including Macedonia, when he was assassinated by Ptolemy Keraunos, the eldest son of Ptolemy I who had been dispossessed of his rights. Not losing a moment, Keraunos had himself proclaimed king of Macedonia by Lysimachos's army.

He was not able to enjoy this kingship for long. Macedonia was invaded by a wave of Gauls, called 'Galatians' by the Greeks — whence the word 'Celts' — (279 BC), Ptolemy's army was annihilated, and he himself was killed in battle. The conquering Gauls (fig. 57) set themselves to pillaging the countryside, whose inhabitants took refuge behind the ramparts of the cities. After a period of confusion and anarchy, the kingship was offered to a Macedonian noble, Sosthenes. He refused the title, but not to serve his country, and fought successfully against the invaders as military commander-in-chief with full powers. A second wave of Gauls, however, then fell upon Macedonia, crossing it towards the south. Thrown back from central Greece, this wave fell back once more on Macedonia as it forced a way towards Thrace. With Sosthenes dead, two pretenders were in contention for the royal crown, and a tyrant established himself in Kassandreia.

Internal and external consolidation (276-217 BC)

Well before Macedonia fell prey, after the death of Cassander, to anarchy and the Celtic invasions (297-276 BC), the kingdoms born of Alexander's legacy had formed themselves into a system of Hellenistic powers. Macedonia ultimately found her place in this system, thanks to Antigonos Gonatas, a son of Demetrios Poliorketes, who succeeded in liberating and stabilising the country.

After his father's death, Antigonos attempted to take possession of Macedonia from southern Greece, but was repulsed by Sosthenes. Later, he succeeded in getting a foothold in Thrace and winning a victory over the Gauls who had occupied the country, annihilating one of their strongest bands.

The prestige he derived from this opened Macedonia to him (276 BC), thus sealing its fate for several decades: it was to form the central and dominating part of a kingdom that embraced a number of annexed territories, notably the bigger part of Thessaly. For, ever since

Philip II had had himself named *archon* of the Thessalian League, the situation had remained more or less the same, in formal terms: the League had continued to exist, with the kings of Macedonia holding the supreme magistracy in Thessaly, which should not be confused with the kingship in Macedonia.

Furthermore, the Antigonids who ruled successively over Macedonia endeavoured to occupy a number of military bases in southern Greece, and to keep under their influence certain cities, whose regimes were favourable to themselves. Thus, Gonatas, and Demetrios II and Antigonos Doson after him, far from being attracted by distant adventures, knew how to match their ambitions with their means. Moreover, Macedonia ceased to be coveted by some king or other drawing his power from the heritage of Alexander. The point of the dispute between the Ptolemies and the Antigonids was the strategic space formed by the south Aegean and southern Greece.

Under Gonatas, the country recovered from the evils from which it had suffered during the troubled period 297-276 BC. With his successors it experienced genuine economic and demographic progress and, thanks to its material and human resources and the organisation of its army, it maintained its military superiority over the states of southern Greece. In short, the Macedonian kingdom regained the importance of the kingdom of Philip II before his expansion into Thrace, though without a king of the same stature. Its rulers, moreover, gave proof of their political qualities by sparing the country from succession crises and internal troubles.

Gonatas

Now king (276-240/39 BC) of a devastated and defeated Macedonia, Gonatas' first tasks were to consolidate his throne by ejecting the other pretenders, restore order in the country and reconstitute the army. Breaking with the policy of Demetrios I, he abandoned the manner of foreign tyrant and all imperial ambitions, and acted as a Macedonian king completely occupied with Macedonia and not concerned with giving the appearance of an adventurer squandering his talents in the pursuit of unattainable designs like his father and grandfather. Though he had been born and spent the whole of the first part of his life outside Macedonia, he adopted a bearing in conformity with the traditional picture of the simple, accessible king, in an attempt to reestablish contact with the Macedonian past. It was probably with this intention that he had the burial mounds of the

Temenid kings at Aigeai restored, which, as we shall see, had been damaged by Pyrrhos.

Educated in Athens, he was a cultured man and readily surrounded himself with philosophers, poets and historians (fig. 58), who came from foreign countries to enjoy his hospitality. He himself was a follower of Zeno and professed Stoic ideals, telling his son Demetrios that kingship was 'glorious slavery'.

Gonatas was hardly established in Macedonia when his title was challenged by Pyrrhos of Epirus, just returned from Italy and financed by subsidies from Ptolemy II (275 BC). His position was still precarious and, significantly, 2,000 of his soldiers went over to his rival, to whom some cities opened their gates. The King of Epirus then subdued the biggest part of Macedonia and Thessaly, but alienated the Macedonians by allowing his troops to violate the royal tombs at Aigeai. In the end, ever the adventurer, he abandoned Macedonia to his son, Ptolemy, and went off to wage war in the Peloponnese (273 BC).

Like the skilful strategist he was, Gonatas was reconciled with his old enemy, Sparta, thus limiting its expansionism, profited from the respite to recapture the territory lost in the Peloponnese, and confronted the other foreign power that had entered the same space, Ptolemaic Egypt. The Antigonids and the Ptolemies thus embarked on permanent confrontation, most often conducted through the agency of other Greek states.

Before becoming king of Macedonia, Gonatas had inherited a number of possessions in southern Greece from his father, Demetrios: Demetrias, Chalkis, Corinth (fig. 59) and possibly Piraeus. The king and his descendants did all they could to keep garrisons in these places, which fulfilled a dual purpose: bastions from which they kept the Macedonian possessions in which they were stationed under their thumb, while also keeping an eye on other states, and also relay stations in a maritime route linking Macedonia, Thessaly, Euboia, Attica and the Peloponnese. This was the only route to southern Greece available to the Macedonians after the Aitolian League had pushed as far as the Malian gulf.

In fact, a first coalition hostile to Macedonia was not long in forming. Disturbed by Gonatas' brilliant success, Sparta (fig. 60) and Ptolemy II, along with a number of Peloponnesian states and Athens, entered into a league against him. The point at issue for Ptolemy was not to be excluded from Greek affairs; for the Greek states, it was to assert their independence from Macedonia and preserve their internal freedom. The conflict, known as the 'Chremonidean War' (267-261 BC) ended in Gonatas' favour. Later, his fleet won two victories over the naval forces of Alexandria which tolled the death-knell of Ptolemaic supremacy in the Aegean.

Gonatas, however, had to return in haste to the Peloponnese. Twelve years after the attack by Pyrrhos, he had to face his successor, Alexander II of Epirus, whom he drove out of Macedonia without much difficulty. Complications were not long arising on another front, however. Gonatas had entrusted Corinth to his brother, Krateros, with wide powers. After the Chremonidean war he further consolidated the chain of bases that he held in Greece, in particular imposing on Athens a puppet government and the military occupation of all its territory.

When Krateros died (249 BC), however, his son Alexander declared himself independent. The Achaean League took advantage of this weakness in the Macedonian system of surveillance covering the Isthmus region to strengthen its position. Gonatas nonetheless succeeded in recovering Corinth from the widow of his revolted nephew, and placed the town under his direct control. The fortunes of war turned once more in favour of the League, however, which recaptured the stronghold, the key of the Macedonian strategic arrangements in the Peloponnese. The Achaean League thus became a foe to be reckoned with, whereas previously only Sparta had been able to trouble the Macedonians in the Peloponnese.

While the Macedonian kings endeavoured to assert their control over southern Greece through the agency of governments that they supported in various cities, the League contributed to the fall of a number of tyrannical regimes favourable to Gonatas, thus securing the adherence to the Achaean League of free cities, and gaining new strength.

At the same time, the Aitolian League, which had succeeded in driving back the Gauls who had penetrated as far as Delphi (279/8 BC), was also strengthened by the adherence of new members. At first its expansion did not constitute a serious threat to the Macedonians but this situation soon changed. The Aitolian League expanded to the Malian gulf, and thus found itself in a position to control land communications between Macedonia and its sphere of influence in southern Greece, forming a danger to Macedonia both on land and at sea, where the Aitolians engaged in piracy.

Under pressure from the Achaeans, however, Gonatas did not hesitate to form an alliance with the Aitolians, in the hope of divid-

58. Boscoreale, villa of Fannius Synistor. Wall-painting, after an original of the middle of the third century BC, in which can be recognised Antigonos Gonatas and his mother Phila, listening to the teaching of the Cynic philosopher Menedemos (not in this part of the picture); between them, a shield with an eight-point star at the centre.

ing with them the territory of the Achaean League. The Aitolians, however, considered it in their best interests to conclude peace with the Achaeans (241/40 BC) and, on Gonatas' death, the positions he had lost in the Peloponnese remained in the hands of his foes.

Demetrios II

When called upon to succeed Gonatas, Demetrios II was at a fairly advanced age. He had shouldered, alongside his father, a number of duties involving great responsibility, and thus had the experience necessary for his role as king. Throughout his reign (239-229 BC) he had to contend with the two Leagues, Achaean and Aitolian, supported by Ptolemy III in the 'Demetrian War', which he provoked in his attempts to contain the Aitolians.

We have seen that Gonatas had sought an alliance with the Aitolians in southern Greece, despite the risks of such a policy. Demetrios decided to spare these turbulent peoples no longer. When they attacked western Akarnania, which was in the hands of the Epirotes, he posed as protector of the latter, whose royal house was in decline (239 BC). Alexander's widow, looking for support, offered him the hand of her daughter, Phthia, but the marriage failed to save either the dynasty or the kingship, which was replaced by a republican regime. It was this attempt by Demetrios to protect Epirus from the Aitolians that unleashed the 'Demetrian War', with the Aitolians forming an alliance with the Achaeans, who could only expand at the expense of the Macedonian positions in the Peloponnese and Attica. Demetrios II defeated the Aitolians in central Greece, but the Achaeans met with some successes and received the support of new allies in the Peloponnese. When the Aitolians resumed their attacks on the Epirotes in western Akarnania, Demetrios sought the aid of the Illyrians. They effectively defeated the Aitolians, but then turned against the Epirotes who, in desperation, entered the Aitolo-Achaean alliance. To add to Demetrios' misfortunes, the Dardanians, who had not stirred for several decades, invaded Macedonia. Demetrios moved to this front, but perished before he was able to drive them out. He left his country invaded by a barbarian army, and his throne to an infant.

Antigonos Doson

Against all expectations, the succession did not lead to any disorder. Antigonos, the son of a half-brother of Antigonos Gonatas, was designated guardian of King Philip V, a minor. Antigonos married the queen mother and

59

60

59. The Acrocorinth. This rock which, from its height of 575 m, dominates the Isthmus at Corinth, commanded a major crossroads of the communication routes running north-south and east-west; it was for this reason that the Macedonian kings always considered it an essential base of operations for their policies in southern Greece.

60. The plain of Sparta. Confident in the strength of their army, the Lacedaemonians built their city on the fertile land watered by the Eurotas and dominated by Taygetos, without protecting it with fortifications, at least until a late period.

adopted the king. He later also assumed the crown himself, though without eliminating his nephew and adoptive son, and was therefore given the surname 'Doson' — 'he who will hand on power'. In addition to this exemplary loyalty, he gave proof of his undoubted political and military talents and restored to Macedonia the place that the other powers had stolen from her.

The abrupt departure of the Macedonians from the Peloponnese and their reverses at the hands of the Dardanians, against whom Antigonos Doson had launched all his available forces, was the signal for the anti-Macedonian movements from Thessaly to the Peloponnese.

The Thessalians benefited from the active support of the Aitolians, who were themselves financed by Ptolemy II, but Doson was not slow to restore the situation in the field, obliging the Aitolians to conclude peace with him.

It was next the turn of the Boiotians to secede from Macedonia, while the Athenians ejected the Macedonian garrison occupying Piraeus. Although the garrison at Chalkis remained intact, the entire Peloponnese was lost to the Macedonians. Their garrisons there withdrew, and the tyrants friendly towards them were obliged to restore internal freedom to their cities and throw in their lot with the Achaean League.

61

61. Scenery in Arkadia, the gorge of Gortynios near Gortys. This site possessed, as a result of the quality of its water, a famous Asklepieion to which Alexander came in person to consecrate his spear; it also controlled a major access-route to Arkadia, and the Macedonians built strong fortifications there, deploying their new techniques.

Very happily, the expansionist policy of Sparta was conducted at the expense of the Achaean League. The Spartans, maintained by subsidies from Ptolemy, recruited an army of mercenaries, and their king, Cleomenes III, won the sympathies of the lower classes in the Achaean cities by distributing land and awarding citizen rights to numerous *perioeci*. Unable to resist the Spartans, the Achaean League resigned itself to seeking Macedonian aid (224 BC).

Antigonos Doson seized this unexpected opportunity and re-established the system of Macedonian garrisons and alliances in the Peloponnese, thanks to the very Achaeans who, a short time previously, had pushed him to the edge of the abyss. Finally, he presented them with a heavy bill for his aid: the Achaeans were required to put their land and sea forces under his control, not to enter into relations with other kings, and not to pass any laws that conflicted with the treaty they concluded with him — all measures designed to prevent any further changes of alliance. Meanwhile Doson, breaking with the foreign policy pursued both by himself and his predecessors, had undertaken a naval expedition in Caria.

Doson deployed all his skill and energy to restore Macedonian influence in Greece. He occupied Corinth and Argos, pressed on as far as Arkadia (fig. 61), and exhorted his allies to found a permanent league under his command, consisting from the outset of the Achaeans, the Epirotes, the Phokians, the Boiotians, the Akarnanians, the Thessalians and the Macedonians. Doson was proclaimed *hegemon*, or supreme military commander of the allies. The member states of the league were represented by delegates, not plenipotentiaries, who formed a kind of federal council that met under the presidency of the *hegemon*.

In 223 and 222 BC Doson again campaigned in the Peloponnese at the head of the allies. He recovered from Cleomenes the land that the latter had won outside Lakonia, and ended by inflicting a crushing defeat on him at the battle of Sellasia (222 BC), thereby ensuring his domination of southern Greece.

Doson had reached the pinnacle of his power. At the head of the armed forces of the League that he had founded, he had reconquered Corinth, taken two cities in Arkadia, placed Sparta under a Macedonian governor and had won some strong sympathies in Greece. However, the Illyrians took advantage of his long absence from Macedonia to invade the country once more. He returned in haste to face this threat, but died of tuberculosis (221 BC).

Philip V

His successor, Philip V, was only seventeen years old. He had acquired a good knowledge of affairs in southern Greece during a stay with Aratos, the experienced leader of the Achaean League, and, in his political testament, Doson had appointed counsellors to assist him. Philip, however, who had an independent and authoritarian character, lost no time in disembarassing himself of them.

With the Spartan danger removed, the entente between the Achaean League and Macedonia continued to be in the interests of both partners, for they still had another common enemy — the Aitolian League, which profited from the death of Antigonos to resume its activities. Pirates intensified their attacks on Macedonian ships, and armed bands began to ravage the coasts of the Achaean League and Messenia. A war between the Achaeans and the Aitolians (221-220 BC) ended badly for the Achaeans, who then appealed to the young king.

Philip V went to their aid, convened the assembly of Doson's League, and had it vote for a war against the Aitolians (219 BC). This was the 'War of the Allies' (the expression in the Latin authors is *bellum sociale*, whence the expression 'Social War'). He was not quick to intervene, occupied as he was with keeping an eye simultaneously on the Dardanians, who were threatening Macedonia, and the Romans, who had carved out a protectorate in Illyria that also included the island of Corcyra. Meanwhile, the Aitolians, in alliance with the Spartans, won some successes in the Peloponnese, reached the heart of Epirus, where they sacked the sanctuary of Dodona, and then pushed on as far as Lower Macedonia, where Dion suffered the same fate.

Once the Dardanian danger was removed, however, Philip defeated the Aitolians in Aitolia itself and the Spartans on their own territory, so comprehensively that the former concluded the peace of Naupaktos with him (217 BC). Elsewhere, Philip seized Paionia. This country, which had made itself independent at the time of the troubles following upon the death of Cassander, had been reunited with the kingdom by Gonatas and then regained its freedom. He had had to repel three attacks by the Illyrians in the space of two years, however. These conflicts had significant consequences. Philip's involvement in the affairs of the Illyrians brought him up against the Romans, which lured him into an expansionist foreign policy[4], in contrast with that followed by his Antigonid predecessors since Gonatas.

Organisation of the Kingdom

The literary sources tell us almost nothing of the functioning of the Macedonian institutions during the period stretching from the reign of Cassander to that of Philip V. The field was thus clear for hypotheses that were at once arbitrary and contradictory. For some, the Antigonids formed from the outset an absolute monarchy comparable to the 'personal' kingships of the Seleucids and Lagids. For others, in contrast, the titles used by the last representatives of the line marked an extension of the rights of the *ethnos* in relation to the king. Still others have even supposed that Macedonia had by then been transformed into a federation of cities. Nothing of this emerges from the numerous epigraphic documents recently discovered from this period. What these do reveal is the strengthening of the civic institutions and the development of political life within the cities and the regions. At the end of the reign of Philip V, in particular, an important reform appears to free the cities from royal tutelage. They enjoyed a greater role in the process of appointing the kings and both they and the regions were accorded the right to mint coins. Moreover, the office of *strategos,* the chief magistracy in each region, seems to have become elective.

This strengthening of the role of the cities would not have been possible without the flourishing of urban life in Macedonia. At the end of the Hellenistic period, the country counted more than a hundred cities and, from an economic, social and cultural point of view, was very different from the kingdom inherited by Philip II two centuries earlier.

The essentially rural world composed of stock-breeders and farmers had given way to a largely urbanised, highly differentiated society, in the bosom of which the development of secondary and tertiary activities went hand in hand with the emergence of paid work and slavery. An amazingly innovative society in certain respects, yet one attached to ancestral virtues and prejudices, and also to the archaic institutions of the monarchy and the assembly of the *ethnos,* which were still associated with memories of grandeur. Their replacement by a federal *synedrion,* imposed by the Romans, was to be accepted only reluctantly.

The economy

The soldiers of Alexander did not return to Macedonia empty-handed. They brought with them from their conquests gold, silver, precious stones, and many other valuable objects. A considerable proportion of these riches was injected into the Macedonian economy[5], though this was soon to suffer from the pillaging of the Epirote armies (288, 274, 262 BC) and, above all, from the devastation inflicted on the countryside by the bands of Gauls (280-276 BC). It had to wait for Gonatas to reestablish normal economic and social conditions. The character of this economy had not changed, moreover, since the time of the Temenids. The agricultural product and stock-raising were sufficient to meet consumption. Under the heading of exports of organic raw materials, we may note timber for construction, resin, pitch, hemp and flax, and mineral products exported included iron and copper. It is not known whether gold and silver continued to be extracted as at the time of Philip. Macedonia had ports at Dion, Pydna, Pella, Thessalonike, Kassandreia and Neapolis, those at Dion and Pella being located on navigable waterways, and this activity was a source of wealth of which there is still clear evidence today[6].

Nonetheless, and despite these by no means negligible economic flows, the kingdom of the Antigonids was poor in comparison with the other Hellenistic kingdoms. In principle, finances had scarcely changed since the Classical period, as is clear from our main source of information: the coinage[7].

The coinage

Like its political history, the monetary history of the period after Alexander is one of a long erosion, the detail of which is far from having been clarified[8]. The Persian treasures, added to the considerable mining revenues, had enabled Alexander to bestow upon his empire a stable monetary system, sustained by a whole series of mints from Pella to Alexandria and Babylon.

The main denominations of this system

62. 63. 64

were the silver tetradrachm (figs 53, 54), on the Attic standard, which was in the process of displacing the Athenian tetradrachm as the Greek, or perhaps one should say international coinage; the gold stater, which weighed two drachms; and the double stater. These were supplemented by an important bronze coinage.

It was the economic role of this coinage, as much as the political uncertainty of the situation, that prevented the generals who assumed power on Alexander's death from following the Macedonian tradition of changing the monetary types upon the accession of a new king. Like those in the rest of the Empire, the mints of Macedonia, Pella and Amphipolis, continued to strike the same types until about 270 BC, with a late resurgence towards 180 BC: the head of Herakles wearing a lion skin, and Olympian Zeus on the silver coins (figs 53, 54), and the head of Athena and a Victory on those of gold.

However, just as in the other Hellenistic kingdoms, the Macedonian sovereigns desired, for reasons that escape us (prestige? financial efficiency?) to have their own coinage. Cassander was content to introduce his own types on certain bronze issues. Demetrios Poliorketes, for his part, imported his system into the part of Macedonia that he conquered. For the first time, his coins bear the likeness, on the obverse, of the king — a king whose bull's horns underline his divine character, the image thus asserting his claim to be the son of Poseidon, who figured on the reverse (figs 55, 56, 62). His successors, Antigonos Gonatas, followed by Doson (figs 63, 64), were to show greater restraint in their iconographic programme. The head of Pan in a Macedonian shield, associated with the traditional representation of Athena Alkidemos, recalled the first victory by the

former over the Galatians, while the head of Poseidon and Apollo on a trireme were references to the traditional pantheon.

The bronze coinage attests to the same duality. Bronze coins with traditional Macedonian types, like the horseman greeting, or the Macedonian shield, though accompanied the name of the ruling king, circulated at the same time as coins struck in the types specific to each king, such as the satyr lifting up a trophy celebrating the victory of Gonatas.

The simultaneous circulation of coins with the same diameter and the same average weight, which must therefore have had the same value, but with different types, seems clearly to indicate that the money supply of the kingdom was sustained by coins originating from mints of differing status.

The variety of types and the beauty of the images cannot, however, mask an indisputable financial decline. We know of no coins of Demetrios II, though he reigned at a date when the Macedonian mints were no longer striking Alexandrians. And if, in the absence of a corpus, we do not know exactly how many stamps (that is to say, how many matrices used to strike coins) were in use, the volume of the silver coinage is far less than that of the Seleucid or Lagid kings. Between the reign of Poliorketes and that of Philip V, gold ceased to be struck: that is to say, it was no longer normally used to sustain the circulation of coins, but was again used for emergency issues under these bellicose kings, whose finances were tangled.

The apparent revival of the coinage under the two last reigns should not deceive us. The images, like the portrait of Philip V (fig. 194), or that of Perseus (fig. 197), are once more of some quality, as are the types on the reverse, such as the powerful eagle in an oak wreath on the tetradrachms of Perseus. But the reduction in weight — particularly noticeable when Perseus was obliged to abandon the Attic standard — the appearance of silver coins in the name of the Macedonians, and the striking of Rhodian imitations; all these manipulations of the coinage betray the financial difficulties and expedients of a king on the brink of bankruptcy.

Society

Macedonian society continued in some respects to be archaic, like the balance of power within its ranks. It was the same with mental attitudes. The small land owners formed a solid class, while the aristocracy of merit, consisting of the 'Companions', later the 'Friends' of the king, still respected and influential, did not accumulate excessive wealth, and its influence did not weigh heavily on the conduct of the affairs of the realm.

There is every indication, moreover, that society, still imbued with military values, had not allowed the traders and artisans to achieve genuine social or political advancement. In the Hellenistic period, farmers of Illyrian, Thracian, and Gallic origins settled in various parts of the country, a policy favoured by several of the kings[9]; their social condition is unknown. Slaves, whose existence is attested by several epigraphic documents, do not seem to have been very numerous, as is to be expected in an economy in which there was no large-scale development of agriculture or craft-industries.

The king and the court

The successive masters of Macedonia, starting with Antipatros, had every interest in leaving untouched the institutions of the Temenid state, the principle source of their legitimacy. The extravagances of Demetrios Poliorketes and the republican power of Sosthenes were mere interludes that had no effect on the tradition. So much so that the royal power under the Antigonids conforms to one's picture of the kingship under the Temenids. This continuity, which might be called constitutional, did not prevent individual kings or exceptional circumstances from setting their seal on history.

The Macedonian state preserved to the end its ancient character and organisation, and continued to consist of the national community (the *koinon*) of the Macedonians and the person of the king. The assembly and the king acted either together or separately, according to the circumstances. The assembly, for example, was competent to decree honours for the king. The system of royal titles, the absence of a dynastic cult, and of the view that kingship stemmed from divine favour, give some idea of the king's position *vis-à-vis* the community.

Official documents preserve three variants of his title: 'king' (without qualification), 'King so-and-so, the Macedonian', and 'King of the Macedonians'. The fact that during the Antigonid period the third form only appears under Philip V has led some to see in it a desire on the part of the king to represent himself as 'master of the Macedonians'. It has properly been observed, however, that the same king is also designated by the other two formulae, and that, besides, the title 'King of the Macedonians' should not be interpreted differently from the title 'King of the Lacedaemonians', and the semantic connotations of the latter expression certainly do not refer to a conception of the king as master of the community of the Lacedaemonians. Thus, the Macedonian Hellenistic kingship did not evolve in the same way as that of the Lagids or the Seleucids, in which legitimacy derived from the favour shown by a god towards the king. And although the Macedonians celebrated the festival of the *Basileia* in honour of the kingship, they never deified the king.

The king possessed vast domains and, according to some documents, had the power to dispose of them in order to found cities. It was to him that the mines in the kingdom belonged, whence his prerogative to strike coins, which remained his alone until the very last years of Philip V (who ceded the privilege of striking coins of small denomination to the regions and the cities). The king intervened in internal affairs by means of orders that took the form of personal letters addressed to royal officials and local magistrates or circulars, known as *diagrammata*. He enjoyed certain prerogatives in matters of justice. As commander of the armed forces he decided on appointments and decreed the mobilisation of the army, directed campaigns in general and the decisive actions in particular, and sometimes risked his own life in battle (fig. 65). He was the only one competent to conclude treaties.

A certain fluidity can be detected, however, with regard to his position amongst the contracting parties. The only treaty known to us from the reign of Demetrios II involves the king himself; in two treaties from the period of Doson, the Macedonian side is defined as 'King Antigonos and the Macedonians'; one treaty from the time of Philip V mentions the king without the 'Macedonians', while in another he

65. Iron cuirass with applied gold decoration (medallions with lion's heads and strips with leaf and dart pattern) found at Vergina in the Tomb of Philip; it was completed at the bottom by pieces of leather, also adorned with gold plaques. Strongly recalling the one worn by Alexander on the famous mosaic of a battle found at Pompeii, this cuirass allows us to imagine the ceremonial dress of a Macedonian king in the field.

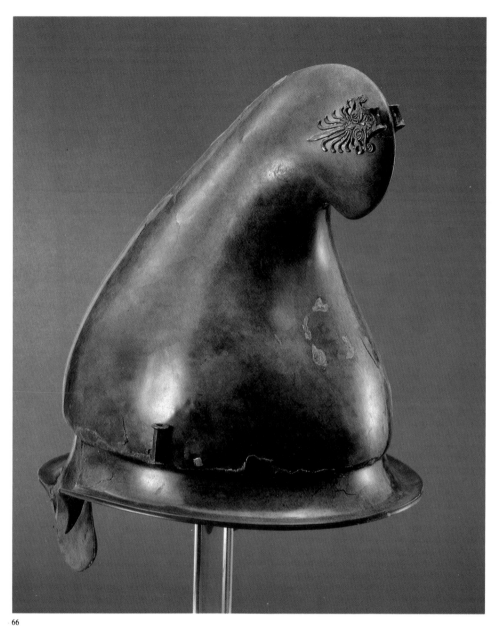

66

age also included the queen, the couple's children and other members of the dynasty. The Macedonian court was able to play an important role in the cultural sphere when it was sufficiently open to artists, men of letters and scholars.

The army

We have seen that the Macedonian armies occasionally intervened in affairs of state[10]. Nothing of this kind is attested in the sources for the period of the Antigonids. The fact that these actions occurred without exception in circumstances in which legitimacy was disputed has led some to doubt whether the assembly of the Macedonians under arms traditionally possessed this prerogative. The question remains an open one, but account must be taken of the following incident: when the peltasts learned that Philip V had decided to put their commander Leontios to death, they wrote to the king to invite him 'not to proceed to judgement without them'; if their demand were not granted, they insisted, 'they would consider that they were being treated with neglect and contempt'. And Polybius comments: 'For the Macedonians had always enjoyed complete *isegoria* (right to address as equals) with regard to their king.'

Their demand thus appears to be an assertion of a right that reverted to the peltasts by virtue of their membership of the Macedonian army, and which Philip V was in the course of trampling under foot. This shows beyond doubt that the Macedonian army was competent to intervene in matters of penal law involving the death penalty. Evidence of this kind for the participation of the 'Macedonians' in affairs of state is very rare, however. We have already noted that they are sometimes mentioned and sometimes not, alongside the king, in the official texts of treaties surviving from the period of the Antigonids.

In principle, there were no major changes in the Macedonian army after Philip II[11]. It had the same establishment (not more than 30,000 men), the same organisation, the same equipment (fig. 66), the same discipline, and continued to employ Balkan troops and mercenaries. We note however, an increase in the importance of the naval forces under Philip V, but the Romans, after their victory in 197 BC, imposed a reduction of the fleet to six ships of low tonnage.

Local administration

The kingdom was divided, it seems, into

66. Helmet of the Macedonian type, also known as a 'Phrygian' or 'Thracian' helmet, bronze, fourth century BC. With its tall crest curving forwards and adorned with a flame palmette, to which a plume was fixed, it was normally worn by the Macedonian infantry.

takes the oath both in his own name and in that of the Macedonians and their allies. For their part, the Romans regarded King Philip, or King Perseus, and the Macedonians as a single entity.

As far as the *koinon* of the Macedonians is concerned, the documents contain only rare indications of its prerogatives, which do not seem to cover the full extent of its power. The royal court was the main centre of government in the land. The title 'in charge of correspondence' probably indicates the king's chief secretary or chancellor. The king was also assisted by his 'Friends', who had no official capacity and acted as private counsellors or ambassadors. They were more or less powerful to the extent that they enjoyed the confidence of the king and exercised influence over him. The royal entour-

territories with cities in Lower Macedonia, where economic and social conditions were more advanced and where there were numerous urban centres, and territories of 'peoples' (*ethne*) in Upper Macedonia. These basic units were grouped together in four large regions.

Urbanisation evolved in Macedonia in the Hellenistic period. Cities appeared, urban economic activities flourished, and the accumulation of wealth and the development of the urban tissue quickened pace. Cassander founded two cities: Kassandreia and Thessalonike. The former, situated outside Macedonia proper, was built on the Pallene peninsula and peopled by the survivors of Olynthos and a few citizens from neighbouring cities. The latter, at the head of the Thermaic gulf, absorbed the inhabitants of twenty-six townships of the surrounding region.

The sites chosen are revealing: it was Cassander's intention to create maritime commercial centres linking the hinterland of Macedonia, and even of the Balkans, with the Aegean basin. History has justified this decision. As for the cities founded in the interior of the kingdom, these were to contribute to the development of local commercial life, but their population was above all occupied in rural work.

The Macedonian cities enjoyed the right of self-government. In fact, their sphere of action was at once geographical and legal — geographical, in that a city possessed its own territory; legal, in that each one had people under its administration, its own courts and laws, and owned landed property. The institutions were those of Greece: an assembly, *ekklesia,* a council, *boule,* whose members originally had the traditional title [peliganes], and magistrates such as the *epistatai, 'archontes', tagoi, skoidoi, dikastai, nomophylakes, tamiai, agoranomoi, exetastai,* etc — the *politarchai* came later — and also eponymous priests, all of them elected for one year. The cities controlled their own finances, which derived from locally levied taxes. Philip V granted his capital, Pella, and also two other cities, Thessalonike and Amphipolis, the right to strike coins in their own name.

Finally, we meet the *strategoi* in charge of the regions. Originally, these had to be appointed by the king, but the office probably later became elective.

Urbanisation was in part tied to another characteristically Hellenistic phenomenon: the transfer of populations. This operated in three ways. In the case of Kassandreia and Thessalonike, Macedonians and other Greeks came from the neighbouring towns, and their dislocation did not take them outside the boundaries of Macedonia. In other cases, we are dealing with cities founded outside Macedonia, in Paionia and elsewhere, but peopled by Macedonians. Finally, groups of Thracians, Illyrians, Gauls and others, were transplanted to the plains of Macedonia under pressure from Cassander and the Antigonids, whose aim was in this way to enlarge the rural population, increase the production of food and raw materials, and also reinforce the military establishment of the kingdom.

The language: the origins of the *koine*

It was, as we know, a common Greek language, the *koine,* that prevailed in the Hellenistic period, becoming, through its influence on Latin and through its role as the common language of Christianity, one of the foundations of western civilisation. In the absence of adequate documentation, however, the history of the formation of the *koine* has long been obscured by a number of false ideas: the *koine* was only formed after the conquest of Asia by Alexander the Great; it was formed in the major cosmopolitan centres such as Athens and some of the Ionian cities; it borrowed its constituent elements from the Attic dialect and, to a lesser extent from the various Ionic dialects. Furthermore, the specialists had a tendency to play down the contribution of Macedonia, the motherland of the great conqueror, since it was too little known, and was thought to be barbarian before his reign.

The spectacular enrichment of the archaeological, and particularly the epigraphical evidence (figs 67, 200) in recent years has revealed that Macedonia was the home of a brilliant civilisation from as early as Philip II. Since some of these epigraphic documents go back to the beginning of the fifth century, we now have a perceptibly different picture of the origins of the *koine*[12]. It emerged during at least the first half of the fourth century, the Macedonian region was one of its main cradles, and the Macedonian dialect also contributed to its formation.

We have already seen[13] that Macedonian was a Greek dialect, similar to Thessalian and the so-called north-west Greek dialects. The scant documents from Macedonia proper before the reign of Philip II, esentially a number of inscriptions on coins, epitaphs and the well-known dedications by Queen Eurydice to the goddess Eukleia, are in fact written in a Greek dialect close to the dialects of the north-west, and which is certainly not Attic. The situation changed under Philip II who, judging from the only two official documents surviving from his reign, adopted Attic as the language of his administration. As in the sphere of institutions, the conquest of Amphipolis and Chalkidike exercised a decisive influence on the Macedonian king: we now know that even before the expansion of Macedonia in these regions the Attic dialect had strongly penetrated the northern periphery of the Aegean basin, which in the fifth century had belonged to the Athenian empire. The Athenians had continued to retain their interests, their ambitions, and even their bases here into the first half of the following century.

Although in the official documents of Amphipolis and the Chalkidian League the Ionic dialect was normally used, albeit tinged with Atticisms, the private documents, in contrast, are written in the Attic dialect, which preserves only a few elements of the local Ionic speech — more numerous in Chalkidike and rarer in Amphipolis. In other words, in the regions conquered by Philip, the current language was already a form of *koine.*

Although fewer in number, the documents allow one to believe that a similar situation prevailed in the more cosmopolitan urban centres of the Macedonian kingdom, such as Pella. Philip's conquest of the 'new territories', where Ionian populations of diverse origins had to live side by side with peoples of Macedonian origin, could not fail to accelerate the process of the elaboration and dissemination of this common language which, while based on the Attic dialect, absorbed into it a number of elements of the local Ionic dialects, and also of the Macedonian dialect.

The documentation for Amphipolis, which is richer than that for the other cities, allows us to follow this process. Here, the acts of sale dating from after the conquest are written in Attic, just like those of the preceding period, but the phonetics and morphology, especially of the proper names, thereafter bear traces of the influence of the Macedonian dialect alongside the Ionic features still present. It is possible to discern, in particular, the large-scale introduction of an original inflexion of masculine nouns of the first declension ending in *-as* which, according to one of the leading experts in the *koine,* was to be widely used in later Greek.

This was the form of the *koine* introduced by the soldiers and administrators of the following generation into the kingdoms of Asia and Egypt that emerged from the conquests of Alexander of the Great. Macedonia was thus the cradle of the Hellenistic world not only in the political and institutional sphere, but also in the linguistic sphere and, as we are increasingly discovering, on the cultural plane in general. For though it is still true to say that Athens was the school of Greece and that Hellenistic civilisation is essentially the civilisation of Athens, it was the Macedonian version of that civilisation, or rather its adaptation of it, that the conquests of Alexander spread throughout the *oikoumene.*

Artistic life

The long century stretching from the accession of Alexander to Philip V was for art truly the golden age of Macedonia. We shall here do no more than recall the more obvious successes, described in the following three chapters. In the case of urbanism, these are, in addition to the creations already discussed[14], the remarkable growth of cities such as Pella, Dion and Amphipolis[15], the construction of palaces at the two capitals of the Kingdom[16], and the astonishing architecture of the 'Macedonian tombs' with their painted decoration and the funerary offerings that they contained[17]. They include, possibly even more remarkably, the development of the art of mosaic which, after a brilliant start at Olynthos, confirmed its status as a major art[18].

We may also note the pursuit, outside Macedonia, of the policy instigated by Philip II, who used works of art as a means of propaganda, and this in the major religious centres of the Greek world. Delphi and the monument of Krateros[19], the structures on Samothrace[20], and offerings at Delos[21] and elsewhere all attest to this intention on the part of the Macedonian kings.

There is still some uncertainty concerning the relations between some of these works and Macedonia, but enough is known to form a precise idea of their character: a composite style with certain strongly accentuated tendencies, such as emphasis and the baroque, which must have been so admired that one finds them afterwards throughout Hellenistic, and then Roman art.

67. Inscription from Dion. It contains the text of a treaty between Philip V and the city of Lysimacheia in Thrace, dating from 202/01 BC.

4

THE CITIES AND SANCTUARIES OF MACEDONIA

68. Vergina, palace, end of the fourth century BC. Room A and the south-east corner of the courtyard. This picture gives an idea of the size of the structure and its organisation, with the rooms distributed around a huge central courtyard, on a terrace dominating the fertile plain and dominated in turn by hills abounding in game.

The Palaces

To speak of royalty is to speak of palaces, an architectural form which had been more or less forgotten in southern Greece since early times. Macedonia presents a picture of prestigious palaces — certainly more impressive than the famous palaces of Pergamon, though less splendid than that of Alexandria, if the surviving descriptions of this can believed. The palaces in question are those of Vergina and Pella, But we should not forget that a Macedonian king, Demetrios Poliorketes[1], had a palace erected at Demetrias in Thessaly of a very different type, since it was directly fortified, whereas the other two were simply protected by the defence walls of their cities[2].

The palace at Vergina

It is now accepted that the palace at Vergina is the palace of Aigeai, the first capital of Macedonia[3]. It occupies a remarkable position, exactly on the dividing line between the plain, with its rich agriculture and animal-breeding, and the hills covered with Mediterranean forest, which are hunting territory (figs 68, 69). To the north, beyond the last slopes covered by the city, it dominates a vast plain, through which rolls the Haliakmon after it emerges from the gorges of Mount Bermion a few kilometres to the west, and which stretches as far as heights on which Pella stands, and down to the sea. It seems likely that, above a retaining wall over 6 m high, a terrace along the north side of the structure directly overhung this immense landscape. Conversely, the palace could be seen from all sides, a majestic symbol of royal grandeur[4].

We are faced here with a type of structure rare in the Greek world since the early kingships had been transformed with the passage of time. Its uniqueness finds expression first of all in its dimensions. It is effectively a house on the traditional plan with an internal courtyard, but a house on a grand scale. The main building (fig. 70) occupies a rectangle 104.50 m long, with a depth only slightly smaller, at 88.50 m. The central courtyard was a square bordered by

69. Vergina, palace. The aerial photograph shows the relationship between the two palaces (the smaller can be seen at the top, towards the middle of the picture) and also their connection with the theatre, erected on the natural slope; it was in this place (though probably before the building that can now be seen) that Philip II was assassinated in 336 BC.

69

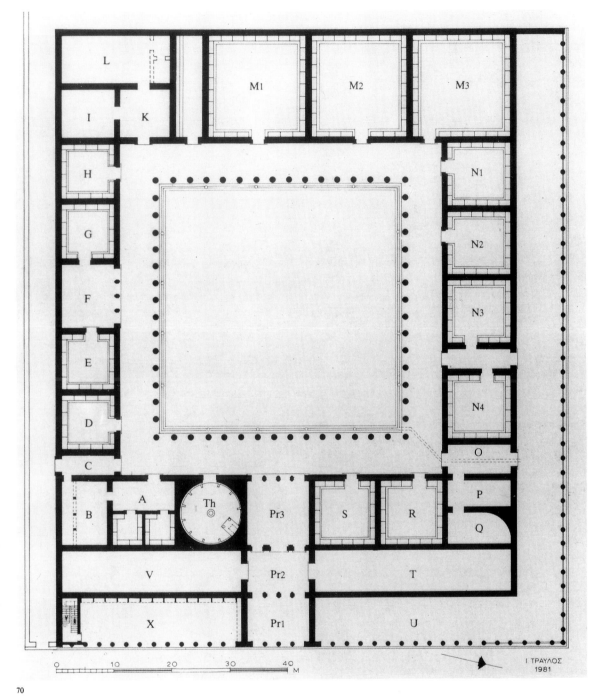

70

an interior peristyle (fig. 71) of a size without equal in Greek architecture. The free space in the centre, about 2000 square metres, was surrounded by a colonnade with sixteen columns on each side, whose Doric sobriety must have lent balance and grandeur to the whole. A large stone channel ran in front of the stylobate, but otherwise the entire space seems to have been left free. This peristyle (fig. 68) was itself bordered on all four sides by rooms to which it afforded direct access, thus acting as a distribution corridor for the complex, since these rooms were in a single row to the north, west

and south, and only on the east formed three rows, access to the innermost being via the stoa.

In fact, the entrance to the building was on this east side, in the middle of the façade — though not precisely centred, since the existence of the stoa at the north already mentioned meant that the east-west axis of the building coincided not with the axis of the entrance but with its north wall. It was a monumental approach in every way, and especially because it comprised a series of three rooms between the outside and the interior courtyard, each 10 m wide, and corresponding with the three rows of

71

rooms that form the east side of the building. The first ante-room (Pr1) is 7 m deep, as is the second (Pr2), and the third (Pr3) 10 m — truly regal dimensions. The doorway between the second and third had a huge threshold, consisting of a single block of marble 8.50 long, with fine mouldings. It had a triple opening, the central door being wider than the others, and the doors were separated by austerely elegant pillars that were a combination of two Ionic half-columns.

The elongated compartments that extend on either side of the second ante-room (T and V) have given rise to differing explanations. But, on the façade the entire side is taken up by a long colonnade (X, U), forming a continuation of the one running along the north side. This stoa, with a bench against the back wall, may have housed the gate-keepers; a staircase at the west end made it possible to ascend to the upper storey. It appears, in fact, that the Doric portico (with some surviving traces of dark blue and red paint) carried a second, Ionic portico. We would thus have a superposition of styles well known in the architecture of the late Hellenistic period (as in the Stoa of Attalos in Athens) and subsequently in the Roman world, though it appears here for the first time. There

will undoubtedly have been false windows in the upper storey, like those in the Great Tomb at Lefkadia[5] emphasising the façade even more — a theatrical décor very popular in Macedonian architecture.

Still in this wing, though now opening onto the courtyard, there are on one side, to the right of the entrance, two large almost square rooms with a side of 10 m (S and R), and also, immediately to the left, a rotunda (Th) set in a square. Sanctuary, throne-room, or banquet room (in which case the circular form would have made it easier for the men, stretched on their dining couch to play the game of *kottabos*[6], it may have been all three at once, and an inscription was found in it with a dedication to Herakles Patroos, the mythical ancestor of the royal family.

The rooms in the row to the south are certainly the most impressive in their arrangement. The lay-out is perfectly symmetrical (Manolis Andronicos has spoken of the 'royal suite'): at either end, opening onto the courtyard, and therefore facing north, is a single square room (D and H), with a group of three rooms between them, of which the two side-rooms (E and G) open only onto the central room (F)

71. Vergina, palace. View of the complex looking south-west. At the left can be seen the row of rooms on the south of the courtyard, with the 'royal suite' between D and H.

(figs 71, 73). This last communicated with the stoa through a wide bay equipped with three pillars formed of two very elegant half-columns. The side rooms E and G had mosaic floors, the one to the east, the only one that is well preserved, being of great artistic value[7]. Along the walls a slightly raised strip, 1.20 m wide, covered with red mortar was intended for the dining couches. Each of these rooms was thus an *andron*, the room reserved for male banquets.

What is surprising is that we meet in the west wing three more almost square rooms of the same type (M1, M2, M3), this time with a floor made of small marble slabs and with the raised strip around the walls decorated with a pebble mosaic. The dimensions of these rooms are considerable: 16. x 17.66 m, giving a surface area of about 300 square metres each, which is completely exceptional for a banquet room. Another noteworthy feature is that these rooms were roofed (a bed of fallen tiles has been found *in situ*), yet there are no evident traces of supports, demonstrating that Macedonian carpenters were capable of executing roofs of astonishing boldness.

The north wing, where the hill slopes down to the plain, has unfortunately suffered badly. We may suppose that it too comprised, in addition to corridors giving access to the exterior portico, four almost square rooms (N1-N4), of more modest, though still impressive dimensions (10.55 x 10.85 m).

The palace thus seems to have been a complex of multi-purpose meeting rooms, designed for the king's seasonal receptions[8]. We must also take account of the existence of an upper storey, at the very least over the east wing. Originally attributed to Antigonos Gonatas (279-239 BC), the building is now dated more securely, particularly by M. Andronicos, to the end of the fourth century.

It was completed on the west by a second building of smaller dimensions, but which also consisted of a large courtyard having stoas with nine columns on each of the four sides, bordered by rooms on the north and west. The quality is not that of the large palace, and the state of the ruin scarcely permits anything more than conjecture. As at Pella, we are without doubt dealing with the system current in the east, with one palace added to another, to suit the circumstances. The inscription on the tholos of the larger building proves that this was certainly in use until the reign of Perseus[9]. It is difficult to see why a smaller, second-rate palace would have been built next to it at a later date; by contrast, everything becomes clear if

72

73

72. Vergina, palace. Entrance to anteroom F. The bases can be seen in it of three pillars formed of two half-columns, very elegant bearing elements, of which these are amongst the earliest examples.

73. Vergina, palace. Threshold of room E. This enormous block, with its sockets for the associated doorframe, shows the exceptionally high quality of the lower part of the structure; above the stone socle, however, the walls were made simply of sun-baked bricks, in keeping with the custom of the period.

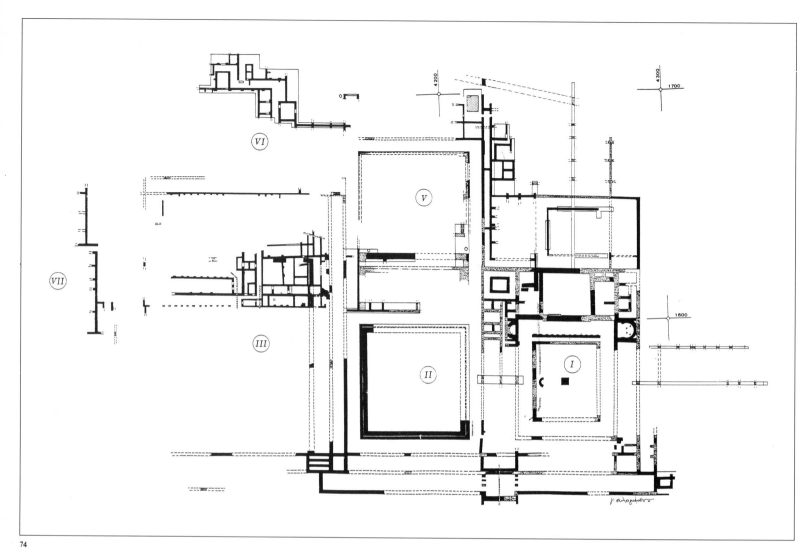

74

this plainer structure is the earlier, preserved out of loyalty to the past.

The palace at Pella

Like the palace at Vergina, this occupied a privileged position, dominating the city (this time to the south) and beyond it a lake open to the sea, which in the Hellenistic period extended further to the west. It crowned the central of three hills bordering the city to the north, and covered a huge area — in the order of 60,000 square metres. In the present state of the excavations, however, we can present only a provisional picture[10]. The building was part of the city's fortifications, which bordered it on the north, though the citadel proper of Pella rose on an islet to the south, and was connected to dry land by a wooden bridge. Interestingly, the palace is inscribed precisely in the geometric plan of the city[11].

As at Vergina, a number of architectural complexes are juxtaposed. At Pella the number is greater, with three successive complexes from east to west, each in two rows, giving a total of six buildings; now, however, there is talk of

building VII to the west, and two others to the east. Buildings I, II, III, and V, at least, are here too characterised by the arrangement of the rooms around a huge courtyard (fig. 74).

Building I, at the south-east, the first to be excavated, seems to have covered an area of 7,500 square metres and acted as a reception complex. The central courtyard, with sides of 35 x 30 m, was surrounded by a peristyle, the north stoa of which had an apsidal room at each end. A huge, almost square room directly behind it, set between two large rectangular rooms, probably formed the heart of the composition. To the north, building IV, the exploration of which is just beginning, although less ambitious in conception, occupies a slightly more elevated level.

Further to the west, a second group of structures included building II on the façade. This had a larger courtyard than that of I, covering an area with a side of 50 m, and surrounded by a Doric colonnade with a double foundation, involving two juxtaposed walls, one of them, 1.20 m thick, girdling a second, 2.20 m thick, on which rested the stylobate.

Building V, to the north of this complex, had a courtyard of the same size and also surrounded by a Doric portico. It also had a complex dubbed 'the great baths' by the excavators, which had a pool with sides of 7 x 5 m, with a waterproof lining on the bottom and the sides still preserved to a height of 0.90 m. The depth of the pool in antiquity is estimated to have been about 1.65 m, and there was a staircase in one corner to afford access. The apparatus for filling and emptying the pool can be seen quite clearly. This arrangement suggests that building V is probably to be identified with the palaestra of the palace, which was devoted to physical exercise[12].

The complex furthest to the west doubtless consisted of building III to the south, organised around a courtyard, followed at the rear by a complex known as building VI. It seems, however, that it did not prove possible to construct the huge peristyle court intended for building III. A few decades later, a number of irregular rooms of small dimensions were erected, at less expense, on the original plan. Building VI, like building V, housed a bathing complex, in this case known as 'the small baths', the excavation of which is still in process.

To the south of this building complex, facing the south, and in any case in front of buildings I and II, rose a large stoa, standing on a stylobate more than 2 m high. At least 153 m long, it directly dominated the city and had a monumental tripartite propylon, 15 m wide, at the junction between the two buildings[13]. The effect must have been even more impressive

than that created by the stoa along the north side of the palace at Vergina.

The dating of this imposing complex poses a problem. There are some pieces of evidence suggesting that the site was occupied in the first half of the fourth century, and one might therefore think of the reign of Amyntas III. It was Amyntas, indeed, who, according to some scholars, made Pella the capital of Macedonia[14]. The erection of these large buildings with peristyle courtyards is to be attributed to Philip II[15]. A number of coins and the forms of the architectural elements (figs 75-77) have led the excavators to suggest a date in the second half of the fourth century for buildings I and II. Thereafter, the palace will have been enlarged to match the growth in the administration of the kingdom and in court life. Building V, with its bath, is to be dated to the turn of the fourth to the third century, in the reign of Cassander, who also seems to have played a major role in the expansion of the city[16]. For the unfinished stoa of building III, the pottery seems to point to the beginning of the third century, and for the poorer structures later erected on it, the second half of the century. Whatever the case, we are here in the presence of a group of buildings of impressive size and complexity. This was no longer, as at Vergina, a palace for entertainment, designed for meetings and festivals, but an arrangement which, in addition to the life of the court, housed the political and administrative machinery of the kingdom.

75

76. Pella, palace. Three-quarters capital of an engaged column, of Ionic style, which has some notable features: the flutings on the shaft end some distance below the echinus which, between the two half-palmettes carved in relief, did not have egg and dart pattern as one would expect (it was probably painted). On the baluster, two rows of horizontal pointed leaves are separated by a band.

77. Pella, palace. Sofa capital. This type of capital is very often used in northern Greece; this one, of a somewhat dry elegance, has unfortunately lost the side volutes that completed the motif of the sofa.

76

77

The Cities

The period of Philip II, and particularly the first century of the Hellenistic period, were marked by the evolution of cities[17]. Pella, Dion and Amphipolis are important and relatively well-known examples of this development, but many other cities (or settlements which became cities at a certain point in their history) are equally deserving of attention. This is true of the ancient capital Aigeai (Vergina), the systematic excavation of which is just beginning[18], and of smaller but just as instructive conglomerations such as Aiane, already important in the sixth and fifth centuries[19], Akanthos in Chalkidike[20], Morrylos in Krestonia[21], Petres (in the process of investigation)[22], Potidaia[23], Beroia[24] and Thessalonike[25], the 'Hippodamean' plan of which we shall encounter again. It would be desirable also to resume the excavation of the Nymphaion at Mieza, where the young Alexander was amongst the pupils of Aristotle, and which may have played a major role in the formation of a particular architectural type[26].

Pella

Capital of the Macedonian kingdom from the beginning of the fourth century, Pella quickly became an important Hellenistic political and artistic centre[27], and was considered 'the largest of the cities of Macedonia'[28].

Archaeological research on the site began in 1914, when Greece regained its sovereignty over this territory[29], and systematic excavations were conducted between 1957 and 1963[30], and were resumed in 1980[31].

None of the written sources mentions the transfer of the capital from Aigeai (Vergina), but the excavation data, though quite scanty at the moment, have led some to place this about the end of the fifth century — that is, at the time of King Archelaos (413-399 BC) — and this date was long accepted. It now seems more likely, however, that this event, of such importance for the kingdom of Macedonia, occurred at the beginning of the fourth century[32].

Remains from the earliest period are rare. The most notable is a cemetery of the end of the fifth and first half of the fourth centuries. This lay beneath the east and south-east area of the agora, but its exact boundaries have not yet been identified. It was abandoned when the city spread to the east in the second half of the fourth century[33].

The most important moment in this expansion came during the reign of Cassander, as is revealed both by the structures discovered in the main area of the excavation, and also by a number of chance finds[34]. The city will have been completely reorganised at this time, and the Roman conquest did not mark the end of its prosperity, which continued until the beginning of the first century, when the city was destroyed by an earthquake. The decline was accelerated with the troubled times of the first quarter of the first century[35]. The city gradually shifted to the west, to a site with a better water supply, where the Roman settlement called Pella Colonia was established. Later, during the Byzantine period, a fortified settlement rose on the site[36].

It has proved possible to repair and excavate some sections of a defence wall belonging to the ancient city, made of unbaked square bricks with a side of about 0.50 m, standing on a stone socle. The northern section of this rampart, reinforced by square towers, follows a continuous line to the west of the modern cemetery. It then skirts the hill of the acropolis and runs along the north edge of the palace and as far as the hill opposite in the west. Another section of the wall has been repaired to the south of the earliest blocks of residences, where a door has been discovered that belongs without doubt to an intermediate wall, for there must have been a wall further to the south, on the edge of the lake. All these remains probably to go back to the last quarter of the fourth century[37].

The city itself was built on 'the latest system, the Hippodamean system'[38]. The whole of the sector explored to date was divided into rectangular *insulae* of residences (figs 78, 79), roughly 45 m wide and in length, successively, 125 m, 111 m, 125 m, (twice), 152 m and finally 125 m. Streets oriented north-south and 9 to 10

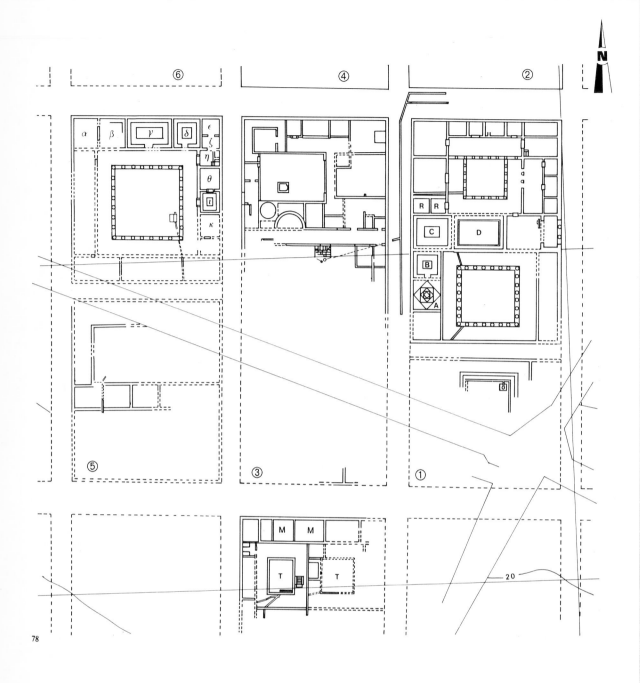

78

78. *Pella, the city. Plan
of the building insulae
excavated so far. To the
north of the modern
road, insula 1 is
occupied by the House
of Dionysos, with the
following rooms: A,
anteroom with mosaic of
inscribed squares; B,
mosaic of Dionysos and,
on the threshold, a
griffin attacking a stag;
C, Lion Hunt and, on
the threshold, two*

*Centaurs; D, chequer-
board of lozenges; RR,
rooms with floors of
mortar. In insula 5, to
the north of the modern
road, House of the
Abduction of Helen: γ,
mosaic of the Abduction
of Helen; δ, Stag Hunt;
ι, Amazonomachy. To the
south of the road, at MM,
floors of marble slabs,
at TT, floors of tesserae
and fragments of tiles.*

79. *Pella, the city.
Aerial view, looking
west; at the bottom, in
the foreground, the
House of Dionysos.
Some of the columns
have been re-erected
and the mosaics
replaced in position
after restoration.*

80

m wide are intersected at right angles by others of the same width[39].

The main street of the city, a 15 m wide avenue that crossed the agora from east to west, formed the axis of the design. The series of streets, however, is also relieved by at least two avenues 10 m wide, running from north to south, paved and equipped with raised stone pavements, which undoubtedly led from the port to the agora. Under the streets and avenues ran a water-supply and drainage system, so that individual houses could be supplied with drinking water, either directly or through public fountains.

This urban layout seems to have been in place from the very beginning. Unequivocal evidence dating from the foundation is lacking, but several house remains datable to the first half of the fourth century have the same orientation as the later structures.

Each of the *insulae* of residences consisted

of two or more houses, depending on the part of the city in which it was situated. The richer houses are of the type organised around a peristyle courtyard (occasionally two) with stoas of Doric or Ionic columns onto which opened the rooms, with the reception rooms normally situated on the north side. The latter, like their ante-rooms, generally had mosaic floors and walls covered with rich stucco decoration. The north part of the house also had an upper floor (as at Olynthos), access to which was by a staircase in the north-east corner. The door in the courtyard opened onto the street.

The wealthiest houses have been discovered in the main part of the excavation, and the investigators estimate that they date from the period immediately after Alexander[40]. We may note, amongst the most luxurious, the House of Dionysos and the House of the Abduction of Helen, so called after the subjects depicted on their mosaic floors[41]. The former (fig. 80) be-

80. Pella, the House of Dionysos. At bottom room A; above left, room B, in which the positions of the dining couches can clearly be made out around the central mosaic; at the right, room D; at the back, the north peristyle with its Ionic colonnade.

longs to the most complex type described by Vitruvius with two peristyles, a Doric one to the south and an Ionic one to the north. At least two banqueting rooms opened onto the Doric peristyle, adorned with mosaics depicting Dionysos on a panther, and a Lion Hunt, while the ante-rooms had geometric motifs. To the north, the private quarters and the staircase ascending to the upper storey gave onto the Ionic peristyle.

The House of the Abduction of Helen is notable for its large Doric peristyle and the banqueting rooms bordering it on the north side which have, from west to east, a mosaic with floral decoration, the mosaics of the Abduction of Helen and the Stag Hunt, signed by Gnosis, and, on the east side, the Amazonomachy.

Another residence, excavated in 1976-78 to the south of the House of the Abduction of Helen, was constructed around a Doric peristyle. Wonderful wall-paintings with architectural motifs adorned its ante-room and a room to the north of the peristyle in which the decoration reached a height of 5 m[42]. Another, smaller house, to the south of the house with the frescoes, belongs to the type of the 'pastas-house', of which numerous examples are known at Olynthos[43], and to which the house discovered by Oikonomos in 1913-1914 also belongs[44].

To the north of these houses, the agora of the city (fig. 81) has been excavated since 1980[45]. It consists of a complex of structures set around an area measuring slightly more than 200 m from east to west and 181 m from north to south. Together with its stoas, the complex measures almost 262 m from east to west and 238 m from north to south and corresponds to five *insulae* on the original plan in length and two in width, giving a total of ten blocks of the ancient city, into the tissue of which it is harmoniously integrated. The five small *insulae* bordering on the agora to the south clearly belong to the same design.

Men and vehicles made use of the large avenue crossing the agora from east to west, and other access roads led to the central square. Two of the latter have been recognised in the north stoa and at least two others to the south. Drainage pipes and clay pipes carrying drinking water ran beneath these streets.

The porticoes were supported on a row of columns in the south wing, and pillars in the north wing, and their superstructure was of timber. Behind them were two areas communicating with each other and connected to the central square, and two others, unconnected with the first two, which opened onto the

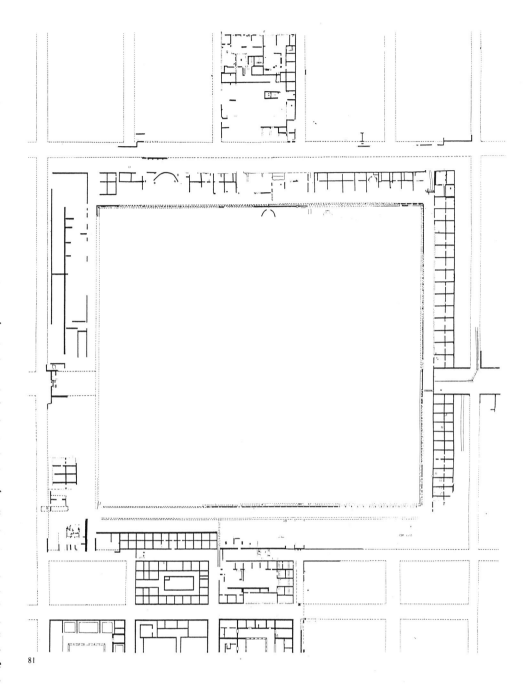

81

81. Pella, the Agora. Plan. The free area in the centre, with its considerable dimensions and its stoas, is virtually enclosed by the structures bordering it, the only opening in them being to accommodate a large east-west street.

82

streets and avenues running around the square, at a higher level in the north and a lower level in the south.

The various sectors of this agora were given over to a large number of artisan and commercial activities. In the south part of the east wing (fig. 82) were pottery workshops and shops. Further to the north were workshops producing terracotta figurines, as in the south wing, where a row of shops offered fresh produce, with a number of butcher's shops. Iron was worked in both the south-west area and the north-west corner. In the north part of the west wing was a row of shops selling aromatic products and further to the south, around the west gate, there were figurine workshops.

The north wing of the agora had a more official character. In front of the stoa, a row of foundations of honorific monuments has come to light, along with some fragments of bronze and some marble dedications. A number of large bases in the rooms of this stoa must have been for votive monuments, as suggested by the fragments of inscriptions. An apsidal room

may have been used for meetings of the body that regulated the proper use of this wing for official, as well as for religious functions, the latter attested by the existence of the sanctuary of Aphrodite and Cybele to the north[46]. A room in the south-west corner of the agora, with a Doric peristyle at the lower level and an Ionic one on the upper storey, housed the public archives. A series of seals and other characteristic objects were found here[47].

The place thus represents a closed complex of unusual dimensions and organisation. The excavation of the four wings is still in progress but, in the light of the first stratigraphic data, we may consider that the agora of Pella, in its present form, was built not after the Roman conquest, but at the time of Philip V.

Dion

The site of Dion was identified at the very beginning of the nineteenth century by W.M. Leake and visited by L. Heuzey towards the middle of the same century. The excavation,

82. Pella, the Agora.
The buildings of the
East wing with their
two rows of rooms.
One of the most
notable pieces of
information yielded by
the recent excavation is
the specialisation of
functions in this huge
complex, with sections
allocated to different
types of shops or
workshops.

conducted by the University of Thessalonike in 1928 under the direction of G. Sotiriadis, brought to light, in particular, a 'Macedonian tomb'. The excavation was resumed in 1963 by G. Bakalakis, who devoted himself mainly to the study of the city's defensive wall, and, above all, by the present excavator, D. Pandermalis, beginning in 1973[48]. Located in the heart of Pieria, a large richly-watered plain, and dominated by Mount Olympos, the city stretched along a river that flowed directly into the sea and which, in the Hellenistic period, was navigable for a distance of just over two kilometres inland.

Dion was in some way the religious capital of Macedonia, and its name was connected with that of Zeus, who was the object of a special cult there, together with the Muses[49]. The sanctuary of Zeus has been thought to have been identified outside the walls of the city (as have sanctuaries of other deities, and also the theatre and the stadium) with a wall 100 m in length, directly to the south, that may have belonged to its precinct, not far from the place where the Roman theatre was later to be built. It seems highly probable that the sanctuary housed the images of the kings of Macedonia (two bases have been found, one for a bronze statue of Cassander, and the other for a marble statue of Perseus) as well as inscribed stelai, a number of which have been preserved, bearing official texts, treaties of alliance or honorific decrees.

The sanctuary of Demeter[50] (fig. 83), also to the south of the city, though much nearer to the walls, experienced a brilliant phase throughout the entire Hellenistic period and beyond. Certain remains date from the very end of the sixth century: two 'megara', a kind of small temple with a pronaos and cella, constructed very carefully of ashlar blocks bound by a simple earth mortar.

The buildings of the Hellenistic period, on the other hand, were constructed in heavy masonry and form an impressive group, oriented north-south. The two small temples that will have replaced the two earlier ones towards the end of the fourth century, were slightly larger, though still of relatively modest size (7 x 11 m), and had no exterior colonnade. In one of them have been found a number of ritual vases and also a beautiful female head, which perhaps belonged to the cult statue of Demeter (fig. 35). To the east of these two buildings stood a whole row of *oikoi*, simple open rooms like the small temples. On the floor of one of these the paving slabs in which the supports for an offering table were embedded are still *in situ,* and behind them, near the back wall, is a base that was intended to receive a cult statue.

A little further to the east, immediately to the south of the south-west corner of the city walls, the sanctuary of Isis[51] consisted of a notable group of buildings, with four temples from the period of the Severi, but also with a sculp-

83. Dion, the Sanctuary
of Demeter. Despite the
complexity of a site
made particularly
difficult by a
subterranean expanse of
water, the
archaeologists have
distinguished the
successive phases of the
two temples.

83

ture dating from the second century. Beneath the podium of the main building have been identified the remains of an earlier structure, that belonged without doubt to the late Hellenistic period, when the cult of Isis replaced that of Artemis Eileithyia.

Still outside the walls at the south of the city, though this time directly to the west, the Hellenistic theatre[52] (fig. 84) was built, as one might have expected, not far from the sanctuary of Dionysos. In the absence of any hill in the neighbourhood, the tiers of seats could not rest on the natural slopes of the ground, the current practice in Greek theatres; and the technique (employed a short distance away on the same site for the theatre built in the second century of the present era) that involved supporting the rows of seat on a radiating series of

vaults had not yet been mastered. The builders were here content to pile up earth to give the necessary gradient, as in the theatre of Eretria, for example. Sherds and coins issued by the Macedonian kings, dating from the fourth to the beginning of the second centuries, help to date its construction to the period of Philip V.

The rows of seats set on the earth fill have suffered badly. They were built of bricks distinctly thicker than those of the Roman period, and obviously made specially for this purpose, set in position with a mortising that dispensed with the use of mortar — a technique completely unknown at this period in the construction of theatres and in Greek building in general, though the use of baked brick is sporadically attested at other sites before the imperial period.

84. Dion, the Greek theatre. The aerial view shows clearly that it was not constructed on a natural slope, as was usual in Greece, but on an artificial embankment.

The orchestra, which has a diameter of about 26 m, was surrounded by a wide, shallow, stone channel, designed to receive the surface water and lead it off to the north. The orchestra circle is broken by the projecting proscenium, from which an underground axial passage led to the centre of the orchestra, an arrangement very rare in Greece, being found in this precise form only at Eretria and Sikyon. It is generally thought that this 'Charonian passage' was to enable actors playing characters from the underworld to make their appearance, though this interpretation has recently been disputed.

Of the proscenium itself, which was 8.50 m deep, the only surviving remains are a few fragments of engaged columns and of the Doric frieze. Between the *paraskenia*, the *skene* was divided into two aisles by a row of pillars, and had a raised floor about 2.65 m above the orchestra.

The city itself was enclosed within defensive walls[53], the total length of which exceeds 2,600 m, with the earliest phase dating from the end of the fourth century, and more precisely from the period of Cassander (fig. 85). Three sides are straight and at right angles, but the fourth, to the east, had to follow the course of the river. This at least, was its Roman form, for an as yet unproven theory claims that originally it was straight, thereby giving the city the form of a perfect rectangle.

To date, five gates have been discovered, at the points of exit of the major streets. The best known, gate B II to the north, was protected externally by two strong towers, 14.20 m apart, and led to a first courtyard, 5.20 x 2.50 m, and then into a second, 8.50 x 5.70 m, which ensured a system of reinforced control and protection. The walls had a series of rectangular towers, thirty-three metres (that is, 100 feet) apart, except where, for some reason, they had to be closer together. The lower part of the entire wall is built of Olympian conglomerate, with facing blocks slightly convex and rusticated (fig. 86). These were probably surmounted by a structure of unbaked bricks. The wall was repaired as early as the Hellenistic period, at the time of Perseus. Under the empire it was completely remodelled.

Within this enceinte the city seems to have been laid out on the geometric plan that we have already encountered at Olynthos, Thessalonike and Pella, with major arteries, set at right angles to each other, leading directly to the gates. The best known is a north-south street in the east part of the city, paved with Olympian conglomerate.

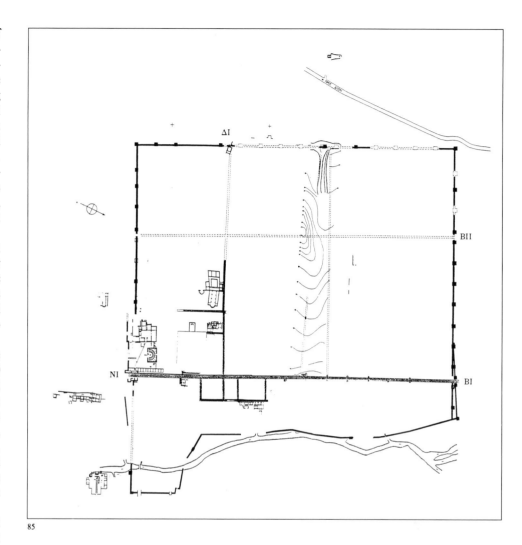

85

Along the side of one of the streets at right angles to this, are a number of architectural remains of a monumental Hellenistic building (fig. 87) adorned with relief shields and breastplates. A good number of other structures has also been identified and awaits excavation. Recent investigations have revealed walls in this area constructed with a fine ashlar masonry, and belonging without doubt to a building of the Hellenistic agora.

Several cemeteries[54] have been located, one of which has yielded the funerary stele of a young girl from the middle of the fifth century discussed above[55]. And a number of chamber tombs, set in a dry stone *peribolos*, are to be dated to the fourth century.

Of the five 'Macedonian tombs' excavated (these structures are studied as a group elsewhere)[56], the most interesting from the architectural point of view is undoubtedly the one dating from the end of the fourth century, discovered by Sotiriadis (fig. 88). Behind a very severe façade (with an architrave forming a lintel above the door, surmounted by a Doric frieze),

85. Dion, the city. Plan of the Hellenistic ramparts. They form three sides of a rectangle, the fourth side following the course of the river, at least from a certain period onwards. The positioning of the gates and the first streets uncovered suggests an organization of Hippodamean type, with a system of rectangular blocks like that at Pella.

86

87

86. Dion, the city. The
fortification wall.
Constructed of fine
isodomic masonry in
the Hellenistic period, it
thereafter underwent a
whole series of
modifications.

87. Dion, the city.
The 'monument of the
shields'. One of the
first streets uncovered
on the site was
bordered by a
structure of fine
appearance, with
walls carved with
shields and cuirasses,
which it may be
supposed were
painted and bore
Macedonian emblems;
this must have been a
Hellenistic public
building, the only one
to be discovered so
far.

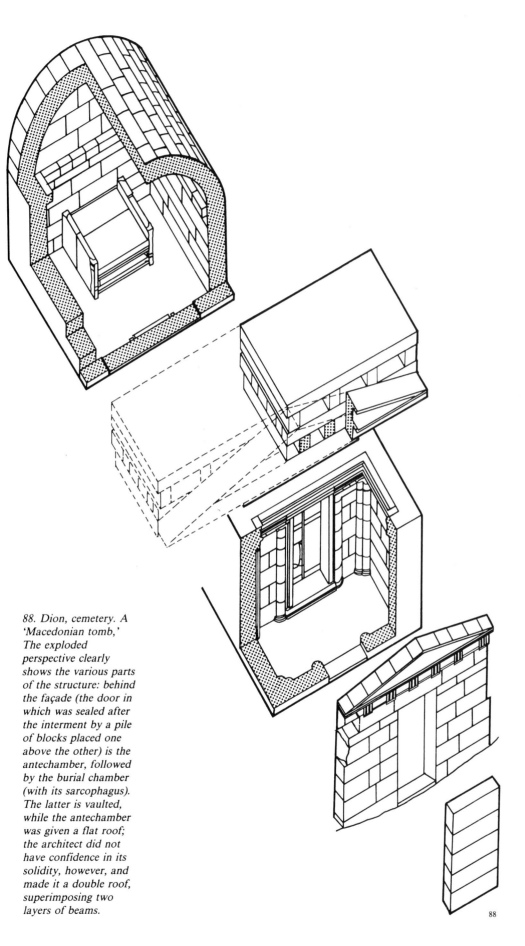

the ante-chamber is adorned with Ionic half-columns on either side of the two axially placed doors, supporting an architrave with fasciae, and with double quarter-columns in the corners — a very unusual arrangement. The ceiling is not vaulted, but flat, and the architect, as though not having confidence in its solidity, made it double: on top of a series of slabs carried on stone beams, he placed a second row of stone beams carrying a second series of slabs. The funerary chamber itself, which has a barrel vault, had a wide marble bed.

Amphipolis

The site of Amphipolis possessed a number of advantages for the establishment of an important city[57]. Occupying a group of hills to the south-west of Mount Pangaion, it was bordered by the Strymon, a navigable river that served as a naval base and connected it with the port of Eion on the north coast of the Aegean. The city was thus located at the crossroads of the communication routes between Macedonia and Thrace, and between the sea and the rich territories of the interior, routes which, most importantly of all, gave access to the gold and silver mines of Pangaion and to the forests famous for the timber that they supplied for the construction of ships.

Founded as an Athenian colony in 437 BC[58], Amphipolis, after a period of independence[59], was conquered in 358/7 BC by Philip II of Macedonia[60]. It then acted as a base of operations for the king, and also for Alexander before his expedition to the East, and housed an important royal mint. It was on its acropolis that Cassander imprisoned Roxane and Alexander IV, the son of Alexander the Great. Under Philip V it struck its own coinage. After the battle of Pydna in 168 BC it was Perseus' last *point d'appui* before he was captured. When the Macedonian state was dissolved by the Romans, Amphipolis found itself elevated to the rank of capital and mint of the first *meris* (administrative region) until, in 148 BC, Macedonia became a Roman province.

The site was explored by D. Lazaridis between 1956 and 1984, and by his daughter Kalliopi Lazaridou since 1985, and important work was carried out over the huge area occupied by the city and its cemetery. The two fortification walls — the 'Long Wall' of which Thucydides speaks (an outer enceinte 7,480 m long that encircled the entire city) and the inner defence wall, 2,200 m long, that protected the acropolis — were erected at the time of the foundation of

88. Dion, cemetery. A 'Macedonian tomb,' The exploded perspective clearly shows the various parts of the structure: behind the façade (the door in which was sealed after the interment by a pile of blocks placed one above the other) is the antechamber, followed by the burial chamber (with its sarcophagus). The latter is vaulted, while the antechamber was given a flat roof; the architect did not have confidence in its solidity, however, and made it a double roof, superimposing two layers of beams.

88

89. Amphipolis, fortifications. The structure, with its pseudo-isodomic masonry, is of great beauty for the Hellenistic period; it also had, in addition to towers and monumental gates, devices to lead outside the walls the water that accumulated at the edge of the city.

90. Amphipolis, the Gymnasium. The aerial view makes it possible to make out the palaestra, at the left, with its rooms grouped around a peristyle court; above, the long horizontal lines of the xystos for track-events.

91. Amphipolis, the Gymnasium. The bathroom was equipped with rectangular basins in which the athletes washed themselves; some of these can be seen here, with their supports, along the walls.

91

the city. These same walls, with repairs, additions and restorations, continued to function in the Hellenistic period (fig. 89). Reinforced by square or round towers, bastions and fortified gates, the lower parts were constructed of poros in isodomic masonry of the Classical period, while on top of these pseudo-isodomic masonry was laid in the Hellenistic period, with courses of low blocks placed lengthways alternating with courses of tall, square and rectangular blocks. The most impressive section is the length of the north wall, preserved to a height reaching 7.50 m, with an unusual system of culverts for leading off water outside the city, and three fortified gates.

As well as two earlier sanctuaries, two open-air sanctuaries dating from the late Hellenistic period have been identified: that of Attis, in the west part of the city, had bases for dedications, large terracotta protomes, and statuettes of the Phrygian god; the other, outside the east wall, was dedicated to Cybele and Attis and yielded a quantity of figurines of these gods, dedications and a votive relief of Cybele.

A second-century house in the south part of the city was adorned with wall-paintings. A room painted with vivid colours (fig. 93) has panels of lozenges between columns, and garlands with young Erotes, cornices and coffers,

modelled in plaster. In another room (fig. 92), the decoration featured pseudo-isodomic masonry in coloured rows[61].

In the south-east part of the city, the first public building has come to light — the gymnasium (fig. 90), in Doric style and constructed of fine isodomic and pseudo-isodomic masonry. Its heart consists of a palaestra, 47 x 36 m, with two entrances, approached from the east by a monumental staircase 8.70 m wide and from the west by a paved road. It is organised around a peristyle courtyard, on to which give two porticoed halls and eight rooms, all of which were used for meetings, teaching and physical exercise. Amongst the most important discoveries may be cited a decree of Philip V, a very detailed ephebic law, a number of honorific decrees, a basin on a stand dedicated by a gymnasiarch, some bases for votive statues and a some herms. A number of socles were probably designed to support wooden benches, and four oval floors, made of small clay tiles, were certainly training areas for the great test of wrestling.

The baths were housed in two rooms in the north corner (one measuring 12.17 x 7.10 m, the other with a side of about 7.15 m). Along the walls were bases supporting rectangular basins, four examples of which, in marble, have been

92

93

93. Amphipolis, the
city. The same house
had another room, this
time adorned with
paintings featuring a
more complex system,
with large rectangular
panels, and also with
columns painted to
appear as though they
stand in front of the
wall.

92. Amphipolis, the
city. A Hellenistic
house has fairly well-
preserved wall
decoration, with an
interesting imitation of
pseudo-isodomic
masonry.

94. Amphipolis, the
Lion. It clearly recalls
the Lion of Chaironeia.
It may be a funerary
monument for one of
the Companions of
Alexander the Great.

discovered on the paved floor (fig. 91). To the
north-west of the palaestra, a structure with
two rectangular basins set side by side, measuring 4.60 x 2.50 m and with a floor of coloured
pebbles, was perhaps used as a swimming pool.
To the north-east, the *xystos*, a track protected
by a stoa with a Doric colonnade facing the
south, made it possible to train for track events
in bad weather. No more than 80 m have been
uncovered, but it probably had the regulation
length of one stade. Its internal width is 7 m,
and it was designed to train six runners, though
the starting line, set obliquely, seems to have
been made for races involving three athletes
competing in the 'double stadion' or 'long
race'. Alongside the *xystos*, the *paradromis* was
the open-air track for fine weather. The starting
line at the beginning of the track had twenty
sockets, in which were set the wooden posts
between which the runners took up their positions. Other sockets made it possible to define
their lanes. The same building also had two cult
areas for sacrifices and banquets, very probably
in honour of the patron gods of athletes, Herakles and Hermes, whose cult is attested by inscriptions.

The gymnasium was founded in the second
half of the fourth century, and continued to
enjoy great prestige until the end of the first
century of the present era.

The cemeteries of Amphipolis covered a
large area, well outside the city walls, or along
their course. On an elongated hill, two kilometres to the north-east of the modern village,
have been found over four hundred tombs of
different types, dating from the middle of the
fourth century to the middle of the second, in
which a quantity of valuable grave offerings,
gold jewellery, figurines, protomes of female
deities, terracotta plaques with relief decoration, vases, and funerary stelai have been
found.

At a number of places, ranging from 1 to 4.5
kilometres away from the city walls, seven built
tombs have been brought to light amongst the
grave groups, beneath tumuli dating from the
third and second centuries. And from the end
of the fourth century dates the 'Lion of Amphipolis' (fig. 94), a famous funerary monument
erected on the west bank of the Strymon in
honour of an important person, probably
Nearchos, Alexander the Great's admiral.

Cults and Myths

The sanctuaries

One searches in vain in the Macedonian cities for the silhouettes of columns and pediments, so familiar in Greece, that signal the presence of a temple. Does this mean that ancient Macedonia did not have sanctuaries for the gods, or that these had a completely different aspect in this country?

A number of indications should already have counselled caution, and the archaeological and above all epigraphical discoveries of recent years have demonstrated the futility of such hypotheses. The lack of significant remains must be accounted for differently. The alluvial plains of Macedonia are poor in durable building materials. Marble, the noble material used mainly for major buildings, was only quarried on the slopes of Mount Bermion, hence the relative rarity of monumental structures, the extensive use of tufa, or brick, occasionally covered with stucco in imitation of marble, and the systematic plundering of durable materials which, with rare exceptions, has effaced even the memory of the monuments.

The earliest and most instructive sanctuaries are located at Dion, the religious centre of the kingdom, in the shadow of Mount Olympos[62]. Here, towards the autumnal equinox, was celebrated the cult of Olympian Zeus, at once the father of the gods and the mythical ancestor of the Macedonians, and, with him, the nine Pierian Muses. The celebration of sacrifices and athletic and musical gatherings, which probably coincided with one of the two meetings of the Macedonian assembly, was the occasion of an extraordinary concourse, for people came from the four corners of Macedonia to be present at the ceremonies.

The postwar excavations have made possible the identification of the enclosure sacred to Zeus in the plain outside and to the south of the city walls[63]. The temple, the stoas and the gymnasium mentioned in the inscriptions and the literary texts will no doubt eventually be discovered.

The earliest temple at Dion known at present belonged to the sanctuary of Demeter (fig. 95), who was no doubt an indigenous mother-goddess Hellenised under this name by the conquering Macedonians. It consists of two buildings from the end of the sixth century which were succeeded in the Hellenistic period by two rather more monumental structures[64]. The cult areas of Artemis Eileithyia and Aphrodite Hypolympidia, which were later absorbed into the complex of the sanctuary of Isis, undoubtedly date from this same period.

The excavations are beginning to give us a more precise picture of the religious landscape of the two capitals of Macedonia. At Aigeai[65], we are seeing the progressive emergence of the temple of Eukleia, from the Classical period. The very recent discovery of a series of statues, one of them of the goddess herself, supplements the information furnished by the fine dedications by queen Eurydice, wife of Amyntas III and mother of Philip II. The identification, also very recent, of a sanctuary of the Mother of the Gods confirms the early vitality of the 'indigenous' cult, which we shall encounter again in other Macedonian cities.

As for Pella[66] we had for a long time only indirect knowledge of the cults, through the literary sources and through archaeological and epigraphical discoveries without a context. Thanks to the discovery of the Archaic megaron and the mysterious large Classical tholos, we now have direct access to a sanctuary in the new capital — possibly that of Herakles. More recently, a sanctuary has been found *extra muros* and attributed to Demeter, and near the agora have been located the sanctuaries of the Mother of the Gods, of Aphrodite, and of Dionysos.

In view of the wealth of material remains from the Macedonian sanctuaries, we shall refer here only to the most important of them, before examining in greater detail those of Beroia, for which we possess unique and relatively abundant documentation.

Until the Roman conquest, Pydna was the most important city in Pieria. Rescue excavations on the site, which has been given over to property developers, have not yet brought to light the traces of an early sanctuary, but the

95. Head of Demeter, found at Dion, end of the fourth century BC. This work possibly belonged to the cult statue of the goddess; its highly Classical features must have been enhanced by the metallic elements, diadem and jewellery, of which all that remains are the attachment sockets.

discovery of a decree reused in a late tomb[67] furnishes excellent evidence for one of its temples, that of Apollo Dekadryos, which was probably located *extra muros*. The cult statue, damaged in circumstances that escape us, but which may be related to the invasion of Pieria by the Romans in 169 BC, was restored by two craftsmen from Demetrias, in whose honour the decree was voted.

At Edessa[68], columns and antae, frequently covered with inscriptions registering acts of manumission from a temple of the Mother of the Gods, invoked in the Roman period under the name of Ma, were reused during the restoration of the south gate of the city and the wide street with stoas that led to it. The temple was probably located close to this gate, outside the ramparts. Another unpublished inscription indicates that this sanctuary was already functioning in the Hellenistic period.

We know from a passage in Diodorus that Alexander the Great planned to erect a sumptuous temple to Athena at Kyrrhos. This Macedonian city and its sanctuary were so little known that the first editors of the historian doubted the reliability of the manuscript tradition of this passage. The recent discovery of an anta from a temple[69], covered with inscriptions going back to the Hellenistic period, has furnished striking confirmation of this unique literary testimony.

We are badly informed about the sanctuaries of pre-Roman Thessalonike. The only exception is that of the Egyptian gods, preserved almost intact from the zeal of the Christians, and restored to us thanks to the great fire of 1917. However, a recently published boundary-stone from the territories of the small townships that were to form the future Thessalonike, dating from the reign of Philip II, offers a glimpse of the cult areas that dotted the surrounding countryside: the Hermaion, the Dioskoureion, and the sanctuary of Artemis.

During the interwar period, a sanctuary of Demeter and Kore *extra muros* was excavated in the gorge near ancient Lete. The finds, from the Hellenistic period, were never published[70]. They reveal a cult connected with the rites of passage of young girls, and shed some light on the origins of manumission through consecration in Macedonia.

It is also thanks to the excavations of the period between the wars, which remained for so long unknown to the public, that the existence has been discovered of an important sanctuary of Asklepios at Morrylos near Kilkis[71], with a series of statues of the god and his family. The wealth of epigraphic evidence (supplemented by subsequent excavations) permits us to reconstruct the functioning of the sanctuary: offerings of cattle, and rural festivals to which pilgrims flocked from the neighbouring cities.

The presence in this list of small towns such as Kyrrhos or Morrylos, and the absence of important centres like Amphipolis, Kassandreia, or even Apollonia, throws into relief the essentially fortuitous character of our documentation. Amphipolis has suffered from the remodelling in the Early Christian period of the area of the sanctuaries, and particularly that of Artemis Tauropolos[72], and Kassandreia from the construction of the modern village of Nea Potidaia on its site, while Apollonia, despite the accidental discovery of remains of great interest, has not yet been systematically explored.

Beroia is not a site that is easy to investigate. Its continuous occupation from antiquity to the present day makes archaeological exploration extremely difficult. The relative wealth of information relating to its sanctuaries is due to the importance of the city under the Antigonids, whose cradle it was, and to the proximity of the marble quarries of Mount Bermion, from which an abundance of durable, quality material was extracted. We also possess testimony dating from the Hellenistic period for at least four sanctuaries[73], the approximate location of which we can guess with some probability, if not certainty.

The main sanctuary at Beroia was that of Herakles Kynagidas, the mythical ancestor of the kings of Macedonia. It is attested by several royal letters, a list of priests called *kynegoi*, and a series of dedications. Some of these documents were inscribed on an anta of the temple which was reused in a late burial. The place in which the majority of the others were found suggests that the sanctuary was located towards the west edge of the city.

Of almost equal importance was the sanctuary of Asklepios, which was shared with Apollo and Hygeia. The priests of this sanctuary were the eponymous officials at Beroia, as at other Macedonian cities. Thanks to a fragment of the accounts that they rendered towards the end of the third century, and also to a slightly later dedication, we may presume that the sanctuary stood near the ancient agora, and that it was provided with an *enkoimeterion* and an *exedra*.

We are less well informed about the sanctuary of Dionysos, even though a fragment of its magnificent marble epistyle has been preserved, together with part of the dedication. A column that perhaps comes from the temple itself affords evidence for the names by which the god was invoked, which were extremely archaic and highly original: the False Man, the Savage, the Very Hidden.

Finally, a royal dedication has revealed the existence of a sanctuary of Athena. It informs us, in fact, that Philip V had some stoas constructed for the goddess, perhaps close to one of the two main axes of both the ancient and the modern city, where the slab bearing the dedication was reused in the Roman period[74].

Iconography of gods and myths

To what degree would it be right to speak of a 'Macedonian religion'? Iconography helps us to answer this question, which does not arise only for the period under consideration here. May we regard the deities worshipped in Macedonia, and the cults and rituals practised there since the earliest times as different from what we find elsewhere in the Greek world? Do we not rather see there phenomena that are common to the whole of Greece — perhaps with some features more pronounced according to the region, or, for example, with certain gods enjoying special favour, accounted for sometimes by the nature of the countryside and the cultivation practised there, in which certain gods intervene more directly.

There is considerable evidence for this phenomenon, notably in Arkadia[75], where the attributes of deities are not exactly the same as in Attica or Epirus, for example. It is therefore of some interest to establish which deities were most successful, so to speak, in a region such as Macedonia, and also to determine the individual characteristics of the heroes and heroines that were particularly in favour there.

We have known for some time that the Macedonians, just like the other inhabitants of Greece, worshipped the Olympian gods, and recent excavations have uncovered several sanctuaries dedicated to them, even though religious buildings are still quite rare in comparison with discoveries of palaces and cities[76].

We must, naturally, first consider the contribution made by the excavations at Dion, where the great festival of Zeus, the Olympia, probably went back to a very early date. Philip and Alexander continued this tradition, and the celebrated group by Lysippos was erected there, depicting the twenty-five companions of Alexander killed at the battle of Granikos[77]. This sanctuary of Zeus, outside the walls of the city[78], was either close to a sanctuary dedicated to the Muses, or dedicated jointly to Zeus and the Muses, his daughters. So much is clear from

96. Poseidon, bronze statuette found at Pella, Late Hellenistic period. The god holds his trident, now lost, vertically in his left hand and rests his right foot on a support which is also missing. This object, a version of the well-known statue preserved in the Latran Museum in Rome, derives ultimately from the creation of Lysippos for the temple of the god at the Isthmus of Corinth.

96

97

97. *Athena with bull's horns, terracotta statuette found at Pella, second century BC. The goddess wears the peplos with a gorgoneion on her chest, as is normal; the two horns on her helmet, which evoke the power of the bull, perhaps allow us to see in this image a copy of the cult statue of Athena Alkidemos, whose cult is attested at this site.*

98. *Aphrodite seated, holding a winged Eros, terracotta statuette found at Beroia, beginning of the second century BC. The goddess's clothing leaves her left breast bare, and she is preparing to suckle the young Eros, whom she draws tenderly towards her, playing the role of 'kourotrophos'. This statuette, which is at this early date a forerunner of the theme of the Virgin and Child, was found in a woman's tomb.*

a statue of a Muse found there, perhaps depicting Terpsichore holding a lyre made from a tortoise-shell[79].

Poseidon, another major Olympian god, appears at Pella, which may be thought of as a seaport, in the form of a bronze statue (fig. 96) in the type of the 'Poseidon of Latran', attributed to Lysippos[80].

We also know at present that, at least from the end of the Archaic period, Demeter was honoured at Dion in a sanctuary[81] that has yielded a large number of finds, the earliest going back to about 500 BC. On display in the site Museum is a splendid head of a goddess (fig. 95), that comes from one of two small temples and, according to D. Pandermalis, probably belonged to the cult statue. It depicts Demeter, with the back of her head covered with a veil, and wearing a diadem and earrings, attested now only by the holes into which they fitted[82]. Dating from the end of the fourth century, the head is of a quality that suggests that it is the work of one of the greatest of the masters at the court of the Macedonian kings.

Other sculptures of deities have been discovered in this same sanctuary, one possibly depicting a small-scale Demeter, the other a fragmentary Aphrodite carrying an Eros on her left shoulder. Both are from the third century and the presence of Aphrodite should not surprise us, for she is also — we shall return to this point — a *kourotrophos* deity, who cared for children as well as the animal and plant kingdoms, and was thus close to Demeter. At Pella, towards the north-west of the city, a Thesmophorion has come to light — a sanctuary in honour of Demeter, where the autumn sowing was celebrated, and where the offerings are connected with the cult of this goddess.

Other excavations have produced their evidence for rural and *kourotrophos* divinities, so important in a society in which agriculture and stock-raising played such a major role. The deity most venerated in Macedonia was perhaps Artemis, as suggested by a whole series of recent discoveries. The most notable is that at Vergina where, since 1982, the sanctuary of Eukleia has been uncovered, one of the epithets by which Artemis was invoked. She had a temple there from the Classical period onwards, and the cult statue itself has recently been found — a work of very high quality dedicated by Eurydice, the mother of Philip II. Hellenistic Macedonia invoked this Artemis under several other names, however: she was Tauropolos at Amphipolis, and Eileithyia at Dion, and had other names, corresponding with the particular attribute to which the dedicator wished to ap-

peal, such as Artemis Digaia Blaganitis, the 'frog' of the wetlands loved by the goddess[83]. Athena, too, who had the surname Alkidemos was the protector of herds and flocks at Pella. She was depicted[84] in the traditional manner with a *gorgoneion* on her chest but also with bull's horns on her helmet[85] (fig. 97).

Finally, the images of Aphrodite herself sometimes also evoke the animal world. A bronze preserved in the Museum of Beroia shows her as 'Epitragia', seated on a goat[86]. More traditionally, though in baroque taste, a group found in a tomb at Beroia[87] depicts her with her right shoulder bare, carrying a winged Eros on her left shoulder, while a young girl at her right holds a dove. Or again, seated, she holds the infant Eros tightly in her arms in a very maternal gesture[88] (fig. 98). At Pella, a statuette depicts her with a standing Eros[89].

It is notable, however, that an entire series of documents from tombs at Beroia depicts the goddess with naked torso holding up a mask of Silenus in her right hand, and a bowl of fruit or a cornucopia in the other (fig. 99). The idea of fecundity is here accompanied by evocations of fertility[90].

These female Macedonian divinities are probably to be connected with the Mother of the gods, who was frequently worshipped in these regions and who often seems to be confused with Cybele. The cult of the latter, well-known in neighbouring Thrace, is equally well attested at both Dion and Vergina. To the north-west of the palace of the latter city, Manolis Andronicos partially uncovered the sanctuary of the Mother of the gods, probably Cybele, as perhaps indicated by a statuette found next to the threshold[91]. This sanctuary functioned from the beginning of the third century until towards the end of the second, and probably housed mystery rituals. In the vicinity of a ditch with a clay pipe, coiled clay serpents call to mind the *Agathodaimon*[92]. At Pella too, the excavations of recent years have revealed the presence of a Mother of the gods, together with Aphrodite, in a sanctuary to the north of the agora dated by the finds to the third or second century. Statuettes of Cybele have been found in some of the shops in the agora[93], as also at Olynthos, from where comes a characteristic mould of the beginning of the fourth century[94] depicting a protome of the goddess crowned with palmettes and rosettes, heavily burdened with jewellery, and striking her tympanum with her right hand.

The presence of this musical instrument, the masks of Silenus held by the Aphrodites of Beroia, and the masks of Silenus on the fine pot-

100

101

102. Cult statue of
Aphrodite
Hypolympidia from
Dion, second century
BC. This work, in
which the drapery,
rendered as though wet,
reveals the beauty of
the body, is a
representation of
'Aphrodite who lives
below Olympos.'

101. Herakles dressed
as Omphale. Bronze
from the decoration of
a bed from Dion, first
century BC. This is a
rendering in Hellenistic
taste of a well-known
theme from myth.

tery of Vergina[95], all serve to remind us how the cult of Dionysos prospered in Macedonia, rich in vines and wines. At Dion, his sanctuary was located near the Hellenistic theatre, as was natural, and D. Pandermalis draws particular attention, amongst the numerous epigraphic and other finds, to a Hellenistic statue of a Hermaphrodite[96].

It is likely that the god's character had certain special features in Macedonia, of which we may perhaps form some idea, for an early period, from literary texts such as the *Bacchae* of Euripides, written at the end of the poet's life, when he was guest of King Archelaos at the Macedonian capital[97].

This cult was in any case welcomed with great fervour by the Macedonians. It was also practised at Pella (like the cult of Pan, who is frequently associated with Dionysos), and its importance is attested by a number of iconographic testimonia of exceptional quality, amongst them the wonderful reliefs on the Derveni krater[98], or the ivory group from the Tomb of the Prince at Vergina[99]. The latter very probably depicts Dionysos holding his thyrsos in one hand and embracing Ariadne with the other, both of them preceded by a small Pan playing the *aulos.* (We should also note that a marble statuette of Alexander found at Pella depicts him with small horns of Pan in his hair[100] (fig. 100).) But this iconography, which reveals a particular interest in the Dionysiac cycle, hardly helps us to discern in what respect the cult of the god differed from that practised, for example, in Attica at the same period. A silver alabastron from the end of the second century[101] at least evokes a quite distinctive *ambiance*, depicting beneath a frieze of Eros a rarer scene — the presentation of the young Dionysos to the Nymphs who are to bring him up.

Chthonic deities also seem to have played a major role in Macedonia. Hades is portrayed on several occasions after the middle of the fourth century at Vergina, in the Tomb of Persephone[102] and the Tomb of Eurydice[103], and then at Lefkadia[104]. We thus see once more that the rural regions (such as neighbouring Epirus) accorded special importance to the divinities who had the power to bring them wealth or famine.

The divinities of health were equally honoured. One of them seems to have been particularly dear to the Macedonians — Asklepios, to whom Alexander himself made offerings in his sanctuary at Gortys in Arkadia[105]. The god is portrayed already in the Hellenistic period at Morrylos[106], and his cult became firmly established in this city, as also at Amphipolis and

elsewhere. It is noteworthy that a group has been found at Dion depicting Asklepios and his family, the Asklepiadai, all of them named by inscriptions. These sculptures date from the Roman period, but it is highly likely that the cult was established at Dion much earlier, at least in the Hellenistic period. A statue of Hygeia, found near the Asklepieion though outside its perimeter wall, probably dates from the fourth century[107].

It was at this period, too, that new cults made their appearance in Macedonia, frequently introduced under the influence of the Ptolemies. Occasionally they involved a renewal of earlier cults. At Dion, for example, the sanctuary of Artemis Eileithyia and Aphrodite Hypolympidia ('she at the foot of Olympos')[108] (fig. 102), Hellenistic statues of whom have been discovered, was set in the superb complex dedicated to the goddess Isis, an Isis-Tyche who is depicted in a statue holding a cornucopia in one hand. A votive relief of the second century shows the holy trinity: Serapis, Isis and Anubis. A fine head of Serapis wears in its hair the modius — the grain-measure indicating the fertility of the earth. Syrian cults were also popular in Hellenistic Macedonia: thus the goddess Atargatis, from the third century, is depicted wearing a tower on her head and seated on a fish[109].

Herakles, who in Macedonia was thought of as a god celebrated by his own priests, rather than as a hero[110], enjoyed a cult there all the more popular because the kings of Macedonia, claiming to be his descendants, took the skin of the Nemean lion as their emblem[111]. The person of the god is frequently depicted. At Beroia, it was in the form of Herakles Kynagidas. At Dion, several portraits of him have been found, dating from the end of the Hellenistic period, one of them a bronze from the first century BC which depicts him dressed in female clothing, as he appeared in the legend of Omphale (fig. 101). A more traditional rendering is found in heads of Herakles wearing the skin of the Nemean lion on his head, on silver vases from a tomb at Vergina[112], and in a small head from the second half of the fourth century found at Derveni[113].

The heroes of the Homeric legends, too, played an essential role in Macedonia, above all Achilles. It seems that the scene in the centre of the large shield in Philip's tomb[114] depicts not merely some hero killing an Amazon, but Achilles, at once lover and murderer of Penthesilea.

The iconography of the heroic world is known also from more modest documents. The workshops on the edge of the main area in the agora at Pella, which formed a large part of the commercial centre that has now been systematically explored[115], have yielded a great wealth of material relating to figurine-production (moulds for relief bowls, fragments of actual bowls). These illustrate many Greek legends, especially subjects drawn from the Sack of Troy[116] (fig. 127), and attest to the importance, even in the second century and later, of an iconography connected with the Homeric poems, in a country where the heroes of the Trojan War continued to be regarded as models. At the foot of Mount Pangaion, however, it was the hero Auloneites, in the type of the 'Thracian horseman', who was honoured in a recently explored sanctuary[117].

Other myths appear in the mosaics of Pella, sometimes connected with the same cycle, like the mosaic of Helen. A large panel[118] (fig. 105) portrays Theseus carrying off the young woman who, in her struggles, holds out her arms to a companion identified by an inscription as Deianeira. No person of this name occurs in the literary texts in the episode of the rape of Helen by Theseus (nor, indeed, in that of her abduction by Paris).

Was this an invention by the artist — a version different from that recorded by the rest of the evidence; It should be noted that here it is Phorbas who is driving Theseus' chariot, and according to one literary tradition he also accompanied him in the episode of the rape of Antiope, queen of the Amazons. Antiope is the name of an Amazon who fought against Herakles. It has therefore been suggested[119] that an original work of art, probably a large-scale painting, must have depicted Deianeira, identified by an inscription, during the abduction of Antiope by Theseus, assisted by Phorbas. Deianeira and Phorbas may thus have been transferred from one scene of abduction, that of Antiope, to another, that of Helen by the same hero. The iconography of other mosaics at Pella evokes the royal hunt, the importance of which is known[120], and other themes connected with the world of Dionysos[121], a further indication of the major role played by the god in Macedonia.

The Setting of Everyday Life

It is still too soon, in the present state of excavation and publication, to attempt to present a synthesis of Macedonian sculpture in the Hellenistic period. By contrast, the major features of artistic creation are already clearly evident in mosaic, parietal art and pottery.

Mosaic

During the course of the last few decades just under twenty mosaics of the Hellenistic period have been brought to light in Macedonia. Their artistic quality has guaranteed their reputation, and their study has considerably enriched our knowledge of Greek mosaic.

The most important group was found at Pella[122]. About ten floors are from the large houses located to the south of the acropolis, and two more have been discovered on the other side of the modern road, in a house and a tholos whose purpose is not clear. All these mosaics are made of small natural pebbles set in mortar. Almost contemporary with each other, they are dated to the end of the fourth century on the basis of certain stratigraphic indications. The poor state of preservation of the early levels in the palace on the same site undoubtedly accounts for the fact that the mosaics that probably adorned at least some of the rooms have so far eluded our investigations.

As for the palace at Vergina[123], the large banquet rooms in the west wing (M1-M3 fig. 70) have a floor consisting of an *opus segmentatum* pavement formed of small slabs of stone with irregular outlines, in a single colour and bordered with a band of black pebbles. A smaller banquet room in the south wing (G), however, was decorated with a very rich pebble mosaic that was probably contemporary with those at Pella[124], and the same type of floor probably covered the banquet room located symmetrically with it (E) (figs 103-104, 115) and also the ante-room shared by them (F). Nothing of these survives today[125].

The floors of tombs at Amphipolis[126] and Dion[127] were also decorated with pebble mosaics in geometric designs. On Samothrace, however, the pavements decorated with lozenges in the *'Altar Court'*[128], and in 'building 24' dedicated by Philip III and Alexander IV[129] are in an unusual technique that is probably related to *opus sectile*, with each lozenge consisting of a single block of dressed porphyry or marble. We shall return later to this kind of pavement.

Irrespective of the type of decoration (choice of figured, floral and geometric motifs, and their stylistic treatment), type of composition, techniques and material employed, this group of pavements is sharply distinguished from other pebble mosaics laid at the same period, or even earlier, in the fourth century, at Olynthos, Corinth, Sikyon and Eretria.

Iconography

The number of mosaics with figure decoration is relatively limited. One has been found at Vergina and seven at Pella.

The Vergina mosaic[130] (fig. 103) has a basically floral decoration. The composition sets a circle within a square, the circle being completely filled by a floral composition that will be discussed below[131]. Only the corners are adorned by figures, and even these are composite, with a face and torso of a woman ending below in a double floral scroll (fig. 104). This type of figure, which is often called the 'goddess with scrolls', comes from a long tradition.

At Pella, the most famous of the mosaics adorned two large houses called the House of the Abduction of Helen (House I 5) and the House of Dionysos (House I 1), after the most important mosaics in them (fig. 78). The former[132] has three floors with figure scenes, all adorning banquet rooms. In a large room situated to the north of the north stoa on the axis of the courtyard, an exceptionally large panel (8.48 m long and 2.84 m wide), surrounded by a zone of meander pattern and a wide band of overlapping leaves, depicts the Abduction of Helen[133] (fig. 105). At the right Helen, lifted off the ground by Theseus who carries her off to the left in a violent movement, turns with her arms outstretched to her companion, Deianeira, who flees to the right at the edge of the picture. The entire left part of the composition

103

103. Vergina, palace. Mosaic in room E, overall view. This mosaic, like those in the following illustrations, possibly dates from the end of the fourth or the beginning of the third century BC. The circle inscribed in a square, with a border of wave pattern and a meander, encloses a complex floral composition based on a central rosette with eight petals, from which spring interlaced stems, volutes, tendrils, leaves and flowers.

104. Vergina, palace. Mosaic in room E, detail. Each corner has the figure of a woman, ending at the bottom in a floral element recalling an inverted lotus flower, from which spring floral scrolls that the figure holds in each hand; this motif is known as the 'goddess with the scrolls'.

(over half of its area) is taken up by the chariot, pulled by four horses leaping three-quarters to the left, and barely held in check by their driver Phorbas, who turns back to wait for Theseus. The names of the characters are given in a light colour against the dark background of the scene, and the ground on which they stand is represented by a band of grey. These inscriptions raise a number of problems, for in the fairly rare depictions of the abduction of Helen by Theseus, the charioteer is never Phorbas, and the character of Deianeira is nowhere connected with the myth. The figure does not fit into the expected scheme, and may have been borrowed by the mosaicist from another scene[134]. Whatever the case, this composition, of rare beauty, was no doubt inspired by a large-scale painting dating either from the se-

cond half of the fourth century[135], or perhaps the beginning of this same century, which may perhaps be attributed to Zeuxis[136].

In the neighbouring room to the east an almost square panel (figs 3, 106) depicts a stag hunt[137]. It is bordered by a wide band with a floral scroll (this will be discussed below)[138] followed by a wave pattern. The stag, in the centre, is already falling to the left onto the triangular rock, its tongue out. A dog bites it in the flank, and to the right a young man, with his chlamys on his back, seizes it by the horn with his left hand and prepares to strike it with his sword. Another youth to the left, his sword in its scabbard, brandishes a double axe. In the violence of the movements, the chlamys of the hunter on the left is flying up, while his comrade's hat has flown off. Above the scene, on

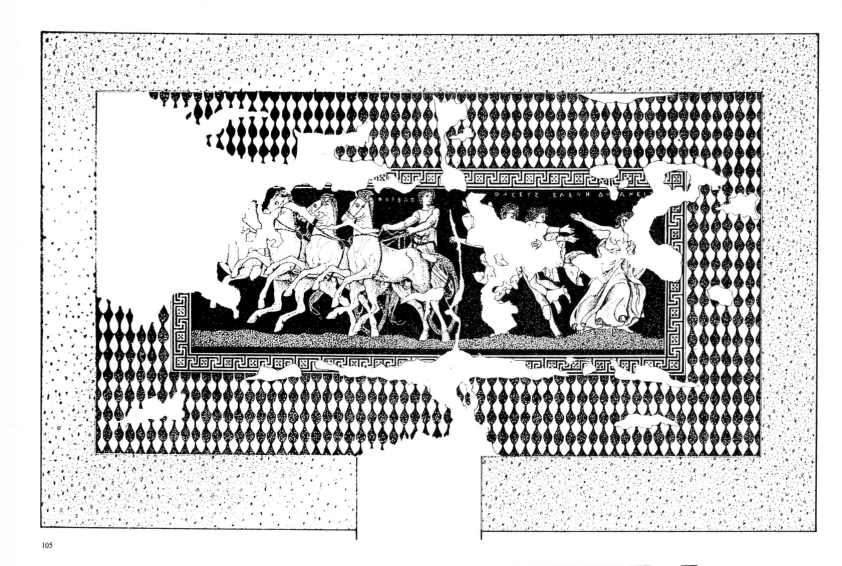

105

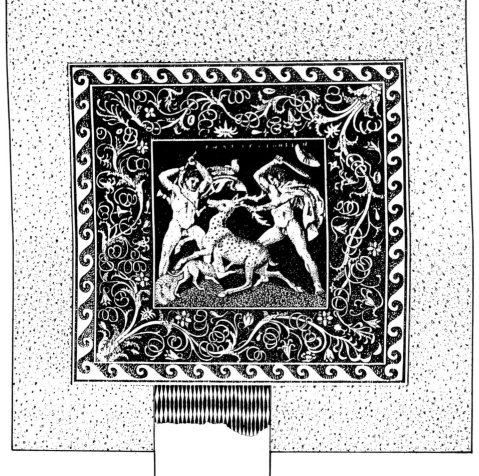

106

105. Pella, House of
the Abduction of
Helen. Mosaic of
the Abduction of
Helen, overall view,
drawing. The huge
central panel is
surrounded by a
band of meanders
and squares, and
stands out against a
background of
overlapping leaves.

106. Pella, House of
the Abduction of
Helen. Mosaic of
the Stag Hunt,
overall view,
drawing. The central
panel is here
bordered by a wide
band of scrolls
consisting of
tendrils, flowers and
palmettes, followed
on the outside, close
to the positions of
the dining couches,
by a band of wave
pattern.

the dark ground, can be read the signature: 'Gnosis made'. A resemblance has been detected between the youth on the right and portraits of Alexander, and it would then be legitimate to compare it with another work, also deriving from large-scale painting, the stag hunt from the famous 'Alexander sarcophagus' in the Istanbul Museum.

Finally, in a third banquet room, this time to the east of the courtyard, we may admire an Amazonomachy scene[139] (fig. 107), bordered by a thin braiding of two strands, a wider band of palmettes and lotus flowers, and an even wider figured band with confronted animals (boar panthers) separated by groups of palmettes and semi-palmettes. The composition is triangular, like that of the stag hunt (fig. 109). To the right a Greek warrior, with cuirass, helmet, greaves, and circular shield, uses his sword to attack an Amazon, fallen to the ground, who tries to protect herself with her shield. Behind her, a second Amazon comes to her aid. Both wear a short chiton, close-fitting trousers, and a tiara.

As for the 'House of Dionysos', this is so called because of the existence, again in a banquet room, to the west of the first courtyard, of an almost square mosaic (with a side of about 2.70 m) in which we see[140] Dionysos riding side-saddle on a panther that is leaping to the left. The god, naked and crowned with vine-leaves, holds onto the animal's neck with his right hand and in his left holds aloft a thyrsos decorated with a ribbon (fig. 111). The picture, elegant and slightly affected, stands out in light colour on a dark background, with no indication of the ground on which the panther moves. The threshold of this room, which also has a figure composition, shows a griffin attacking a stag to the right from the rear (fig. 110), a common subject in the fourth century, whether in mosaic or in other art forms.

Still in the same house, a large rectangular mosaic depicts a Lion Hunt[141] bordered by a double band with bead and reel and complex floral scrolls, unfortunately badly damaged (fig. 112). In the centre, the lion, standing three-quarters left in a menacing attitude, turns his head towards the young hunter at the right who, with a sweeping movement that makes his chlamys fly in the air, prepares to attack it with his sword, holding the scabbard in his left hand. At the left another hunter, also dressed in a chlamys and wearing a petasos on his head, and with his left hand on the scabbard of his sword, is about to strike the beast. The question has obviously been raised as to whether this picture should be connected with the famous *ex voto* of

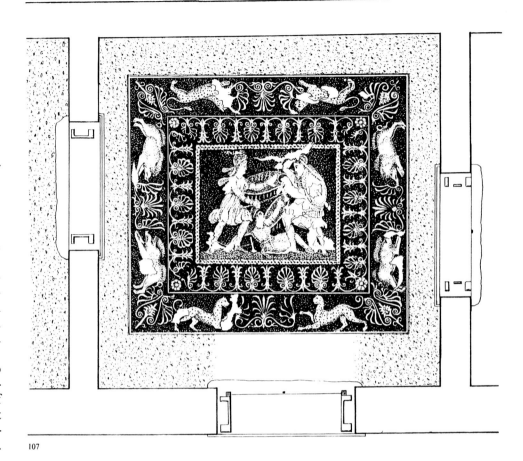

107

Krateros at Delphi[142], and we should also think of the great lion hunt in the tomb of Philip at Vergina[143]. Here, too, the threshold of the room had a figure composition, with a scene of a Centaur and Centauress. The former, on the right, is holding a bowl in his left hand, and the Centauress a vase. The scene appears to be unique in Greek art[144].

In a house located directly to the south, a figure panel (fig. 108) once again serves as the threshold to a banquet room, itself adorned by a very badly preserved mosaic with floral decoration[145]. A Centauress proceeds to the left, in the direction of a natural grotto, the large triangular opening of which is surrounded by rocks. She is preparing to make a libation, overturning the contents of a rhyton in the form of an animal (perhaps a dog) in a fluted patera that she holds in her left hand. Behind her is a tall tree with some branches but no leaves. The subject is unusual, like that with the Centaurs on the threshold of the preceding mosaic, but the presence of Centaurs should occasion no surprise at the entrance to banquet rooms, where there will have been numerous libations.

Finally, a round room (fig. 116) belonging

107. Pella, House of the Abduction of Helen. Mosaic of the Amazonomachy, overall view, drawing. Around the central panel is first a braiding, then a band decorated with alternating palmettes and lotus flowers, and finally a band with, on each side, a central motif of a palmette between two half-palmettes, flanked by two heraldically confronted animals.

108

108. Pella, South
House. Threshold
mosaic: the Centauress.
The centauress raises an
animal's head rhyton in
her right hand, in order
to pour a libation into
the patera which she

holds in her left hand;
at the right, a dead tree
trunk evokes a rural
landscape with, at the
left (out of the picture),
the entrance to a grotto
in front of which the
rite is unfolding.

109

109. Mosaic of the Amazonomachy, central panel. Although the pyramidal composition recalls that of the Stag Hunt, with an Amazon fallen to the ground defended by a companion armed with a shield and spear against a Greek brandishing a sword, the quality of the work is inferior from every point of view to that in the other figure panels: the clumsiness of the drawing and the poverty of the rendering are out of keeping with the group of mosaics from Pella, and even with the quality of the border.

110

110. Pella, House of
Dionysos, threshold:
griffin attacking a stag.
The rapacious griffin,
with its characteristic
bird's beak, pointed
crest, and widely spread
wings, attacks its prey
from behind.

111. Pella, House of
Dionysos. Mosaic of
Dionysos, central panel.
The god, seated side-
saddle on a panther
leaping to the left, is
clasping its neck with
his right arm and holds
the thyrsos in his left
hand; the curves of the
ribbon on the thyrsos
combine with that of
the animal's tail.

KYNHΓION ΛΕΟΝΤΟΣ
LION HUNTING SCENE

112

to a building also located in the southern sector of the city, whose main decoration, a fine floral composition, will be discussed below[146], has a figure panel with a griffin to the left, and to the right a panther attacking an animal fallen to the ground.

We thus see that the iconography consists partly of subjects that were current in this period, such as combats of animals and griffins, and partly of others that were related to the function of the banquet room. It is notable that two hunt scenes have been discovered in these rooms[147].

Composition

In the majority of ancient mosaics, at Olynthos or Eretria, for example, the entire surface is covered by a decor organised in a number of concentric bands surrounding a central surface of restricted dimensions.

This type of decoration, at once abundant and fragmented, undoubtedly attests to the influence of the art of textiles on the composition of the earliest mosaics. In fact, it was to replace textile carpets that pavements made of pebbles, 'which could be washed' and were therefore

112. Pella, House of Dionysos. Mosaic of the Lion Hunt. In the scene, which decorates an elongated space, the legs of the two hunters repeat almost exactly the same pose, and the obliques of their torsoes balance each other; but the figure at the left, in a defensive attitude,

brandishes a short weapon in his right hand, the sheath of which he holds in his left, while the other hunter attacks with his sword. Some have identified these figures with Alexander the Great and Krateros, in a hunt which is in every way royal.

oration in the room was the Amazonomachy, placed in the centre with a unique orientation and framed by a series of bands executed according to the earlier scheme[148].

In the other banquet rooms in this house, the composition is even more strongly centralised, again because the only piece of figure decoration is placed in the centre — a panel of large dimensions and a unique orientation. It is, of course, framed by a number of bands, or stands out against the background[149], but the decoration of the latter, invariably either geometric or floral, does not compete with that of the main scene.

In the two banquet rooms of the House of Dionysos, this type of composition is even more marked, since the central figure panel has either no decorative frame at all or only a slight one, and stands out against a broad undecorated background of large pebbles[150]. In each banquet room, a second figure panel, of more modest dimensions and less carefully executed, adorns the entire width of the threshold. In both the room with the Lion Hunt and that of Dionysos, the mosaicist has chosen a type of composition completely original for his period, and well adapted to realising the figure panels, and has treated them in the manner of paintings set on a neutral ground.

The two other paved floors in this same house of Dionysos, decorating the huge rooms giving access to the banquet rooms, present yet another type of composition in which almost the entire surface is covered by a single geometric motif. In room A the entire mosaic, which does not have a border, is decorated (fig. 114) with a series of seven squares inscribed one inside the other[151]. The paved floor in room D has a border of wave pattern, but the biggest part of it is decorated with a chequer pattern of green and white lozenges, executed very carefully with large pebbles[152] (fig. 118). A similar chequer pattern of lozenges adorns the main chamber and antechamber in the tomb at Amphipolis, and also the buildings on Samothrace referred to above.

Using these examples from Macedonia and a number of other, later examples as a basis, it has been possible to show[153] that this type of composition with a uniform surface, invariably formed of lozenges, cubes (themselves consisting of three lozenges) or squares, is to be explained in terms of the influence exercised on mosaics from the very beginning by the decoration of paved floors, which are relatively poorly known, because they are badly preserved. In fact, the paved floor of the tholos at Epidauros[154], and those in the two buildings on Samo-

eminently practical, were used to adorn the banquet rooms. The mosaicists were naturally inspired by carpets, therefore, for their earliest decorative schemes. Furthermore, this type of composition in concentric bands made it possible to allot the figure decoration to the bands and to orientate it on each side towards the diners seated on the beds along the wall, without giving prominence to any single viewpoint.

At Pella, this traditional scheme was only adopted once, in the banquet room of the House of the Abduction of Helen, and even then only in a partial manner, for the main dec-

113. Pella, House of
Dionysos. Aerial view,
with rooms A, B, C, D,
and, towards the
bottom right, the large
south peristyle.

114. Pella, House of
Dionysos. room A:
mosaic with inscribed
squares, detail.

114

thrace prove that these *opus sectile* floors with geometric decoration existed at a date earlier than had hitherto been thought, and that they are at least contemporary with, if indeed not earlier than, the earliest pebble mosaics. Some of the latter are thus imitations of these very costly paved floors, which have today almost completely disappeared.

The use of floral compositions is itself very notable in Macedonia. Of the dozen pavements known at Pella, six have scrolls with flowers of various kinds, and of these, three are in a centralised composition and three a linear composition. The finest example of this latter arrangement frames the stag hunt in the mosaic signed by Gnosis[155], but a similar composition also formed the border of the lion hunt and a pavement with floral decoration in room B of the House of the Abduction of Helen[156].

The centralised compositions are themselves worthy of attention. From a central rosette with petals and sepals spring sinuous, intertwining shoots, with a profusion of sheathing leaves, tendrils, volutes and above all different kinds of flowers. Taking this same scheme as a starting point, the compositions vary in the number of shoots and axes of symmetry.

At Pella, we can admire the circular floor of the tholos[157] and the square one in a house in the same quarter[158] (fig. 117). But the finest of them is to be found at Vergina[159], where the mosaicist has depicted a large number of different kinds of flowers, both natural and imaginary (figs 103, 115). He has designed both single ribbon volutes, double volutes and tendrils, and the intertwining of the shoots, and the view above and below the flowers renders the depth of the motif in linear perspective. Moreover, the mosaicist has made use of chiaroscuro to suggest the volume of the floral elements. The use of colour is discreet, as at Pella, with a few touches of red and yellow amongst subtle shades of white and grey standing out against the dark ground. The composition, which is even more complex than those at Pella, discreetly withdraws before the suppleness, the richness and the exuberance of the floral elements organised by it.

It has been shown[160] that this Macedonian type of floral, centralised composition was the most accomplished achievement of a series that began at Sikyon, Corinth and Eretria, and subsequently spread to Athens, and that the pebble mosaic of Dyrrachium-Epidamnos (in modern Albania), adorned with a female head surrounded by sinuous shoots with flowers, is very close to these Macedonian mosaics. It thus attests to the influence exercised by Macedonia on this city in Illyria towards the end of the fourth century.

In these large, luxuriant floral compositions, the place of figured ornamentation is secondary. At Pella, only the floors of the thresholds have figures[161], and at Vergina, the

115

116

corners were adorned with goddesses with foliate scrolls, an excellent transition from the figural to the floral. We are here dealing, therefore, with yet another different type of composition. Should this type be connected with paintings on vaults[162] and/or with floors strewn with flowers[163]? The question remains unanswered. Whatever the case, however, the origin of these large-scale floral compositions with many flowers is probably to be sought in Sikyon, even if the model thus created is thenceforth mainly attested in Macedonia.

From this point of view, one cannot but be attracted by the hypothesis formulated by M. Robertson, on the basis of a passage in Pliny: these floral compositions with flowers will have been the invention of Pausias, a Sikyonian painter of the fourth century, who then worked in Macedonia and will have 'exported' the motif there — a motif also found, in various regions, used in pottery, in the wall-paintings of the Macedonian tombs, and in the goldsmith's and toreutic arts.

Style and technique

From a stylistic point of view, the characteristic feature of the mosaics of Pella is the rendering of the third dimension, with use both of linear perspective and of colour shading to represent chiaroscuro. The mosaics of Corinth, Sikyon, Olynthos and Eretria already made use of linear perspective, but at Pella the figure compositions are more compressed, the foreshortening of the figures and the sumperimposition of several planes graphically indicating the depth of the scene, as in the depiction of the chariot of

115. Vergina, palace. Mosaic in room E: detail of the centre, floral decoration.

116. Pella, tholos building. Mosaic of the tholos, drawing. The area of the circle, which is bordered by a wave pattern like the threshold with a griffin
and panther attacking their prey, is occupied by a floral composition with scrolls, volutes and large flowers.

117. Pella, South House. Mosaic in the andron, overall view, drawing. The central panel, unfortunately badly damaged, has a
floral composition skilfully arranged around a central rosette with sinuous, interlaced stems on eight radiating axes, bearing a profusion of volutes and flowers and ending in flame palmettes in the corners, with groups of two half-palmettes in the middle of the sides.

Phorbas, or the 'pyramidal' structures in the Amazonomachy, and especially in the Stag Hunt by Gnosis.

It is above all for their pictorial style, however, that the Pella mosaics are distinguished from other pebble pavements, whether earlier, contemporary or later, and this pictorial treatment applies as well to figure decoration as to geometric or floral decoration.

In the sphere of figure decoration, it was at Eretria, as far as we can tell at present, that a mosaicist for the first time rendered the rounded volume of the shield of a Nereid, with shades of brown and yellow suggesting chiaroscuro. This pictorial treatment, however, is reserved for the threshold panel, and the main panel of this same mosaic was still treated graphically with flat colours[164].

At Pella, by contrast, shading was used systematically to render the volumes of the figures. Its use there is completely masterful, especially in the House of the Abduction of Helen, where the hues are subtler and richer than in the House of Dionysos. The rendering of light in the shades of grey makes one think of the 'grisailles' of Apelles, known to us only from the literary texts[165].

The same observations may be made of the geometric and floral decoration, as we have shown for the naturalistic compositions. To them should be added the non-naturalistic floral motifs, like the palmette framing the Amazonomachy, in which the volume of each element is indicated by shades of grey, just as in geometric motifs — the braid belonging to this same mosaic, or the bead and reel of the Lion Hunt.

The use of colour in the mosaics is always discreet, however, with a few touches of red and yellow enlivening the light figures on a dark background. This quite special, pictorial treatment, like the quality of the compositions, attests very clearly to the influence of large-scale painting on the Pella mosaics. This has already been studied for the figure representations[166], and with respect to the floral compositions, we have already referred to M. Robertson's hypothesis. The same is true, however, of the geometric decoration and the non-naturalistic floral decoration.

Whereas the braid and the palmette are generally given a flat treatment in black on white, in the pebble mosaics of Eretria, for example (as in architectural terracottas), the volume of these motifs is here rendered by shading, a technique also used in the wall paintings

118

118. Pella, House of Dionysos. Room D, mosaic with a chequerboard of lozenges and a border of wave pattern.

on the false façade of the Tomb of Eurydice[167]. The mosaicist, like the painter, attempted to give the impression of sculptural decoration. Thus, the two major features of Hellenistic mosaics — the illusionistic element in the perspective treatment of geometric decoration, and the pictorial element — first make their appearance at Pella.

It was at Pella, too, that mosaicists first played with their materials to achieve particular effects. First, they turned the shape of the pebbles to good advantage. In the Stag Hunt, and especially in the Lion Hunt, the ground on which the figures stand is executed with larger and more irregular pebbles, in terms of both colour and shape, than those used for the background, and the same is true of the grotto in the mosaic with the Centauress[168]. The chequer pattern of lozenges is made of pebbles cut much larger than the wave pattern bordering it, which meant that they had to be placed in position very carefully in order to preserve the clarity of the contours — the touchstone of the quality of the motif — but the resulting discontinuity in the interior surfaces of the lozenges animated each element, like veins on stone paving slabs.

In the mosaics with strips of lead, the eyes of the figures have now disappeared. The sockets for them, however, show that they were made of large, round elements, placed flat in the mortar, perhaps semi-precious stones, as some have suggested[169]. The mosaicists, in any event, did not hesitate to insert artificial materials into their pavements to represent the green leaves in the crown of Dionysos, and his thyrsos[170].

In fact, it was a problem to find natural materials of a light green colour, whether for pebble mosaics or tessellated mosaics, and other solutions were therefore adopted[171]. Blue posed a problem, and for the ornaments on the harness of the chariot, the mosaicist used pieces of opaque blue glass[172]. In using these artificial materials, the mosaicists of Pella were making another innovation, at least in the present state of our knowledge. There is nothing surprising in this, since these mosaicists were the first who wanted to render the colour, and possessed the necessary means to use the corresponding materials.

Another innovation made at Pella was the use of strips of lead and terracotta. In the Lion Hunt the mosaicist used only terracotta strips, of a brown colour, to outline the male figures, to pick out the major features, and to stress details such as locks of hair or the lion's mane. In the depiction of Dionysos (fig. 120), the hair is rendered by pieces of terracotta, but lead

119

119. Pella, mosaic of the Abduction of Helen, detail: head of Phorbas, the charioteer. The face is seen slightly foreshortened, since the figure is mounted on a chariot.

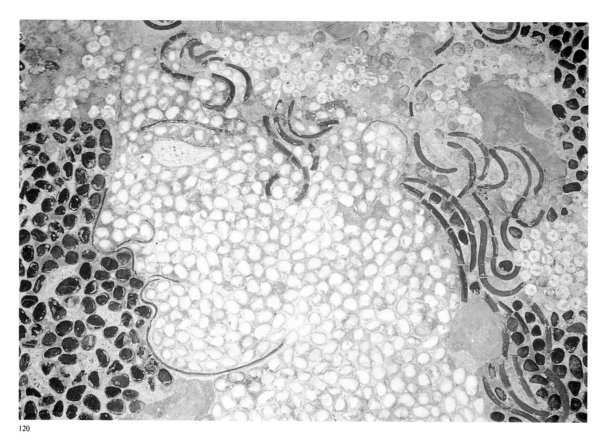

120

120. *Pella. Mosaic of Dionysos, detail: head of the god, strictly in profile. Here, all that counts are the curves of the lines, the precision of which is achieved by strips of terracotta and lead.*

121. *Pella, mosaic of the Stag Hunt, detail: head of the hunter at the left. The modelling is achieved by subtle shades of grey; the eyes and the nose are picked out by fine lines of black pebbles.*

strips are used on both of the god's shoulders and for his face, hands and feet. The threshold scene of animals in combat associated with the panel of Dionysos does not include any of these strips. By contrast, the Centaurs associated with the Lion Hunt are completely outlined by strips of lead.

In the neighbouring house, neither the Stag Hunt (fig. 121) nor the Amazonomachy have any lead or terracotta pieces, but strips of both materials are used to stress the details of the various figures in the Abduction of Helen (fig. 119).

Why were these pieces of terracotta or lead used? Undoubtedly to introduce an element of graphic continuity into a material that was by its nature discontinuous[173]. Another possible explanation is that this was a technique used by the mosaicist to render the dark outlines that were a feature of the earliest paintings.

There are none of these strips in the Stag Hunt. The few dark features are drawn in black pebbles, while the volumes are made the object of a much more subtle pictorial treatment. The Abduction of Helen is close to the Stag Hunt in stylistic terms, and yet the scene includes lead and terracotta to stress the details. The Amazonomachy has none, but its artistic quality is not on the same level as that of the Stag Hunt. It is not possible, therefore, to use the presence or

absence of lead and terracotta to distinguish the 'hands' of the mosaicists. The geometric motifs and floral compositions are executed without this additional material. The Lion Hunt and the Stag Hunt are both bordered by a floral scroll, and neither of these have any lead or terracotta. The presence or absence of terracotta or lead strips in the figural panels cannot, therefore, be interpreted as a characteristic of the particular mosaic workshop — the entire floor of the Lion Hunt will necessarily have been by the same workshop, and even by a single craftsman — but must rather reflect the different styles of the paintings that served as models.

In figured decors such as the lion hunt, the lead or terracotta strips must have been set in place according to a prepared scheme, and then acted as a guide for positioning the pebbles. Generally speaking, however, they were used rather to indicate details than to pick out the main lines of the composition. The terracotta pieces must in any case have been modelled before firing, and therefore prepared in advance, unlike the lead strips which could be modelled as the laying of the floor proceeded. This is undoubtedly the reason why the mosaicists henceforth used only the latter, in mosaics of both pebbles and tesserae. In tessellated floors, moreover, they were reserved for other kinds of use[174].

Mosaic in Macedonia

The Macedonian mosaics basically adorned houses and tombs. In the tombs, they were imitations of paved floors[175], as they were in the two large rooms in the House of Dionysos at Pella. In the three houses at Pella and the palace at Vergina, and undoubtedly also in the tholos at Pella, they adorned the floors of banquet rooms. This was their traditional use from the very first mosaics, but the artists changed the compositional scheme, giving pre-eminence to a figured decoration of pictorial type, with a unique orientation, turned invariably towards the entrance. Apart from their practical character, the presence in the banquet rooms of these rich mosaics is to be accounted for by the role played by meetings of this kind amongst the Macedonian élite.

Splendid witnesses to daily life in Macedonia, these floors are true works of art that set their seal on the history of mosaic about one century after its beginnings in Greece. An entire series of innovations found at Pella were then repeated. Are we to suggest, with some researchers, that *opus tessellatum* — mosaics made of small, cut stones — was also invented in northern Greece? With the exception of the floors on Samothrace, which are related more to *opus sectile* than *opus tessellatum,* it has to be admitted that we know of no Hellenistic mosaic in the *opus tessellatum* technique in Macedonia. Caution is therefore recommended. But, from the point of view both of iconography and of technique, the influence of the Pella mosaics is undeniable on the Alexandria mosaic depicting Erotes hunting (newly dated by W. Daszewski to the first third of the third century[176]), and this confirms the importance of the latter in the controversial question of the origins of *opus tessellatum.* It is certainly true, of mosaic as of other spheres of art, that the birth of Hellenistic art, which was disseminated by the successors of Alexander over the entire Mediterranean basin and even beyond, owed much to the works executed by the best Greek artists invited to the Macedonian court[177].

Parietal art

We shall deal here not with the frescoes adorning the Macedonian tombs, which are related directly to large-scale painting[178], but with the mural decoration of the houses. It is certain, in fact, that the walls of the rooms, both in the palaces and in the more carefully finished houses, were covered with painted plaster.

The mode of construction of the walls invited the wide use of this technique, for it should not be forgotten that, even in the richer buildings of domestic architecture, the walls consisted of a stone socle supporting masonry of unbaked bricks, which it was better to conceal. In fact, excavations have yielded numerous examples of this plastering, which undoubtedly played a major role in the aesthetic of the buildings.

Generally used in layers that were superimposed one on the other during redecoration in ancient times, the plaster frequently took the form of continuous coloured surfaces, with four main colours, white, black, yellow and red, and sometimes intermediate tones, such as grey. Notably, imitations of marble are not rare — proof of the desire attested on several occasions in Macedonia to play with appearances in order to give slighter materials a richer architectural aspect. It is, of course, the lower parts of the walls that have most frequently preserved their decoration. In a house at Pella[179], for example, we see an imitation of a structure with large-scale masonry, with the plinth at the bottom represented by a white band, surmounted by black orthostates, the joints of which are rendered by grooves. Above these was the crowning member of this dado, followed by the main body of the wall in regular courses. This copy, less expensive but very suggestive, of a meticulously executed stone structure, constitutes what is called the 'structural style' or, in a vivid expression 'masonry style', and we can recognise in this kind of decoration an antecedent of the 'first Pompeian style'[180].

Another house at Pella, the 'House of the Painted Plaster' has yielded some of the richest evidence[181]. The entrance hall itself was given a decoration that it has proved possible to restore to a height of 2 m. A white band, 10 cm high, recalling a plinth, supported a zone imitating marble orthostates, and this dado was crowned by black and white bands with incisions. Next followed the principal zone of the wall featuring isodomic masonry, the yellow, green and red elements of which are chiselled around. At the top, a thin band imitated marble and a white projecting cornice. We thus find here again the arrangement in five zones, one above the other, typical of the 'structural style'.

The decoration of the large exedra opening to the north of the peristyle, restored for the entire height of the room, or about 5 m, contained some new elements. The lower half of the wall was a strict imitation of a solid wall, with a plinth supporting a dado of orthostates surmounted by two bands one above the other, followed by isodomic masonry, which was in

122

122. Lefkadia, Great Tomb, the burial chamber. The treatment of the walls with pilasters in low relief, standing on a socle and supporting an entablature with an Ionic architrave, is designed to give the impression of an open space, simply surrounded by a peristyle.

turn crowned by a band and a projecting cornice. This type of composition, then, like that of the corridor, belongs to the structural style.

Above it, the second half of the wall has a completely different character. It is enlivened by a representation of a row of tall pilasters, whose capitals support a complete entablature. Between the pilasters, the lower part of the space is filled by an imitation of a parapet with large red panels surmounted by a relief band. Above this, the blue colour of the plaster evokes the sky, and thus an open space that increases the dimensions of the room infinitely.

This composition on two levels, with a solid dado at the bottom and an open, albeit fictional, gallery above it, was also used to organise the painted decoration of the Hieron on Samothrace[182] and, also on Samothrace, the stone architecture of the Rotunda of Arsinoe, with, in this case, a real parapet between the columns[183].

The same illusionistic intent can be seen in

other decorative schemes, notably those of the 'Macedonian tombs', such as the pilasters in light relief that punctuate the space above the dado in the interior of the Great Tomb of Lefkadia[184] (fig. 122); or the *trompe l'oeil* pillars of the Tomb of Lyson and Kallikles[185], whose perspective rendering produced an opposition between the two short sides of the room, with the shadows corresponding to lighting supposedly coming from either the main axis of the room, or the two sides (figs 149-150).

Mural decoration in architectural style in Macedonia thus not only attained a quality quite remarkable from the purely pictorial point of view, but also opened the way to an illusionistic system that would reappear at a later date on some of the walls of Delos[186].

Some scholars have placed these walls at the beginning of what is known as the 'second Pompeian style'[187], and it is now easier to understand how a famous theory, recently repeated, could adduce this style as evidence for Alexandrian architecture[188]. Again, it should not be forgotten that the 'first style' of Pompeii could also make use of an open gallery above an imitation of a solid wall[189]. Better still, just like the example at Pella, it might employ the technique of dividing the wall into two parts, with a solid wall beneath an imitation of an open gallery, and offering a very realistic representation of a parapet between the columns[190].

We may perhaps go further. A house at Amphipolis has produced two rooms[191] adorned with painted decoration. In one (fig. 92) we find the structural style in its simplest form, though very carefully executed. Above a plinth are four courses of pseudo-isodomic masonry, rising to a height of over 2 m, with blocks 0.97 m long. Black lines indicate the joints, inside which a red band portrays the chiselling encircling the panel.

The decoration of the neighbouring room (fig. 93), however, preserved to a height of almost 2.60 m, introduces a notable innovation. The wall here is treated in the structural style, with a plinth at the bottom, then a dado of orthostates, then a number of vertical panels 1.40 m high, alternately empty and decorated with lozenges, the whole being crowned by three low courses, the first and third of them red, the middle with smaller elements imitating alabaster. But this solid decoration appears *behind* a row of columns 2.22 m high, also painted in *trompe l'oeil* (the Ionic capitals must have been completed in plaster) supporting an entablature[192]. We thus recognise here the desire to deepen the visual space, though now not by piercing the wall with simulated openings, but by projecting optically, in front of a back wall, painted bearing elements — one of the main features of the 'second Pompeian style'[193]. The house has been dated by the excavators to the second century. If its frescoes go back to this date, they mark a stage in the development of parietal art in Macedonia.

The pottery

When Manolis Andronicos in 1955 published a tomb at Beroia, dating from the second century[194], with its vases and terracotta lamps, this first systematic study based on all the available excavation data opened a significant chapter in the history of Hellenistic pottery, and at the same time of archaeology in Macedonia.

The decades that followed have increased in unexpected fashion the number of second-cen-

tury rock-cut chamber tombs rich in ceramic material, particularly at Beroia, though also at Edessa and Pella. To this material is to be added the finds produced by other excavations, mainly of 'Macedonian tombs' and cist graves, dating mainly from the fourth and third centuries.

The chronological horizon of this material, which is very abundant between the death of Philip II and the end of the second century is thus broadened. Unfortunately, stratigraphic data relating to this material are still relatively rare and poor in quality, especially for the urban sites, and the study of the finds has hitherto concentrated mainly on the rich funerary groups, for which there are special chronological indications.

The first systematic study of Macedonian Hellenistic pottery, involving research into a chronology based on coins, lamps and other excavation data, was undertaken by S. Drougou and Y. Touratsoglou in 1980, with the publication of a group of Hellenistic tombs of Beroia. These same scholars then presented a general survey of Hellenistic pottery in Macedonia[195]. At the same time, the publication was proceeding of material from sites such as the agora at Pella, with the discovery, published by I. Akamatis[196] of terracotta moulds for making relief vases. These yielded new, essential data not only for our knowledge of Hellenistic pottery, but more generally for our approach to the economic and social life of this Macedonian city.

This information has gradually defined a new geographic unit within the broad sphere of Hellenistic pottery, alongside the groups already defined by research, such as those of Asia Minor, centred on Pergamon, and those of Athens, Delos etc. The aim of research is to define this unit and its relations within a group at once common and diverse.

The chronological framework for Hellenistic pottery in Macedonia is thus defined. Its geographical extent is wider than that of the kingdom itself, and also embraces the regions under the economic and political influence of the King of Macedonia as far as the Nestos in the east and the source of the Axios in the north. But, at least in the present state of our knowledge, the centres of production continued to be in the old country of the Macedonians, Lower Macedonia. Here were the workshops that determined the features of the pottery, as of other products and, in general, of the economic life of the kingdom.

Of the many conditions that gave Hellenistic pottery its character, the most important are

123. Two black-glaze bowls, Pella, Agora, last third of the third century BC. They were found in a well in which the refuse from the pottery workshops grouped in the east stoa was thrown. The 'West Slope' decoration is very simple, a row of arches and leaves above two incised lines, separated by a row of white spots for the figure at the bottom, a garland summarily painted in a dilute brown clay for the figure at the top.

124

124. Black-glaze kantharos. Pella, same date, same provenance. The elegant, functional shape of this drinking vessel is emphasized by the very simple 'West Slope' decoration, a garland suspended between the upper handle attachments with a bunch of grapes either side.

skyphoi, small plates and perfume containers. Moulded motifs still adorn the bottom of the open vases, but lose their importance, set without any real organisation in the centre of the surface. These features continue to predominate during the second century without any change of shape, but the quality deteriorates and, above all, the black glaze tends to disappear.

Towards the end of the fourth and the beginning of the third century, a period of prosperity but also of economic change in Macedonia, we note the introduction, soon after their appearance at Athens, of floral and other decorative motifs executed in white or yellow clay applied to black-glaze vases. This technique is known as the 'West Slope' style, a creation of the Athenian pottery workshops, though it swiftly became international and pan-Hellenic, and eventually came to be a basic characteristic of Hellenistic pottery in general. In Macedonia, it was predominant in the third and second centuries, although it is difficult to form a precise idea in the absence of any systematic study. What is certain is that, although the technique is Attic in origin, it here became directly connected, about the middle of the third century, with the craftsmen and workshops of Asia Minor, a phenomenon that continued until the middle of the second century.

To begin with, the rich floral motifs are rendered (figs 123-125) in a white or pale yellow colour and, in the second half of the third century, incisions were added, making the motifs more linear. In the second century, this technique became general and formed one of the main features of 'West Slope' motifs, the majority of which, at the same time, became more simplified and tended to be rendered as geometrical forms.

The shapes also contribute to defining this category. In its first phase, at the end of the fourth century and throughout the great part of the third, they were above all kantharoi, small vases such as askoi, 'salt-cellars', perfume containers, and especially pyxides and oinochoai, with amphorae as well.

During the course of the third century the old shapes persisted but their decoration changed and one senses the dawning of an interest in the renewal of the products in this sphere. This involved especially, towards the end of the third century and later, pyxides, small plates and perfume containers, while kantharoi are found in new variations, known as 'Hellenistic'. This new category also had a very significant element, namely, the combination of painted and relief decoration, as it appeared on

historical. In the second half of the fourth century, the pottery products of Attica held the favour of the Macedonian buyers, but very quickly, beginning at the end of this same century, the shapes and decoration of these Attic black-glaze vases were imitated or copied by the local workshops, as is clear from the offerings in the tombs of the fourth and third centuries at Vergina and Pella. The technique of metalworking that flourished in Macedonia in the fourth century makes its appearance in the decoration of Hellenistic pottery. We may recall, as a characteristic example, the technique that involved covering black-glaze vases in a burial at Methone, probably from Attica[197], with gold or silver, in order to give them the touch of luxury indispensable at this period.

Black-glaze pottery continued to be produced and utilised during the course of the third century. Fewer shapes are used, however, and the quality of the glaze becomes blackish and brownish-red. In general, they are small vases, skyphoi, kantharoi, small handleless

125. Lid. Pella, same provenance, same date, same technique. Apart from some circles on the rim, the decoration consists only of the undulating line of a white scroll with ivy leaves either side, in dilute brown clay. We are here in the presence of local production, designed to respond to modest needs, but which does not lack charm.

125

pyxides with their characteristic medallions (e.g. pyxides from Beroia).

We may note the group of small plates from the tombs at Aiane, with painted floral compositions in the middle of the bottom and small decorative motifs around the edge, all executed in a thick white colour[198]. These date from the end of the third century, proving the existence of an important local workshop with its own original methods. In the absence of a comprehensive study, however, it would be difficult to define this production of 'West Slope' pottery in Macedonia, since few examples of it have survived.

The use of moulding brought about a fundamental change in Hellenistic pottery. Relief ornamentation was, of course, already used for

some shapes, such as the 'West Slope' pyxides in the third century. But the making of whole vases, and other small objects such as lamps, in moulds became common, as far as we can tell, at the end of the third century at Athens, where these relief vases were invented, as the finds from the Athenian agora have shown. In Macedonia, we have to wait for the second century, and moreover the middle of that century, before the use of this technique is attested. These products of Macedonia, especially the hemispherical bowls, form the majority of the pottery in the second half of this century and down to the end of the first half of the first century.

Our knowledge of this category of relief vases has started to become more systematic

126

and richer with the discovery of moulds in the agora at Pella by I. Akamatis, who dates them to the beginning of the first century. At the same time, sporadic finds of the same kind at Vergina, Thessalonike and Florina reveal obvious affinities, and attest to the commercial circulation of these moulds over a large part of Macedonia.

At the same time, however, their shapes and the composition of the floral and geometric decoration are evidence for a close link with the production centres of Asia Minor, or at least those which appeared on the international market of Delos, and also reveal relations with similar objects at Athens. The relief bowls are characterised by floral motifs, long leaves and stems with rosettes, braids on the rim and rich rosettes in the middle of the lower part (fig. 126). Similar motifs also cover the surface of larger vases, such as the krater, which occupy a special place in the active centres of Macedonia.

In this category, the relief bowls with iconographic motifs depicting mythological scenes borrowed from the epic cycle, from ancient theatre and from contemporary poetry are evidence for the culture of the advanced second century (fig. 127). These vessels, known as 'Homeric' bowls[199], are preeminently Macedonian products, found in Macedonia and the lands influenced by it. The scenes with their inscriptions, drawn both from the Homeric epic and from the dramas of Euripides and other tragedians, reveal a narrative style with stereotyped forms in small compositions repeated on the surface of the vase, and demonstrate the importance of the Classical tradition in the

country, which was itself now under the domination of Rome.

The problem of the dating of these relief vases is a complex one and does not depend solely on the evidence of excavations and their finds. The nature of their production also enters into consideration, for the moulds could be reproduced, sold and used in different regions. The discovery of the moulds in the agora at Pella attests to a late phase of this production, at the beginning of the first century, but it is certainly the case that these 'Homeric bowls' were already being produced at least in the second half of the second century.

These two categories do not, of course, give a complete picture of Macedonian pottery in the Hellenistic period. It included a great variety of other shapes and types, such as undecorated oinochoai, perfume containers, lagynoi, and especially large tripod pyxides, and was related to other production centres in the Hellenistic world.

All these creations, with the vast quantity of material, the repetition of shapes, and their low market value, shed light on a significant aspect of the economic life of the country, combined with the growth of large fortunes and the tendency to ostentation, the need to satisfy a numerous community of individuals having a minimum of economic means and demanding low-priced goods.

Other objects, such as lamps, followed the same evolution as the rest of the pottery, with their origins in the 'Attic' ware of the fourth century, their independent production in the third and second centuries, and a role in the technique of moulding, which influenced their production.

Despite the incomplete state of our documentation, and the uncertainty relating to the dating and existence of workshops, our present knowledge, acquired in a relatively short time, even though not directly concerned with the major political events, or large-scale art, furnishes much information on the daily economic and social life of Hellenistic Macedonia. Macedonian pottery, without having the originality and quality of Attic works, for example, reveals both an independence of the Classical centres, and connections with tradition. It formed the link between metropolitan Greece and the centres of the north and Asia Minor[200]. Thus, the study and dating of this rich material provides archaeological research not only with a useful tool for excavation, but also with a method enabling us to approach some fundamental problems relating to society.

126. Fragment of a hemispherical 'Megarian bowl' found at Pella, second half of the second century BC. These relief moulded vases might have floral decoration, with a leafy rosette on the bottom, or motifs with living beings, such as the griffins borrowed from the repertoire of orientalising art.

127

127. 'Megarian' bowl
with a representation of
the Sack of Troy, from
Pella (mould). The
Trojan horse can be
seen, and Kelados
blowing his trumpet;
other objects of this
type also have scenes
taken from tragedies,
such as the Iphigeneia
in Aulis of Euripides.

5

THE 'MACEDONIAN TOMBS'

128. Vergina, façade of the Tomb of Philip, about 336 BC. The uncovering of this building and its completely preserved contents by Manolis Andronicos, in 1977, marked a turning point in our knowledge of Hellenistic art. The Doric order of the façade, with two half-columns between two antae, supports a plain architrave and a frieze with blue triglyphs above a red taenia; beneath the first cornice is the imposing famous fresco of the Hunt, itself protected by a supplementary cornice.

Architecture and Rituals

Definition of the 'Macedonian tomb'

'Their tomb shall be constructed under ground, in the form of an oblong vault of spongy stone, as long-lasting as possible, and fitted with couches of stone set side by side; in this when they have laid him who is gone to his rest, they shall make a mound in a circle round it and plant thereon a grove of trees, save only at one extremity, so that at that point the tomb may for all time admit of enlargement...'[1].

This description by Plato (*Laws* 947 d-e) is the earliest, and perhaps the most precise, of the 'Macedonian tomb', even though it ante-dates all the 'Macedonian tombs' discovered to date[2]. In effect the monuments to which this name is applied by archaeologists, since the majority of them have been found in Macedonia, consist of a subterranean building covered by a vault; they are almost always built of very durable blocks of poros; the structure is almost invariably covered with a circular tumulus; and the presence of one or two couches is also very common (fig. 131).

Plato's description, however, makes no mention of another essential feature of this type of building, the door in the façade (figs 128, 130, 146, 148, 151). We may assume that the philosopher did not see fit to mention an opening, since he considered it to be indispensable in order to admit the body. One might finally note that Plato also ignores the architectural decoration of the façade, but such a definition of 'Macedonian tombs' would exclude a number whose façade is of great simplicity[3]. It should therefore be concluded that the main feature of the 'Macedonian tomb' is the vault. We shall see that this type of covering was imposed by the dimensions of the building.

A total of some seventy 'Macedonian tombs' has been discovered to date, sixty-two within the borders of ancient Macedonia in its greatest extent, under Philip II, six in southern Greece, and two in Asia Minor.

This geographical distribution not only justifies the name 'Macedonian', but also demonstrates that the tombs reflected social structures and funerary customs that were themselves Macedonian. It might also be noted that the majority are to be found in 'Lower Macedonia'

130

129. Vergina, Tomb of Philip, model. From right to left, just behind the façade, can be seen the antechamber, with a first chest for the ashes of a deceased person, then the burial chamber with a second chest; the two rooms, which communicated through a marble door, are roofed with barrel vaults.

130. Door of a tomb from Hagia Paraskevi, marble. Detail of the metal elements.

(according to the ancient terminology), or modern Central Macedonia. In fact, the most numerous and most imposing 'Macedonian' tombs have been discovered at two sites: eleven at Vergina, ancient Aigeai, and seven at Lefkadia. A single tomb has been identified so far in the region of Pella, and even this is four kilometres outside the city, but it should not be forgotten that the tumuli in this area, which in all probability also cover Macedonian tombs, have not yet been excavated[4].

The dating of 'Macedonian tombs'

These tombs cannot always be precisely dated, for the majority of them had been pillaged when they were discovered. There is no doubt, however, that the earliest appeared just after the middle of the fourth century, while the latest are no later than the middle of the second century.

The earliest known is the tomb with the magnificent throne discovered at Vergina in 1987 by Manolis Andronicos, who called it the 'Tomb of Eurydice'. The pottery finds enable us to date this tomb about 340 BC. The tomb of Philip at Vergina is a little later, and this is followed by the 'Tomb of the Prince' at the same site. All three were royal tombs, according to the excavator.

One of the latest (middle of the second century), in the same region, is small and plain, as are the later monuments in general. The largest tombs, which are the most important from the architectural point of view, may be placed between the end of the fourth century and the first half of the third, although the dates of some of these are based on fairly inconclusive evidence.

Attempts have been made to seek a chronological indicator in the ratio between the diameter of the vault and the height of the tomb, but wrongly. Finally, even the morphological study of the architectural elements (capitals, mouldings etc) does not make precise dating possible, for two reasons: we do not yet have enough monuments in Macedonia to allow secure points of reference to be established; and the Macedonian tombs, covered, as a general rule, by a tumulus, do not always have the precision of execution normally found in surface buildings, especially public buildings. Furthermore, since they were not visible, they did not give birth to architectural forms exhibiting a continuous evolution (we shall even see that no two of them have the same architecture on the façade).

Origins and morphological evolution

These tombs made their first appearance just after the middle of the fourth century, but it is necessary to go back to earlier times to understand the needs that led to the conception of the vaulted roof, which was until then unknown in Greece. The efforts that have been made to explain this usage[5], and also the fittings of the façade, in terms of the simple imitation of foreign models, do not seem to be methodologically appropriate. According to a recent study[6], the vault which is a characteristic feature of the roofing of these tombs became necessary when their width exceeded a certain limit, since horizontal stone beams were incapable of supporting the weight of the earth accumulated above them to form the tumulus. This means that the vault (and by the same token, the Macedonian type of tomb) was justified by the need to construct tombs with dimensions larger than those known hitherto.

Of course, this only concerned a minority, of a very elevated social rank and wealth, for in Macedonia, as in the rest of Greece, ordinary people were buried in pit graves or cist graves (with side walls faced with slabs), with dimensions roughly those of a body, and marked simply by stelai, very often with painted decoration.

The excavations of recent years in Macedonia have already furnished a large number of funerary monuments that reflect the social structure of the kingdom. The imposing cist tombs discovered at Aiane, and also those at Vergina, dating from the fifth century[7] are the earliest examples of structures with dimensions significantly larger than usual, which posed difficult problems of roofing. Two large tombs with flat roofs, found recently at Katerini and Palatitsia, near Vergina, attest to tentative efforts to solve these problems.

The tomb at Katerini[8] is securely dated to before the middle of the fourth century by a coin of Amyntas III (394-370 BC) and the pottery finds. It is intermediate in form between the chamber tombs and the 'Macedonian tombs'. Although the interior arrangement is that of the latter, with an antechamber separated by a door from the burial chamber, it lacks two characteristic elements — the vault and the door in the façade. The rectangular building is divided by a partition wall into a main chamber (3.66 x 2.32 m, height 2.95 m) and an antechamber (3.66 x 1.95 m, height 3.32 m). The door between these two rooms has two marble leaves, and a low rectangular structure (2 x 1.10 m with a height of 0.46 m) against the back wall of the chamber, a little to the right of the axis, was probably a stand for a wooden couch.

The tomb at Palatitsia dates from the third quarter of the fourth century[9]. In the form of a large cist grave (4.10 m x 3.10 m internally), it has an unexpected feature: it was divided into two parts by two square pillars supporting an architrave, with the larger area containing a sort of table.

The covering of these two tombs is made of horizontal slabs. At Katerini, those over the main chamber were laid in position first, between the back wall and the dividing wall, with a span of 2.32 m. The slabs over the antechamber were set in position later, and were supported upon the slabs roofing the main chamber, above the dividing wall, and upon the front wall. The antechamber thus had an internal height more than 0.37 m greater than that of the main chamber, corresponding to the height of the blocks covering the latter.

In the tomb at Palatitsia, the roofing blocks were also laid in two rows, the first supported on one of the long walls and the architrave above the pillars, the second on the blocks of the first row above the architrave and on the other long wall. In both cases the builders were concerned to reduce the length of the roofing blocks to make them stronger, but their efforts went unrewarded: a large number of them had split.

A gold ring from the hilt of a sword, and a dagger demonstrate beyond any doubt that the Katerini tomb was intended for a man. The couch, a piece of furniture typical of the banquet room, was also made for him. We thus see that the main room of the tomb is no longer the earlier 'chest' of traditional tombs. We are here dealing with a substitute for the space in which a man really had a couch, a banquet table and the utensils necessary for daily life. What remains of the grave offerings after the plundering of the tomb suggests that the deceased man occupied an elevated rank in Macedonian society. The valuable armour and the gold jewellery, with eagles and heads of Herakles, are indications not merely of wealth but of a high grade in the military hierarchy, and he may even have been a close companion of the king.

We may conclude from this that the tomb at Katerini was constructed in response to the same funerary conceptions and the same needs as the vaulted 'Macedonian tombs'. The use of horizontal slabs for the cover meant that the interment could take place from above, making an outer door unnecessary. This link between

the external door and the form of roofing is also attested by the fact that only two tombs that were not vaulted, one at Olynthos[10] and one at Sedes near Thessalonike[11], had such a door, and both of these had a pitched roof.

The large cist tombs dating from the fifth or the fourth century recently discovered in Macedonia are thus evidence for a development amongst the ruling class that was to lead to the creation of the 'Macedonian tomb'. And it was the demands of construction that led — after the attempts attested by the tombs of Katerini and Palatitsia, of Olynthos and Sedes — to the conception of the vault, the only effective and reliable solution, it seemed. This type of architecture was thus not directly borrowed in its final form from a culturally foreign area and implanted into Macedonia as though by chance. It has been noted[12] that the existence of a vault in the tomb of Philip II, which has all the features of a structure that had matured over a long period, suggests that there were other earlier experiments. The excavations at Vergina have very recently brought to light another tomb that can be securely dated to around 340 BC[13]. This is undoubtedly the earliest 'Macedonian tomb' known at present, and forms a good starting point from which to form an idea of some of the most representative of these monuments[14].

Characteristic elements of the architectural form

Although no two 'Macedonian tombs' are the same in terms of their architecture, they nevertheless share a number of common elements, in addition to the vault that is their main feature. All of them have a large burial chamber. The smaller tombs are restricted to this chamber, and the larger additionally have an antechamber, which generally communicates with the main chamber by means of a door with two leaves (fig. 129). Only the tombs at Pydna[15], as well as another at Kirklareli in Eastern Thrace, had a second antechamber. Some of them had a passageway leading to the façade.

A door, often framed by doorposts and a lintel, opened in the façade of the smaller and plainer tombs. The larger and more luxurious ones have an advanced architectural composition, the outstanding feature of which is the engaged half-column supporting an Ionic or Doric entablature, surmounted most frequently by a pediment, and occasionally by a wide band forming a kind of additional frieze.

Inside, the walls were coated with plaster of good quality, often coloured, and quite frequently imitating isodomic masonry. In a number of rare cases, the walls had painted decoration. Three of the interior rooms also have an architectural structure, while in a fourth the architectural arrangement is merely suggested by painting, in a *trompe l'oeil.*

The painted decoration

Some of the 'Macedonian tombs' had painted decoration, either on the interior walls[16], or on the façade, and more rarely on both. Tomb I at Vergina (the Rhomaios Tomb)[17] has both a frieze on the façade and a band in the main chamber, both of them with floral decoration. The interior walls of the Tomb of Lyson and Kallikles at Lefkadia (Lefkadia III according to Gossel's terminology)[18] were adorned with very rich 'still life' frescoes (armour, garlands etc.).

In another tomb at the same site (Lefkadia VII, known as the Tomb of Rhomiopoulou)[19], the main chamber has very well-preserved floral decoration with a great wealth of colour and invention. The tympanum of the pediment on the façade has unfortunately very worn decoration depicting a man and a woman on a couch. A scene of combat in low relief could be seen in a wall-painting in the interior of the Kinch Tomb (Lefkadia II[20]) at the time of its discovery by the Danish archaeologist, but it has since been completely destroyed. The Great Tomb at Lefkadia (Lefkadia I) excavated by Ph. Petsas[21] has the richest decoration on its façade. Paintings can just be made out on the tympanum of the pediment, but beneath the scenes of combat adorning the frieze on the upper storey, the painted metopes and the large figures in the intercolumniations are much better preserved.

It is the tombs at Vergina, however, that contain the most remarkable paintings[22], especially those in the royal tombs. One of these, with no vault but of large dimensions, may be mentioned here because its interior walls are adorned with some of the most important frescoes in Greek antiquity, one of them a masterpiece: the Abduction of Persephone by Hades[23]. The frieze on the façade of the Tomb of Philip, a multi-figural hunting scene, is of equally fine quality[24]. The Tomb of the Prince[25] also had an external frieze which has not been preserved, though its loss is compensated for, partly at least, by the frieze with the chariot race in the antechamber. And a notable painting on the façade of one of the tombs in the 'Bella tumulus' depicts human figures[26].

The painted decoration of these tombs offers us the best, and sometimes the only, examples of Greek large-scale painting. Some of the works may be attributed with great probability to known painters of the fourth century — the glorious period of Classical painting — and they reveal to us an art that had hitherto been considered definitively lost.

The funerary furniture

The most characteristic piece of furniture in the 'Macedonian tombs' is the couch, most often a stone imitation of the wooden couch placed in the banquet room of a house[27] (fig. 131). It is not certain whether it represents a sort of intermediary between the banquet couch and the coffin, though the existence of a sarcophagus-couch in some of the tombs reinforces this hypothesis.

The presence of a throne is rare. In a 'Macedonian tomb' at Eretria[28], which had two couches and two thrones, the inscriptions on the couches give the names of men, and those on the thrones the names of women, Since, in reliefs depicting funerary banquets, the men are lying on couches and the women are seated, it could be inferred that thrones belonged to women's tombs and couches to men's tombs. However, the three burials with thrones found to date at Vergina do not entirely confirm this view. The sex of the deceased in the first (Rhomaios Tomb) is not known with certainty[29]. In the second (Tomb of Eurydice)[30] (figs 135, 136) the grave offerings left behind by the robbers demonstrate that the dead person was indeed a woman. In the case of the third, however (Tomb II of the Bella tumulus) (fig. 146), the warrior in the wall-painting on the façade suggests rather that it was a man.

Certain tombs contained fittings that lead one to think of offering tables, even though the excavators identified them, in a quite vague way, either as couches, or as stands for wooden couches. Some tombs also have structures along the walls resembling benches. In the Tomb of Phoinikas at Thessalonike[31], two very carefully worked elements have been interpreted as stands on which couches will have been placed, but this hypothesis does not seem very probable.

Only one monument, the Tomb of Philip, had a marble coffin, both in the main chamber and in the antechamber, in which was placed the gold chest containing the ashes of the deceased. Two tombs, finally (that at Amphipolis and the Tomb of Lyson at Lefkadia), had

131

burial niches. In the Lefkadia tomb[32], these number no less than twenty-two, with six in the back wall and eight in each of the side walls. According to the inscriptions recording the name of the dead person in each niche, the tomb appears to have been used by four generations. The last five niches remained empty, no doubt because the family had no further descendants.

Funerary customs

Burial.

In Macedonia of the fourth and third centuries, as indeed in the rest of Greece, both interment and cremation were practised. The coexistence of these two customs suggests that the choice lay with the families, but economic considerations may have intervened, since cremation involved additional expense.

In the tumulus cemetery at Vergina[33], interment of the body was the rule, as it was in the six tombs dating from the sixth and fifth centuries so far discovered in this region[34]. Although all the 'Macedonian tombs' that have been excavated had been plundered (with the exception of two royal tombs at Vergina), thus depriving us of information relating to the modes of burial, they housed both sarcophagi and ossuaries containing burnt bones, proof that burial of the body and of ashes were practised indifferently.

It is not always possible to locate the site of the funerary pyre, which was probably erected well away from the tomb. In rare cases, the excavators mention traces of fire above the tomb or in its vicinity, but even then it is possible that these were not traces of the funerary pyre itself, but of the remains of the pyre, which were taken and placed above the tomb after the burial. There are a number of examples of this, the most notable relating to the Tomb of Philip: on the extrados of the vault have been found bricks that formed the base of the pyre, and a whole series of burned objects that appear to have been placed on the pyre with the dead king's body — two swords, the remains of a shield, a horse's rein and several fragments of ivory figurines that recall the 'images in ivory and gold' mentioned by Diodoros in his description of the cremation of Hephaistion (XVII, 115, 1). The burials of Philip and Hephaistion, of course, were exceptional ceremonies, but there are examples of ordinary tombs where humbler offerings such as vases were found in the remains of the fire.

No 'Macedonian tomb' has so far produced a funerary stele or any other indication of the

131. Funerary couch, right end. Vergina, tomb in the Bella tumulus. Carved stone (palmettes, stylised rosette) embellished with painting and inlays (for the nine small rectangles at the top of the upright), like the wooden couches that this marble bed is imitating; on the horizontal frieze is a row of gilded griffins on a red background.

132

133

name of the dead person, apart from the Tomb of Lyson at Lefkadia where, as we have seen, names were inscribed above each niche[35]. However, the pan-Hellenic custom of erecting a stele over the tomb was also practised in Macedonia, where we encounter it in stelai from the beginning of the fifth century. And at Aiane[36] in Western Macedonia, fragments have even been found of an Archaic *kouros*, an Archaic *kore* and a lion, which must have belonged to funerary monuments. The existence has also been noted of several painted funerary stelai[37] in the cemetery at Vergina, preserved because they were reused in the large tumulus covering the royal tombs. These recall the stelai of Demetrias.

We naturally have no evidence for the ceremonies that will have followed the burial and will have been repeated at regular intervals at the tomb. The only exception here relates to the Tomb of Philip and the neighbouring one known as the 'Tomb of the Prince' at Vergina. Next to the Tomb of Philip may be seen the foundations of an important building, undoubtedly those of the 'heroon' where religious ceremonies were held in honour of the dead king.

Grave offerings

It is scarcely necessary to note that all the tombs discovered so far have yielded the same kinds of grave offerings — vases (figs 132-134), weapons, jewellery, figurines — as those found in tombs in other regions of Greece, Asia Minor and Magna Graecia. The number of these gifts, as well as their quality, obviously depended on the means at the disposal of the deceased person's family. It is apparent, however, that the objects discovered in the tombs of Macedonia are more numerous and more valuable than those in southern Greece. Thus, jewellery is very rare in tombs of the Classical period in Athens[38], whereas things were very different with the tombs of Macedonia, from the first period of the Iron Age to the late Hellenistic period. Tombs of women, in particular, have produced all kinds of jewellery, notable not only for their number but above all for their artistic quality and the richness of the materials. From the tombs of Sindos in the sixth century[39] to those of Neapolis or Thessalonike in the second[40], dozens of burials contain extremely valuable offerings. It is no exaggeration to conclude that belief in a life after death was much stronger and more profound amongst the Macedonians than elsewhere, and that desire to please the dead person was much greater. Euri-

134

132. Silver cup. Vergina, Tomb of Philip. The working of the metal has made it possible to achieve a delicacy and purity of form that it would have been difficult to achieve in pottery.

133. Silver strainer. Vergina, Tomb of Philip. The circular band of braiding is enhanced by a gold zone; the elegance of the forms and the richness of the material proclaim the quality of the artist and the importance of the homage accorded to the deceased, and also the splendour of the table of the living.

134. Silver oinochoe. Vergina, Tomb of Philip. The vase is decorated with egg and dart pattern on the rim, and a palmette on the handle, which is supported on an exceptionally expressive head of Silenus, with a slightly swollen face and a hairy beard, a masterpiece of Greek toreutic art.

pides might declare, through the mouth of Hecuba: 'In my opinion, the dead do not care for the wealth of the offerings they receive: this is only the vainglory of the living'[41], and this reasonable opinion was probably that of many Athenians of his day. It does not seem, however, to have been shared by the Macedonians, who remained very attached to their ancestral beliefs.

It is, indeed, the archaic structure of both Macedonian society and the political system[42] that perhaps explains the striking difference, in terms of dimensions and contents, between these tombs and those of southern Greece, and also the differences among these tombs themselves. It may be safely said that some of the objects found had been used for ordinary purposes (vases, weapons, jewellery etc.), while others were genuinely 'grave offerings' — that is, objects offered to the person specifically for the afterlife (white-ground lekythoi, figurines, objects of a religious nature) or objects made for the burial (funerary chests, couches, sarcophagi, etc). To these were added objects belonging to the family of the deceased, deposited in the tomb to perpetuate the links between the generations (the fifth century tripod found in Philip II's tomb).

The Tombs at Vergina

In the vicinity of Vergina have been discovered not only the most numerous 'Macedonian tombs', but also the earliest and most important. The wealth of the offerings in some of them, which were unplundered, enables us to say without question that they were royal tombs. This is also true of another which had, however, been pillaged.

Three of them contained a marble throne, which is not found in any other burial in Macedonia. The only 'Macedonian tomb' with a free-standing colonnade on the façade is also at Vergina, and this is also the only one, with a single exception, that has been destroyed, the majority of the blocks having been removed. Finally, four of these tombs have wall-paintings, of which two are certainly the work of master painters of the fourth century. According to Manolis Andronicos, the wealth, characteristics and antiquity of these tombs is to be explained by the fact that they belonged to the royal cemetery of Macedonia. Even when it had been supplanted by Pella, the ancient capital at Aigeai will have occupied a predominating position in the kingdom, and some of the wealthiest families from the ruling class probably continued to live there.

Of the eleven 'Macedonian tombs' at Vergina, only two stand isolated, three are part of the sector with the royal tombs, three others share a common tumulus (the 'Bella tumulus'), from which a fourth (the Heuzey Tomb) is separated by only a few metres. The last two are located side by side outside the north rampart of the city, in the cemetery of the sixth and fifth centuries. Although most of them are of some special interest, we will content ourselves with examining two in detail, and allude briefly to some of the characteristic features of the others.

The Tomb of Eurydice

Barely four metres to the east of the Rhomaios Tomb, M. Andronicos discovered another monument in 1987, the façade of which has not yet been completely uncovered, but which has already attracted attention for the unusual nature of its construction and the unique fittings in the burial chamber[43].

From the outside the building presents the appearance of an irregular rectangular block 10.60-10.70 m long and 7.50-7.95 wide. The vault did not, therefore, project outside the building, though in the present condition of the monument, it can be detected in the horizontal courses of the façade, where the plaster has fallen away as a result of the activities of the robbers. Was it the builders' intent to give the tomb this roughly rectangular volume to recall the very ancient tradition of cist graves? Or was it to reinforce the side walls of the structure,

which received all the thrust of the vault? This would imply that we are here in the first phase of construction of subterranean vaulted tombs, with the builders, not completely sure at this stage of the solidity of their work, taking extra steps to ensure additional protection. The indications that this tomb is the earliest of the 'Macedonian tombs' argue in favour of this latter hypothesis, though this does not, of course, preclude the former. Whatever the case, this arrangement, unique for the moment, undoubtedly represents a stage in the evolution of this type of building.

Although the excavation of the façade, which faces south, has not yet been completed, it can be seen that its only feature is a wall of poros covered with white plaster, not very carefully applied. In the centre is a door with two marble leaves, still *in situ*, the rear face of which — the only face visible at the present time — was worked with a great deal of care. Neither the door, nor the frame, posts or lintel, have suffered any damage.

The tomb consists of an antechamber 2.50 m deep and 4.48 m wide, and a main chamber of the same width and 5.51 m deep. The interior height reaches 5.80 m. The two rooms communicate by way of a second axial door, 3.01 m high, found half-open (opened no doubt by the robbers). Both the outer and the inner door were bolted after the burial with iron bars, that the robbers removed, but traces of which, in the form of oxidation, can clearly be seen on the marble leaves. Since they must have been bolted from the inside, the builders had made provision for one of the lower blocks of the partition wall and of the outer wall to be removed and then replaced in position once the man responsible for putting the iron bar in position had made his exit. The fact that the robbers were able to open the marble door suggests that the hinges were still functioning normally and had not yet rusted, and this suggests that the tomb must have been violated shortly after the burial.

Near the east wall of the antechamber, beneath the opening, a heap of earth from the break-in covered the skeleton of a man lying on his stomach, probably one of the intruders. A second skeleton, again probably one of the intruders, lay at the level of the roofing, some of the blocks of which had been removed by the robbers so that they could enter the tomb. There is nothing to indicate that any objects had been deposited in the antechamber. The plaster in this room, a large part of which had collapsed, was of excellent quality and that on the walls imitated isodomic masonry. Over the entire surface of the vault have been found iron nails, set at regular intervals in the shape of the Greek letter Π.

The main chamber is the largest and most carefully worked, from an architectural point of view, of all the 'Macedonian tombs' so far known. Its rear (that is, north) wall, had a full architectural decoration on its inner surface recalling the façade of an Ionic building (fig. 1). The perfect preservation of the plaster, which has retained the full richness of the colours, gives it a striking appearance without equal in any other Greek architectural structure.

In the centre of the wall is a false door with a threshold, posts and lintel. A mortar of excellent quality imitates the marble leaves of the door connecting the main chamber and antechamber so perfectly that the robbers were deceived by its appearance and tried to break it down, striking it in the middle with an iron bar and thereby uncovering the poros blocks of the north wall. It should be noted that this wall was of double thickness behind the false door, and triple thickness, that is, with three rows of course-blocks, in its lower part, to the right and left of the false door, which accounts for the exceptionally good state of preservation of the mortar and the colours.

The false door occupied the central intercolumniation of an order with four elegant Ionic half-columns crowned with capitals painted in blue and red. Two false windows, in the form of small doors, opened in each of the side intercolumniations, just below the architrave. The entablature consisted of an architrave with three *fasciae*, a frieze adorned with a white anthemion on a dark blue ground, dentils painted on a green and red ground that made their white volume stand out, and a cornice.

The quality of this very elegant architecture is almost eclipsed by a veritable masterpiece in the north-east corner of the chamber, which occupies the entire width of an intercolumniation and has a height of 2 m, rising just higher than the level of the bottom of the window: a marble throne (figs 135, 136), unique not only for its dimensions (2 m wide at the front and 1.18 m deep) but above all for the superb decoration that covers all the visible surfaces.

On the front, the two legs are crowned by a sort of capital with relief volutes, decorated with gilded palmettes, also in relief, and with decorative details in red. Between the legs, in a shallow recess just below the seat, is a frieze with a pair of confronted griffins at each end and two griffins in the centre devouring a stag, all executed in low relief and gilded, against a red ground. There is a similar frieze along each

136. Vergina, Tomb of Eurydice: the throne, seen from the front. This piece of marble furniture is very impressive, for its size, and the richness and quality of its decoration; the sphinx and the female figures between the small columns are particularly notable.

Following page:

137. Vergina, Tomb of Eurydice. The back of the throne has a veritable painted tableau depicting Hades and Persephone in their glory, a creation whose type was hitherto unknown in Greek art.

of the sides, with a lion in the centre feeding on a stag and a griffin at each end leaping towards the centre. On the band above the frieze, two seated women flank the Macedonian star. At the base of the back and at the sides, where these form the arms of the throne, are two superposed rows of small columns, the gilded bases and capitals of which define cutaway panels, two rows of four on the back and two of three on each arm. In the lower row, each panel contained a relief sphinx and in the upper row, slightly higher, a female figurine, also in relief, which appears to be supporting the architrave above it with its raised arm (several of these statuettes were unfortunately removed by the robbers).

The most important decoration on the throne, however, is the veritable 'painting' (fig. 137) which occupies the surface of the marble back. This is surrounded on three sides (apart from the base) by a coloured band in low relief with a wonderful scroll painted against a dark ground, and outside this by bead and reel moulding and on the exterior by an Ionic moulding with gilded egg and darts. The band at the top is surmounted by a Lesbian moulding with leaf and dart, which is also gilded.

The main scene is undoubtedly by a painter of great talent and inspiration. Unique in the whole of Classical art for its technique and its subject, as well as for its state of preservation, this find from Vergina is a superb addition to Greek large-scale painting, though unhappily one blemished by spots of a dark red colour in several places (they cover the bigger part of the face of the male figure). The blame here should perhaps be attributed to the presence on the throne of a purple cloth, which in time will have started to decompose. This may also account for the stains on the arms of the throne.

The scene depicts two figures in a chariot. The artist has chosen to show them frontally, a difficult solution and one rare in the field of painting. He was motivated by the desire to portray the two figures, who are without doubt deities, standing in the chariot, in the same manner and in their full majesty. At the left a bearded man, wearing a chiton and himation, holds the horses' reins in his left hand and the goad in his right. At the right is a young woman, also wearing a chiton and himation, with her head veiled by the himation, which she is raising in the traditional gesture called the 'Hera gesture' by archaeologists. In her left hand she holds a sceptre that ends in a fleur-de-lis.

In order to avoid the bigger part of the figures being concealed by the bodies of the horses, the painter has not hesitated to resort to the device of separating them obliquely, two at either side, so as to free the two deities completely and present them in all their majesty. This device has also allowed him to depict the horses at a gallop in a most expressive fashion, which would have been impossible had he depicted them frontally. Colour effects have been freely used for the animals (cover illustration). The two inner horses, with their white volume, flank and emphasise the red capes of the two figures, while the strong brown colour of the outer horses closes the entire composition very solidly.

The identity of the two figures is clear: they are Hades and Persephone, the fearful yet venerated gods of the Underworld. The depiction of these two, who here appear for the first time in an official tomb, and also in inscriptions of a slightly later date, reveals that these gods were the object of a cult, which is quite rare in Greece, and that the Macedonians believed deeply in life after death and did their best to try to satisfy the needs of their dead.

A footstool in front of the throne, covered with ornamentation, also has painted and gilded decoration. On the throne was found a marble slab, which had covered the funerary chest, and had been placed here by the robbers when they had emptied it of its contents. Both this cover and the marble sides of the chest bear traces of colour from the purple cloth that covered the bones of the dead. It seems likely that its contents were very valuable.

Apart from a number of terracotta and alabaster vases that they broke, the robbers themselves removed all the offerings in the tomb, which without doubt consisted of gold, silver and bronze utensils, and also jewellery. This can be conjectured from an examination of the traces on the west wall, against which the chests were apparently placed, and from the quality of the alabaster vases and a number of red-figure sherds. In particular, it has proved possible to restore two large squat lekythoi of excellent quality. The first, depicting an Eleusinian scene, is attributed to the Eleusis Painter, which not only enriches the *oeuvre* of this artist by the addition of a magnificent example, but also gives us a criterion by which to date the tomb. The date is confirmed by the fact that the initials of the eponymous archon can be read on a sherd of a panathenaic amphora, found outside the tomb, but certainly belonging to it: ΛΥΚ..., no doubt Lykiskos who held the office in 344 BC. The date 340 BC may be considered fairly probable. This dating, which is also that of the vaulted roof over the tomb, disproves the theory according to which the Great Tomb at Vergina cannot be that of Philip II, on the grounds that the vault was not introduced in Greece before Alexander's campaign in the East. The Tomb of Eurydice affords evidence that a subterranean vaulted edifice could perfectly well have been constructed before this campaign.

This tomb is not only the earliest of all the 'Macedonian tombs' known, but also the largest. It housed only a single burial, which is known with certainty to have contained the burnt bones of a woman. The size and quality of construction of the tomb, and the presence of an exceptionally rich throne suggests that this was a royal tomb. Its dating to 340 BC, and the connection that can be established with three inscribed bases from this same period which belonged to offerings made by Eurydice, daughter of Sirrhas and mother of Philip II, suggest that the tomb should be attributed to this highly active queen, who must have been seventy years old at this time. For this reason, Manolis Andronicos proposed, with reservations, that it be called the Tomb of Eurydice[44].

The Tomb of Philip

This is the most important Macedonian tomb known to date[45]. It was discovered in 1977 by Manolis Andronicos in the south-west sector of the large tumulus, a gigantic mound 110 m in diameter and 12 m high that rose at the west edge of the tumulus cemetery at Vergina.

A short distance to the north is another 'Macedonian tomb', a few metres to the southeast a cist grave, and finally, about thirty metres to the east, another 'Macedonian tomb' with a free colonnade on the façade, of which almost all the blocks have been removed. The foundations of a building 9.60 x 6 m in this same area have been interpreted as a heroon dedicated to the cult of Philip[46].

Certain features of the Tomb of Philip can only be due to the need to construct it as quickly as possible after the king's assassination. The hasty obsequies were naturally conducted in the presence of Alexander, who then had to repair to Pella to regulate the problems of the succession. It is certain that the tomb was constructed in two stages — to begin with the main chamber and only after this the antechamber. This is clear from the break in the masonry of the vault and that of the side walls above the wall dividing the two rooms. This interruption is confirmed by the existence, unique in this type of tomb, of plaster covering the exterior of the vault, a strong lime mortar that was as thick as

10 cm in places, in which can be traced the order in which the work was carried out.

The same difference can be seen in the interior plaster. That in the chamber was applied very quickly, as though for some provisional work, while that in the antechamber is of excellent quality and was painted very carefully with a band decorated with rosettes.

Some of the finds, which are also of an exceptional nature, attest to the hasty nature of the burial. On top of the vault was a pile of bricks amongst which were objects often blackened by the flames[47]. The bricks left their imprints on the vault, obviously because the plaster was still wet when they were placed there, and they probably came, like the rest of the finds, from the pyre on which the dead king was cremated. They must have been placed on the tomb after the interment of the bones of the deceased, immediately after the construction of the chamber and the application of the plaster on the vault.

Six gold acorns and a small fragment of a gold oak leaf, belonging to the crown placed in the gold chest containing the burnt bones, were discovered in the pile of bricks, proof that the dead king was still wearing the crown when he was placed on the pyre. It was removed at the very moment of incineration, and some of the leaves and acorns fell into the pyre. The majority probably melted and vanished, but a few survived. When the door to the chamber was closed forever after the ceremony, the remains of the fire must have been taken and placed on the vault, which is how the excavator came to find the fragments of melted crown in the bricks. All these details relating to the burial are important in determining the occupant of the tomb. Some scholars have thought of Philip III Arrhidaios rather than Philip II, but the foregoing observations preclude this hypothesis, for there was no need for haste in the burial of Arrhidaios[48].

The façade is the most imposing feature of the tomb (fig. 128). An order with antae that have slender capitals and a Doric half-column either side of the door is crowned with an entablature consisting of an architrave, a frieze of triglyphs and metopes (two above the side intercolumniations and four above the central one) and a cornice. Colour and painted decoration are preserved on all these elements: dark blue, red and white on the capitals, a white maeander on the red taenia of the architrave, dark blue for the triglyphs, regulae and guttae, and red for the band emphasising the cornice. The most notable feature, however, is the preservation *in situ* of the marble door with two leaves, which gives us a more accurate idea of the appearance of these ancient buildings.

Above the cornice of this Doric order one would expect to find a pediment, but the entire width of the façade, 5.56 m, is occupied up to a height of 1.16 m by a frieze, protected by the second cornice, which projects prominently above the entire structure, and is itself emphasised by a red band and a whole series of painted decoration, in particular a magnificent anthemion with palmettes and lotus flowers on the sima, in white on a blue ground.

The final and most important feature of this large frieze was its decoration, which has remained in quite good condition despite its twenty-three centuries of interment. It depicts a hunt in a forest, with seven hunters on foot and three on horseback, five or six wild beasts and nine hunting dogs, in a landscape with four trees, a tall stele in the form of a pillar and rocks against a hilly background.

Four or five scenes can be isolated in the composition, which depicts the dramatic moment at which the lion was about to be killed. At the top left, is a deer running behind rocks, wounded in the flank by a spear. Below this, a hunter has seized another deer, on which a dog has leapt, by the antlers. Immediately to the right is a superbly painted horseman, armed with a spear and depicted three-quarters from the rear in a bold perspective (fig. 138). A bushy tree is followed by two hunters, one portrayed from behind, the other frontally. They are preparing to strike a boar, which is being attacked by four dogs, with their spears. Between them, a stele in the form of a pillar supports three objects, probably statuettes, while behind the boar and the hunter depicted *en face* rises a dead tree. In the centre of the composition a young horseman, at full gallop to the right in front of a bare tree, points with his spear to the decisive episode of the hunt. In front of a bushy tree, a hunter on foot armed with a spear, a second brandishing an axe with both hands, and an imposing horseman of mature age coming from the right, with their three dogs, have surrounded a lion, wounded in the flank, which is raising its head in a violent movement towards the horseman, who is preparing to despatch it.

Further to the right again, a hunter, in a statuesque pose raises his spear obliquely. Behind his back a dog is leaping towards rocks where a bear, wounded by a blow from a spear, has a second, broken spear in its mouth. Finally, at the right edge, a young man is pulling a net. Hills are depicted faintly but clearly in the background.

The large stele with the three statuettes (?), and the ribbons and the picture tied to the first tree are undoubtedly cult elements, but there is nothing to indicate that this is a scene from mythology. Quite the reverse: everything suggests that both the hunt and the landscape are real.

It is clear that the artist desired to centre attention on the dramatic scene around the lion, towards which is moving the young horseman who, although the main figure in the scene, is dominated by the mature horseman. Is this Alexander and his father Philip? Their presence would not be surprising in a 'royal' hunt of this kind — for this is the proper interpretation of a lion hunt with so many participants, probably the young princes who took part along with the king in hunt meetings[49]. Far from being improbable in Macedonia, the lion hunt is attested there by a series of ancient testimonia[50]. The most important figure in the whole scene is thus quite probably the king who occupied the tomb and, in fact, the painter has deployed all his art to throw the hero of his composition into relief. The galloping motion of the horse of the rider in the centre and the direction of his spear both lead to the main scene, and the long spear of the foot hunter, which is touching the animal's neck, points in the same direction. The tension characterising this episode creates an impression of continuity, whereas the other figures in the fresco are spaced out almost independently of each other, and are much more tranquil.

The creator of this fresco was a complete master of perspective, colour and the rendering of volumes, and possessed a sure sense of composition. He was also a pioneer, for landscape, which used to be thought of as a conquest of the Late Hellenistic period, appears here for the first time in Greek painting in a most notable fashion. This work should be compared with the famous mosaic depicting the Battle of Alexander and Darius, and its creator with the creator of the original painting reproduced in that mosaic. The fresco in this tomb could have been a youthful work of the same painter[51].

The interior of the tomb.

The tomb consisted of a square main chamber, with a side of 4.46 m, and an antechamber of the same width and 3.36 m deep, with a height of 5.30 m. In both rooms the grave offerings were found in the spot where they had been deposited, or displaced slightly to one side as a result of the decomposition of the wooden furniture supporting them.

138. Vergina, Tomb of Philip: fresco of the Hunt, detail of the left part. This picture of a horseman seen from the rear, seated on a horse depicted obliquely to the left and starting to turn to the right, is striking for its freedom of conception.

Against the back wall of the chamber, on the axis of the room, a cubic marble sarcophagus contained the gold chest (fig. 139) enclosing the bones of the dead man, wrapped in a purple cloth (fig. 140) on which had been placed the gold wreath with its oak leaves and acorns (fig. 142). In front of the sarcophagus, there must have been a wooden couch, and probably a small wooden table. On the couch were placed the dead man's sword and dagger next to a support holding his gilded iron cuirass, and next to this, an iron helmet, his diadem and a pair of greaves — in fact, the complete defensive panoply of the deceased, apart from his shields.

The table probably held the silver, bronze and terracotta vessels used for banquets, a krater and a whole series of drinking cups in various shapes, a spoon and a ladle, all of them in silver (figs 132-134), a pitcher, a bronze patera, a pitcher and four clay 'salt-cellars'.

In the corner of the room two tripods were found, one of iron and the other of bronze, a bronze bowl and a bronze lantern with a terracotta lamp, followed by a number of objects for bathing — a basin with a sponge, a jug, and a number of bowls, all of bronze. Against the west wall was leaning a round bronze object recalling a large shield, with two pairs of bronze greaves at the side.

On the floor, behind the round object, was a mass of pieces of ivory, a few fragments of gilded silver, and some pieces of glass. These were, in fact, fragments of a sumptuous shield with chryselephantine decoration — that is, of gold and ivory, and it thus became clear that the round bronze object was the cover to protect this fragile ceremonial shield.

The antechamber was of an unusual depth for a tomb of this type, since it housed a second burial very similar to the one in the main chamber: an oblong marble sarcophagus (1.01 x 0.56 m, with a height of 0.68 m) containing a gold chest with the burnt bones of a woman wrapped in a superb purple cloth. To the side was found a magnificent gold diadem (fig. 143).

Just in front of the sarcophagus, the ground was covered with a thick layer of decomposed organic material, from wooden furniture richly decorated with gold and ivory. All around were scattered small gold roundels with the eight-pointed Macedonian star, and, between the sarcophagus and the dividing wall lay a gold wreath (fig. 141) of superb art, with myrtle leaves and flowers. Many of these were scattered over a fairly large area, the wreath having doubtless originally been suspended from one of the nails driven into the wall.

139. Vergina, Tomb of Philip. The main chamber contained, inside a marble sarcophagus, this gold funerary chest mounted on lion's paws, with the lid decorated by a sixteen-point star, and the four sides with three superposed bands: at the bottom a double scroll with volutes and flowers, then a row of five rosettes in blue glass paste, and finally a frieze of palmettes and lotus flowers. The corner uprights have rosettes.

139

140

The majority of the finds, however, were grouped in the recess formed by the communicating door and its posts. In the left corner a gold quiver had been placed against the door, still full of arrowheads. Next to it, two gold greaves, two iron spear- or javelin-heads were found on the threshold, as well as fragments of at least ten alabastra with a clay amphora. On the north side of the antechamber were the remains of painted wood, a gold pectoral, two gold gorgoneia, some silver rings and rosettes, and an iron spearhead.

The identification of the dead

In the light of his researches, Manolis Andronicos concluded that the tomb should be dated to the third quarter of the fourth century, that it is a royal tomb, and that the bodies are very probably those of Philip II (360-336 BC) and one of his wives, a hypothesis confirmed by anthropological examination of the male skull. On this, English experts have identified a wound to the right eye and Philip is known to have lost his eye in the siege of Methone in 354 BC.

The hypothesis advanced by some scholars that it is rather to be considered the tomb of Philip III Arrhidaios and his wife Eurydice must be ruled out, because it is certain that in our tomb the bones were interred immediately after the cremation, as proved by the traces of fire, while the official interment of Philip III, his wife and his stepmother did not take place until several months after their assassination. This decisive feature, and several others (such as the haste with which the walls of the funerary chamber were plastered) cannot have been taken into account by the protagonists of this theory.

The Tomb of the Prince

A short distance to the north-west of the Tomb of Philip, Manolis Andronicos discovered another, smaller tomb with a simpler façade, which he called the Tomb of the Prince[52]. Examination of the burnt bones has shown that in fact they belonged to a young man of thirteen or fourteen years, and every indication is that this tomb was also a 'royal' one. The dead boy may have been Alexander IV, son of Alexander the Great, who was assassinated by Cassander in 310/09 BC when he was roughly this age, though there is no archaeological evidence to confirm this hypothesis.

The tomb had a main chamber (3 x 4.03 m) opening onto the antechamber via a marble door with two leaves (one of them had fallen inwards). Its construction does not exhibit the same details as that of the Tomb of Philip. The simple façade had only an anta at each end, and the marble posts of the door with two leaves, also of marble. Between the antae and the door,

on the upper part of the wall, two relief shields, worked in stucco, had poorly preserved painted decoration. A small cornice projects above the frieze with the triglyphs, and above this one finds, as in the Tomb of Philip, a frieze, in this case 5.06 m long and 0.63 m high, surmounted by a second cornice with antefixes. This frieze did not have a fresco, but the excavator deduced from some of the traces that it was covered by a panel of wood, which was painted. This hypothesis is supported by the traces, at the springing of the vault over the chamber, of a wooden frieze, the nails for which are preserved *in situ.* In the case of the frieze on the façade, there was no need to fasten it in place, since it was known that after the interment the tomb would be covered with earth, which would hold the picture in place.

The upper part of the walls of the antechamber are decorated with a frieze 0.24 m high depicting a chariot race all around the walls (fig. 144). Despite the confined space at his disposal, the painter gave proof of all his considerable skill. Material in a very poor state of preservation lay scattered about on the ground. Towards the north has been found what is thought to be a leather uniform, some pieces of which were crumpled. Towards the south more organic remains have been found, and gilded bronze and iron strigils. Next to them, was the butt of a spear — the only gilded butt known from Classical antiquity — the head of which, found on the ground, also has traces of gilded decoration. At the back of the burial chamber was a sort of table, 1.10 m long, 0.67 wide and 0.54 high, with a circular cavity in the centre holding a silver hydria that contained the burnt bones of the deceased, wrapped in a purple cloth; on the shoulder of the hydria was placed a gold wreath (fig. 145). Some decomposed remains in front of the table may come from a wooden couch, and some silver vases were found on a piece of leather.

In the corners of the room was a rich harvest: silver-plated bronze vessels, a lampstand, two gilded bronze greaves, a gilded bronze wreath and two small gold plaques with decoration in low relief that were no doubt the remains of the cuirass. Other vases were the vessels used for banqueting, as in the Tomb of Philip. The majority were found in pairs, two kantharoi, two cups, two plates, etc. One of the most notable vases is a silver patera, the handle of which terminates in a superb ram's head.

These objects, of excellent quality, form a valuable group both in terms of their number and because of the variety of their shapes, but comparison with those from the tomb of Philip

142

144

144. Vergina, Tomb of the Prince. The walls of the antechamber were crowned by this chariot race, beneath a red band and a row of egg and dart pattern; the

conception of the gallop in its different stages, and the variety of the perspective treatment attest, even in this minor composition to a genuine mastery.

reveals the clear artistic superiority of the latter.

The tomb contained two more reliefs that belonged to the ivory decoration of the couch. The first is a bearded male figure whose body ends in an acanthus flower at the bottom. The second is a group of three figures (fig. 2): at the left the young goat-footed god Pan is accompanying a couple on his pipes — a bearded mature man holding a torch (or a thyrsos), who supports himself on a young woman following him. Even if this is not necessarily Dionysos and Ariadne[53], the figures are manifestly votaries of the god of wine. The quality of the relief is wonderful, and it is no exaggeration to recognise in it a masterpiece of Greek miniature sculpture.

Other tombs at Vergina

Four other 'Macedonian tombs' in the region were discovered between the villages of Vergina and Palatitsia. One of them, excavated in the last century by L. Heuzey, was the second tomb of this type known after the one at Pydna[54]. Relatively small, the burial chamber measured 3.85 m wide and 3.10 m long, while the antechamber, of the same width, was 1.45 m deep. The antechamber communicated with the main chamber by means of a door with two marble leaves, and the burial chamber contained two stone couches. The dating of the tomb to the end of the fourth century has been confirmed by the stamp of a Thasian amphora discovered on the façade in 1981, when Manolis Andronicos had undertaken its systematic investigation.

The other three tombs were discovered a short distance to the south-west, under a very low tumulus[55]. The largest was approached by a passageway 7.80 m long. Its façade had Doric architectural elements, with four half-columns, an entablature and a pediment surmounted by a high cornice that recalls the Egyptian throat. The tomb consists of a main chamber 3.60 x 3.04 m and an antechamber measuring 1.23 x 3.02 m. Its originality lies in the difference in treatment of the roofing[56] over the main chamber, and the antechamber, which has a horizontal ceiling with false beams imitating the wooden beams of a real ceiling.

In the vestibule, the white plaster at the bottom imitates the courses of ashlar masonry, above which the plaster is red. In the main chamber, the plaster is yellow at the bottom and white at the top. Against the back wall, a stone couch-sarcophagus (poros with white plaster) is covered with blocks imitating a red

146

mattress; the two pillows were depicted and painted in the same manner. The outer feet of the couch had relief decoration of volutes, palmettes and rosettes, whose colours emphasise the relief element. Between the legs runs a painted frieze, with a border also decorated with small scenes. The tomb may be dated with some probability to the second half of the third century.

The second tomb has a single chamber, 3.50 x 3 m, and its façade gives the appearance of a continuous wall crowned by a cornice, with no special architectural arrangement other than the marble door-frame (fig. 146). Above the door, however, are three wonderful figures from a fresco. In the centre, the striking representation of a young warrior, no doubt the deceased (fig. 147), depicted frontally with a spear in his raised right hand, and wearing a cuirass beneath which a short blue chiton can be seen, and he holds in his left hand the red himation rolled up to his waist. To his left (the viewer's right) a large female figure in profile —perhaps a personification of Macedonia, or martial Virtue —holds a gold wreath out to him in her right hand. On the other side, seated on a pile of shields, a young warrior raises his left hand

147

while with his right he touches the hilt of his
sword. A circular shield leans against his seat.

In the burial chamber, which was violated
by robbers, fragments of a marble throne[57], and
also of its foot-stool, have been discovered. The
back of the throne was simply a painted area of
the wall. A poros chest was also found, along
with a badly damaged poros head and an
enormous pillar, the presence of which is difficult to explain. The few sherds and the fresco
allow the group to be dated to the end of the
fourth or the beginning of the third century.

The third, and smallest, tomb, measures
only 2.53 x 2.32 m. Its construction and fittings are very plain, and it contained a large
sarcophagus.

All these tombs had been plundered, as had
the one excavated by K.A. Rhomaios in 1938 a
few metres to the west of the Tomb of Eurydice[58], at the north extremity of the plateau
on which the city of Aigeai stands, outside the
north rampart of the city and in the area of
the Archaic and Classical cemetery (fig. 148).
Sherds from Corinthian pots discovered in the
earth that had fallen inside this tomb suggest
that its construction involved the destruction of
a number of Archaic tombs. The tomb, which
very skilfully combines a façade in the form of a
temple with vaulted rooms, is one of the largest
(the third after the Tomb of Eurydice nearby
and the Tomb of Philip) and the most elegant
of those discovered to date. The façade, resting
on a low plinth, has four Ionic half-columns
supporting an architrave with two fasciae.
Above this, a narrow frieze bore a decoration
of white, red, yellow and green flowers on a
dark blue ground, beneath the cornice and the
pediment. The door was made of marble, with
two leaves, and set in a frame also of marble.

The interior was divided into two rooms
— the antechamber, measuring 4.56 x 2.50 m
with a height of 4.34 m, and the burial
chamber, a square of 4.56 m with a height of
4.44 m. A painted band of flowers adorned the
walls of the antechamber. The main chamber
had a similar band, though in this case undecorated. At the back of this chamber was a built
table, which Rhomaios, with some reservation,
called a couch, and also a large marble throne,
unique for its size and painted decoration until
the truly royal throne of Eurydice was discovered in the neighbouring tomb. Despite the
austere style of the former, these two finds form
a homogeneous pair.

The only chronological criteria are the architectural elements of the tomb, which allow it
to be placed with great probability in the first
half of the third century.

147. Vergina, tomb in
the Bella tumulus,
detail of the façade: the
central figure, probably
a representation of the
heroised dead man
between two allegorical
figures (possibly Ares
and Virtue), is depicted
here in the glory of the
young warrior.

148

148. Vergina, Rhomaios Tomb, reconstruction of façade. Its subtle elegance depends upon the four soaring Ionic half-columns, whose bases have simplified profiles, affixed to pilasters in low relief which support a light entablature: the architrave has only two fasciae, and the narrow frieze is enriched with a vividly painted scroll, with a great variety of leaves, volutes and white flowers on a deep blue ground; the entablature is crowned by a cornice with dentils beneath a low pediment. The trapezoidal door, set in its marble frame, imitates a wooden closure with two leaves reinforced by rows of large-headed nails.

The Tombs of Lefkadia

Seven 'Macedonian tombs' have been discovered so far in the region of Lefkadia[59], some of them of great importance. Already in last century the Danish archaeologist K.F. Kinch had identified one of them[60], decorated with a fresco depicting a horseman attacking an infantryman, but unfortunately almost nothing of this has been preserved. In three other tombs in the region the painted decoration is quite well preserved and allows us to complete the picture presented by the Vergina tombs, though they are far from having the artistic quality of the royal tombs.

The Tomb of Lyson and Kallikles

A small 'Macedonian tomb', the Tomb of Lyson and Kallikles[61], discovered in 1942, is unique in several respects. The names of the two brothers are inscribed on the lintel over the entrance —the only case in which we have an inscription for the tombs. A small antechamber, 0.89 x 0.86 m, leads through a relatively narrow entrance, to the burial chamber, 3.05 m wide, 3.95 deep and 1.92 m high. In the wall at the back six niches open, in two rows of three, and in each of the side walls eight niches in two rows of four. Above each cavity are inscribed the names of the dead, which go back to the fourth generation, both on the side of Lyson and on that of Kallikles. The five last niches were empty, indicating that the family was abruptly extinguished or had departed. If the first burials are dated to about 250 BC, it follows that the end of the family coincided with the troubled years of the Roman occupation.

The tomb is lavishly adorned with painted decoration, leaving no surface free and preserved in good condition; garlands with ribbons above the niches, between which painted pillars[62] carry a smooth architrave surmounted by mutules with guttae.

In the antechamber on one side a *perirrhanterion* and on the other an altar with a serpent is depicted. The most interesting decoration, however, occupies the lunettes — the semicircles defined on the front and rear walls by the curvature of the vault. The centre of the back wall is occupied (fig. 145) by a Macedonian shield with the star emblem, beneath which are two greaves, flanked by two helmets, and finally two swords, which seem to be suspended symmetrically from the vault. In the centre of the entrance wall there is also (fig. 150) a Macedonian shield, this time between two cuirasses, followed by two swords, as on the back wall. These frescoes thus confined themselves to depicting a number of pieces of the armour of the dead warriors, who were undoubtedly two brothers and will have been the first to be buried in the tomb. The good state of preservation of the frescoes, however, and the richness of the colours wins them a privileged place in the study of Greek painting.

The Great Tomb

Much more important for our knowledge of Greek painting are the frescoes of the Great Tomb of Lefkadia, excavated by Ph. Petsas in 1954, a short distance away from the preceding tomb[63].

This tomb presents noteworthy features (figs 152-153), in particular the rich architectural order on the façade, which has two levels. We may also note the great width of the antechamber (6.50 m, for a depth of 2.12 m) in comparison with that of the burial chamber (4.80 m for a depth of 4.72 m), and the difference in height between the two rooms — 7.70 m for the antechamber, 5.26 m for the main chamber. The large dimensions of the entrance are to be explained by the need for it to sustain a façade that it was desired should be monumental.

The fittings of the burial chamber are equally carefully worked (fig. 122). The walls are covered with stucco decoration, and the lower part of them has a podium with a base and a relief crowning member, on which pilasters worked in low relief appear to stand, supporting an architrave with three fasciae, surmounted in turn by a cornice. This gives the suggestion of a peristyle surrounding the room. The podium was white, as were the pilasters, and the wall between the latter was a bright red colour, making the supports stand out and contributing to the pictorial illusion[64].

The most impressive feature however, is the size of the façade (fig. 151), which is practically a square, 8.68 m in width and 8.60 m in height. The lower storey is Doric, with four half-columns *in antis.* In the entablature, the triglyphs

149. Lefkadia. Tomb of Lyson and Kallikles: burial chamber, rear lunette. In the middle, a shield with an eight-pointed star in its centre; beneath it, as though placed on the entablature, are two greaves and two helmets; at either side, a sword (the hilt of one of these is a bird's head) seems to be hanging from the vault (even the nail is depicted in perfect detail).

150. Lefkadia, Tomb of Lyson and Kallikles: burial chamber, front lunette. Here, again, is a shield, decorated with circles, between two swords hanging from the vault; this time, however, it is two complete cuirasses that are placed on the entablature, each surmounted by a helmet with a visor and cheek-pieces.

149

150

151

151. Lefkadia, façade of the
Great Tomb (reconstruction,
drawing), beginning of the third
century BC. At the lower level,
four Doric half-columns
between two antae support an
entablature with bright blue
triglyphs. The metopes have a
trompe l'oeil depiction of a
Centauromachy and, between
the columns and above a
screen-wall, the dead man is
shown, with Hermes and two
judges of the Underworld.
Higher up, a plinth showing a
battle between Macedonians
and Persians supports eight
Ionic half-columns, between
which are represented false
windows. The whole was
crowned by a painted pediment.

are dark blue, and the metopes have painted
scenes from a Centauromachy[65]. The face of the
cornice has a band decorated with floral motifs
on a dark blue ground. In the upper storey, a
podium has a wide frieze of a battle between
horsemen and infantrymen, probably between
Macedonians and Persians, in which the relief
figures (lime mortar) with painted clothes and
armour, stand out against a deep blue ground.
Above this podium is an Ionic order, with six
half-columns *in antis*. The seven compartments
so defined are occupied by false windows with
closed shutters, beneath the architrave and the
cornice. Finally, the entire façade is crowned by
a triangular pediment, in the tympanum of
which are a few traces of relief decoration of the
same type as that on the frieze on the podium.

The most important paintings of this façade

which, until the discovery of the royal tombs at
Vergina, were the most notable in Greek painting, are those between the Doric columns, set at
a height of 2.06 m above the stylobate, and
above an imitation of a screen-wall in isodomic
masonry[66].

There is a figure in each intercolumniation
—beginning from the left, a standing warrior,
then Hermes, then, after the door, a seated old
man who, we are informed by the inscription
over his head, is Aiakos, and finally a mature
man resting on his staff, Rhadamanthys according to the inscription. Although each figure appears to be independent and separated from the
others by the half-columns, the painter has,
without any doubt, integrated them into a
unique subject, the judgement of the dead
man, which accounts for the presence together
of a mortal, a god, and two mythical figures
believed to be the judges in Hades: Hermes,
the conductor of souls, leads the warrior towards the judges Aiakos and Rhadamanthys.

The dead man is portrayed standing, and
almost frontally, though slightly turned, as
though preparing to move to the right, towards
Hermes. His left hand rests on the sheath of his
sword, while in his right he holds his spear,
pointing downwards. He wears a short red
chiton, with a white cuirass over it, and from
his right shoulder hangs a yellow chlamys that
covers his back and falls behind to his right leg.
His boots, high and fastened, are the same colour as the chlamys. Hermes is also depicted
standing, almost *en face*, moving to the right
towards the judges, but turning his head towards the dead man, to whom he holds out his
right hand as though inviting him to follow,
while in his left hand he holds the caduceus. He
is dressed in a chiton of a dark red colour, beneath a pale blue chlamys with mauve edges,
and his boots are yellowish and tall, like those
of the deceased. He is thus wearing neither the
familiar petasos nor the winged sandals.

Aiakos is sitting on a cubic seat, in profile to
the left —that is to say, looking at Hermes and
the dead man. His right hand rests on his thigh,
while in his left, which is raised above his head,
he holds a long rod. A brown himation covers
his body, leaving bare only the right shoulder
and the greater part of his chest, and he wears
sandals on his feet. The age of the figure is
rendered realistically, his beard is not well
groomed but his hair is held by a ribbon diadem and a wreath with pointed leaves. Above
his head can be distinguished the letters of his
name [ΑΙΑ]ΚΟΣ.

Finally, Rhadamanthys is portrayed three
quarters, standing, with his weight on his left

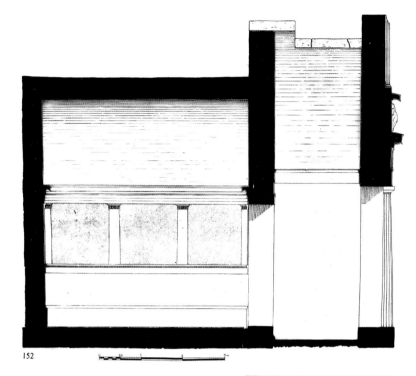

152

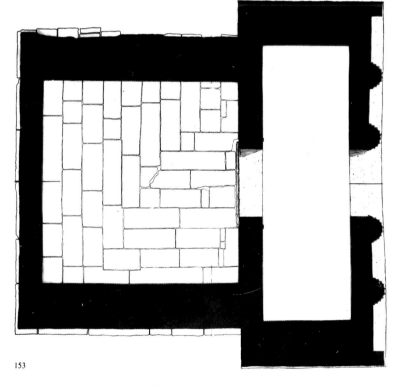

153

152-153. Lefkadia, the Great Tomb, plan and longitudinal section. The unusually great width of the antechamber was designed to allow the construction of a truly monumental façade, *which has no structural connection with the burial chamber; the vault over the antechamber is, as a result, itself higher and goes up to the level of the pediment.*

leg, the right crossed over it. His body is leaning forward, supported by a long staff, and, like Aiakos, he wears a himation, though of a paler colour, which leaves the upper part of his body bare, and also sandals. His face is also rendered in realistic manner, with his beard in disorder and, in his hair, the green leaves of a wreath. His aspect his serious and profound, and his features, taken as a whole, indicate a mature man, though somewhat younger than Aiakos. Above his head can be read the inscription PA-ΔAM[A]NΘΥΣ. This last figure has been compared with the philosopher in the famous Boscoreale fresco, the figures in which are thought to be taken from Macedonian history; for M. Andronicos, however, the only two points in common are the posture of the man leaning on his staff and the realism of the rendering.

The two young figures, those of the dead warrior and of Hermes, are rather idealised by the use of pale, bright colours, while the figures of the Judges, mature men, are penetratingly realistic. One might say that the first two figures are inspired by an earlier tradition, which may be related to Classical models, while the other two express more immediately the currents of the Hellenistic period, which turned to man's inner world. For Manolis Andronicos, we are here dealing with two artists. Ph. Petsas shares this conviction, but attributes to the first the figures of the dead man and Rhadamanthys and to the second the two central characters — a highly debatable hypothesis, given the differences of design and colour treatment.

Whatever the case, these works are of remarkable technical quality, though they do not reveal any great inspiration or any exceptional level of creativity. Petsas notes, not without justification, that 'the painter of the tomb may be compared with the journeyman painters of a small Campanian town'. The tomb very probably dates from the beginning of the third century.

The Tomb of Rhomiopoulou

Another tomb in the area of Lefkadia is of particular interest for its painted decoration, and also for the large number of fragments of ivory, belonging to the decoration of wooden furniture, which were found on the ground. Unfortunately, we have only a brief report, with little illustration, for this tomb, which was discovered in 1972[67]. Its façade was that of a temple, with four Ionic half-columns supporting an architrave with two fasciae, a cornice and a pediment with antefixes, which are rare in 'Macedonian tombs'. Traces of paint can be seen on the pediment, depicting a couple on a couch.

The tomb consists of an antechamber 4.10 m wide and 2 m deep, and a burial chamber 4.05 m wide with a depth of 5.10 m. It is thus bigger than the Tomb of Eurydice at Vergina. The two rooms communicated by means of a door with two marble leaves.

The walls of the antechamber are painted yellow. The decoration of the vaulted roof is unique. On a pale blue ground is a rich floral composition with scrolls, anthemia, acanthus leaves and flowers. The colours used are white, brown and red, the shades of which give a relief effect. The lower part of the walls of the main chamber is black and the upper part red, and the ceiling is yellow.

This tomb had also been plundered, but the robbers had left behind a large number of fragments of ivory scattered over the floor, which probably belonged to the decoration of one or more pieces of wooden furniture that have decomposed. Amongst them twenty-one heads and several limbs were found, which suggests that the compositions involved scenes of battle and Dionysiac scenes.

In view of the scanty nature of the published information, this tomb clearly cannot be dated with any certainty: perhaps the end of the third century, with reference to the floral decoration on the ceiling of the antechamber.

The Tomb of Langada

For the other 'Macedonian tombs' we frequently have no information beyond the fact of their discovery, but two monuments, of particular interest, have been published in detail — the tombs of Langada and Pydna.

The Tomb of Langada[68] was situated under a very high (19.50 m) and very extensive (76 m diameter at the base) tumulus, 9 km outside Thessalonike on the road leading to Langada. Found by chance in 1910, it was excavated the same year by Th. Macridy. Some damage had been caused to it by earthquakes and robbers. The unusually high façade (7.83 m) had an Ionic order, with two half-columns on either side of the central door and, in the corners, a quarter-column and pilaster. Above these was a complete entablature, with architrave, frieze and cornice, and a pediment. The door must have been of wood with some bronze elements, since sixty nails have been found, along with a knocker in the form of a lion's head, a handle with two opposed anthemia, a gilded Medusa's head, and a disc. These elements have made it possible to make a reconstruction of the door, which is now in the Istanbul Museum.

The tomb has an antechamber 5.38 m wide and 2.55 m deep with a height of 6.35 m, and a burial chamber 4.41 m wide, 4.07 m deep and 5.29 m high. The thickness of the walls is notable: while that of the façade is the usual 0.46 m, the side walls of the antechamber and the dividing wall are 0.92 m thick, and those of the main chamber reach a thickness of 1.25 m.

The door between the two rooms was of marble, with two leaves decorated with convex discs imitating the nails of wooden doors. One of the leaves had a relief head of Medusa towards the top, and a disc lower down was used to attach a handle. This disc, the nails and the head of Medusa were mostly covered with gold leaf, found intact, according to the excavator. Pale blue colour was also preserved in the eyes of the Medusa.

At the back of the chamber was a sarcophagus, occupying its entire width, made of marble slabs and divided into two parts, the larger to the left (2.20 m long). The tomb proper, however, beneath the left part of the sarcophagus, consisted of a pit dug into the ground and revetted with plastered blocks of poros, and with a lid also of poros, on which the wooden coffin was placed. The remains of this monument indicate that it was one of the most carefully executed and richest of the 'Macedonian tombs' known to us. It, too, should be dated before the end of the fourth century.

The Tomb of Pydna

The Tomb of Pydna[69], which has some very rare fittings, was one of the first tombs of this type discovered in the last century, in a region that has since produced two others for which we do not yet have much information. It is in the north-west part of a tumulus 10.70 m high and 60 m in diameter. Access to it was by a vaulted passageway 11 m long, an arrangement otherwise only found in the tomb at Stavropolis near Xanthe (where, however, the passageway is only 4.65 m long)[70]. The entrance to this *dromos* was closed by a door, and immediately after the threshold began the descent by a sloping surface covered with red plaster. The width of the *dromos* is 1.98 m at the beginning, but it grows steadily narrower until it is 1.58 m at the entrance to the tomb. The funerary building consisted of three rooms, the first two of which were not very deep: 1.48 and 1.49 m with widths of 2.88 and then 3.03 m. The burial chamber was 4.03 m deep and 4.09 m high. Against the left wall a marble couch had legs covered with decoration, with a lion carved in relief between them. A second couch, at right angles to the first, leaned against the back wall, with the same decoration, but with a relief serpent instead of the lion. The French excavators removed one of the couches, a door post and a bronze lion's head that acted as a knocker, to the Louvre, where they are now on exhibition. Only one other 'Macedonian tomb' with three rooms appears to be known at present — the one discovered at Kirklareli (Saranda Ekklisies) in East Thrace (Turkey)[71]. There is not much evidence by which to date the Tomb of Pydna, but the date proposed, at the end of the of the third or beginning of the second century, seems probable enough.

Monumental cist tombs

Another type of tomb was erected in Macedonia, in the fourth century, that might be called a monumental cist tomb, since, like the cist grave it formed a sort of completely closed oblong box, though its dimensions relate it rather to the chamber tomb. This was not a 'Macedonian tomb', however, since it had neither an entrance door in the façade, nor a vaulted roof. We shall examine two examples here, which are valuable for our knowledge both of funerary customs and also of painting and the goldsmith's art in fourth century Macedonia. The tombs in question are one discovered near the Tomb of Philip at Vergina, and a group of tombs at Derveni, about 10 km north-west of Thessalonike.

The Tomb of Persephone at Vergina

Manolis Andronicos gave this conventional name to the monumental cist tomb that he discovered a few metres to the south-east of the Tomb of Philip[72], in view of the fresco adorning one of the walls, whose subject is the Rape of Persephone.

The four-sided edifice is built of poros. Its internal dimensions are 3.50 x 2.09 m with a height of 3 m. It is closed on all four sides, like all cist graves, and roofed with slabs of poros set in position after the burial. It is very probable that there was a timber ceiling under this roof. Only a few potsherds and a marble shell were left behind by the robbers. Fortunately, however, they were unable to remove the most important items, the frescoes that decorated three quarters of the wall surfaces.

The lower part of the walls is painted 'Pompeian' red. At a height of 1.50 m above the ground, a band 0.19 to 0.22 m high runs around three of the walls (but not the west wall, where nails have been found *in situ*). On a pale blue ground is a repeated decorative motif of two confronted griffins flanking a flower. Above this band, the walls were white, but occupied by frescoes. On the long south wall three female figures can be seen. The first from the right is that of a woman of mature age seated and turned slightly to the right, and the central fig-

154

ure had almost the same pose. Both are badly damaged. The figure on the left is in a better state of preservation, at least as far as the outline is concerned. This was a woman depicted in profile, with the left hand raised almost to the height of the shoulders. The line is tranquil and noble, and of genuine beauty, and her youthful bearing contrasts with the austere expression of the other two figures. The excavator is of the opinion that this could be a depiction of the three Fates.

The middle of the east side is given over to a single female figure, seated on a rock, which is in quite a good state of preservation, though the colours have almost entirely disappeared. The woman is of mature age, and the himation, which covers her head as well as her body, emphasises the austere, venerable expression on her face. This is almost certainly Demeter, seated on 'the stone that does not smile', in the expression of the Homeric hymn, and deeply saddened by the loss of her daughter, carried off by the god Pluto.

This is in fact the subject treated on the long north wall (fig. 155), towards which the goddess is turned. The composition covers a surface of 3.50 x 1.01 m. The first figure from the left is that of Hermes (not shown here) who, almost flying, with his caduceus in his right hand, the Macedonian petasos on his head and sandals on his feet, escorts the god's chariot. In his left hand he holds the reins of the four galloping white horses. The chariot is depicted three quarters.

Pluto, with his sceptre in his right hand, is holding Persephone around the waist with his left arm, while she extends her arms behind in a desperate effort to escape. The god has his right foot on the chariot and the left still in space, just above the ground, on which can be seen the

155

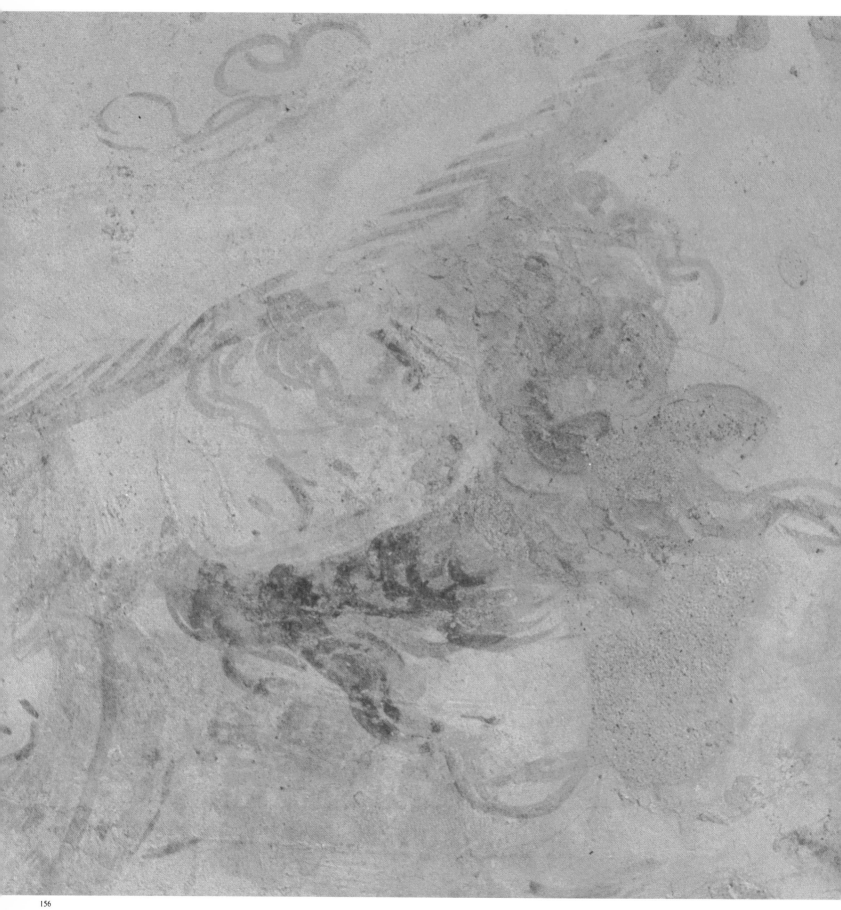

156

Preceding pages:

154. Vergina, Tomb of Persephone, preliminary drawing of the wall-painting. These rapid lines reveal the hesitations and changes of mind by the artist in his preparatory design.

155. Vergina, Tomb of Persephone, wall-painting of the Abduction of Persephone by Hades. The other two painted walls depict Demeter seated and the three Fates. Here the god, one foot already in the chariot, and holding the reins and his sceptre in his right hand, firmly grasps the young girl who attempts to resist, flinging herself backwards; behind, one of her companions makes a gesture of terror.

156. Abduction of Persephone, detail. In this picture, with its bold perspective, the rapid touches and hatching convey the agitation of the scene.

157. Oinochoe found at Derveni, tomb B, partially gilded silver, second half of the fourth century BC. The rich decoration has a triple crown of water-lily leaves encompassing the bottom of the belly and supporting open palmettes beneath a row of egg and dart pattern.

flowers that the young goddess and her companions were gathering at the time of the abduction. One of the latter, kneeling behind the chariot, turns in a frightened movement towards Persephone, raising her right hand in despair.

The painter, who must have been a major artist, has executed the design with inspiration, precision and assurance (fig. 156). It is quite certain that he is not reproducing an already prepared model in this fresco, but is creating his work directly on the surface of the wall. This is shown by the incised traces that can be seen in the final composition, which give several alternatives for each figure (fig. 154) —just as in some of the works of Leonardo da Vinci. The quality of the line, however, detracts in no way from that of the colours, which were used with great virtuosity. Manolis Andronicos believes that this fresco is not only plausibly, but almost certainly to be attributed to Nikomachos the famous painter of the middle of the fourth century[73].

Tomb B at Derveni

In 1962, during work on widening the national road linking Thessalonike with Kavala, two unplundered monumental cist tombs were discovered at Derveni, 10 km outside Thessalonike. Since then, the Archaeological Service has brought to light four others, also intact.

The funerary offerings in these tombs were extremely rich, above all in bronze and silver vases, which form a valuable group for the study of toreutics in Macedonia towards the middle of the fourth century. Unfortunately, apart from a brief report[74], only one of the large kraters has been published[75]. Most of these tombs are over 2 m long, and tomb B, the richest of them, reached 3 m, though their width does not exceed 2 m.

Although the form of the tombs suggests that they might have held a complete body, the archaeological data show that the deceased were first cremated, and only their burnt bones deposited in the tombs, closed in vases of precious metal. The excavator's note that 'the incineration was carried out on the blocks of the roof', is certainly far from the truth, for once the tomb was covered, it was difficult to place the bones of the dead in it, and yet these were found inside. In fact, the pyre was erected elsewhere, and the remains of it carried and placed on the tomb after the burial, a custom attested at several tombs in Macedonia, whether cist tombs or 'Macedonian tombs' (Tombs of Philip, Eurydice, etc.)[76].

157

Alongside the bronze vases have been found silver banqueting vessels, and even gold wreaths and diadems, with the bronze and iron weapons of the deceased. Tomb B, the largest of them, has yielded the richest harvest, including twenty silver vases (fig. 157). The remains of the fire in this tomb contained a charred papyrus, the first to be discovered in Greece (others have been found since). If this is not the earliest papyrus that has come down to us, it must be almost contemporary with the earliest, which has preserved the *Persians* of Timotheos. The contents of the papyrus are of fundamental importance for our knowledge of Orphic texts, for it contains one of the earliest of these with, according to Burkert, a pre-Socratic commentary on the *Theogony* of Orpheus.

A second find is that of the large bronze krater that contained the bones of the deceased (fig. 158). The height of this up to the rim is 0.766 m, and together with the handles it reaches 0.905 m. Magnificent embossed decoration, inspired by the cult of Dionysos, covers its entire surface. In addition to the main decoration on the body, there are also reliefs adorning

158

both its base and its neck and the centre of the volutes of the handles, while four statuettes worked in the round decorate the shoulder.

The composition of the main scene reflects Bacchic celebrations (figs 158-160). Dionysos and Ariadne are featured on the main face, flanked by dancing Maenads followed by a Silenus. It is more difficult to explain the presence of a bearded man, under one of the handles of the vase, depicted with only one shoe. He holds a spear and carries a sword in its sheath. He moves in time with that of the Maenads, but his identification with Pentheus or Lykourgos is far from certain, and it is not easy to concede that he represents the dead man as an initiate of the Dionysiac cult.

One of the four statuettes on the shoulders depicts Dionysos, and a second Silenus. Alternating with them are two Maenads. Finally, in the centre of the volutes (fig. 159) are four bearded figures representing Herakles, a god 'with bull's horns' and two other deities, which have been interpreted as Hades and Dionysos.

The egg and dart pattern around the rim of the vase has an inscription in silver-plated letters, in which can be read: ΑΣΤΙΟΥΝΕΙΟΣ ΑΝΑΞΑΓΟΡΑΙΟΙ ΕΣ ΛΑΡΙΣΑΣ, which means: 'I am (the krater) of Astion, son of Anaxagoras of Larisa'. It is quite possible that Astion was the dead man in tomb B, which is to be dated to about 330 BC.

'Macedonian tombs' and Greece

The excavation of a very large number of graves in Macedonia, dating from the Archaic period to the Hellenistic period, has furnished, in addition to much information on points of detail, as well as a number of fairly certain general conclusions.

The form taken by the vast majority of the graves is that known throughout the Greek world: pit graves, which became cist graves by virtue of the use on their walls of a revetment of poros blocks. The manner in which the burial was conducted is also the same. There were in-

158. Krater found at Derveni, tomb B, bronze with silver inlays, about 330 BC. The main face of the body depicts Dionysos in a sensual posture and Ariadne lightly raising her veil, in the middle

of a group of dancing Satyrs and Maenads.

159. Derveni krater. Handle volute: the head of a god (that of Herakles) is superbly set within it; the snake that coils around it to

the fluted rim, with its head towards the centre of the vase, extends down the entire handle, forming a horizontal spiral at its base. In the angle, a half flame palmette.

terments and cremations, but no chronological distinction between the two methods can be drawn, with one or the other predominating in turn and the two methods occasionally existing alongside each other in the same period and in the same region. The grave offerings exhibit great variety and consist in general of objects belonging to the deceased (weapons and banqueting vessels for men, jewellery for women), vases and figurines, as in all Greek cemeteries. Finally, the funerary monuments discovered to date allow us to assert that a Macedonian cemetery must have resembled any other Greek cemetery. The Archaic sculptures of the tombs at Aiane[77] undoubtedly formed part of funerary monuments similar to those to which belonged the famous funerary *kouroi* of Attica. The stele of Pella in the Istanbul Museum, and the stele of the hoplite at Vergina, works of the fifth century[78], attest to the similarity between the funerary stelai of Macedonia and those of other Greek cities of the same period, and the same is true of the fourth- and third- century funerary stelai discovered at Vergina and in so many other Macedonian cemeteries, with their painted or relief scenes and inscriptions containing the names of the dead or funerary epigrams.

Thus, there was no noticeable difference between the tombs of Macedonia and those of the rest of Greece, as far as normal burials are concerned — in other words, the majority. However, one cannot fail to be impressed by the existence in Macedonia of the large vaulted tombs known as 'Macedonian tombs', and also of the cist graves that we have called 'monumental cist tombs', which are clearly distinct from those of other regions by virtue of their dimensions and their content. And even though almost all the 'Macedonian tombs' had been pillaged, apart from two royal tombs at Vergina, there is no doubt that they housed very rich offerings. The robbers left behind them the clay vases in particular, but they must have taken with them those in bronze, silver and gold. Manolis Andronicos is of the view, quite rightly, that this particular feature of Macedonia cannot be interpreted as indicating a difference in religion, which would reflect an ethnological difference between the Macedonians and the Greeks living further south. It is to be explained in terms of

the social and political structure, with the Macedonians having preserved archaic forms of organisation for historical reasons.

The presence of these very rich, monumental tombs, reflects the existence of a class of wealthy, dominant families, a characteristic phenomenon of Macedonian society which also appears in the written sources. The Archaic tombs already attest to the enrichment of a certain section of the population, and this continued in the fifth century and intensified in the fourth, after the expedition of Alexander. It is even likely that the first 'Macedonian tombs' were constructed for members of the royal family, and subsequently for the 'Companions' of the king who desired to imitate their sovereign.

More important still is the contribution made by the 'Macedonian tombs' to our knowledge of both the architecture and the painting of the early Hellenistic period, for the area covered by the Macedonian kingdom and also for the whole of Greece. These are, in fact, the only architectural monuments of their period that are preserved in their entirety. They allow us to form, for the first time, a direct picture of Greek large-scale painting. Thanks to the frescoes in the tombs of Lefkadia and Vergina, we can understand the admiration in which the Greeks of the time, followed later by the Romans, held their artists.

Moreover, through these tombs we have also learned to appreciate the art of metal-working and the decorative art of the Macedonians, which were themselves heirs to a long tradition, for they did not appear fully fledged in the fourth century. And this tradition has its roots in Macedonia itself. The country possessed the raw material, precious metals, in great abundance, and, since the sixth century, it had not only belonged to the sphere of influence of Ionian art but, according to Manolis Andronicos, had connections with the Ionian world itself which, as part of the vast Persian empire, combined the Greek heritage with oriental delicacy and luxury.

Thus, the 'Macedonian phenomenon' now throws a new light on Hellenistic civilisation as it evolved in the major centres created by the Macedonian successors of Alexander the Great.

160. Derveni krater. The scene of a Dionysiac dance, of which a detail is shown here, with an ithyphallic Silenos and a young woman whirling beneath a vine-shoot, reminds us that it was at Pella that Euripides presented his Bacchae *and, more generally, reveals the importance of the cult of Dionysos in Macedonia.*

6

MACEDONIAN DEDICATIONS OUTSIDE MACEDONIA

161. View of Samothrace with the Hieron.

Macedonian architecture is, fortunately, known to us not only through the buildings of Macedonia, but also from structures erected elsewhere in Greece, especially at the great pan-Hellenic sanctuaries. The erection of a building, particularly if it is notable for some reason, not only contributes to the quality of life but is at the same time an act of political propaganda[1], the effectiveness of which may be judged from the observation that the modern world does not fail to make use of it.

The sanctuaries that seem to have been of most direct interest to the rulers of Macedonia were those at Olympia and Delos, to some extent at Delphi and some other sites, but above all the sanctuary of the Great Gods on Samothrace which, of course, fell directly within their sphere of influence. We shall see that they astutely chose the most prominent locations there, the most prestigious and best adapted types of building, and the boldest architects for creations that set their seal on the future evolution of Greek architecture[2].

Olympia

The Philippeion

The earliest of these edifices is the Philippeion at Olympia[3], erected by Philip II after the battle of Chaironeia in 338 BC, and perhaps completed by Alexander. It stood at what must have been the most frequently used entrance to the sanctuary, next to some of its most venerated monuments, the temple of Hera and the Pelopeion, the sacred temenos of the hero who founded Olympia and great-grandfather of Herakles, whom the Macedonian kings believed to be the ancestor of their family.

It was a tholos, a fairly rare type of building for which Macedonian architecture seems to have entertained a certain favour — we shall later examine the one on Samothrace, and we have already discussed those at Vergina and Pella[4]. Although this rotunda (figs 162, 163) is undoubtedly influenced by the one at Delphi, it is of the Ionic order, an unusual innovation, the validity of which may be questioned, since the rectangle of the Ionic capital harmonises less well with the curvature of the building than the square of the Doric or Corinthian capital. Moreover, beneath the usual torus and scotia, the bases of the eighteen columns (fig. 164) have

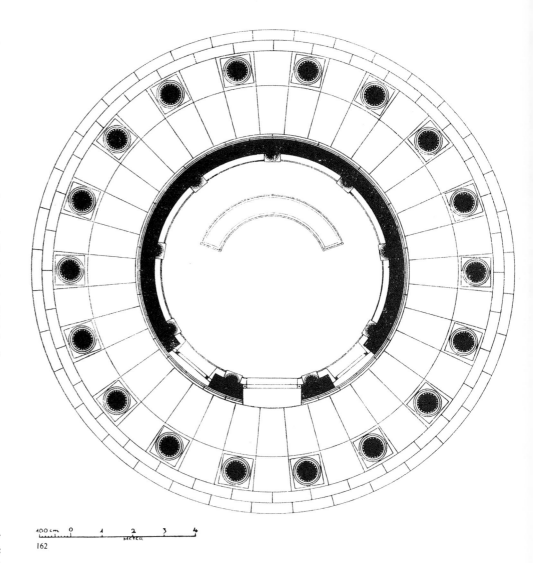

100 cm 0   1   2   3   4
meter
162

a square plinth, which is unusual, though it is also found at Pella.

The capital, too, is reminiscent of certain details found in Macedonia. The architrave has only two fasciae, instead of the three that one would expect, and above all, the entablature combined a frieze (typical of mainland Greece) with dentils (typical of Greece in Asia Minor), which had hitherto been used separately. This is perhaps the first occurrence (apart from an isolated and disputed Archaic example) of this reduplication of the decoration, which was to have a long future. We shall encounter it again in another building of the same date or a few years later, the Propylon of the Temenos on Samothrace.

Higher still, the Ionic cornice is surmounted by a typically Doric moulding, known by the experts as an ogee-type hawksbeak moulding, which here seems to be making its first appearance.

In the interior, above a raised stylobate, the

162. Olympia, the Philippeion, about 333 BC. Plan. Inside the peristyle with its eighteen columns, the wall pierced by a door is decorated on the interior with an order of nine half-engaged columns.

163

163. Olympia, the
Philippeion. Blocks: the
first row belong to the
interior stylobate with
its moulding; behind
the wall, bases from the
exterior colonnade.

164

164. Olympia, the
Philippeion. Base of a
column from the
exterior order: it is of
Ionic-Attic style, but
with a square plinth.

In the interior, above a raised stylobate, the innovative architect applied nine Corinthian half-columns to the wall. 'Applied', because these elements did not actually support the entablature, and were not themselves supported by the stylobate —we have here one of those décors of which Macedonian funerary architecture was so fond[5].

The room housed five statues: Philip, his parents Amyntas and Eurydice, his wife Olympias, and his son Alexander. The sculptor, Leochares, used gold for the drapery and ivory for the flesh —a 'chryselephantine' technique that recalls the cult figures of Athena on the Parthenon and of Zeus in the temple at Olympia to which the Philippeion is so close. The implied comparison tended to elevate to the level of the gods the royal guests in this highly unusual edifice, which it has been suggested should be regarded not as a heroon or a treasury, but as a temple[6].

Megalopolis
The Stoa of Philip II

Still with Philip II, we shall say little of the great Stoa at Megalopolis, a structure dedicated to him, according to Pausanias[7], since we do not know if the king who gave his name to the building provided the finance for it, or contributed in any way to its erection. We may note, however, that it was a stoa, a type of structure widely used by the Hellenistic kings in their public relations. The long colonnaded gallery, protected from the sun and the rain, yet still open to the air and to light and offering a view, was the most practical edifice for housing throngs and thus rendered the greatest service for the least expense (the building is relatively plain) in the most visible manner. This is why, as we shall see at Delos, it was of special interest to the Macedonian kings. It is also true that the building is of impressive, 'regal' dimensions, being over 155 m long and having two rows of interior columns — a quite unusual arrangement, though one not really surprising in the artificial creation that was the 'Great City'. Its plan, finally, with projecting wings (though in this case with nine columns on the façades!) conforms with that of several other Macedonian structures that we shall encounter, and its relationship to the king, even if we do not know its exact nature, is clearly attested.

Oropos
The Stoa of the Amphiareion

The situation is different when we turn to another famous stoa, the one that housed the oracular sleep of the faithful at the Amphiareion at Oropos[8], which was probably dedicated towards the middle of the fourth century, by two Macedonians named Amyntas, of whom one was none other than the son of Perdikkas III (fig. 165).

An entire series of features of this building, which has a Doric colonnade on the façade and an Ionic colonnade on its axis, recalls arrangements that we shall meet again in the orbit of Macedonia: the way the side walls return along the façade, which reappears on Delos in the Stoa of Philip; the scarcely orthodox arrangement of the interior colonnade, with two intercolumniations corresponding, more or less, to five intercolumniations on the façade (whereas the usual ratio is one to two); certain details of the Doric order with, for example, the crowning member of the triglyphs having 'ears' at the corners, which are to be found in many Macedonian buildings, though also elsewhere; the absence of mutules on the returns of the cornice, as in Stoa J on Samothrace[9]. Above all, the timber frame of the roof, which has been restored with some probability, was of the type with sloping cross-beams, the first example of an arrangement typical of the Stoa of Antigonos at Delos and Stoa J on Samothrace.

The connection with Macedonia, however, remains hypothetical for the moment, in the absence of a certain dating of the building. Macedonia was perhaps not yet in a position to give expression to its wealth and grandeur by such lavish expenditure and such technical prowess.

165

165. Oropos, the
Amphiareion: the stoa,
middle of the fourth
century BC. It housed
the oracular sleep of the
faithful who had come
to consult the seer
Amphiaraos, and was
probably dedicated by
two Macedonians.

Delos

This moment came, at a distinctly later date, when the Macedonian stoas were erected on Delos. There are two of these, both superbly situated, and with a wealth of significant features. From the middle of the third century on, the influence of Macedonians from Macedonia itself tends to supplant that of the Ptolemies, as already attested by the foundation of the Antigoneia and Philippeia games[10].

The Stoa of Antigonos Gonatas

The architecture lent its massive assurance to this policy. The earliest Macedonian stoa on the site, that of Antigonos Gonatas[11], dating from the third quarter of the third century, served as the backcloth to the sanctuary of Apollo, just to the north of the temples and the treasuries (fig. 166). Of imposing dimensions (120 m long), its plan was that of the Greek letter Π, Athenian in origin but here implemented on a Macedonian scale, with two projecting side-wings, each with six columns crowned by a pediment, recalling the façades of temples. It has, moreover, a number of peculiarities, such as the difference in the spacing between the columns in the central part of the facade, those on the wings, and those on the returns, and in the corners of the wings there is no contracted intercolumniation, which centuries of Doric architecture had perfected in order to avoid having a section of a metope at the end of the frieze.

A number of the details of the order also seem to be characteristic: for example, the profile of the echinus on the capital — a steep oblique that ended directly on the abacus; higher up, the triglyphs have the 'ears' above the side glyphs that have already been discussed in connection with the stoa at Oropos; and, most importantly, the front face of the metopes is brought forward so far that the face of the triglyphs is in the same vertical plane as the taenia that they surmount, a new arrangement that we shall also find in the Hypostyle Hall on Delos and in certain of the Macedonian tombs, and

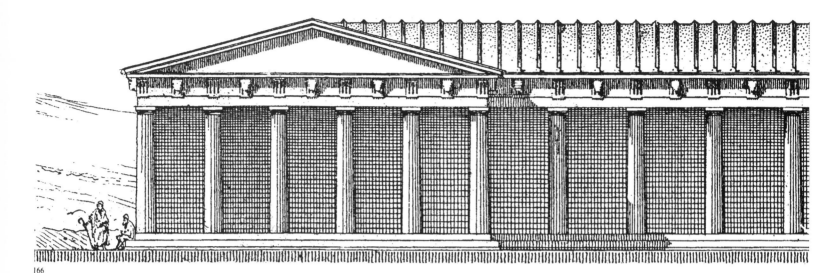

166

which was to become the rule in Roman architecture. Still on the entablature, it is perhaps surprising to find only two metopes per intercolumniation, while the interval between the columns seems to call for three, the metopes thus being unusually wide in proportion to their height (especially on the façade of the building, where the columns are more spaced out). This was to accommodate another unusual arrangement: in the middle of each intercolumniation was placed a triglyph decorated with a bull's head, a motif rich in religious significance[12]. These heads, moreover, which appear to support the cornice, would have concealed a number of mutules, and it was accordingly preferred to omit all the latter. In several of the 'Macedonian tombs', a similar desire for simplification led to the abandonment of this ornament, the original purpose of which must have by then been half forgotten. It was also omitted on the sides and the back of the stoa at Oropos, and of stoa J on Samothrace[13].

Other details also recall the façades of Macedonian tombs, such as the combination of an ogee-type hawksbeak moulding at the top of the horizontal cornice with a plain ovolo on the sloping cornice. This stoa also has a new type of timber roof-frame with a pitched roof created by cross-beams sloping between the Ionic colonnade on the axis and the long sides at the front and back. We have already seen this in the stoa at Oropos, and we shall encounter it again in Stoa J on Samothrace.

This building, remarkable in terms of its dimensions, its decoration and a number of its particular features, was also notable for the sumptuousness of its façade. This was of marble, indeed, but it was the only feature made of this material, as though to combine the taste for ostentation with a certain concern for economy

that also marked several other aspects of Macedonian architecture. Examples are not rare of this double preoccupation, which translates itself, here as in many other cases, into the placing of emphasis on the façade to the detriment of the classical unity of the whole. But the large inscription on the architrave, and the pedestal placed in front of the monument, on which stood twenty-one bronze statues depicting the ancestors of the king, focused interest on the Macedonian dynasty.

The Stoa of Philip V

The second Macedonian stoa on Delos was erected at a later date, about 210 BC, due this time to the munificence of Philip V[14]. It, too, occupied a privileged position, bordering the avenue of the Processions leading from the port and the Agora of the Competaliastae to the south propylaia of the sanctuary, and standing opposite another stoa that was probably also a royal dedication, this time by the Attalids — earlier than that of Philip, which no doubt aspired to surpass it in majesty.

Built entirely of marble, the Stoa of Philip is notable first of all for its plan (fig. 167). In its original form, this was a simple rectangle, though the colonnade of the façade, which was Doric, as in the case of the stoa of Antigonos, was set between two sections of wall, following the example of the stoa at Oropos. In north Greece, the Hall of Votive Gifts on Samothrace[15] and the Stoa of the Thesmophorion on Thasos[16] followed the same formula, but in the Stoa of Philip the walls were themselves enlivened by an 'attic', a row of four windows framed by five pilasters aligned vertically under the triglyphs of the frieze (fig. 168). The two ends of the stoa were thus protected and illumin-

166. Delos, the Stoa of Antigonos (left part of the façade), third quarter of the third century BC. At the ends of the long colonnade were projecting wings surmounted by pediments, like temple façades.

167. Delos, plan of the Stoa of Philip, about 210 BC, and subsequently enlarged in the first half of the second century BC. The part added consisted of the large colonnade at the south, and the room at the north that completed the building on the west side.

168. Delos, the Stoa of Philip, left end of the north façade, reconstruction. The walls, which return on the façade, were of marble like the rest of the building, and were pierced towards the top by windows, whose jambs continue the line of the triglyphs.

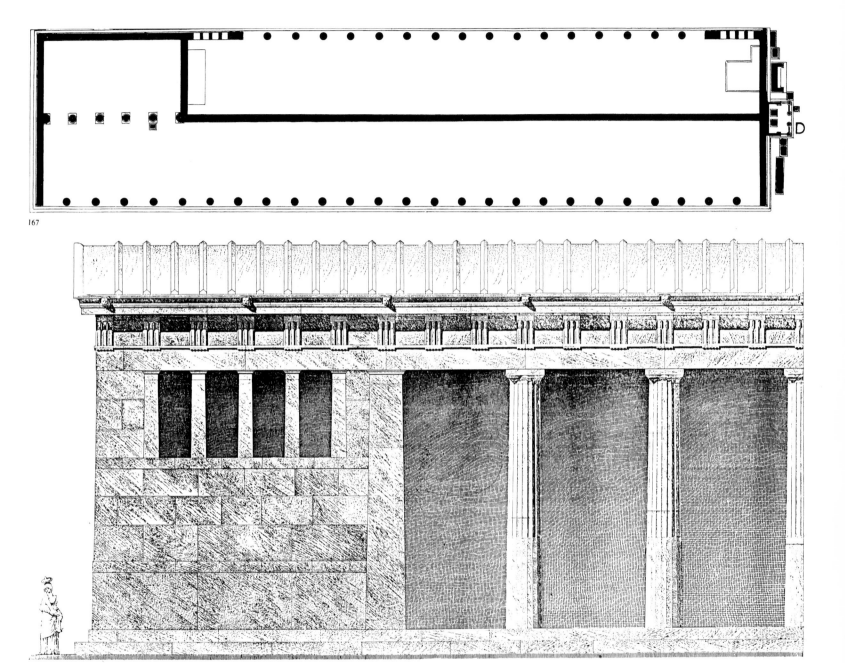

167

168

ated by an arrangement of which we shall encounter an echo in the Neorion on Delos and
the Rotunda on Samothrace, in which there
was similarly a correspondence between pilasters and triglyphs.

Another surprising feature of the building is
its use of huge elements — the orthostates are
over 2.50 m long, and 1.32 m high. These
blocks seem colossal, especially when compared with the Delian construction material of
this period. In the same register, we may note
the size of the timber roof-frame, whose beams
had to span 8.90 m without any intermediate
support, a distance that presupposes timbers
distinctly larger than those generally at the dis-

posal of the builders of Delos, though they are
known to have procured supplies from Macedonia. The sockets in the walls suggest that
these timbers were 0.67 m high and 0.90 m wide
(unless we are to envisage two joined timbers of
0.45 m each). Should not a royal monument
make exceptional timbers available to unrivalled carpenters?

Some of the features of the structural elements are those commonly found at the period,
such as the stiffness of the column, with no
bulge on the shaft, with none of that 'tension'
(entasis in Greek) that breathed life into the
Classical column; and the treatment of the
shaft, too, only the upper part of which was

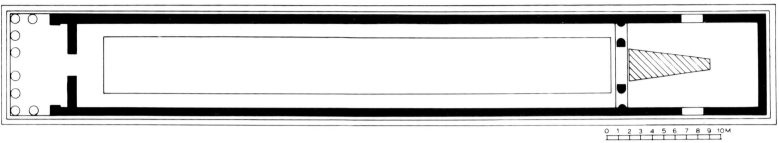

169

fluted, with the lower part simply cut in facets up to a height of 2 m (probably to prevent visitors from damaging the ridges of the fluting as they passed). This Pergamene formula is also found in Stoa S-E on Thasos[17]. But here again the building is connected with Macedonian structures by certain details of the decoration, such as the treatment of the upper end of the flutings, just below the annulets of the Doric capital; or the presence below the soffit moulding on the cornice of a double fascia that we also encounter in Macedonian funerary architecture; or, again, the combination of the two forms of the hawksbeak moulding, with the upper part treated either as an ogee or as an ovolo, which is already an anachronism at this period. These details are scarcely perceptible to even an attentive gaze, but they allow the experts to relate this building to a group of structures, other features of which, this time directly perceptible, were designed to impress and arouse admiration.

It was probably during the first half of the second century that the stoa was enlarged and doubled, this time with a colonnade 89 m long facing the sea. Thus the building henceforth had a double façade, a quite rare formula. Furthermore, this addition involved the construction, at the north end of the original stoa, of a hall separated from the new one by an interior Ionic order. This was a colonnade of quite exceptional type. Its four elements have been described as having 'oval' shafts, though it is more correct to call them 'double half-columns', each of them consisting of two half-columns affixed to the faces of a large rectangular pillar. The earliest example of this formula is perhaps that in the entrance of the Palace at Vergina[18]. At either end, this colonnade ends in a pilaster, formed this time by half of one of these supports affixed to a rectangular pillar, producing two quarter-columns framed by flat vertical bands. These engaged quarter-columns were also used in a tomb at Dion[19] and the tomb at Langada[20]. The imagination of the architects thus gave birth to combinations that are also found in façades at Petra[21], and which

have rightly been described as baroque. It is also clear that the two Macedonian stoas on Delos are very different from each other, even though they are separated by only a relatively short time. It should not be concluded from this, however, that they were not Macedonian creations, or that the donors were content simply to supply the finances. It is a feature of Macedonian architecture to combine elements of diverse origin in a continually changing manner, seeking continuity through constant renewal.

The Monument of the Bulls

At least two other buildings on Delos are interesting in the present context, even though their relationship to Macedonia is less certain than that of the two stoas. The first, traditionally called the Monument of the Bulls[22], has been described by G. Roux as 'the most original monument of Delos, and even of Hellenistic Greece' (figure 169). Situated in the heart of the sanctuary, almost on the axis of the Stoa of Antigonos, it is orientated north-south, like the Hieron on Samothrace and, like it, is not surrounded by a colonnade but has only a single portico (probably with six columns on the façade and one on each return), placing the emphasis on the façade and the entrance (here on the south). Behind this is a surprisingly elongated hall, whose walls are formed of bearing columns connected by slender curtain walls, a formula called 'monoptère cloisonné' by Georges Roux, which is also found in the gallery of the Arsinoeion on Samothrace[23].

This hall has a sort of central basin surrounded by a raised passage, after which a triple opening led to a reserved area to which access could also be gained from two side doors, and on the axis of which stood a structure in the shape of a trapezium. This unusual plan was accompanied by some notable decorative features, such as the roof over the great hall, which consisted of slabs of marble carved with coffers on the under side and in the form of tiles on their upper side; or like the lantern above the room at the end of the building; or, above

169. Delos, the Monument of the Bulls, beginning of the third century BC. The very elongated form of the building accommodated the display of a large battleship, commemorating a victory; and several of the structural features suggest that its creation should be attributed to Macedonia.

all, the treatment of the triple doorway, with side openings flanked by two confronted half-columns. The central passage opened between two pilasters, each crowned by a bull protome — whence the traditional name of the building — and will have been roofed by a triangular in the form of a 'hollow pediment'.

It has been suggested, with some likelihood, that this complex was intended to house a large battleship, as a monument to some naval victory, and that the building will therefore be the 'Neorion' of which the ancient authors speak. But what victory? That of Antigonos Gonatas off Kos towards the middle of the third century? Or that of his father, Demetrios Poliorketes, at Salamis on Cyprus, in 306 BC? Stylistic considerations might suggest an early date — in which case, should we believe that the building was used twice? Whatever the case, it will have been a Macedonian dedication — unless it be thought an Athenian offering, as some

have suggested[24]. But the lack of conformism in its construction, and its composite character, which recalls some Egyptian structures (the lantern, to which we shall return in the context of the Hypostyle Hall, the triangular arch over the central passage, the very concept of displaying a boat in an architectural frame) and oriental influences (with the bulls that we have already encountered in the Stoa of Philip), invite us rather to recognise here another one of those unusual creations that derive from the freedom of spirit of the Macedonian architects.

It is all the more interesting to note that we also find on Samothrace, in the same Macedonian *ambiance*, not only the glorification of a naval victory, as represented by the famous Victory on her ship, in a basin situated below the theatre[25], but also another monument of the same type as that of Delos, the Neorion which, albeit with a different plan, was used to display a celebrated warship.

170-171. Delos, the Hypostyle Hall, about 210 BC, reconstruction, elevation and plan. Its essential feature resides in the 'boxed' rectangles formed by the interior colonnades (Doric followed by Ionic), leaving free at the centre a square of three by three columns beneath the lantern. This composition, probably Macedonian, is a forerunner of the Roman basilica.

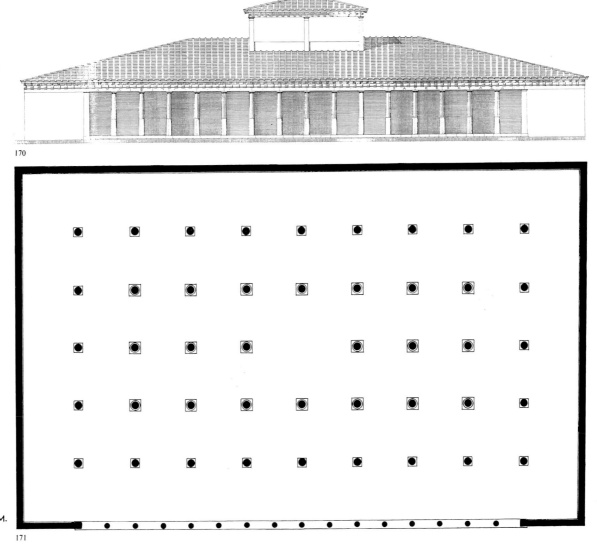

N

0 2 4 6 8 10 M.

The Hypostyle Hall

The final building on Delos that will be discussed, which is traditionally called the 'Hypostyle Hall'[26] is also an unusual structure when compared with Classical Greek architecture, and its very name points, like many of the features of the Neorion, to the Egyptian world. The façade of this huge complex (figs 170, 171), however, whose function can scarcely have been different from that of traditional stoas, immediately calls to mind that of the stoa of Philip on the same site, with a long colonnade (Doric in this case too, but with four metopes per intercolumniation) between two sections of return wall. Instead of an elongated building, however, we have a large rectangular hall, with a ceiling supported by colonnades arranged in two rectangles, one inside the other, the outer a Doric colonnade (9 x 5 columns) and the inner an Ionic one (7 x 3 columns). On the longitudinal axis, there are two pairs of additional Ionic columns, leaving a square in the centre with three columns on each side. This forest of forty-four columns clearly recalls the hypostyle halls of Egypt.

Better still, the central square supported a lantern, a structure with Ionic piers and a pavilion roof raised above the hipped roof covering the rest of the space. This arrangement, which provided perfect lighting for the interior, is clearly borrowed from Pharaonic Egypt — not so much from the Hypostyle Hall at Karnak, whose three axial bays are elevated throughout their length, as from the Jubilee Hall of Thutmosis III[27], in which can be seen the rectangles inscribed inside each other characteristic of the Delian building, and also from the lanterns of houses: the *oecus aegyptius* cited by Vitruvius[28] is in the same vein.

The lantern of the Hypostyle Hall may be compared with the one at the rear of the Neorion, and another example has been restored in the building dedicated by Thersilochos[29] on Thasos. A whole series of architectural details place the Hypostyle Hall in the same *ambiance* as the 'Macedonian' structures: not only the orders of its façade, which has already been mentioned, but also the incongruity of Ionic fluting on the Doric shafts; the treatment of the lower zone of the capitals, beneath annulets, which is the same as that of the stoa of Philip V and the votive column erected on Samothrace in honour of this same king; the forward projection of the triglyphs, which puts the architrave and the metopes in the same plane, already noted in the Stoa of Antigonos and apparently usual in Macedonian tombs from the

end of the fourth century; on the interior Ionic columns, the base is reduced to a plain torus surmounted by a high fascia, separated from the shaft by a pronounced apophyge, a form well known first in Macedonia and then in the Roman world; finally, in these same columns, the simplification of the capitals, treated as roughly dressed rather than sculpted volumes. It is a great temptation to attribute this building, too, to Macedonia. In it we sees the prototype of a certain form, at least, of the Roman basilica, dating from about 210 BC — and thus a quarter of a century earlier than the Porcia in Rome, the first basilica mentioned in the written sources, and about a hundred years earlier than the first preserved basilica, that at Pompeii.

Samothrace

It is above all the site of Samothrace, however, that is of interest in the context of propaganda architecture, for the buildings constructed in the sanctuary of the Great Gods between the end of the fourth century and the beginning of the third were apparently erected under the patronage of the kings of Macedonia (fig. 161).

The prestige enjoyed in the Greek world by the mystery cults practised there is well known, but they became particularly famous in the fourth century, when confidence in the traditional gods grew weaker, and especially after an affair of the heart —the meeting between Philip II and Olympias, from which Alexander the Great was to be born. Henceforth, the sanctuary was to become a sort of national sanctuary for the Macedonian kings, directly connected with their history. It was only natural that they should give proof of their indebtedness by erecting exceptional monuments, which at the same time enhanced their own glory[30] (fig. 172).

The Temenos

In fact, several of these structures are major achievements not only of Macedonian, but also of Greek architecture. This is true of a building attributed to the munificence of Philip II, towards the year 340 BC — the Temenos[31], a simple enclosure fenced in by high walls in which secret ceremonies were held, around two altars.

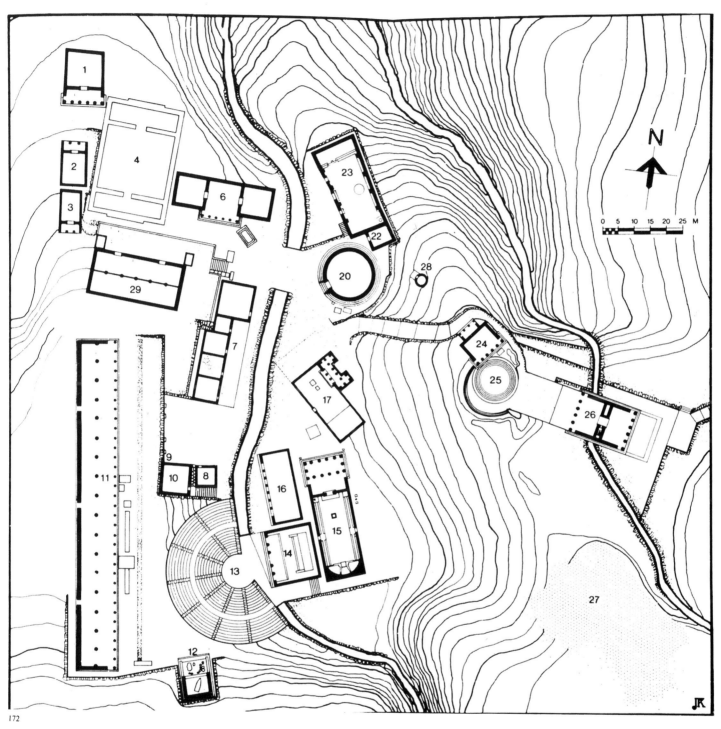

172

Access was by a Propylon (the first marble building, of Thasian marble, erected in the sanctuary) — a monumental gate that it has proved possible to reconstruct (fig. 173). The Propylon has a Π-shaped plan, with two projecting wings, like a stoa (that of Antigonos Gonatas we have seen on Delos, or the Winged Stoa, of the same inspiration, on the neighbouring island of Thasos)[32]. It is not a stoa, however. The sole purpose of the structure is to act as a decoration affixed to the walls. It is a fa-

çade decoration in the Macedonian tradition, and one of remarkable refinement.

In front of the triple door, the shafts of the Ionic columns are crowned by an elegant collar (the ornament is rare in this position, despite the equally notable example of the Erechtheion in Athens), whose flame palmettes are repeated on the bolsters of the capitals. Above these, the entablature has both a frieze and dentils, a new combination that we saw in the Philippeion at Olympia at almost the same date. The frieze

173

depicts a chorus of musicians and young girls dancing, which may be the earliest archaising group in Greek sculpture.

The marble ceiling had recessed coffers, the separately made lids of which were carved with heads that were probably also painted. Since at least one of these directly recalls the style of Skopas, who is known to have worked for the Macedonian court, the question arises whether the entire building, the work of a sculptor as much as an architect, should be attributed to him[33].

The Hieron

Erected about twenty years later, since its construction will have commenced about 320 BC, the building known from an inscription[34] as the Hieron was a kind of temple, but one with a special purpose. The dedication has not survived, but its importance and its richness mean that it can only be attributed to a royal donor.

It is oriented not to the east, but to the north, because of the configuration of the terrain, and also in order to face the sea and a wonderful landscape. The façade overlooking this was given special importance by the architect. The building is not 'peripteral', like the majority of Greek temples, but has a colonnade only on this façade. However, in its second state, at least, this was a prostyle hexastyle col-

onnade connected by a return column at each side with a second hexastyle colonnade, also set in front of the walls *in antis* (fig. 174). This complex arrangement, known in a number of Archaic temples, is repeated here in order to enrich the façade, which stands on three steps (they appear only here, and not on the sides and back, as in Classical temples), and to give depth to the pronaos, which is roofed with a splendid marble ceiling with carved coffer-lids. The façade thus seems to be a major element in the composition.

The long sides of the Hieron and the back wall, deprived of the decoration that would have been furnished by the colonnade, were given as a facing a special treatment designed to avoid the monotony of a smooth surface. The entire height of the wall is occupied by an alternating series of two high courses followed by one low one, in which the blocks were chiselled around the edges, leaving a slightly raised central panel — the first example of an association of formulas destined to enjoy great success.

This richness in the decoration can be seen even in the details, for example in the triglyphs of the frieze, with perhaps the earliest example of the 'ear', which has been discussed on several occasions; or again in the gutter, where the waterspouts, in the form of lions' heads, give rise to scrolls with a triple volute — a typically Samothracian scheme found close by in the Arsinoeion and the propylon of the Temenos

174

173. Samothrace, the Temenos about 340 BC: the propylon, reconstruction, elevation. This entrance-portico, applied against the wall of the enceinte with its three gates opened, has two projecting wings surmounted by small pediments. The Ionic order is very richly decorated.

174. Samothrace, the Hieron, about 320 BC. The columns are those of the entrance-portico, open to the north and to the sea, on which great emphasis was laid. The apse, a segment of a circle, at the rear is set in a thick wall, making it possible to preserve the rectangular plan of the building.

and also in several buildings on Thasos. Finally, above the sculpted pediment over the entrance, a central akroterion flanked by a Victory on each corner had an extraordinary combination of curves and counter-curves extending from a tuft of acanthus to its palmette finial.

The interior of the building has the largest space without any intermediate supports known in the Greek world, with a span of almost 11 m —well in excess of that of the stoa of Philip on Delos. For this reason, one wonders if the architect of the Hieron was not already familiar with the trussed timber frame, which was cap-

able of spanning much greater distances than those attainable by the frame which had been used hitherto. Beneath a wooden ceiling with coffers adorned with bronze, the walls (fig. 175) had a rich stucco decoration[35], forming a relief imitation of the exterior masonry, with three superposed zones in black, red and white, themselves surmounted by a zone of stucco half-columns affixed to the wall —giving a suggestion of space, of which the Arsinoeion supplies another version.

Finally, and most importantly, the room was organised to receive initiates, whereas the

175

175. Samothrace, the Hieron, interior elevation, reconstruction. This huge hall, which the faithful entered by two side doors, had two rows of benches along the walls, leaving the central space free for the processions and the apse for the major ceremonies. The decoration of the walls, imitating pseudo-isodomic masonry, is surmounted by an order of half-columns designed to open up the space visually.

176-177. Samothrace, Rotunda of Arsinoe, first quarter of the third century BC, reconstruction, elevation, external view and section. In both cases, an engaged colonnade is superposed upon a high socle, but this one has pilasters on the outside and engaged columns on the inside. The roofing of a round hall of such great size must have involved a masterpiece of timber-framing.

178. Samothrace, Rotunda of Arsinoe: foundations.

Greek temple is as a general rule the dwelling place of the god alone. Here, two side doors allowed the faithful to proceed to benches set along the sides on two slightly raised platforms in order to see the procession in the aisle passage. This aisle led, after the grand entrance, towards a feature that was another major innovation (if we except the designs of the early Archaic period) — the apse in which the building ended, which probably had a roof in the shape of a tent.

This apse was disguised on the outside by the flat rear wall of the building (and one finds here the disjunction between the external appearance and the reality of the internal structure so evident in the case of the 'Macedonian tombs'), but inside it rose two steps higher than the nave and, like the choir of a church, formed the most holy part of the building. Its form probably evoked the idea of a grotto, and was thus suitable for the chthonic cults of the Great Gods. It is not surprising that a composition like this, known to the entire Greek world and then to the Romans, formed the starting point of a rich series of religious structures.

The Rotunda of Arsinoe

Still in the heart of the sanctuary of Samothrace, the Rotunda of Arsinoe II[36] was constructed of Thasian marble sometime between 289 and 281 BC, a chronological problem that is at the same time a problem of dynasty, so that the link with Macedonia is perhaps not official in this case. This building too has some exceptional features (figs 176-178). It is a tholos (like the Philippeion at Olympia), though here without an exterior colonnade, and there was no colonnade on the inside, either free or engaged, at least at the lower level of the structure. But above the door runs a partially open storey, with Doric pilasters on the outside and Corinthian half-columns on the inside, here engaged to projecting pilasters. This is the first example of a very rare combination, which, according to Georges Roux, may have been based on an invention of Skopas at Tegea.

On the outside, the pilasters are surmounted by a Doric entablature, the triglyphs of which continue the vertical lines of the pilasters. The height of the entablature, moreover, is scaled not so much to that of the pilasters as to that of the overall structure. As for the internal colonnade, it recalls both the interior decoration of the Hieron, and the arrangement with 'attics' discussed in connection with the stoa of Philip on Delos.

The building was even more notable for its dimensions for, at over 17 m in diameter, it is the largest roofed, round building in Greek antiquity. A volume of this size clearly involved a superior technique for the timber roof-frame.

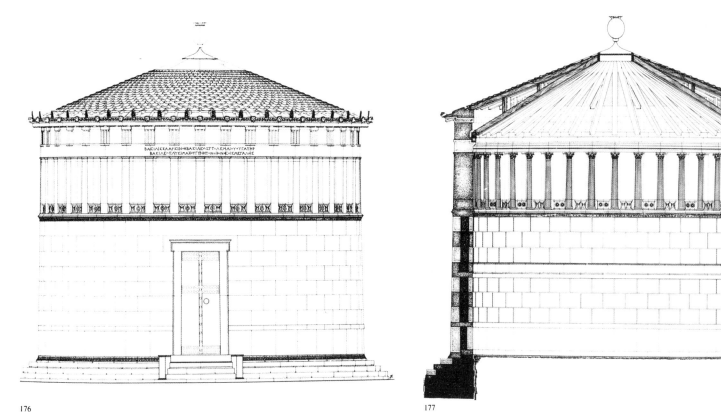

176

177

178

179. Samothrace,
Rotunda of Arsinoe:
interior elevation. The
engaged colonnade of
the upper storey recalls
the one that adorns the
upper part of the
interior walls of the
Hieron; here, however,
between the supports,
are parapets decorated
with pateras and
bucrania.

180

180. Samothrace,
Rotunda of Arsinoe:
exterior elevation.

Above, the roof, made of scale-shaped tiles that decreased in size towards the top, ended in a hollow marble cylinder, flared at the bottom, whose form has been compared with that of a pagoda roof. It has been suggested that it was designed to allow the building to be ventilated and perhaps to extract the fumes produced by the fire for the sacrifices, but the American excavators now think that it was rather the base of the acroterion crowning the roof in its second state (under the Roman empire).

The function of this tholos remains uncertain. According to Karl Lehmann, it may have served as a meeting hall for the *theoroi*. The parapets between the columns of the clerestory were carved with altars (figs 179, 180), with alternating pateras and bucrania, which certainly attest to the religious nature of the complex. And the building presents, once again, a combination of formal innovations and technical achievements characteristic of prestige and propaganda architecture.

The Propylon of Ptolemy II

Although undoubtedly of lesser importance for the history of architecture, but very attractive in many respects, the Propylon of Ptolemy II Philadelphos[37] (fig. 181), dating from the years 285-280 BC, may seem to be less directly

of interest to us since it was a donation by another dynasty, albeit one closely linked with Macedonia. A number of technical and decorative details, however, suggest that it was perhaps from the same workshop, and possibly even by the same architect, as the Arsinoeion just discussed[38]. For Georges Roux, the sculpture is here too of a superior quality, especially in the Corinthian capital. Since the building also served as a bridge over a seasonal torrent, a long, oblique, barrel-vaulted tunnel (figs 182, 183), 2 m wide, was created in the substructure to allow the passage of water. The vault of the Macedonian tombs is here put to a different use, though one already attested in the stadium at Nemea, about 320 BC[39].

The building has a monumental air, with practically the same width as the north Propylon at Epidauros. It had only a single, relatively narrow, door, to allow effective control of those entering the sanctuary for the mysteries, or perhaps the enactment of certain rituals. But on either side, this door was preceded by a deep stoa, each of large dimensions with a hexastyle prostyle colonnade at the front crowned by a pediment. The colonnade to the east of the door is Ionic, and that to the west has Corinthian capitals (fig. 184). If the combination of these two orders is itself interesting, the use of the Corinthian for the façade of an import-

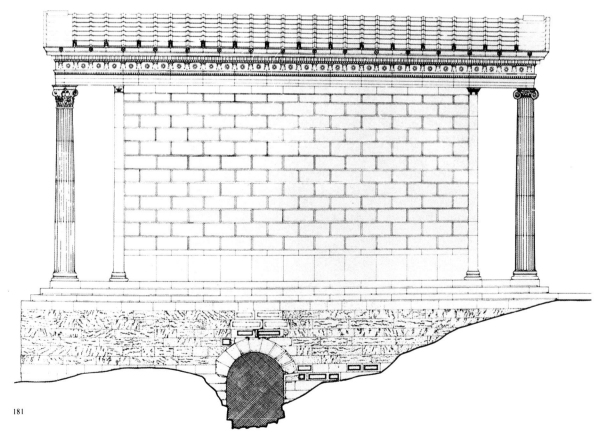

181. Samothrace, Propylon of Ptolemy II, about 285-280 BC, reconstruction, elevation. The two façades are different, Ionic on the exterior, Corinthian facing the sanctuary; the use of the Corinthian order on the façade is an innovation.

181

182

*182. Samothrace,
Propylon of Ptolemy II:
infrastructure of the
building, with the
subterranean passage
for the winter torrent.*

ant building (of which we probably have here the earliest example) is all the more notable in that this order seems to have been little used in Macedonia, though it was common in Ptolemaic Egypt.

The carved decoration is exquisite, with some of the details quite new. The 'canal' of the volutes of the Ionic capitals is decorated with a relief floral motif reminiscent of structures in north-west Asia Minor, an ancestor of which has been recognised in the rosette placed in the same position in a capital from the beginning of the fifth century found at Kavala, ancient Neapolis[40]. Finally, the antae were crowned with elegant sofa capitals. The form seems to be of Peloponnesian origins and, practically abandoned in its homeland in the Hellenistic period, it enjoyed some success in Macedonian architecture.

The Hexastyle Building and Altar Court

Other structures erected by the kings of Macedonia in the sanctuary of Samothrace, though lacking innovations of this kind, illuminate certain aspects of Macedonian architecture.

A building[41] dedicated by Philip III Arrhidaios and Alexander IV, half-brother and posthumous son of Alexander the Great respectively, had a plan recalling that of an Archaic treasury, long fallen out of fashion, with several traces of Peloponnesian influence[42]. Its walls are of Thasian marble, which is normal in the architecture of Samothrace, while its façade, a delicate Doric hexastyle prostyle colonnade, was of a superior quality marble that has not been certainly identified (Pentelic has been suggested) — another example of the special treatment accorded to the façade, which is distinguished from the rest of the building by its richness.

The same holds for another building that will have been dedicated by Philip Arrhidaios before 323 BC, which is known as the Altar Court[43]. In this limestone structure marble has been reserved for the façade, here again deemed worthy of special treatment. Of particular note was the 'colonnade-screen' of the entrance, dividing two open areas, and the back wall with a trapezium-shaped pediment. These restorations, and even the restoration of the dedication, have been contested, however[44]. It is nonetheless true that we see here, probably for the first time, the well-developed form of the 'ears' at the top corners of the triglyphs, which we have already

183

184

183. Samothrace, Propylon of Ptolemy II. The barrel vault is one of the earliest in Greece, apart from those of the 'Macedonian tombs' (and here, too, it is buried).

184. Samothrace, Propylon of Ptolemy II: the Corinthian capital (reconstruction).

185

185. Samothrace. The
Hieron, at the left, and,
in the background, the
terrace of Stoa J, a
magnificent belvedere
dominating the
sanctuary complex.

186. Samothrace, Stoa
J, first half of the third
century BC, overall
view. With its thirty-
five prostyle columns
on the façade, two
intercolumniations of
which corresponded

with a single one of the
axial colonnade, this
building, of
considerable size, was
also probably due to
the munificence of a
Macedonian king.

observed in a number of buildings of Macedonian inspiration.

The Neorion

Finally, we now know that the sanctuary, like that on Delos, also had a Neorion, a display gallery for a ship. This time it was a rectangular structure[45] divided into two aisles by a row of five columns. In one of them, a double series of marble blocks at right angles to the long sides had their upper surface dressed to a concave shape in order to receive the hull of the ship, whose keel sat in the space between them. Given the date of the building — the first half of the third century — it has been attributed to Antigonos Gonatas, and connected like perhaps, the Neorion on Delos, with his victory over the fleet of the Ptolemies.

Stoa J

The last of the buildings from this sanctuary that we shall discuss here is Stoa J[46], dating from the first half of the third century. About 200 BC, a column was erected in front of it, in honour of Philip V, which, at the very least, connects this building with the Macedonian royal house (figs 185, 186). Unusually, the columns do not stand between antae, according to the most usual formula, but project in front, according to the prostyle formula found on a number of sites including, not far from Samothrace, a building in the Agora on Thasos[47]. The shaft of these Doric columns is simply polygonal up to a certain height, as in the Stoa of Philip on Delos (and also at Pergamon and elsewhere at this period). There is a Doric cornice without mutules on the back and sides of the building (as in the stoa at Oropos, and on the façade of the Stoa of Antigonos on Delos)[48].

It also had the timber roof-frame with sloping cross-beams that we have encountered on several occasions in Macedonian buildings. Above all, it is a very imposing building, by virtue both of its length (about 104 m) and of its location on an artificially widened terrace, creating above the theatre a splendid backdrop to an entire area of the sanctuary — as the colonnade of the palace must have done above the theatre at Vergina[49]. In both cases the building itself formed a magnificent belvedere, like the one in front of the palace at Pella, which dominated the entire landscape[50].

186

Other notable buildings

The list of buildings presented briefly above, though already long, does not of course comprise the entire series of Macedonian creations outside Macedonia. It should not be forgotten that the Hellenistic structures erected in the new kingdoms after Alexander were all buildings willed and controlled by Macedonians, albeit in different *ambiances,* in the heart of countries that might themselves already have very strong traditions. We have tried here simply to draw attention to a number of monuments, all notable in several respects, erected by the Macedonian powers in pre-eminent meeting places, mainly in sanctuaries, where they must have been very effective instruments of propaganda.

One could also mention a number of buildings of lesser importance, like a structure at Perachora[51] intended for symposia, which has been attributed to Demetrios Poliorketes[52]. On the same site the Stoa in the harbour has also been related[53] to the interest evinced by Demetrios in neighbouring Corinth, on the occasion of the reconstitution of the Hellenic League in 303 BC[54]. The building is notable for its L-shaped plan, the only one, in fact, of its type on mainland Greece, for its superposition of two colonnades, with an Ionic order above a Doric[55], and for certain significant features[56].

Furthermore, the South Stoa at Corinth (fig. 187) itself has been attributed to Philip II[57], probably incorrectly given its date, but it is now explained, probably correctly, in terms of the need to organise on the site a building large

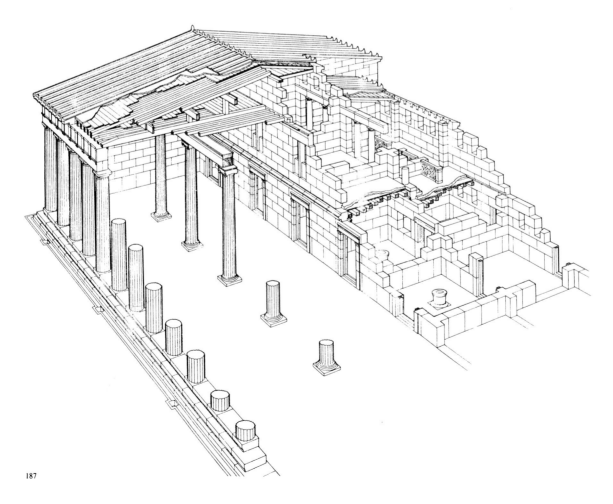

187

187. Corinth, South Stoa, turn of the fourth to the third century BC, reconstruction of the left end. This stoa has some notable features, such as the two rows of rooms behind the aisles, and the two levels behind a colonnade that appeared, as a result, to belong to a 'colossal order.'

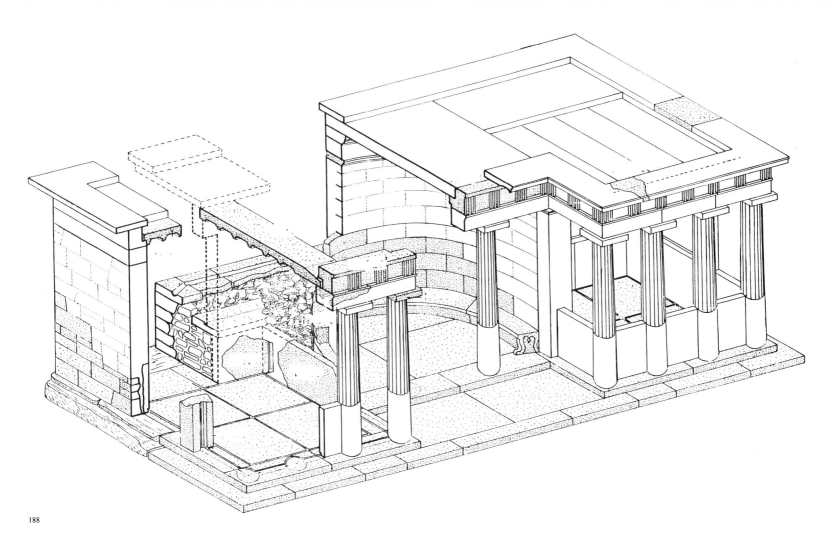

188

188. Tenos,
monumental fountain-
exedra, reconstruction.
This original structure
has also been attributed
to the Macedonians,
particularly in view of
the star adorning the
coffers in the ceiling.

enough for the purposes of the League[58]. In fact, the stoa must have been the most impressive in the city, with a length of almost 165 m (10 m longer than the Stoa of Philip at Megalopolis) and a depth of 25 m, and with its unusual arrangement of two rows of rooms (33 in each) behind the two aisles. This plan is repeated on two levels, while the front of the building presented only a single level with a colonnade of remarkable height on the façade. This disposition was never to be repeated, but a single order standing in front of two levels of rooms is what is known as 'colossal' in baroque architecture, and here makes its first appearance.

This building thus attests to a desire for grandeur, to a spirit of innovation, and to technical and financial means that can hardly be attributed anywhere other than to Macedonia, concerned to entertain members of the League in the best possible conditions.

We shall not dwell on those other Macedonian structures outside Macedonia, the 'Macedonian tombs'. Even though they were not intended to be seen, these must have made a great impression. The one dated about 300 BC, for example, that crowns a hill above Eretria[59], had a passageway leading to a single vaulted chamber inscribed in a cube with a side of practically 3 m, which contained two couches (set in such a way that the diners, resting on their left elbows, faced each other), two thrones and a chest. It is in any case generally agreed that a structure such as the vaulted tunnel leading to the stadium at Nemea is to be explained in terms of the imitation of the barrel vaults on these tombs[60].

Military architecture should also be mentioned in this context. Macedonian engineers seem to have known how to make use of solutions such as those in which towers are replaced by set-backs in the rampart, a formula at once quick and economical to construct and effective for defence. A fine application of this has been found on the site of Gortys in Arkadia, which must have been from the beginning one of the Macedonian strong points in the Peloponnese, and which seems to have been occupied and adapted by Demetrios Poliorketes[61]. It is significant that the façade of a baths building on the same site has been compared with that of a Macedonian tomb[62]. On the island of Tenos, the sanctuary of Poseidon (a deity particularly revered by Demetrios Poliorketes) was given a fountain adorned with a highly original façade, the coffers in the roof of which bear the Macedonian star. Its construction took place in the period of Antigonid domination, which 'was perhaps not unfamiliar with the launching of major schemes of improvement in a sanctuary'[62] (fig. 188). Mention should also be made of a structure less notable for its architecture than for its content, this time at Delphi.

189. Athens, the
Monument of
Lysikrates. Made of
Pentelic marble, this
monument, standing on
a poros plinth
commemorates a
choregic victory in
335/4 BC. Between the
columns, a screen-wall
supports a frieze of
tripods, the prize
awarded to winners at
the games.

189

190. Athens, the Monument of Lysikrates, the Corinthian capital. Now very badly damaged; above a crown of unusual water-leaves it has not two but a single crown of acanthus leaves interspersed with rosettes. The volutes are supported by acanthus leaves; above the central volutes are two more supporting a palmette.

Delphi: *ex-voto* of Krateros

In the heart of the sanctuary of Apollo, the most famous in the Greek world, just behind the temple, Krateros, the son of one of Alexander's lieutenants, had a veritable tableau erected on a huge platform raised above the paved street[63] —an episode from a lion hunt, during the course of which Alexander, at grips with the beast, was aided at a critical moment by Krateros.

Fruits of the combined talents of Lysippos and Leochares, the statues of the characters, horsemen, horses, dogs, and lion were in bronze and formed, probably for the first time, a sculpted group, frequently imitated thereafter, and rivalling the scenes of large-scale painting. By recalling the bravery of the king and the loyalty of his companions, the group exalted the grandeur of the Macedonian court in a new and highly expressive manner[64].

Athens: The Monument of Lysikrates

Certain other structures, possibly less marked by political propaganda, may be considered in this same perspective. The famous monument of Lysikrates at Athens, for example, has been ascribed by some to Macedonian architecture[65] (fig. 189).

Amongst its other features, this construction was the first example of a monopteral tholos known in Greece, and for a long time the only one. Its form recalls that of the rotundas of Samothrace, but it had columns connected by a screen-wall, added during the course of construction, which stopped beneath the capital and gave the columns the appearance of half-columns. We may also note the Corinthian order on the exterior (fig. 190), the combination of friezes and dentils, the false tiles in the form of scales, up to the crowning member, which is similar to that of the Philippeion at Olympia — features which long ago led to the monument being described as 'baroque'[66].

Macedonian baroque

May we not apply the term 'baroque' to the entire range of Macedonian architectural creation, both with direct reference to the forms of the baroque of modern times, and with respect to a certain spirit that has been called 'Hellenistic baroque'[67]?

As we know, baroque is first of all, in opposition to Classicism, the abandoning of formulas employed by a long tradition, a certain spirit of freedom that gives the rotunda of the Philippeion at Olympia not Doric but Ionic columns, and at Samothrace erects rotundas completely without columns, both outside and inside, thereby redeploying the form of the tholos in the Athenian agora. It is also a certain disdain for tradition. On the Ionic base, the lower torus is replaced by a square plinth, the Doric frieze is carried forward at the level of the architrave, the mutules are dispensed with on the cornice if necessary, and throughout, mouldings are used in breach of the long established rules.

But the baroque spirit, in architecture, is much more the glorification of perceptible effects, the placing of stress on impressions and emotions rather than reason, by means of structures of exceptionally large dimensions (the widest building without interior supports is the Hieron, the greatest diameter is roofed in the Arsinoeion), with elements that are no less exceptional, both in terms of the huge timbers used for the roof-frame and the length of the orthostates in the Stoa of Philip at Delos. We here encounter the taste for competition, for the 'masterpiece', which manifested itself from the Archaic period in the large temples of Ionia and southern Italy.

There was also some insistence on effects of richness, created by an overuse of decoration, as in the small 'ear' on the Doric metopes, and the double half-columns and double quarter-columns in the Stoa of Philip on Delos, the combination of Ionic frieze with dentils in the Philippeion at Olympia and in the Propylon of the Ptolemaion on Samothrace, and the treatment of the exterior facing of the Hieron with rusticated masonry having drafted margins.

Finally, the baroque spirit triumphed when the decoration became independent of the structure — 'atectonic' in Wöllflin's expression — with the use of half-columns that supported nothing, standing on a podium on which they do not bear down, as in the Philippeion at Olympia or in the upper zone of stucco decoration in the Hieron of Samothrace. Stucco was used to supplement stone architecture, which itself sometimes had simplified forms — many examples of this are to be found in the Macedonian tombs — and the use of painting made it possible to play with *trompe l'oeil*. With this decoration, applied to the building, the essential idea of the baroque of modern times[68] is born — the concept of the 'monumental façade', a complex architectural composition, one of the major features of which is that it does not correspond to the structural reality that it covers — or dissimulates. We have noted the importance attaching to the façade in all the prestige buildings erected by Macedonians in the major sanctuaries of Greece, and also in the 'Macedonian tombs'[69], in the rock-cut tombs that succeeded them[70], and in the palaces at Vergina and Pella[71].

It is notable that, on the site of Thasos, which we have good reason to believe was directly subjected to the influence of Macedonian architecture[72], we encounter another remarkable example of a decorative façade, in what is called the Gateway of Zeus and Hera[73]. This gate, which had from early times been part of the defence wall of the city, was given applied monumental decoration in the last quarter of the fourth century, with a lower row of four columns crowned by a Doric entablature (with the cornice without mutules with which we are familiar) supporting, on a second level, a colonnade of Ionic half-columns affixed to pilasters and itself crowned by a pediment. The complex strongly recalls the façade of the tomb at Lefkadia[74], but above all we have here a decoration applied to an architectural reality with which it has no connection. It is for this reason that this kind of composition and the buildings in which it was used have been regarded as 'the true starting point of Hellenistic architecture and its Roman developments'[75]. It is not surprising, therefore, that we find echoes of it as far away as the façades of the tombs at Canossa[76], in a region whose connections with Mace-

191. Petra, wall of Kasr el Bint. The date of this structure is debated, but it seems certain that it gives us at least an idea of the baroque element of Alexandrian architecture, with the use of stucco to supplement the carved elements and, above all, a superabundance of characteristic decorative elements.

191

192. Petra, rock façade. These superposed orders, entirely cut into the rock, are set before a burial chamber of small dimensions and without any structural connection to the grandiose exteriors.

donia we have already noted[77]. It would be difficult, too, not to mention at least the tombs of Petra[78], whose façades (figs 191, 192), cut into the rock and therefore totally independent of the architectural reality that they at once proclaim and conceal, are one of the pinnacles of Hellenistic baroque.

If we have recognised the first manifestations of this in Macedonia (not forming a style, properly speaking, but attesting to a genuine community of inspiration), it is because the architects there worked at the heart of very specific economic, political and psychological conditions which to some extent recall those surrounding other baroque creations in the world[79]. They worked in a region and in an *ambiance* free of the weight of the Classical tradition, and open, in contrast, to the major currents of the East (making use of the vault, though still restricted to certain functions) and Egypt (for the Hypostyle Hall, the screen-wall, the lantern, the triangular arch, and the architectural framing of a ship, probably also the use of stucco and more generally the *trompe l'oeil* of false doors and false windows). They responded to the demands of princes eager for prestige, spurred on by the competition of their rivals, wishing to dazzle, to strike the imagination by effects of grandeur, richness and decoration. And to do so, they had at their disposal, it is true, the considerable financial resources of Macedonia.

Dardanians

• Astibos
• Bylazora
Stoboi

Alkomena
Derriopos   Paionia
• Styberra
Dassaretis   • Idomenai
Lychnidos   • Bragylai
Herakleia   MACEDONIA   • Serrhai
Lake Lychnitis   Krestonia
Europos   Tyrissa   Philippoi   Dikaia   • Stryme
Kyrrhos   Bisaltia   Neapolis   • Abdera   Doriskos   • Kypsel
Lynkos   Edessa   Pella   Mygdonia   Amphipolis   Maroneia
Bottiaia   • Lete   Lake Bolbe   Edonis   • Ainos
Keletron   Beroia   Aloros   Thessalonike   • Thasos   Lysimac
Eordaia   • Aigeai   Apollonia   Kardia
Argos Orestikon   Pydna   • Arethousa   Thasos   Kallipolis
Orestis   Haliakmon   • Akanthos   Lampsako
Pieria   Chalkidike   Samothrace   Sestos
Aiane   Perrhaibia   Dion   Madytos   Aby
Paravaians   Doliche   • Herakleion   Kassandreia   Imbros   Eleous
Azoros   Pythion   Hephaistia   Sigeion   TRO
Phoinike   Oloosson   Herakleion   Tenedos   Ilion
Tymphaians   Gonnoi   Peneios   Homolion   Lemnos
Bouthrotos   Aiginion
Korkyra   Dodone   Larissa
Trikka   Krannon   Antissa
Korkyra   EPIRUS   Gomphoi   THESSALY   Eresos   Mytilene
Skotoussa   Pherai   Lesbos
Pharsalos   Demetrias
Ambrakia   Thebes   Skiathos   AEGEAN
Kassope   Dolopia   Peparethos
Lamia   Skyros
Leukas   Thyrreion   Ainis   • Oreos
Herakleia
Leukas   Stratos   AITOLIAN LEAGUE   Euboia   Chios
Thermos   Aitolia   Doris   Phokis   Elateia
Sami   Oiniadai   Lokris   Delphi   Chalkis   Chios
Ithaca   Kalydon   Naupaktos   Thebes   Eretria   Erythrai
Patras   Aigion   Boiotia   Oropos
Kephallenia   Dyme   Achaia   Sikyon   Megara   Attica   Karystos   Andros
ACHAIAN   Corinth   Athens   Sam
Zakynthos   Elis   LEAGUE   Korinthia   Piraeus
Orchomenos   Keos   Tenos   Ikaros
Olympia   Heraia   Argos   Epidauros
Arcadia   Argolis   Troizen   Mykonos
Megalopolis   Tegea   Hermione   Kythnos   Delos
Messenia   Sellasia   Seriphos   Paros   Naxos   Patmos
Messene   Sparta   Sikinos   Amorgos
Laconia   Melos   Ios
Methone
Gytheion   • Epidauros Limera
Boiai   Astypa

Anaphe

Kythera

Crete   • Knossos   Itan
Gortys

193

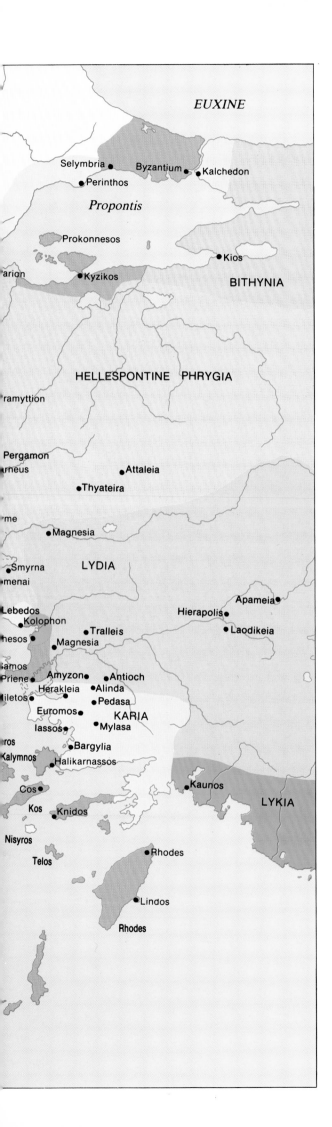

7

THE END OF THE KINGDOM OF MACEDONIA

193. Map of Macedonia
on the eve of the
Second Macedonian
War, about 200 BC.
The kingdom of
Macedonia and the
possessions of the
Antigonids are shown
in beige; the kingdom
of the Seleucids and
Seleucid possessions in
pink; the kingdom of
Pergamon and the
possessions of the
Attalids in khaki; the
independent Greek
states in green; the
States in the political
sphere of influence of
Philip V in light orange;
the regions under the
protection of the
Romans in violet; the
possessions of the
Ptolemies in dark
orange.

In 217 BC, the history of Macedonia entered into a new phase, as a result of a number of significant and simultaneous changes, closely connected with each other, which made themselves felt up to the end of Macedonian independence. At the very time that he was signing the treaty of Naupaktos[1], Philip V was erecting projects on the grand scale and dreaming of extending his sphere of interests well beyond that with which his predecessors had contented themselves, as far as the Adriatic, and before long to the Dardanelles and Karia. By so doing, he made new enemies: Rome, Pergamon and Rhodes were added to the Aitolians, the Spartans and others (fig. 193). Rome, moreover, combined in herself alone several new characteristics: she was not Greek, she did not belong to the Balkan or Near-eastern space, she was much richer in resources and military potential than the ancient enemies of Macedonia, and she gave proof, in her expansionist policy, of an implacable determination and will. Moreover, the Macedonians were to find themselves in a position of inferiority in the balance of powers thus created. Finally, since the Romans were to seek the alliance of other opponents of the Macedonians, the conflict was to extend to all the territories and all the seas of Illyria and the east Aegean, thus covering a huge unified area.

The Romans intervened in Illyria in order to protect shipping using the strait of Otranto from Illyrian pirates, placing Corcyra under their protection, as well as the Greek cities and some small Illyrian tribes between Epirus and Lissos (229 BC). A few years later, the adventurer Demetrios, who had become master of Pharos thanks to the Romans, adopted an independent policy that led to the second Illyrian war (219 BC). Expelled by the Romans, he took refuge with Philip V, which did not fail to displease the Senate.

During the negotiations leading to the peace of Naupaktos (217 BC), Agelaos, one of the Aitolian delegates, had besought the Greeks to cease their fratricidal quarrels and turn their gaze to Italy where Rome and Carthage were locked in a confrontation, which presaged a greater threat; if Philip had ambitions, it was there that he should attempt to satisfy them. We do not know if Philip (fig. 194) allowed himself to be seduced, but it is certain that he hastened to make peace with the Aitolians and to expand in the direction of the Adriatic on the news of the defeat of the Romans by the Carthaginians at Trasimene (217 BC). The election of Agelaos by his fellow-compatriots as *strategos* of the League opened the way to a truly pan-Hellenic *entente* against the Romans, of which Philip was to be the leader. Rome was to deploy all her might to thwart his designs.

Philip led a large fleet into the straits of Otranto, but retired on the approach of a Roman flotilla. It was only after a second Roman defeat at Cannae (216 BC) that he decided to collaborate with Hannibal. The treaty they concluded (215 BC) stipulated, amongst other things, that they would remove from the Romans their protectorate of Illyria. But Philip had to wait a year before moving to the attack, for he had first to deal with serious troubles in Messenia, where he suffered a number of reverses and, through his acts of brutality, lost the sympathies he had hitherto enjoyed in the Peloponnese.

The first 'Macedonian War' — from the Roman point of view — (214-205 BC) began in the protectorate of Illyria, but spread across the whole of Greece, where the Greeks fought amongst themselves without the Romans intervening directly in the land operations. Within the bounds of Macedonia and Illyria, Philip succeeded in conquering the territories of the Atintanes and the Parthinoi, friends of the Romans, and in seizing Lissos from the Illyrians.

The Romans then looked for Greek allies, whom they found, naturally enough, amongst the enemies of the Macedonians, the Aitolians and Sparta. The Aitolians brought with them their friends, the Messenians and Attalos I of Pergamon. Philip, for his part, mobilised the members of the League to his advantage. The operations took place in Thessaly, central Greece and the Peloponnese, and Philip was obliged to rush from one front to the other, and sometimes also to Illyria and Thrace. Some of the neutral Greek states tried in vain to reconcile the belligerents. Then the Aitolians, frustrated at finding themselves abandoned by the Romans, decided to conclude a separate peace with Philip, who had led his army as far as Thermos, their religious and political capital (206 BC). Philip regained the parts of Thessaly that had been won from him by the Aitolians, and also wrested Epiknemidian Lokris from them, thus securing control of the strategic land route linking Thessaly with Boiotia, Attica and the Peloponnese.

The following year, a compromise peace was signed between Philip and the Romans themselves, at Phoinike in Epirus. Neither of the adversaries could claim a decisive victory. Philip, who kept control of a zone between the Aoos and the Apsos rivers, emerged the gainer from a war of nine years. In Greece, he had extended his sphere of influence at the expense of the Aitolians, and confirmed his authority over the League founded by Doson. In Illyria, he took possession of half the Roman protectorate and an outlet on the Adriatic.

His Illyrian adventure over, Philip strengthened his fleet in order to throw himself without delay into a number of conquests in the heart of the Aegean basin. Here, it was not a question of protection but of overtly expansionist activity. In agreement with Antiochos III to strip Ptolemy of his possessions outside Egypt, Philip laid hands on the Ptolemaic bases in the Aegean, and annexed on his way some of the cities associated with the Aitolian League, not without giving proof of his cynicism and cruelty. In order to strengthen his troops and crews, he hired pirates on all sides, including a number of Cretans, and bound himself to the Confederation of Cretan cities.

Faced with his will to hegemony, the two most powerful states in the Aegean area, the Rhodians and Attalos I of Pergamon, entered into alliance in order to check him. Having inferior sea forces, Philip concentrated his efforts on land operations, ravaging the area around Pergamon and pushing as far as the Rhodian territory in Karia. Unable to deal with Philip, Attalos and the Rhodians resigned themselves to seeking the aid of Rome.

The Romans had already experienced Philip's ambitions, and feared his resources. They also reckoned that they would have to stop him, if not make him withdraw, before it was too late. A senatorial commission sent to Greece to arouse anti-Macedonian sentiments went beyond the terms of their mission and summoned Philip on two occasions to submit himself to the Senate's arbitration with respect to the harm he had done to Attalos and the Rhodians. The king's refusal and a propaganda campaign accusing him of aggression against some of Rome's friends strengthened the current of feeling in favour of a recourse to arms.

Neither Philip nor the Romans enjoyed the advantage of any solid alliances during the war. Philip was still the head of the league founded by Doson but the Achaean Confederation, the second power in Doson's league, was preoccupied with the threat represented to it by Nabis, the tyrant of Sparta. The other members, the Boiotians, Akarnanians, and Epirotes, made little effort to fight on Philip's behalf, and the Greek ruling classes nurtured no great sympathy for the king, who was suspected of favouring the popular masses.

The Romans, for their part, were at a disadvantage because they were foreigners. At the beginning of hostilities, only the Athenians rallied to them, and this by chance. The Aitolians, ancient allies of the Romans, only decided to take up arms on the news of a Roman victory, which was, in any case, exaggerated. Outside Greece proper, the Romans could count on the Rhodians and Attalos, as well as the Dardanians — all unwavering in their hostility to Philip.

The disembarkation of a Roman army in Illyria opened operations in the 'Second Macedonian War' (200-197 BC). Philip succeeded at one and the same time in preventing this army from penetrating Macedonia and in driving the Aitolians back from Thessaly and the Dardanians from Paionia, but he lost the cooperation of the Epirotes, who hesitated to confront the Romans. The Roman fleet met with only a few limited successes. At the beginning of 198 BC, Philip made is known to the Roman general Quinctius Flamininus (fig. 195) that he was ready to buy peace by abandoning his recent conquests. He was called upon to restore liberty to the Greeks, however —that is, to abandon even Thessaly, which had been governed by the Macedonian kings since Philip II. He accordingly rejected these conditions, but his situation deteriorated. Evaded by the Romans in Epirus, he had to fall back on Thessaly, soon to be invaded not only by the Romans, but also by their allies, the Aitolians and the Athamanians. Some of the Achaean cities then also ranged themselves on the side of the conquerors. Negotiations for peace were reopened (198 BC). The Romans, pressing their advantage, demanded the evacuation of the Illyrian territories. Philip attempted to save half of Thessaly and the three 'fetters of Greece', Demetrias, Chalkis and the Acrocorinth. When discussions broke down, he sought out the enemy in Thessaly and was defeated at Cynoscephalae (197 BC).

Judging by the concessions that the Romans demanded from Philip before and during the war, it seems likely that they had from the beginning intended to cut off from the kingdom all its dependencies to the south of Olympos and to the west of Pindos. After their victory, they showed themselves neither more lenient, nor more severe. To the Aitolians, who were pressing him to invade Macedonia and evict Philip, Flamininus retorted that Macedonia must not cease to form a rampart against the barbarians of the north. But the Romans deprived Philip of his fleet, with the exception of a handful of ships, and imposed a war indemnity of one thousand talents upon him. In return, they accorded him the status of *amicus*.

Of all the territories that they had occupied in the past, the Aitolians only recovered Phokis

194. 195

and the west half of Thessaly. Out of the rest of Thessaly, Flamininus formed four republics. He solemnly proclaimed the freedom of the Greeks at the Isthmian Games in 196 BC, which was greeted with enthusiasm by the audience, who were celebrating the end of Macedonian domination. Two years later, the Romans demonstrated that they had no aspirations to hegemony in Greece by withdrawing the last of their armed forces. Meanwhile, Philip had had the opportunity to offer the first proof of his loyalty by collaborating with Flamininus against Nabis of Sparta.

According to the order established in Greece by the Romans, Macedonia had to be strong enough to contain the northern barbarians, and the Aitolian League not strong enough to threaten Macedonia. The Achaean League was to play the role of a third power in a system of balanced forces. This reckoned without the Aitolians who, frustrated that the Romans had not satisfied all their demands, turned against Rome and sounded out Philip to see if he was disposed to make common cause with them. An alliance with the Macedonian was also sought by the Seleucid king Antiochos III.

Philip declined these offers (193 BC), fought on the side of the Romans against the armies of the Aitolians and Antiochos in Thessaly (191 BC), and opened his territory to the Romans who were on the way to confront Antiochos in Asia Minor. During the course of these operations, he himself occupied Perrhaibia, Dolopia, Magnesia, Demetrias and other places in Achaia

Phthiotis, which he kept in part after the peace, the Romans remitting the rest of the war indemnity that he owed them.

The Aitolians found themselves in the camp of the vanquished. The peoples subjected by Philip demanded of Rome a return to the terms of the peace of 196 BC, and the Romans decided that he should evacuate some of the territories in dispute. Other complaints against the king, brought before the Senate by certain Greek cities, were rejected.

The ancient tradition saw in this leniency, albeit relative, the hand of Demetrios, the son of Philip who, sent to Rome to plead the Macedonian cause, was able to put to profit relations of friendship that had developed during his sojourn in Rome as a hostage. The Senate did not respond in the same way when Eumenes II, king of Pergamon and a loyal friend of Rome, complained in his turn. This time it condemned Philip to evacuate two cities in Aegean Thrace, but was tolerant once again when he was slow to obey. Thus, Philip, free to act in Thrace, repelled an invasion by the Dardanians, undertook a number of expeditions against different tribes, and consolidated his gains. At the end of his life, he was contemplating appealing to a Germanic tribe established near the Danube in order to evict the Dardanians.

Alongside these external preoccupations, Philip was engaged in strengthening the economy, finances, demography and military power of his kingdom. He sought to secure a better yield from his mines, increased his fiscal

194. Tetradrachm of Philip V: the head of the king is encircled by a diadem.

195. Gold stater, head of Titus Quinctius Flamininus.

196.197

196-197. Tetradrachm of Perseus, with the head of the king encircled by a diadem. On the reverse, within an oak-wreath, an eagle and the name of the king.

revenues with the aid of taxes on real estate and trade, and added to the size of the coinage. As for his demographic policy, this consisted of a group of converging measures: the encouragement of marriage, penalties on the exposure of newly born infants, and the transplanting of Thracians to certain parts of the kingdom.

However, Philip had to face a crisis of a different kind. In 183/2 BC, for reasons that remain unknown, he executed several dignitaries of high standing, who were accused of treason. We are better informed about another drama that arose from the confrontation both between two trends in Macedonian foreign policy and between two of Philip's sons, Perseus and Demetrios. We have seen that, thanks to his good relations in Rome, Demetrios had achieved a diplomatic success. He was suspected, rightly or wrongly, of conspiring with Roman support to eliminate his elder brother from the succession and was executed, but Polybius relates that Philip was consumed with doubts. His reign came to an end in 179 BC. He appears genuinely to have tried to collaborate with the Romans, and it was only the implacable hostility of the latter that obliged him to take measures of self-defence. With Philip out of the way, Rome was to impose war on his successor.

At his accession, Perseus (figs 196, 197) was concerned to restore his image, which had been tarnished by the death of his brother Demetrios, and hastened to be recognised by the Romans, both as King of Macedonia, and as a party to the treaty of 196 BC. He also decreed

the recall of exiles, the cancellation of debts and an amnesty, in an attempt to improve a situation that had become difficult towards the end of his father's reign, and thus to secure greater support for himself in Macedonian society.

Convinced that he had won the confidence of the Romans, Perseus felt he had enough room for manoeuvre to attempt to strengthen his influence in southern Greece. He improved his position in the Delphic Amphictiony, concluded an alliance with the Boiotians, was invited to intervene in the internal affairs of a number of Greek states, and attracted to himself the sympathies of the common people. But since the latter were ill-disposed towards the Romans, the all-powerful ally conceived some resentment at this, especially as the king, giving proof of his rashness, campaigned against the Dolopians who had tortured and killed his governor, and was bold enough to undertake a 'pilgrimage' to Delphi at the head of his army. In order to neutralise the traditional hostilities and the intrigues stirred up by Eumenes II of Pergamon, he arranged bonds of matrimony with the families of Prusias II of Bithynia and Seleukos IV of Syria.

Rome closed her eyes for a time until, in 174 BC, she seems to have begun to feel uneasy on learning of the armed pilgrimage to Delphi. As complaints and accusations followed one upon the other, senatorial commissions were sent to investigate on the spot and demand explanations. The king turned a deaf ear, being little inclined to renounce his Greek policy. At the end of 173 BC, a motion was introduced to the Senate demanding that Macedonia be declared a Roman 'province' (that is, in this case, a theatre of military operations). It did not achieve a majority, but some months later the Senate bowed before the accusations that flowed from various parts of the Greek world and yielded to the arguments in favour of military action. The Romans then stirred up anti-Macedonian movements and this time it was they who rejected Perseus' offers. The king, in fact, received only limited help from the Epirotes and some of the cities of Boiotia. Everywhere the ruling classes were hostile to him, and inclined towards the Romans as guarantors of the established order. However, the latter also did not have many enthusiastic allies. The Achaean League made only a small contingent available to them, and Eumenes and the Rhodians contributed only a few warships and transports. The game was played out on land, where the Romans had several armies, the operations were slow and were drawn out over three years, at the end of which Perseus was crushed at Pydna (168 BC) (fig. 198).

Rome had decided, this time, to have done with Macedonia. She deprived the nation of its traditional leadership by deporting Perseus and the dignitaries of the kingdom to Italy. She even suppressed the Macedonian state (though its unity was maintained at the level of the *synedrion*), substituting for it four political entities, the *merides* (portions). The very term, and the fact that each *meris* was designated by an ordinal number suggest that the Romans had no intention of considering them as states, but the *merides* were also explicitly forbidden to have economic or juridical relations, including those of marriage.

At the economic level, Rome appropriated fabulous riches as war booty and imposed an annual tribute, which was of the order of one hundred talents. On the other hand, she deprived the Macedonians of important resources by withdrawing from them the right to exploit the gold and silver mines, and to produce timber for the construction of ships, the key to the country's wealth.

Nevertheless, twenty years later an adventurer called Andriskos passed himself off as Philip, the son of Perseus, and easily had himself accepted in Macedonia. He even seized Thessaly and succeeded in repelling the first Roman military intervention, but the second (148 BC) cut short his career, and along with it the final attempt by the Macedonians to recover their liberty. Rome then proceeded to annex Macedonia as a province.

198. Reconstruction of the monument of Aemilius Paulus at Delphi. The pedestal originally formed the monument of Perseus, to which were added in 168 BC, after the battle of Pydna, the pillar with a base and capital and the Ionic entablature with a cornice with dentils; above this, the plinth supported the equestrian statue of the Roman general.

198

MACEDONIA
IN GREEK HISTORY

The foregoing chapters will have shown, we hope, the contribution made by the researches of the last twenty years to our knowledge of Macedonia and, above all, will have shown the contribution made by Macedonia, as we now know it, to Greek civilisation and more generally to the civilisation of Classical antiquity.

When the Macedonian kingdom vanishes, we are a long way from the groups of transhumant shepherds moving between the mountain pastures of Olympos and the winter grazing in the plains of Pieria and Emathia, where they ultimately settled in order to undertake the exploitation of the agricultural resources and the natural resources, the minerals and forests. We begin to form a better understanding of the first occupants of these lands at the start of the Palaeolithic period. Already in the Neolithic period, their contacts with Thessaly are certainly attested. It is undoubtedly with the transition to the Bronze Age, at the turn of the third to the second millennium, that groups arrived speaking an Indo-European dialect that was to become Greek. And the most recent archaeological discoveries show that we must henceforth push the boundaries of the 'Mycenaean' settlements further north, to Pieria and Elimeia.

It may be admitted that the Macedonian kingdom was already established in what was to be its historical heart when the earliest tumuli rose at Vergina, about 900 BC and it seems that, from the beginning, these Macedonians were 'hellenophones', speaking a Greek dialect somewhere between Thessalian and the northwest dialects.

During the Geometric and Archaic periods, and down to the middle of the fourth century, Macedonia evolved a culture which, though clearly on the margin of that of southern Greece and Ionia, was nevertheless illuminated by it. The coinage attests to the originality of the Macedonian and Thracian tribes, who did not adopt independent systems, like the Greek cities, but had a regional monetary system down to the second Persian war. Macedonia was then, 'in terms of the utilisation of coinage, more advanced than many of the Greek cities' (O. Picard), and the striking of a bronze coinage with pieces of low value facilitated the small exchanges of everyday life without imposing a burden on the public finances.

Recent excavations have yielded evidence of a comparatively rapid development of urbanism. Towards the end of the fifth century, the Hippodamian plan was brilliantly applied to Olynthos in Chalkidike. Olynthos, of course, was not Macedonian, but it is notable that the system was used, apparently at almost the same period, for the new Macedonian capital at Pella, at Dion, the religious capital, and also at Thessalonike. The site of Aiane reveals that very soon a different type of urbanism was deployed, this time in Upper Macedonia, involving terraces with retaining walls — a type that the Hellenistic world was to implement on a grand scale at Pergamon.

For the sculpture of the Archaic period, the recent discovery at Aiane of statues of *kouroi* and *korai* confirms what was already suggested by a number of finds in northern Greece, and in the second half of the fifth century, an art influenced by Ionia produced works that have their own spirit. Finally, still in the Archaic period, and the early Classical period, the tombs of Sindos and of Vergina attest to the piety towards the dead of an influential and wealthy social class of refined tastes.

The enormous, multi-faceted work of Philip II, who went from the unification of the country to the reorganisation of the army, to the remodelling of the kingdom by the transfer of populations and to the exploitation of new territories, foreshadowed a great idea, openly expressed after the victory at Chaironeia: the need for a general peace between the Greeks, who had been torn by the rivalries between the cities. In fact, the pan-Hellenic Congress of 338 BC, which proclaimed the freedom and autonomy of every city, forbade war between Greeks. And if the king proposed to launch them against the Orient, this was as much to unite them in a grand common ambition as to prevent Persia from fomenting troubles in Greece and exacerbating their internal divisions.

It was during this brief reign that the 'Macedonian tomb' received its definitive form and a number of prestige and propaganda structures were erected outside Macedonia, the first examples of a composite architecture that may be called 'Macedonian'. The tombs of Persephone, Eurydice and Philip attest to an astonishing flowering of painting, and to an equally impressive development of toreutic art, the products of which have modified our picture of Greek art.

Prepared by Philip, the conquest of the East was the work of Alexander, and had consequences that transcend Macedonia and even Greece. Its world-wide implications are due to the fact that, from the very outset of an extraordinary expedition, whose success was dependent in large measure on the exceptional gifts of the king, it was Alexander's desire to construct a multi- national empire covering the known world, with the intention of reuniting and amalgamating West and East. His death, and the disorders that followed it, have left nothing of this dream, though history is still nourished by it.

The Hellenistic period followed. Recent studies have given us a better understanding of Macedonian political institutions, especially the role played by the cities, and of the nature of a society much of which was now urbanised, but which remained loyal to the ancient virtues and ideals. Its administrative organisation, economy and finances are now better known and light has also been shed by recent research on the role played by Macedonia in the formation of the *koine*, the common Greek language that prevailed in the Hellenistic period.

As for the confrontations between the Macedonians and their neighbours, especially those of southern Greece, the policy of the kings seems neither worse nor better than those of the cities, Leagues, and other kingdoms with which they were faced in a world compounded of violence, intrigue and treason. And in the final conflict that set the Macedonian kings in opposition to the Romans, the fault was far from having been entirely on the side of the former, as has for too long been believed. It was Rome who, on many occasions, drove Macedonia into the war that was to be its ruin.

Moreover, we now know that the long cen-

tury following the death of Alexander was, in the sphere of the arts, a golden age for Macedonia, and at the same time a golden age for Greece. The pebble mosaics of Pella and Vergina are masterpieces in which, alongside splendid figure compositions, appear new types of geometric designs, a wonderful flowering of floral decoration and an original rendering of the third dimension. Subtle shades of colour give the images a pictorial character and, for the first time, artificial materials were used for some colours, as well as small pieces of lead and terracotta to indicate outlines.

Wall-painting, too, has not merely given us the wonderful frescoes so justly famous. To decorate the walls, the artists not only excelled in a structural style also found on Delos and in the 'first Pompeian style', but also used formulae which, in opening the wall to a distant plane, or in depicting architectural elements in a *trompe l'oeil*, probably contributed to the formation of what is known as the 'second Pompeian style'.

In the sphere of architecture, it is scarcely necessary to recall the flowering of the cities, characterised by their unified organisation, the width of the communicating streets, and the extent, on a site such as Pella, of a closed agora covering, with its stoas, more than 60,000 square metres. Crowning these cities, the palace, a form forgotten since early times for obvious historical reasons, was reborn on an outstanding scale and with great richness.

Sanctuaries were erected at the heart of the cities, or outside their walls. We are beginning to appreciate the number and variety of these —those of Beroia, for example, none of which has been found, but for which the inscriptions give us a fairly detailed knowledge.

Finally, Macedonian architecture outside Macedonia erected structures whose 'baroque' features have already been discussed, in an environment which, moreover, in many respects foreshadows the conditions of modern baroque: independence of the forms used by tradition; the glorification of sensual, emotional effects in buildings of exceptional dimensions, and with exceptional elements; effects of richness, linked with a decorative excess which did not hesitate to make use of stucco to supplement stone, or painting for *trompe l'oeil* effects; independence above all of the decoration from the structure, with the 'monumental façade' applied to the front of the palace, the Macedonian tomb, or the propaganda building. Thus, Macedonian architecture, through what it shatters, through what it combines, through what it invents, opens the way to some of the most original developments in architecture in the

199

199. Head of Medusa, Vergina, antechamber of the Tomb of Philip. This gold appliqué transforms the image of a monstrous creature, whose repulsiveness, large eyes and serpents in the hair should have been terrifying, into a masterpiece of serenity and composure.

Hellenistic kingdoms and in the Roman empire.

The contribution made by Macedonia is far from confined to this. Alexander's empire began to disintegrate the day after his death, it is true, and of all the kingdoms that were pieces of it, Macedonia was the first to be seized by Rome —the first in a series that was brought to completion with the annexation of Egypt in 30 BC. Nonetheless, the Hellenistic world continued, no doubt not deliberately, and certainly without being conscious of it, to realise Alexander's dream: the fusion of the West and East, through the spreading of a Greek civilisation that retained its essential values, first and foremost among them the blossoming of the individual.

The great line of division in Classical antiquity is thus not situated between the Greeks and the Romans. It is Alexander's expedition, which inangurated a new civilisation — the civilisation conquered by Rome when she conquered the Greek kingdoms, and which made the Roman empire the heir of Hellenistic Macedonia.

NOTES

INTRODUCTION
(pages 12-15)

1. On the rediscovery of Macedonia, see the articles by HATZOPOULOS 1981 and by BORZA 1982-1, the introduction to PAPAZOGLOU'S monograph and also HATZOPOULOS 1990.

THE EMERGENCE OF MACEDONIA
(pages 16-43)

1. For the study of the historical geography and natural resources of Macedonia, several recent works are available: the chapters devoted to these subjects in the monumental work by HAMMOND 1972, which also appeared in a more concise form in HAMMOND 1989; the relevant chapter in SIVIGNON 1983, and the articles by BORZA 1979, 1982-2 and 1987, the last repeated in BORZA 1990.
2. See *infra*, pp. 121 and 162.
3. For this 'common language', see *infra*, pp. 79-80.
4. For the history of Macedonia in general, see the many recent publications, including the monumental work by HAMMOND 1972; HAMMOND, GRIFFITH 1979; HAMMOND, WALBANK 1988; the collective volume edited by SAKELLARIOU 1982; the manual of ERRINGTON 1986 and that of BORZA 1990. For the early period of Macedonian history, see especially the incomplete work of KALLERIS 1954, 1976, the article by EDSON 1970, and, amongst the many important publications by this author, PAPAZOGLOU 1977; see also notes 5, 6 and 7 below. Several points of view expressed in the present text reflect opinions developed by its author in his course on Macedonia at the University of Paris X.
5. For the Neolithic period, see GRAMMENOS 1988, 1991, with recent bibliography.
6. For the Bronze Age, see KOUKOULI-CHRYSANTHAKI 1988.
7. VOKOTOPOULOU, KOUKOULI-CHRYSANTHAKI 1988.
8. See *infra*, pp. 32-35.
9. For explanations of this phenomenon, see *infra*, p. 106.
10. BAKALAKIS 1963, pp. 30-34.
11. LAZARIDIS 1969, pp. 17-20.
12. Unpublished: see ANDRONICOS 1988-2, p. 96.

---

200. Funerary stele, painted marble, from the great tumulus at Vergina, second half of the 4th century B.C. Scene of farewell. On the pediment, against a blue pediment, against a blue ground, a small representation of the 'goddess of the scrolls'.

13. See *infra*, pp. 97 and 106.
14. ANDRONICOS 1988-2, pp. 93-94 and fig. 56; FLOREN 1987, p. 323.
15. FLOREN 1987, p. 323, with no. 1 for the earlier bibliography.
16. KARAMITROU-MENDESSIDI 1988, 1989-1, -2.
17. For the discoveries at Sindos, see the fine catalogue SINDOS 1985. For the site, see HAMMOND 1972, pp. 183-ff. and 1979, p. 116; A. DESPINIS in SINDOS 1985, pp. 11-ff, HATZOPOULOS, LOUKOPOULOU 1987, p. 60, n. 171. For special studies, see DESPINI 1982, 1983; TIVERIOS 1986 and 1988.
18. ANDRONICOS 1988-1; KOTTARIDOU 1989.
19. See *infra*, p. 50.
20. For this site see the 14-volume publication by the American archaeologists including, for the architecture, volumes II, VIII, XII, ROBINSON 1930, 1938 and 1946.
21. On the architect and this type of urban planning, see MARTIN 1974, pp. 97-126, 296-301; HOEPFNER, SCHWANDNER 1986. A relationship has been suggested between this plan and the democratic regimes; see SCHULER, HOEPFNER, SCHWANDNER 1989, but the plan was also adopted in a whole series of royal foundations, especially in the Greek East.
22. See *infra*, pp. 87 and 117.
23. See *infra*, pp. 117-136.
24. See *supra*, pp. 40 and 41.
25. See *infra*, pp. 91-96.
26. See *infra*, pp. 101-105.
27. ANDRONICOS 1988-2, p. 99.
28. KOSTOGLOU-DESPINE 1979, p. 69.
29. This is the interpretation of ANDRONICOS 1988-2, p. 95.
30. STEPHANIDOU 1975.
31. ANDRONICOS 1988, p. 96.
32. AKAMATIS 1987-1.
33. See the calendar *Makedonia-Dion* 90, 15-20 October.

THE MACEDONIA OF PHILIP II
(pages 44-57)

1. See ELLIS 1976; CAWKWELL 1978; HATZOPOULOS, LOUKOPOULOU 1981.
2. See *supra*, p. 42.
3. See *supra*, pp. 23, 40 and 41.
4. Pending the forthcoming publication of the monograph by HATZOPOULOS, the most balanced recent synthesis on this question may be read in MOOREN 1983. On the detailed questions, see also the monograph by HAMMOND 1989, pp. 16-36, 49-70 and 382-95.
5. See *infra*, pp. 154-161.

6. For the Tomb of Philip, see *infra*, pp. 161-166.
7. See *infra*, pp. 147-190.
8. See *infra*, pp. 183-187.
9. See *infra*, pp. 187-188.
10. See *infra*, pp. 202-204.
11. See *infra*, pp. 194-196.
12. See *infra*, p. 196.
13. See *infra*, p. 196.

ALEXANDER AND THE DIADOCHI
(pages 58-81)

1. See *supra*, p. 54 for the justification for his project.
2. See *supra*, pp. 55-57.
3. See the Glossary.
4. See *infra*, p. 222.
5. For the evidence afforded by coins, see *infra*, same page.
6. For royal and private architecture, see *infra*, pp. 84-104; for funerary architecture, *infra*, pp. 147-190.
7. See *supra*, pp. 21-22, for revenues from royal property, whether mines or forests, and also fiscal revenues and taxes.
8. NEWELL 1927; PRICE 1974, 1991; MARTIN 1985.
9. See *infra*, p. 79.
10. See *supra*, p. 64.
11. See *supra*, pp. 46-49.
12. On this question, see BRIXHE, PANAYOTOU 1988; HATZOPOULOS 1988-3 and 1991; PANAYOTOU 1990.
13. See *supra*, p. 22.
14. See *supra*, pp. 78-79.
15. See *infra*, pp. 91-104.
16. See *infra*, pp. 84-89.
17. See *infra*, pp. 147-190.
18. See *infra*, pp. 117-136.
19. See *infra*, p. 217.
20. For the buildings on Samothrace, see *infra*, pp. 202-213.
21. For Delos, see *infra*, pp. 197-202.

CITIES AND SANCTUARIES OF MACEDONIA
(pages 82-143)

1. See *supra*, p. 66.
2. LAUTER 1987, p. 347 and n. 10, with bibliography.
3. For a description of the ruins see above all HEUZEY, DAUMET 1876; for recent works RHOMAIOS 1954; ANDRONICOS, MAKARONAS, MOUTSOPOULOS, BAKALAKIS 1961; ANDRO-

NICOS 1964; and mainly ANDRONICOS 1984-1, pp. 38-46. The restored plan is by J. TRAVLOS. The letters designating the rooms are used in the text.

4. The remains of the building allow the restoration of the tiled roof, and even the volumes of the complex: see PANDERMALIS 1987.

5. PANDERMALIS 1976. For the tomb, see *infra*, p. 178.

6. MILLER 1972. Kottabos is a game of skill involving throwing the contents of a cup into a receptacle.

7. See *infra*, pp. 117 and 129.

8. LAUTER 1987, pp. 345-346, posits a hierarchy of rooms corresponding to that of the courtiers.

9. It has in fact been noted that it contained a dedication by this king which was subsequently erased: HATZOPOULOS 1988-2.

10. For the time being, see the reports by SIGANIDOU 1987-2 and 3; for the swimming pools, CHRYSOSTOMOU 1988-2, with the earlier bibliography. See also LAUTER 1986; 1987.

11. See *infra*, p. 91.

12. CHRYSOSTOMOU 1988-2, p. 121.

13. SIGANIDOU 1989.

14. See *supra*, pp. 41 and 43.

15. CHRYSOSTOMOU 1988-2, p. 114 and note 5. For an early date, see HATZOPOULOS, LOUKOPOULOU 1987, pp. 42-ff.

16. See *infra*, p. 91.

17. See *supra*, pp. 78-79.

18. Let us only mention the discovery, just below the palace, of the theatre of Vergina, connected with the assassination of Philip II; DROUGOU 1989. For the acropolis, see FAKLARIS 1989. For the sanctuaries of the city, see *infra*, p. 106.

19. See *supra*, pp. 29-32.

20. TRAKOSOPOULOU-SALAKIDOU 1987.

21. HATZOPOULOS, LOUKOPOULOU 1989.

22. VELENIS, ADAM-VELENI 1988.

23. ALEXANDER 1963.

24. See for the occupation of its territory, HATZOPOULOS 1986.

25. For the formation of this city by a synoecism, see *supra*, p. 79; and also TIVERIOS 1986-2; and for the 'Hippodamean' plan, VICKERS 1972.

26. For the time being, see PETSAS 1968. We mention here the name of Edessa, which has been identified with Aigeai; see on the fortification wall CHRYSOSTOMOU 1987-1; 1988-1.

27. On Pella in general , see PAPAKONSTANTINOU-DIAMANTOUROU 1971, PETSAS 1978, ANDRONICOS 1976. For the recent excavations, see the convenient presentation in *Pella* 1987.

28. The expression is that of Xenophon, *Hellenika* 5, 2, 13.

29. For the results of these excavations, see OIKONOMOS 1914 and 1926.

30. See the reports of Makaronas in *Arch Deltion* starting in 1960; PETSAS 1960, 1964, 1976 and 1978.

31. See the general presentations in SIGANIDOU 1986; 1987-1, -2, -3; KOTTARIDOU 1987.

32. See e.g. HAMMOND, GRIFFITH 1979, pp. 6 and 139-140; HAMMOND, WALBANK 1988, p. 183 and note 6 and *supra*, pp. 40, 41 and 43.

33. AKAMATIS 1987-1, p. 13 and n. 2; 1989-1, p.

189, note 77; for the anthropological material, see REUER, FABRIZII-REUER 1988, pp. 261-266.

34. TOURATSOGLOU 1975.

35. AKAMATIS 1985, pp. 483-554.

36. GOUNAROPOULOU, HATZOPOULOS 1985, pp. 52-53, with bibliography.

37. SIGANIDOU 1987-1 and 2.

38. The expression is that of Aristotle, *Politics* VII, 10, 4. For Olynthos, see *supra*, p. 43, for Thessalonike *supra* p. 91, for Dion *infra*, p. 99.

39. SIGANIDOU 1983; 1986.

40. MAKARONAS 1970 and TOURATSOGLOU 1975.

41. MAKARONAS, GIOURI 1989; and *infra*, p. 117.

42. SIGANIDOU 1982; for analyses of the plaster, see CALAMIOTOU, SIGANIDOU, FILIPAKIS 1983; and *infra*, p. 136.

43. See *supra*, p. 43.

44. OIKONOMOS 1914 and 1915; KRAUSE 1977, pp. 170 and 175.

45. AKAMATIS 1986, 1987-2, 1988, 1989-1, -2, -3.

46. On the sanctuary, see LILIMBAKI-AKAMATI 1986 and *infra*, p. 106.

47. See the presentation in AKAMATIS 1988, pp. 80-81.

48. For the excavations, see PANDERMALIS 1977; 1989 with earlier bibliography.

49. PANDERMALIS 1989, pp. 12-14; and *infra*, pp. 106 and 109-110.

50. PANDERMALIS 1989, pp. 14-17.

51. PANDERMALIS 1989, pp. 18-23.

52. KARADEDOS 1983; POLACCO 1986; PANDERMALIS 1989, pp. 23-26.

53. STEFANIDOU-TIVERIOU 1987, 1988; PANDERMALIS 1989, pp. 26-29.

54. PANDERMALIS 1989, pp. 35-39.

55. See *supra*, p. 43.

56. See *infra*, pp. 147-190. SOTERIADIS 1932; MAKARONAS 1956.

57. D. LAZARIDIS 1977; 1982; 1983; K.LAZARIDIS 1986; 1987; 1988; 1989. For the cemeteries, see SAMARTZIDOU 1987. For the famous Lion of Amphipolis, see ROGER 1939; BRONEER 1941; STEVENS 1949.

58. See *supra*, p. 40.

59. See *supra*, p. 42.

60. See *supra*, p. 50.

61. See *infra*, p. 138.

62. For the sanctuaries of Dion, we have the articles by PANDERMALIS 1977 and 1989.

63. See *supra*, p. 97. For the festival, see p. 40.

64. See *supra*, p. 97.

65. The excavation of the sanctuary of Eukleia had not been completed at the time of the publication of the fine volume ANDRONICOS 1984-1; more recent information can be found in the annual reports published in E*rgon*, and also in SAATSOGLOU-PALIADELI 1987 and 1989.

66. For the tholos and the megaron of Pella, see HADJISTELIOU-PRICE 1973 and, for the more recently discovered sanctuaries, LILIMBAKI-AKAMATI 1986 and AKAMATIS 1986.

67. The decree of Pydna concerning the restoration of a statue of Apollo has been the object of a communication by BESSIOS 1992.

68. The most recent publication on the temple of

Ma at Edessa is that of VAVRITSAS 1983.

69. For the only report on the temple of Athena at Kyrrhos, see VAVRITSAS 1973, p. 9.

70. There is no report on the excavation of the temple of the Egyptian Gods at Thessalonike, and the excavations in the sanctuary of Demeter and Kore have never been published; see HATZOPOULOS (forthcoming).

71. The sanctuary of Asklepios at Morrylos is the subject of a monograph by HATZOPOULOS, LOUKOPOULOU 1989.

72. But see *supra*, p. 103.

73. There is no comprehensive study of the sanctuaries of Beroia: the published information on them is contained in a thesis by Laurence Brocas, a student of M. Hatzopoulos, on the ancient topography of the city.

74. For the sanctuary of Dionysos at Aphytos, and for the sanctuary of Zeus Ammon, see GIOURI 1974.

75. JOST 1985; her conclusion, especially pp. 545-559, could be broadly applied to Macedonian religion. For neighbouring Epirus, see also TZOUVARA-SOULI 1979.

76. For the sanctuaries, see *supra*, pp. 106-109.

77. See SISMONDO RIDGWAY 1990, pp. 119, 129, 151.

78. See *supra*, pp. 97 and 106.

79. PANDERMALIS 1989, p. 13.

80. *Alexander the Great*, pl. 7.

81. See *supra*, pp. 97 and 106.

82. PANDERMALIS 1989, p. 15.

83. HATZOPOULOS 1987, pp. 397-412, who cites many other epithets by which Artemis was invoked in Macedonia.

84. *Search for Alexander*, fig. 150.

85. For their significance, see *supra*, p. 198.

86. SAKELLARIOU 1982, p. 169, n. 107.

87. Beroia Museum no. Pi 2361. See *Search for Alexander* p. 173, fig. 142.

88. *Alexander the Great*, p. 61.

89. *Ancient Macedonia* 1988, p. 343, n° 302.

90. E.g. Beroia Museum no. Pi 2360.

91. *BCH* 115, 1991, p. 899, fig. 94.

92. *Ibid.*, fig. 95.

93. *Ancient Macedonia* 1988, p. 318, n° 215.

94. *Search for Alexander*, p. 175, fig. 145.

95. *Search for Alexander*, 31.

96. PANDERMALIS 1989, p. 25.

97. See *supra*, p. 40.

98. See *infra*, pp. 187-188.

99. See *infra*, p. 175.

100. Pella Museum, Pi lambda 43; see *Search for Alexander*, p. 179, note 153 and pl. 25. For the deities in favour in Macedonia on late representations at Athens, see also KAHIL 1991.

101. *Search for Alexander*, 17 and p. 157, fig. 110.

102. See *infra*, p. 184.

103. See *infra*, p. 160.

104. See *infra*, p. 180.

105. For this site, see *infra*, p. 215.

106. See *supra*, p. 91 and note 71.

107. PANDERMALIS 1992, p. 20.

108. PANDERMALIS 1992, p. 22.

109. For the spread of this cult, first known in west Macedonia, see CHRYSOSTOMOU 1989.

110. See the letter of Demetrios II dating from

249/8 BC, *SEG* 12, 1955, no. 311. Asklepios appears in it also as a god.

111. See *Search for Alexander*, p. 32 and p. 185, fig. 165.

112. ANDRONICOS 1984, p. 155, figs 119-120.

113. *Search for Alexander* p. 171, fig. 139.

114. See *infra*, p. 164.

115. See *supra*, pp. 95-96.

116. See *infra*, p. 142.

117. KOUKOULI-CHRYSANTHAKI, MALAMI-DOU 1989.

118. See *supra*, p. 95, and *infra*, pp. 117-118.

119. KAHIL 1988 and already ROBERTSON 1965, pp. 79-80 and ROBERTSON 1967, p. 136, note 1.

120. See *supra*, pp. 118, 121 and 162.

121. See *supra*, p. 121.

122. For this site, see *supra*, pp. 91-96. For the mosaics of Pella, one should consult PETSAS 1978 (selection of articles), MAKARONAS, GIOURI 1989. All the pebble mosaics are republished in SALZMANN 1982; earlier articles, which attribute an important role to the mosaics of Pella are RO-BERTSON 1965 and 1967; BRUNEAU 1976. For each of the mosaics of the Greek period cited here, a reference will be given in the notes, just before the main bibliographical references (in capital letters, e.g. VERGINA 1), to the Data Bank *La mosaïque dans le monde grec, des origines à la fin de l'époque hellénistique*, compiled by A.M. Guimier-Sorbets, and distributed by the Research Centre *Archéologie et systèmes d'informations (CNRS et l'Université de Paris X)*; and the detailed description of each paving is associated with photographs and drawings on the video-disc *Images de l'Archéologie*.

123. For this palace, see *supra*, pp. 84-88.

124. VERGINA 1. See ANDRONICOS, MAKA-RONAS, MOUTSOPOULOS, BAKALAKIS 1961, pp. 21-23, pl. 10, 13-1, 14, 17.

125. VERGINA 2. See *Ibid*, p. 23.

126. AMPHIPOLIS 1 and 2. See LAZARIDIS 1960, p. 69, pl. 50A.

127. DION 1. See MAKARONAS 1955, pp. 153-154.

128. For this building see *infra*, p. 211. SAMO-THRACE 2. See LEHMANN, SPITTLE 1964, p. 59, fig. 59, pl. XL.

129. For this building see *infra*, p. 211. SAMO-THRACE 1. See MCCREDIE 1968, p. 228, fig. 3, pl. 69 A-C.

130. See *supra*, same page.

131. See *infra*, p. 129.

132. See *supra*, p. 95.

133. PELLA 1. See MAKARONAS, GIOURI 1989, pp. 124-127, 164, pls 14-17.

134. See *supra* n. 119.

136. MORENO 1965, p. 58; the same attribution also applies to the panel with a male and female Centaur, see *infra*, p. 121. On the problem of the relationship of mosaic to large-scale painting in general, see *infra*, notes 165, 166.

137. PELLA 2. See MAKARONAS, GIOURI 1989, pp. 117-119, 142-143, 165-166, pls 18-22.

138. See *infra*, p. 129.

139. PELLA 4. See MAKARONAS, GIOURI 1989, pp. 130-131, 143, pl. 23.

140. PELLA 5. See MAKARONAS, GIOURI 1989, pp. 133-137, 143-144, pl. 24.

141. PELLA 6. See MAKARONAS, GIOURI 1989, pp. 137-140, 144-145, pl. 25 B-C.

142. See *infra*, p. 217.

143. See *infra*, p. 162.

144. But see *infra*, same page.

145. PELLA 12. See LILIMBAKI-AKAMATI 1987-2; *Ancient Macedonia* 1988, p. 307.

146. PELLA 9. See MAKARONAS, GIOURI 1989, p. 175, pl. 26; LILIMBAKI-AKAMATI 1988-1.

147. On the significance of this subject, see *infra*, p. 162, note 49.

148. PELLA 4. See *supra*, note 139.

149. A composition with a surface of overlapping leaves, for the Abduction of Helen. PELLA 1. See *supra*, note 133.

150. The part of the mosaic occupied by Dionysos, for example, is enclosed only by a thin monochrome band. PELLA 5.

151. PELLA 8. See MAKARONAS, GIOURI 1989, p. 133.

152. PELLA 7. See MAKARONAS, GIOURI 1989, p. 134.

153. GUIMIER-SORBETS 1987.

154. ROUX 1961, p. 160, pl. 38.

155. PELLA 2. See *supra*, note 137.

156. PELLA 6. See *supra*, note 141.

157. PELLA 9. See *supra*, note 146.

158. PELLA 12. See *supra*, note 145.

159. See *supra*, note 124.

160. GUIMIER-SORBETS 1993.

161. PELLA 9 (see *supra*, note 146) and PELLA 12 (*supra*, note 145). In the case of PELLA 3, a mosaic in the House of the Abduction of Helen, the threshold scene is not preserved, see MAKARONAS, GIOURI 1989, p. 132.

162. ROBERTSON 1975, p. 486-489; ROBERT-SON 1982, pp. 241-249; GUIMIER-SORBETS 1993.

163. BÖRKER 1978; GUIMIER-SORBETS 1993.

164. ERETRIA 3. See DUCREY, METZGER 1979, pp. 8, 21, pls 1.3, 2.5 and 6. Pending the forthcoming publication, see the *Guide de la Maison aux mosaïques*, DUCREY 1991.

165. Fr. VILLARD in CARBONNEAUX, MAR-TIN, VILLARD 1970, p. 105; but see also BRUNO 1981, p. 4, note 9.

166. ROUVERET 1989, pp. 172, 244-247, where the author re-examines the theses of MORENO 1965 and BRUNO 1977.

167. See *Ergon* 1987 (1988), pp. 45-50, pl. 46 and *infra*, p. 156.

168. PELLA 12. See supra, note 145.

169. See MAKARONIAS, GIOURI 1989, p. 141, note 53.

170. See *Ibid.*, p. 143, note 60.

171. At the beginning of the second century, mosaicists used faience in order to obtain tesserae of pale green, pale blue, bright blue, or even grey-blue, even though the fragility of this material made it unsuitable for floor decoration; see GIANNOULI, GUIMIER-SORBETS 1988; GUIMIER-SORBETS 1990; GUIMIER-SORBETS, NENNA 1992.

172. MAKARONAS, GIOURI 1989, p. 141, suggested the hypothesis that such pieces were used. After examination, it has been possible to confirm that use was made of fragments of opaque blue glass, probably waste material from glass-workshops, which was used here without any preparation, just like pebbles.

173. BRUNEAU 1972, pp. 27-29; BRUNEAU 1987, p. 64.

174. GUIMIER-SORBETS 1990.

175. The mosaic in the tomb at Dion (see *supra*, pp. 99, 101) is adorned with a ring, like the pavement in the Tholos at Delphi (CHARBONNEAUX 1925, pp. 18-19; BOMMELAER 1991, p. 66). For other examples of mosaics imitating paved floors, and for the Macedonian tomb of Langada, the floor of which is an imitation of *opus sectile*, see GUI-MIER-SORBETS 1987.

176. ALEXANDRIA 1. See DASZEWSKI 1978, pp. 128-135; figs. 116-129; DASZEWSKI 1985, pp. 103-110, pls. C, 4-7, 10-11, 12 B-C.

177. And also, in the Orient, as far afield as the mosaic of Ai Khanoum, in the northern part of modern Afghanistan.

178. See *infra*, p. 150.

179. MAKARONAS, GIOURI 1989, p. 145.

180. For these antecedents, see ROUVERET 1989, p. 166; the walls of houses at Olynthos (see *supra*, p. 43) have already furnished good examples, and the first manifestations of the style are perhaps to be found at Athens from the turn of the fourth to the third century, see BRUNO 1969; but it is now legitimate to ask whether the examples at Delos, although from the 'Athenian' period, derive from direct Athenian influence, or whether they do not also continue a tradition brought to Delos by the Macedonians.

181. Pending the publication of this house, see SI-GANIDOU 1982, p. 35. This decoration must date from the second century.

182. See *infra*, p. 205.

183. See *infra*, pp. 206 and 209.

184. See *supra*, p. 178.

185. See *infra*, p. 178.

186. See the frequently cited example in the House of Dionysos, CHAMONARD 1922, p. 194, fig. 83 and 1924 pp. 385-386; the upper part of the wall represents an open gallery of pillars supporting a complete entablature and even, between the columns, a coffered ceiling in perspective. See also, on the House of the Comedians on the same site, BE-ZERRA DE MENESES 1970, p. 155, this time with an order of half-columns. See, finally, 'la maison de l'épée' ALABE 1987, p. 643.

187. BEZERRA DE MENESES 1970, p. 191; MILLER 1971, p. 119-168; FITTSCHEN 1976; LEHMANN 1979; MILLER 1982; numerous entries in *Pittura Ellenistica* 1985, especially those of BALDASSARE (p. 211-214), COARELLI (pp. 290-292), ROUVERET (p. 293); and the various contributions in DE FRANCISCIS 1991.

188. See SCHEFOLD 1975; and now MCKENZIE 1990, especially pp. 85-104.

189. For an entablature supported by pillars, see LAIDLAW 1985, pl. 14; by Ionic colonnettes, *ibid.* pl. 32 a. The interval between these supports certainly did not depict a solid wall but, even though it was not painted blue, formed an opening into space, achieved in practice, in the former example, by the presence of windows.

190. This is the case in the atrium of the Casa Sam-

nitica; LAIDLAW 1985, pl. 41 c.

191. LAZARIDIS 1982, p. 48, and 1983, p. 35-37. And see *supra*, p. 103.

192. The arrangement is completely different from that found on Delos in the House of Hermes; see LAIDLAW 1985, p. 37 and fig. 8, p. 36, where the representations of blocks with drafted margins stops *against* the corner pilasters, and therefore in the same plane, whereas at Amphipolis, the entire masonry is set *behind* the representations of the columns.

193. Here too, however, it should not be forgotten that the 'first Pompeian style' has produced at least two examples of this arrangement, at Pompeii itself, see LAIDLAW 1985, pl. 33 a and pl. 41, a, b and pp. 31-32 with note 24; it is true that these examples concern the upper zones of walls, like those already discussed *supra*, note 186; and it is also true that the division of the walls of Pompeii into 'styles', the application of which to Greek walls should be avoided at all costs, is related to the state of knowledge of a particular period and does not reflect a strict chronological order.

194. ANDRONICOS 1955.

195. DROUGOU, TOURATSOGLOU 1980, 1991. On the fourth-century pottery of neighbouring Chalkidike, see GIOURI 1972.

196. AKAMATIS 1985. See also, for Vergina, FAKLARIS 1983.

197. M. BESSIOS in DROUGOU 1991, pp. 41-42.

198. KARAMITROU-MENDESSIDI in DROUGOU 1991, pp. 140-143.

199. SINN 1979.

200. On architectural terracottas, see KALTSAS 1985.

THE "MACEDONIAN TOMBS"
(pages 144-191)

1. Loeb translation.

2. The first presentation of the 'Macedonian tombs' was that of HEUZEY, DAUMET 1876; this was followed by the publication of VOLLMOELLER 1901. PANDERMALIS 1972, in the publication of a small tomb at Vergina, gave, with his bibliography, a complete catalogue of the tombs discovered to that date; GOSSEL 1980 describes the 43 tombs known at that time in Macedonia, and Western Thrace (but does not include, for example, the 'Macedonian tombs' of Eretria) with bibliography; her interpretations and dates, however, cannot be completely accepted. See also MILLER 1971 and 1982, TOMLINSON 1974 and 1977. For the complete range of questions posed by these monuments, see now ANDRONICOS 1987-1.

3. Even these tombs do have a façade, and it is notable that this feature also occurs, though in even simpler form, in certain of the rock-cut tombs that succeeded the 'Macedonian tombs' at Beroia; see DROUGOU, TOURATSOGLOU 1980.

4. See, however, CHRYSOSTOMOU 1986; 1987-2.

5. On the problem of the introduction of the vault to Greece, in its form before the discoveries at Vergina, see e.g. BOYD 1978 and now TOMLINSON 1987.

6. ANDRONICOS 1987-1.

7. See *supra*, pp. 30-32 and 35-38.

8. DESPINI 1980.

9. ANDRONICOS 1984, 1985.

10. ROBINSON 1942, p. 117, no. 598, pls. 53-56; KURTZ, BOARDMAN 1971, p. 194, fig. 40.

11. KOTZIAS 1937, pp. 866-895.

12. ANDRONICOS 1987-1.

13. This is the Tomb of Eurydice, see *infra*, pp. 154-161.

14. See *infra*, p. 154.

15. See *infra*, p. 183.

16. See ANDRONICOS 1987-2. This painted decoration might be supplemented by the geometric, floral or figure decoration on wooden or textile panels, the attachment nails for which have been preserved in some of the tombs; it is notable that the motifs on these panels, which came in some cases from the steppes of Asia, were imitated in the frescoes in the tombs; see e.g. BOARDMAN 1970; and also TOMLINSON 1983.

17. RHOMAIOS 1951; and *infra*, p. 176.

18. MAKARONAS, MILLER 1974; TOMLINSON 1983; MILLER 1993; and *infra*, p. 178.

19. RHOMIOPOULOU 1973; and *infra*, pp. 181-182.

20. KINCH 1920; RHOMIOPOULOU, TOURATSOGLOU 1971; and, for the painted restoration of the tomb Ἱστορία 1973, IV, p. 186.

21. PETSAS 1966; and *infra*, pp. 178-181.

22. ANDRONICOS 1984-1; and *infra*, pp. 154-177.

23. The Tomb of Persephone, see *infra*, pp. 183-187.

24. See *infra*, p. 162.

25. See *infra*, pp. 166-175.

26. See *infra*, p. 175.

27. KYRIELEIS 1969.

28. VOLLMOELLER 1901.

29. See *infra*, p. 176.

30. See *infra*, pp. 154-161.

31. TSIMBIDOU-AVLONITE 1988.

32. See *supra*, note 18; *infra*, p. 178.

33. ANDRONICOS 1969.

34. See *supra*, pp. 35-38.

35. But compare outside Macedonia one of the tombs at Eretria, *infra*, p. 215.

36. KARAMITROU-MENDESSIDI 1989-1 and -2 and *supra*, p. 32.

37. ANDRONICOS 1984-1; SAATSOGLOU-PALIADELI 1984.

38. KURTZ, BOARDMAN 1971, p. 101.

39. SINDOS 1985 and *supra*, pp. 33-35.

40. DAFFA-NIKONANOU 1985, 1986.

41. Euripides, *Trojan Women*, 1248-50.

42. See *supra*, pp. 55-57.

43. ANDRONICOS 1987-3.

44. The designation 'Tomb of the Throne' should in any case be avoided, for the Tomb of Rhomaios close by and one of the tombs in the 'Bella tumulus' also have thrones.

45. ANDRONICOS 1980; 1984-1.

46. See *supra*, p. 153.

47. See *supra*, p. 151.

48. For the discussion and related bibliography see PRAG 1990; TRIPODI 1991, p. 146, note 6 and *passim*; BRIANT 1991; PRESTIANNI GIALLOMBARDO 1991, especially p. 286, note 63.

49. This is attested by Arrian, *Anabasis* 4, 13, 1. On the exact capacity of the characters in the scene, see PRESTIANNI GIALLOMBARDO 1991, especially pp. 280-286; on the connection with oriental hunts, see TRIPODI 1991, BRIANT 1991.

50. Compare the accounts in Herodotus 7, 124-126, of lions attacking Xerxes' army as it was crossing Paionia; the testimony of Aristotle *Peri ta Zoa Istoriai* VI 31 (597 b7) and VIII 28 (606 d15); and above all the explicit testimony of Xenophon, *Cynegeticus* II, on the way in which lions, lynxes, panthers and bears were hunted in Macedonia. And see BRIANT 1991 pp. 222-225, 236-240.

51. On this question see also TRIPODI 1991, pp. 148-185.

52. ANDRONICOS 1984-1, pp. 198-217.

53. But see *supra*, p. 114.

54. ANDRONICOS 1984-1, p. 31.

55. ANDRONICOS 1984-1, pp. 35-37.

56. But see also a tomb at Dion, *supra*, p. 101.

57. See *supra*, p. 150.

58. RHOMAIOS 1951.

59. For a presentation of the entire group, see TOURATSOGLOU 1973.

60. See *supra*, note 2.

61. See *supra*, note 18.

62. See *supra*, p. 137 for the apparent incongruity of the perspective.

63. PETSAS 1966.

64. See *supra*, p. 137.

65. BRUNO 1981.

66. See *supra*, p. 150.

67. RHOMIOPOULOU 1973.

68. MACRIDY 1911.

69. HEUZEY 1860, pp. 172-ff; HEUZEY, DAUMET 1876, pp. 243-ff.

70. MAKARONAS 1953-2. A tomb at Nea Kerdyllia should perhaps be added here, but, since it has never been published, it is not certain whether it had a vault.

71. MANSEL 1943, p. 52.

72. ANDRONICOS 1984-1, pp. 84-95.

73. See, already, for this painter, SIX 1925; and THOMAS 1989.

74. MAKARONAS 1963.

75. GIOURI 1978. Some of the finds are illustrated in *Treasures* 1979, nos 157-268, pls 24-37.

76. See *supra*, pp. 151 and 161.

77. See *supra*, p. 32.

78. See *supra*, p. 43.

MACEDONIAN DEDICATIONS OUTSIDE MACEDONIA
(pages 192-219)

1. This thesis was argued by THOMPSON 1982, in an article with the significant title: 'Architecture as a Medium of Public Relations among the Successors of Alexander'; it dealt not only with Macedonians from Macedonia, but with all the Hellenistic kings. See also TARDITI 1990.

2. Many fundamental observations on this Macedonian architecture have already been made, especially by MILLER 1971, pp. 175-227, 1973 and 1982.

3. CURTIUS *et alii* 1892, pp. 128-133; SCHLEIF, ZSCHIETZSCHMANN 1944; MILLER 1971, pp. 179-201; MILLER 1973.

4. See *supra*, pp. 86, 106 and 129; but the rotundas in question there had no peristyle, which presented a difficult problems of statics.

5. See *supra*, pp. 161, 176, 178 and 182.

6. THOMPSON 1982, p. 174.

7. COULTON 1976, pp. 255-256.

8. COULTON 1968; PETRAKOS 1968; MILLER 1971, pp. 222-227; COULTON 1976, p. 269.

9. See *infra*, p. 213.

10. And see *supra*, p. 68.

11. COURBY 1912; COULTON 1976, p. 231; MILLER 1971, pp. 203-207; BRUNEAU, DUCAT 1983, pp. 141-142.

12. With regard to the Monument of the Bulls, see *infra*, pp. 200-201.

13. See *supra*, p. 196, *infra*, p. 213.

14. VALLOIS 1923; COULTON 1976, pp. 233-234; MILLER 1971, pp. 207-212; BRUNEAU, DUCAT 1983, pp. 117-118.

15. LEHMANN 1962.

16. ROLLEY 1965, pp. 480-482 and ROLLEY 1986.

17. COULTON 1976, p. 288.

18. See *supra*, pp. 85-86.

19. See *supra*, pp. 99-101.

20. See *supra*, p. 182.

21. See, e.g., MCKENZIE 1990, index, s.v. *quarter column*, p. 207, and *coupled quarter column*, p. 199. for the idea of baroque, see *infra*, pp. 217-219.

22. VALLOIS 1944, pp. 33-37, 253, 255, 279-280, 373, 397 (Vallois speaks of 'Pythion'); ROUX 1989; BRUNEAU, DUCAT 1983, pp. 138-140.

23. See *infra*, p. 206.

24. For the discussion, see ROUX 1981-2; BRUNEAU, DUCAT 1983, p. 140; TRÉHEUX 1987; ROUX 1989.

25. LEHMANN 1983, pp. 87-88.

26. LEROUX 1909; POULSEN, VALLOIS 1914; COULTON 1976, p. 233; BRUNEAY, DUCAT 1983, pp. 162-163.

27. See, e.g., LECLANT 1979, p. 304, fig. 381.

28. VITRUVIUS 143, 15-26.

29. *Guide de Thasos*, French School at Athens 1967, p. 70, note 23. The building is now studied by J. des Courtils.

30. See in general LEHMANN 1983; FRAZER 1982; THOMPSON 1982.

31. LEHMANN, SPITTLE 1982; LEHMANN 1983, pp. 63-69.

32. For this last building, see MARTIN 1959, pp.

59-91 ('building with paraskenia'); COULTON 1976, p. 288.

33. LEHMANN 1972; LEHMANN, SPITTLE 1982.

34. LEHMANN 1969; LEHMANN 1983, pp. 69-75.

35. LEHMANN 1964; LEHMANN 1969, III, pp. 207-208, 216.

36. CONZE 1875, pp. 77-85; LEHMANN 1983, pp. 53-59; MCCREDIE, ROUX, SHAW, KURTICH 1992.

37. CONZE 1880, pp. 35-45; MCCREDIE 1968, pp. 212-216; ROUX 1981-1; LEHMANN 1983, pp. 90-92; FRAZER 1990.

38. FRAZER 1982, p. 199.

39. MILLER 1979; MILLER 1980.

40. FRAZER 1982, p. 199; and *supra*, p. 29.

41. MILLER 1971, pp. 213-217; LEHMANN 1983, pp. 93-94.

42. On this influence, see MILLER 1971, pp. 15-89.

43. LEHMANN, SPITTLE 1964; MILLER 1971, pp. 217-221; LEHMANN 1983, pp. 77-78.

44. BRONEER 1967; SEYRIG 1965.

45. TOUCHAIS 1987, p. 557; 1988, p. 668; 1989, p. 663.

46. MCCREDIE 1976, p. 76; COULTON 1976, p. 281; LEHMANN 1983, pp. 83-86.

47. MARTIN 1959, pl. B, building II; COULTON 1976, p. 287.

48. See *supra*, p. 196 and pp. 197-198.

49. PANDERMALIS 1976 and *supra*, p. 84.

50. See *supra*, p. 89.

51. TOMLINSON 1970, pp. 311-312.

52. But see the new dating by TOMLINSON 1990.

53. COULTON 1976, p. 56 and *passim*.

54. See *supra*, p. 66.

55. On this subject, Coulton cites the Gateway of Zeus on Thasos, *infra*, p. 218, and the façade of the Great Tomb at Lefkadia, *supra*, pp. 178-181.

56. For example, on the upper storey, the half-column affixed to a pillar and the heart-shaped arrangement [en cœur] on the angle.

57. BRONEER 1954, pp. 98-99.

58. COULTON 1976, pp. 57-58 and *passim*.

59. VOLLMOELLER 1901; SCHEFOLD, AUBERSON 1972, pp. 149-151.

60. MILLER 1979, p. 103.

61. MARTIN 1947, especially pp. 130-147.

62. GINOUVÈS 1959, p. 15 and p. 17, fig. 18.

62 . ETIENNE 1986, p. 191.

63. COURBY 1927, pp. 237-240; BOMMELAER 1991, pp. 225-227; BRIANT 1991, pp. 216-224 with recent bibliography.

64. PICARD 1963, pp. 142-150, 153; and, for its relation to the mosaics of Pella, VASIC 1979.

65. MCCREDIE 1974.

66. LAWRENCE 1957, p. 187.

67. For the idea of baroque in art, see BURCKHARDT 1860; for baroque as a stage in the evolution of styles, WÖLFFLIN 1888 and 1915; E. D'ORS 1935, who distinguishes twenty-two different baroques; FOCILLON 1936, who already recognises Hellenistic baroque. For the last, see mainly LYTTELTON 1974.

68. It has been noted that, in the baroque church, the façade is frequently 'a monument in itself', see LELIEVRE 1963, p. 108.

69. See *supra*, p. 147.

70. See *supra*, p. 147, note 3.

71. See *supra*, pp. 84-86 and 89.

72. This despite the difficulty of establishing the political relations between Macedonia and Thasos; for the period between the fourth century and 196 BC, see POUILLOUX 1954, pp. 422-438; PICARD 1985.

73. MARTIN 1968, pp. 172-176. This complex is also studied by J. des Courtils.

74. See *supra*, fig. 151.

75. MARTIN 1968, p. 176. Reference should be made in this context to the superposition of orders, which is perhaps to be found on the same site on Thasos in the structure of the stage of the theatre; see SALVIAT 1960.

76. MERTENS 1982, pp. 132-133. See also a 'royal tomb' like that at Selce in modern Albania (first half of the third century BC).

77. See especially the dissemination in southern Italy of the floral decoration cited *supra*, pp. 129-130.

78. LYTTELTON 1974; and, now, MCKENZIE 1990.

79. TAPIE 1972, p. 19, pp. 160-165 and *passim;* for baroque since the Renaissance, he cites the triumph of the Church and the monarchies, and the consolidation of landed property: 'Baroque is at once monarchical, aristocratic, religious and related to land'.

THE END OF THE KINGDOM OF MACEDONIA
(pages 220-229)

1. See *supra*, p. 73

BIBLIOGRAPHIE

The books whose titles are in Greek and also in some other language are cited here — for obvious practical reasons — only in this other language. Similarly, when an article in Greek is accompanied by an abstract in some other language, we have cited its title in this other language followed by the indication: (in Gr.). In such cases, we cite the name of the author in the transription which has been used in the relevant publication.

Periodicals are indicated with the followings abbreviations.

AA: Archäologischer Anzeiger.

AAA: Athens Annals of Archaeology.

ABSA: Annual of the British School at Athens.

AJA: American Journal of Archaeology.

AM: Mitteilungen des deutschen Archäologischen Instituts. Athenische Abteilung.

Ant. K: Antike Kunst.

BCH: Bulletin de Correspondance hellénique.

CRAI: Comptes rendus des séances. Académie des inscriptions et belles-lettres.

Deltion: Ἀρχαιολογικὸν Δελτίον.

JdI: Jahrbuch des deutschen Archäologischen Instituts.

JHS: The Journal of Hellenic Studies.

PAPS: Proceedings of the American Philosophical Association.

Praktika: Πρακτικὰ τῆς ἐν Ἀθήναις Ἀρχαιολογικῆς Ἑταιρείας.

RA: Revue archéologique.

RIA: Rivista dell'Istituto Nazionale d'Archeologia e Storia dell'Arte.

AKAMATIS 1985 = Ι. ΑΚΑΜΑΤΗΣ, *Πήλινες μῆτρες ἀγγείων ἀπὸ τὴν Πέλλα. Συμβολὴ στὴ μελέτη τῆς ἑλληνιστικῆς κεραμεικῆς.* Thessalonike, 1985.

AKAMATIS 1986 = I. AKAMATIS, «L'agora de Pella: premiers résultats des fouilles», in *Μνήμη Λαζαρίδη* 1986, p. 175-193.

AKAMATIS 1987-1 = I. AKAMATIS, «Xanthos son of Demetrios and Amadika» (in Gr.), in *Ἀμητός* 1987, p. 13-29.

AKAMATIS 1987-2 = I. AKAMATIS, «Board from the Agora of Pella» (in Gr.), *Μακεδονία καὶ Θράκη* 1, 1987, p. 125-136.

AKAMATIS 1988 = I. AKAMATIS, «The Agora of Pella» (in Gr.), *Μακεδονία καὶ Θράκη* 2, 1988, p. 75-90.

AKAMATIS 1989-1 = I. AKAMATIS, «Additional Excavation Data Concerning the Final Destruction of the Agora at Pella» (in Gr.), *Egnatia* 1, 1989, p. 173-193.

AKAMATIS 1989-2 = Ι. ΑΚΑΜΑΤΗΣ, «Ἀνασκαφή αγοράς Πέλλας», *Egnatia* 2, 1989, chron., p. 423-434.

AKAMATIS 1989-3 = I. AKAMATIS, «Pella, Agora 1989», *Μακεδονία καὶ Θράκη* 3, 1989, p. 76-90.

ALABE 1987 = F. ALABE, «Les revêtements muraux de la maison de l'Epée», *BCH* 111, 1987, p. 642-644.

Alexander the Great = Alexander the Great, History and Legend in Art, Arch. Museum of Thessalonike 1980.

ALEXANDER 1963 = J. A. ALEXANDER, *Potidea, Its History and Remains.* Atlanta 1963.

Ametos 1987 = ΑΜΗΤΟΣ, *Τιμητικὸς τόμος γιὰ τὸν καθηγητὴ Μ. Ἀνδρόνικο.* Thessalonike 1987.

Ancient Macedonia 1988 = Ancient Macedonia, Melbourne, Brisbane, Sydney. Athens 1988.

Ancient Macedonia I 1968 = Ancient Macedonia I, Papers Read at the First International Symposium Held in Thessaloniki, 1968. Thessalonike 1970.

Ancient Macedonia II 1973 = Ancient Macedonia II, Papers... Second International Symposium... 1973. Thessalonike 1977.

Ancient Macedonia III 1977 = Ancient Macedonia III. Papers... Third International Symposium... 1977. Thessalonike 1983.

Ancient Macedonia IV 1983 = Ancient Macedonia IV, Papers... Fourth International Symposium... 1983. Thessalonike 1986.

Ancient Macedonia V 1989 = Ancient Macedonia V, Papers... Fifth International Symposium... 1989. Thessalonike 1993.

ANDRONICOS 1955 = Μ. ΑΝΔΡΟΝΙΚΟΣ, «Ἑλληνιστικὸς τάφος Βεροίας», *Arch. Eph.* 1955, p. 22-50.

ANDRONICOS, MAKARONAS, MOUTSOPOULOS, BAKALAKIS 1961 = Μ. ΑΝΔΡΟΝΙΚΟΣ, Χ. ΜΑΚΑΡΟΝΑΣ, Ν. ΜΟΥΤΣΟΠΟΥΛΟΣ, Γ. ΜΠΑΚΑΛΑΚΗΣ, *Τὸ ἀνάκτορον τῆς Βεργίνας.* Athens 1961.

ANDRONICOS 1964 = M. ANDRONIKOS, *Vergina, The Prehistoric Necropolis and the Hellenistic Palace,* Studies in Mediterranean Archaeology 13, Lund, 1964.

ANDRONICOS 1969 = Μ. ΑΝΔΡΟΝΙΚΟΣ, *Βεργίνα I. Τὸ νεκροταφεῖον τῶν τύμβων.* Athens 1969.

ANDRONICOS 1976 = M. ANDRONIKOS, «Pella Museum», in *Die griechischen Museen.* Athens 1976.

ANDRONICOS 1977 = M. ANDRONIKOS, «The Royal Graves in the Great Tumulus», *AAA X,* 1977, p. 40-72.

ANDRONICOS 1980 = M. ANDRONIKOS, «The Royal Tomb at Vergina and the Problem of the Dead», *AAA* XIII, 1980, p. 168-178.

ANDRONICOS 1982 = M. ANDRONIKOS, «Art during the Archaic and Classical Period», in SAKELLARIOU 1982, p. 92-109.

ANDRONICOS 1984-1 = M. ANDRONIKOS, *Vergina, the Royal Tombs and the Ancient City.* Athens 1984.

ANDRONICOS 1984-2 = Μ. ΑΝΔΡΟΝΙΚΟΣ «Ἀνασκαφὴ Βεργίνας 1984», *Praktika* 1984 (1988), p. 66-70.

ANDRONICOS 1985 = Μ. ΑΝΔΡΟΝΙΚΟΣ, «Τύμβος Παλατιτσίων», *Praktika* 1985 (1990), p. 55-59.

ANDRONICOS 1987-1 = M. ANDRONIKOS, «Some Reflections on the Macedonian Tombs», *ABSA* 82, 1987, p. 1-16.

ANDRONICOS 1987-2 = Μ. ΑΝΔΡΟΝΙΚΟΣ «Ἡ ζωγραφικὴ στὴν ἀρχαία Μακεδονία», *Arch. Eph.*, 1987, p. 361-382.

ANDRONICOS 1987-3 = M. ANDRONIKOS, «Vergina, the Excavation of 1987» (in Gr.), *Μακεδονία καὶ Θράκη* 1, 1987, p. 81-88.

ANDRONICOS 1988 = M. ANDRONIKOS, «Vergina 1988. Excavation in the Gemetery» (in Gr.), *Μακεδονία καὶ Θράκη* 2, 1988, p. 1-3.

BAKALAKIS 1963 = G. BAKALAKIS, «Therme-Thessaloniki», in *Neue Ausgrabungen in Griechenland, Ant. K. Beiheft* 1, 1963, p. 30-34.

BESSIOS 1989 = Μ. ΜΠΕΣΣΙΟΣ, «Μαρτυρίες Πύδνας. Τὸ ψήφισμα τοῦ Ἀπόλλωνος Δεκαδρυου», *Ancient Macedonia* V, Thessalonike 1993.

BEZERRA DE MENESES 1970 = U. BEZERRA DE MENESES, in *Exploration archéologique de Délos* 27, *L'Ilot de la maison des Comédiens,* 1970, p. 151-193.

BOARDMAN 1970 = J. BOARDMAN, «Travelling Rugs», *Antiquity* 44, 1970, p. 143-144.

BOMMELAER 1991 = J. F. BOMMELAER, *Guide de Delphes. Le site.* Athens 1991.

BÖRKER 1978 = C. BÖRKER, «Mosaiken im Hause des Demetrios von Phaleron?», *Zeitschrift für Papyrologie und Epigraphik* 29, 1978, p. 43-48.

BORZA 1979 = E. N. BORZA, «Some Observations on Malaria and the Ecology of Central Macedonia in Antiquity», *AJA* 4, 1979, p. 102-124.

BORZA 1982-1 = E. N. BORZA, «The History and Archaeology of Macedonia: Retrospect and Prospect», in *Macedonia and Greece,* 1982, p. 17-30.

BORZA 1982-2 = E. N. BORZA, «The Natural Resources of Early Macedonia», in W. L. ADAMS, E. N. BORZA (ed), *Philip II, Alexander,* Washington D. C., 1982, p. 1-20.

BORZA 1987 = E. N. BORZA, «Timber and Politics in the Ancient World: Macedon and the Greeks», *PAPS* 131, 1987, p. 32-52.

BORZA 1990 = E. N. BORZA, *In the Shadow of Olympus. The Emergence of Macedon.* Princeton 1990.

BOYD 1978 = T. D. BOYD, «The Arch and the Vault in Greek Architecture», *AJA* 82, 1978, p. 83-100.

BRIANT 1991 = P. BRIANT, «Chasses royales macédoniennes et chasses royales perses: le thème de la chasse au lion sur la Chasse de Vergina», *Dialogues d'histoire ancienne* 17, 1, 1991, p. 211-255.

BRIXHE, PANAYOTOU 1988 = C. BRIXHE A. PA-NAYOTOU, «L'atticisation de la Macédoine: l'une des sources de la koinè», *Verbum* 11, 1988, p. 245-260.

BRONEER 1941 = O. BRONEER, *The Lion Monument at Amphipolis.* Cambridge, Mass. 1941.

BRONEER 1954 = O. BRONEER, *Corinth* I 4. *The South Stoa and its Roman Successors.* Princeton 1954.

BRONEER, LEHMANN, SPITTLE 1967 = O. BRO-NEER, C. R. DE LEHMANN, D. SPITTLE, «Altar Court», AJA 71, 1967, p. 96-98.

BRUNEAU 1972 = Ph. BRUNEAU, *Exploration archéologique de Délos.* XXIX. *Les mosaïques.* Athens 1972.

BRUNEAU 1976 = Ph. BRUNEAU, «La mosaïque grecque classique et hellénistique», *Archeologia* (Warsaw) 27, 1976, p. 12-42.

BRUNEAU, DUCAT 1983 = Ph. BRUNEAU, J. DU-CAT, *Guide de Délos.* Ecole française d'Athènes, Athens, Paris 1983.

BRUNEAU 1987 = Ph. BRUNEAU, *La Mosaïque antique.* Paris 1987.

BRUNO 1969 = V. J. BRUNO, «Antecedents of the Pompeian First Style», *AJA* 73, 1979, p. 305-317.

BRUNO 1977 = V. J. BRUNO, *Form and Color in Greek Painting.* New York 1977.

BRUNO 1981 = V. J. BRUNO, «The Painted Metopes at Lefkadia and the Problem of Color in Doric Sculptured Metopes», *AJA* 85, 1981, p. 3-11.

BURCKHARDT 1860 = J. BURCKHARDT, *Der Cicerone,* Basel 1860.

CALAMIOTOU, SIGANIDOU, FILIPPAKIS 1983 = M. CALAMIOTOU, M. SIGANIDOU, S. E. FILIPPAKIS, «X-Ray Analysis of Pigments from Pella, Greece», *Studies in Conservation* 28, 1983, p. 117-121.

CAWKWELL 1978 = G. CAWKWELL, *Philip of Macedon.* London 1978.

CHAMONARD 1922, 1924 = J. CHAMONARD, *Exploration archéologique de Délos,* VIII 1 et 2, *Le quartier du Théâtre.* p. 357-391.

CHARBONNEAUX 1925 = J. CHARBONNEAUX, *Fouilles de Delphes II. La tholos.* Athens 1925.

CHARBONNEAUX, MARTIN, VILLARD 1970 = J. CHARBONNEAUX, R. MARTIN, Fr. VILLARD, *La Grèce hellénistique.* Paris, 1970.

CHRYSOSTOMOU 1986 = P. CHRYSOSTOMOU, «Topographie du nord de la Bottiée: le territoire de Pella» (in Gr.), in *Μνήμη Λαζαρίδη.* 1986, p. 205-238.

CHRYSOSTOMOU 1987-1 = A. CHRYSOSTOMOU, «Burial Mounds in the Area of Pella» (in Gr.), *Μακεδονία καὶ Θράκη* 1, p. 147-159.

CHRYSOSTOMOU 1987-2 = A. CHRYSOSTOMOU, «The City Wall of Edessa» (in Gr.), *Μακεδονία καὶ Θράκη* 1, p. 161-169.

CHRYSOSTOMOU 1988-1 = A. CHRYSOSTOMOU, «Latest Research on the Wall of Edessa» (in Gr.), *Μακεδονία καὶ Θράκη* 2, p. 55-67.

CHRYSOSTOMOU 1988-2 = A. CHRYSOSTOMOU, «The Baths of the Palace at Pella» (in Gr.), *Μακεδονία καὶ Θράκη* 2, p. 113-126.

CHRYSOSTOMOU 1989 = P. CHRYSOSTOMOU, «On the Cult of the Syrian Goddess (Atargatis) in Western Macedonia» (in Gr), *Μακεδονία καὶ Θράκη* 3, p. 103-117.

CONZE 1875 = A. CONZE, A. HAUSER, G. NIE-MANN, *Archaeologische Untersuchungen auf Samothrake,* I. Vienna 1875.

CONZE 1880 = A. CONZE, A. HAUSER, G. BENN-DORF, *Neue archaeologische Untersuchungen auf Samothrake.* Vienna 1880.

COULTON 1968 = J. J. COULTON, «The Stoa at the Amphiaraion, Oropos», *ABSA* 63, 1968, p. 147-183.

COULTON 1976 = J. J. COULTON, *The Architectural Development of the Greek Stoa.* Oxford 1976.

COURBY 1912 = F. COURBY, *Exploration archéologiqué de Délos V. Le Portique d'Antigone.* Paris 1912.

COURBY 1927 = F. COURBY, *Fouilles de Delphes II, La terrasse du temple.* Paris 1927.

CURTIUS et alii 1892 = *Olympia: Ergebnisse,* II. Berlin 1892.

DAFFA-NIKONANOU 1986 = A. ΔΑΦΦΑ-ΝΙΚΟΝΑ-ΝΟΥ, «Κτερίσματα ἑλληνιστικοῦ τάφου στὴ Νεάπολη τῆς Θεσσαλονίκης», *Makedonika* 25, 1985-6, p. 180-202.

DAFFA-NIKONANOU 1987 = A. DAFFA-NIKONANOU. «Zwei Importvasen aus dem Grab von Neapolis in Thessaloniki», in Ἀμητός 1987, p. 263-277.

DASZEWSKI 1978 = W. A. DASZEWSKI, «Some Problems of Early Mosaics from Egypt», in *Das Ptolemäische Aegypten,* Berlin 1978, p. 123-136.

DASZEWSKI 1985 = W. A. DASZEWSKI, *Corpus of Mosaics from Egypt, I. Hellenistic and Early Roman Period.* Mainz 1985.

DE FRANCISCIS 1991 = A. DE FRANCISCIS, K. SCHEFOLD, A. LAIDLAW, V. M. STROCKA, U. PAPPALARDO, G. CERULLI IRELLI, E. SIMON, W. J. Th. PETERS, ST. DE CARO, F. ZEVI, M. AOYA-GI, *La pittura di Pompei.* Milan, 1991.

DESPINI 1980 = A. ΔΕΣΠΟΙΝΗ, «Ὁ τάφος τῆς Κατερίνης», *AAA* 13, 1980, p. 198-209.

DESPINI 1982 = A. ΔΕΣΠΟΙΝΗ, «Κεραμεικοὶ κλί-βανοι Σίνδου», *Arch.Eph.* 1982, p. 61-84.

DESPINI 1983 = A. ΔΕΣΠΟΙΝΗ, «Χρυσά σκουλαρί-κια Σίνδου», *Ancient Macedonia IV,* 1983 (1986), p. 159-169.

D'ORS 1935 = E. D'ORS, *Du baroque.* Paris 1935.

DROUGOU 1989 = St. DROUGOU, «The Ancient Theatre of Vergina and the Area around it», *Μακεδονία καὶ Θράκη* 3, 1989, p. 13-23.

DROUGOU 1991 = St. DROUGOU (ed.), *Hellenistic Ceramic in Makedonia.* 1. Athens 1991.

DROUGOU, TOURATSOGLOU 1980 = ΣΤ. ΔΡΟΥΓΟΥ, Ι. ΤΟΥΡΑΤΣΟΓΛΟΥ, Ἑλληνιστικοὶ λαξευτοὶ τάφοι Βεροίας. Athens 1980.

DROUGOU, TOURATSOGLOU 1991 = ST. DROU-GOU, I. TOURATSOGLOU, «Hellenistische Keramik aus Makedonien: chronologischen Indizien», *Ant. K.* 34, 1991, p. 13-27.

DUCREY, METZGER 1979 = P. DUCREY, I. R. METZGER, «La Maison aux mosaïques à Erétrie», *Ant. K.* 1, 1979, p. 3-21.

DUCREY 1991 = P. DUCREY, *Erétrie, Guide de la Maison aux mosaïques,* Athens 1991.

EDSON 1968 = Ch. EDSON, «Early Macedonia», *Ancient Macedonia I,* 1968 (1970), I, p. 17-44.

ELLIS 1976 = J. R. ELLIS, *Philipp II and Macedonian Imperialism.* London 1976.

ERRINGTON 1986 = M. ERRINGTON, *Geschichte Makedoniens,* Munich 1986.

ETIENNE 1986 = R. ETIENNE, *Ténos I, Les sanctuaires de Poséidon et d'Amphitrite.* Athens, Paris 1986.

FAKLARIS 1983 = Π. ΦΑΚΛΑΡΗΣ, «Πήλινες μῆτρες, σφραγίδες καὶ ἀνάγλυφα ἀγγεῖα ἀπὸ τὴ Βεργίνα», *Deltion* 38, 1983, p. 213-238.

FAKLARIS 1989 = P. FAKLARIS, «Excavation at the Acropolis of Vergina», *Μακεδονία καὶ Θράκη* 3, 1989, p. 37-44.

FITTSCHEN 1976 = K. FITTSCHEN, «Zur Herkunft und Entstehung des 2. Stils - Probleme und Argumente», in *Hellenismus in Mittelitalien,* 1976, p. 541-563.

FLOREN 1987 = J. FLOREN. *Die geometrische und archaische Plastik,* volume I of W. FUCHS, J. FLOREN, *Die griechische Plastik.* Munich 1987.

FOCILLON 1936 = H. FOCILLON, *Vie des formes.* Paris 1936.

FRAZER 1982 = A. FRAZER, «Macedonia and Samothrace. Two Architectural Late Bloomers», in *Macedonia and Greece,* 1982, p. 191-203.

FRAZER 1990 = A. FRAZER, *Samothrace 10, The Propylon of Ptolemy II.* Princeton 1990.

GIANNOULI, GUIMIER-SORBETS 1988 = V. GIANNOULI, A. M. GUIMIER-SORBETS, «Deux mosaïques hellénistiques à Samos», *BCH* 112, 1988, p. 545-568.

GINOUVES 1959 = R. GINOUVES, *L'Établissement thermal de Gortys d'Arcadie.* Paris 1959.

GIOURI 1972 = E. ΓΙΟΥΡΗ, «Ἡ κεραμεικὴ τῆς Χαλκιδικῆς στὸν 4ο αἰ. π.Χ.», in *Κέρνος Γ. ΜΠΑΚΑΛΑΚΗ.* Thessalonike, p. 6-14.

GIOURI 1974 = E. ΓΙΟΥΡΗ, «Τὸ ἐν Ἀφύτει ἱερόν τοῦ Διονύσου καὶ τὸ ἱερόν τοῦ Ἄμμωνος Διός», in *Neue Forschungen in griechischen Heiligtümnern, Intern. Symposion in Olympia,* p. 135-150.

GIOURI 1978 = E. GIOURI. *Ὁ κρατήρας τοῦ Δερβενίου.* Athens 1978.

GOSSEL 1980 = B. GOSSEL, *Makedonische Kammergräber,* Berlin 1980.

GOUNAROPOULOU, HATZOPOULOS 1985 = L. GOUNAROPOULOU, M. B. HATZOPOULOS. *Les Milliaires de la voie Egnatienne entre Héraclée des Lyncestes et Thessalonique (Μελετήματα 1),* 1985.

GRAMMENOS 1988 = D. GRAMMENOS, «The Neolithic Period in Northern Greece», *Ancient Macedonia* 1988, p. 71-73.

GRAMMENOS 1991 = Δ. B. ΓΡΑΜΜΕΝΟΣ, *Νεολιθικὲς ἔρευνες στὴν Κεντρικὴ καὶ Ἀνατολικὴ Μακεδονία.* Athens 1991.

GUIMIER-SORBETS 1987 = A. M. GUIMIER-SORBETS, «Mosaïques et dallages dans le monde grec aux époques classique et hellénistique». *Vᵉ Colloque international pour l'étude des mosaïques antiques.* Bath, September 1987.

GUIMIER-SORBETS 1990 = A. M. GUIMIER-SORBETS, «Techniques de la mosaïque classique et hellénistique: le trait et la couleur», *VIᵉ Colloque international pour l'étude des mosaïques antiques.* Palencia-Merida, 14-21 October 1990.

GUIMIER-SORBETS, NENNA 1992 = A. M. GUIMIER-SORBETS, M. D. NENNA, «L'emploi du verre, de la faïence et de la peinture dans les mosaïques de Délos», *BCH* 116, 1992, p. 607-631.

GUIMIER-SORBETS 1993 = A. M. GUIMIER-SORBETS, «La mosaïque hellénistique de Dyrrhachion et sa place dans la série des mosaïques grecques à décor végétal». *L'Illyrie méridionale et l'Epire dans l'Antiquité,* II, Paris, 1993, p. 135-141.

HADZISTELIOU-PRICE 1973 = T. HADZISTELIOU-PRICE, «An Enigma in Pella: the Tholos and Herakles Phylakos», *AJA* 77, 1973, p. 66-71.

HAMMOND 1972 = N. G. L. HAMMOND, *A History of Macedonia,* I. Oxford 1972.

HAMMOND, GRIFFITH 1979 = N. G. L. HAMMOND, G. T. GRIFFITH, *A History of Macedonia,* II, *550-336 B.C.* Oxford 1979.

HAMMOND, WALBANK 1988 = N. G. L. HAMMOND, F. W. WALBANK, *A History of Macedonia,* III, *336-167 B.C.* Oxford 1988.

HAMMOND 1989 = N. G. L. HAMMOND, *The Macedonian State,* Oxford 1989.

HATZOPOULOS, LOUKOPOULOU 1980 = M. B. HATZOPOULOS, L. D. LOUKOPOULOU (ed.), *Philippe de Macédoine,* Athens 1980.

HATZOPOULOS 1981 = M. B. HATZOPOULOS, «A Century and a Lustrum of Macedonian Studies», *The Ancient World* 4, 1981, p. 91-108.

HATZOPOULOS 1986 = M. B. HATZOPOULOS, «Territoire et villages de Béroia» (in Gr.), in *Μνήμη Λαζαρίδη* 1986, p. 57-68.

HATZOPOULOS, LOUKOPOULOU 1987 = M. B. HATZOPOULOS, L. D. LOUKOPOULOU, *Two Studies in Ancient Macedonian Topography (Μελετήματα 3). Athens 1987.*

HATZOPOULOS 1988-1 = M. B. HATZOPOULOS, Une donation du roi Lysimaque (Μελετήματα 5). Athens 1988.

HATZOPOULOS 1988-2 = M. B. HATZOPOULOS, *Bulletin épigraphique* 1988, no 861, p. 448-449.

HATZOPOULOS 1988-3 E M. B. HATZOPOULOS, *Actes de vente de la Chalcidique centrale (Μελετήματα 6). Athens 1988.*

HATZOPOULOS, LOUKOPOULOU 1989 = M. B. HATZOPOULOS, L. D. LOUKOPOULOU, *Morrylos, cité de la Crestonie (Μελετήματα 7). Athens 1989.*

HATZOPOULOS 1990 = M. B. HATZOPOULOS, «Les épigraphistes français en Macédoine», in *Actes du colloque international du Centenaire de l'Année épigraphique,* Paris 1990, p. 205-221.

HATZOPOULOS 1991 = M. B. HATZOPOULOS, *Actes de vente d'Amphipolis (Μελετήματα 14).* Athens 1991.

HATZOPOULOS s.d. = M. B. HATZOPOULOS, *Macedonian Institutions under the Kings: a Historical and Epigraphic Study.* Forthcoming.

HEUZEY 1860 = L. HEUZEY, *Le Mont Olympe et l'Acarnanie.* Paris 1860.

HEUZEY, DAUMET 1876 = L. HEUZEY, H. DAUMET, *Mission archéologique de Macédoine.* Paris 1876.

HOEPFNER, SCHWANDNER 1986 = W. HOEPFNER, L. SCHWANDNER, *Haus und Stadt im klassischen Griechenland,* I. Munich 1986.

Ἱστορία 1973 = Ἱστορία τοῦ Ἑλληνικοῦ Ἔθνους, IV. Athens 1973.

JOST 1985 = M. JOST, *Sanctuaires et cultes en Arcadie.* Paris 1985.

KAHIL 1988 = L. KAHIL, «Helene», in *Lexicon Iconographicum Mythologiae Classicae* IV, 1988, p. 498-562.

KAHIL 1991 = L. KAHIL, «Artémis, Dionysos et Pan à Athènes», *Hesperia* 60 (4), 1991, p. 511-523.

KALLERIS 1954, 1976 = N. KALLERIS, *Les Anciens Macédoniens,* I, 1954; II, 1976. Athens.

KALTSAS 1985 = N. E. ΚΑΛΤΣΑΣ, *Πήλινες διακοσμημένες κεραμώσεις ἀπὸ τῇ Μακεδονία.* Athens 1985.

KARADEDOS 1983 = Γ. ΚΑΡΑΔΕΔΟΣ, «Τὸ ἑλληνιστικὸ θέατρο τοῦ Δίου», *Ancient Macedonia IV,* 1983 (1986), p. 325-340.

KARAMITROU-MENDESSIDI 1988 = G. KARAMITROU-MENDESSIDI, «The Cemetery of Aiani» (in Gr.), *Μακεδονία καὶ Θράκη* 2, 1988, p. 19-25.

KARAMITROU-MENDESSIDI 1989-1 = G. KARAMITROU-MENDESSIDI, «The Excavation Research at Aiani», *Μακεδονία καὶ Θράκη* 3, 1989, p. 45-57.

KARAMITROU-MENDESSIDI 1989-2 = G. KARAMITROU-MENDESSIDI, *Aiani of Kozani, Archaeological Guide.* Thessalonike 1989.

KINCH 1920 = K. F. KINCH, «Le tombeau de Niausta», in *Danske Vidensk. Selskab. 7 R. Hist.-Filos. Skrifter. Afd. IV 3,* 1920, p. 283-288.

KOSTOGLOU-DESPINE 1979 = A. ΚΩΣΤΟΓΛΟΥ-ΔΕΣΠΟΙΝΗ, *Προβλήματα τῆς Παριανῆς πλαστικῆς του 5ου αἰ. π. Χ.* Thessalonike 1979.

KOTTARIDOU 1987 = A. KOTTARIDOU, «Excavations at the NW Part of Aigai», *Μακεδονία καὶ Θράκη* 1, 1987, p. 109-113.

KOTTARIDOU 1989 = A. KOTTARIDOU, «Vergina 1989. The Excavation of the Cemetery», *Μακεδονία καὶ Θράκη* 3, 1989, p. 1-11.

KOTZIAS 1937 = N. KOTZIAS, «Ὁ παρὰ τὸ ἀεροδρόμιον τῆς Θεσσαλονίκης (Σέδες) Γ΄ τάφος», *Arch. Eph.* 1937, p. 866-895.

KOUKOULI-CHRYSANTHAKI 1988 = Ch. KOUKOULI-CHRYSANTHAKI, «Macedonia in the Bronze Age», *Ancient Macedonia* 1988, p. 74-78.

KOUKOULI-CHRYSANTHAKI, MALAMIDOU 1989 = Ch. KOUKOULI-CHRYSANTHAKI, D. MALAMIDOU, «The Sanctuary of the Hero Auloneites on Mount Pangaion», *Μακεδονία καὶ Θράκη* 3, 1989, p. 553-567.

KRAUSE 1977 = C. KRAUSE, «Grundformen des griechischen Pastashauses», *AA* 1977, p. 164-179.

KUNZE, SCHLEIF 1944 = E. KUNZE, H. SCHLEIF (ed.), *Olympische Forschungen* 1. Berlin 1944.

KURTZ, BOARDMAN 1971 = D. C. KURTZ, J. BOARDMAN, *Greek Burial Customs*. London 1971.

KYRIELEIS 1969 = H. KYRIELEIS, «Throne und Klinen», *JdI-EH* 24. 1969.

LAIDLAW 1985 = A. LAIDLAW, *The First Style in Pompei: Painting and Architecture*. Rome 1985.

LAUTER 1986 = H. LAUTER, *Die Architektur des Hellenismus*. Darmstadt 1986.

LAUTER 1987 = H. LAUTER, «Les éléments de la Regia hellénistique», in *Le Système palatial en Orient, en Grèce et à Rome*, E. Lévy (ed.), Strasbourg 1987, p. 345-355.

LAWRENCE 1957 = A. W. LAWRENCE, *Greek Architecture*. Harmondsworth 1957.

LAZARIDI 1986 = K. D. LAZARIDI, «Le gymnase d'Amphipolis», in *Μνήμη Λαζαρίδη*, p. 241-273.

LAZARIDI 1987 = K. D. LAZARIDI, «Excavations at Amphipolis» («Le gymnase de l'ancienne Amphipolis») (in Gr.), *Μακεδονία καὶ Θράκη* I, 1987, p. 313-326.

LAZARIDI 1988 = K. D. LAZARIDI, «The Gymnasium of Amphipolis» (in Gr.), *Μακεδονία καὶ Θράκη* 2, 1988, p. 385-386.

LAZARIDI 1989 = K. D. LAZARIDI, «The Gymnasium of Amphipolis» (in Gr.), *Μακεδονία καὶ Θράκη* 3, 1989, p. 547-552.

LAZARIDIS 1955 = Δ. ΛΑΖΑΡΙΔΗΣ, «Ἀνασκαφαὶ καὶ ἔρευναι ἐν Ἀβδήροις», *Praktika* 1955 (1960), p. 160-164.

LAZARIDIS 1969 = Δ. Ι. ΛΑΖΑΡΙΔΗΣ, *Νεάπολις, Χριστούπολις, Καβάλα. Ὁδηγὸς Μουσείου Καβάλας*. Athens 1969.

LAZARIDIS 1977 = Δ. Ι. ΛΑΖΑΡΙΔΗΣ, «Ἀνασκαφὲς καὶ ἔρευνες Ἀμφιπόλεως», *Praktika* 1977 [1980], p. 38-45.

LAZARIDIS 1982, 1983 = Δ. ΛΑΖΑΡΙΔΗΣ, «Ἀνασκαφαὶ Ἀμφιπόλεως», *Praktika* 1982, p. 43-51, 1983, p. 35-41.

LECLANT 1979 = J. LECLANT, *L'Empire des Conquérants, l'Egypte au Nouvel Empire*. Paris 1979.

LEHMANN 1962 = K. LEHMANN, *Samothrace 4.1, The Hall of Votive Gifts*. New York 1962.

LEHMANN, SPITTLE 1964 = K. LEHMANN, D. SPITTLE, *Samothrace, 4. 2, The Altar Court*. New York 1964.

LEHMANN 1983 = K. LEHMANN, *Samothrace. A Guide to the Excavations and the Museum*, 5ᵉ ed., New York 1983.

LEHMANN 1964 = Ph. W. LEHMANN, «The Wall Decoration of the Hieron in Samothrace», *Balkan Studies* 5, 1964, p. 277-286.

LEHMANN 1969 = Ph. W. LEHMANN, *Samothrace 3. The Hieron*. Princeton 1969.

LEHMAN 1972 = Ph. W. LEHMANN, *Skopas in Samothrace*. Northampton, Mass. 1972.

LEHMANN 1979 = Ph. W. LEHMANN, «Lefkadia

and the Second Style», in *Studies in Classical Art and Archaeology. A Tribute to P. H. von Blanckenhagen*, G. Kopcke, M. B. Moore (ed.), Locust Valley, N. Y., p. 225-229.

LEHMANN, SPITTLE 1982 = Ph. W. LEHMANN, D. SPITTLE, *Samothrace 5, The Temenos*. Princeton 1982.

LELIEVRE 1963 = P. LELIEVRE, *L'Architecture française*. Paris 1963.

LE RIDER 1977 = G. LE RIDER, *Le Monnayage d'argent et d'or de Philippe II*. Paris 1977.

LEROUX 1909 = G. LEROUX, *Exploration archéologique de Délos*. II, *La salle hypostyle*. Paris 1909.

LILIMBAKI-AKAMATI 1986 = M. LILIMBAKI-A-KAMATI, «Sanctuaires de Pella» (in Gr.), in *Μνήμη Λαζαρίδη* 1986, p. 195-203.

LILIMBAKI-AKAMATI 1987-1 = M. LILIMBAKI-A-KAMATI, «A New Pebble Mosaic Floor in Pella» (in Gr.), in *Ἀμητός* 1987, p. 455-469.

LILIMBAKI-AKAMATI 1987-2 = M. ΛΙΛΙΜΠΑΚΗ-Α-ΚΑΜΑΤΗ, «Ἀνασκαφικὴ ἔρευνα στὴν περιοχὴ τοῦ Καναλιοῦ τῆς Πέλλας», *Μακεδονία καὶ Θράκη* 1, 1987, p. 137-145.

LILIMBAKI-AKAMATI 1988 = M. LILIMBAKI-A-KAMATI, *Ancient Macedonia* 1988, no 260, p. 306-307.

LYTTELTON 1974 = M. LYTTELTON, *Baroque Architecture in Classical Antiquity*. London 1974.

Macedonia and Greece 1982 = B. BARR-SHAR-RAR, E. N. BORZA (ed.), *Studies in the History of Art, 10, Macedonia and Greece in Late Classical and Early Hellenistic Times*. Washington 1982.

MACRIDY 1911 = T. MACRIDY, «Un tumulus macédonien à Langada», *JdI* 26, 1911, p. 193-215.

MAKARONAS 1953-1 = X. I. ΜΑΚΑΡΟΝΑΣ, «Λευκάδια», *Makedonika* 2, 1941-1952, p. 634-636.

MAKARONAS 1953-2 = Ch. I. MAKARONAS, *Praktika*, 1953, p. 133-140.

MAKARONAS 1955 = X. I. ΜΑΚΑΡΟΝΑΣ, «Ἀνασκαφὴ μακεδονικοῦ τάφου εἰς Καρύτσαν Πιερίας», *Praktika* 1955, p. 151-159.

MAKARONAS 1956 = X. I. ΜΑΚΑΡΟΝΑΣ, «Ἀνασκαφικὴ ἔρευνα μακεδονικοῦ τάφου ἐν Δίῳ Πιερίας», *Praktika* 1956, p. 131-138.

ΜΑΚΑΡΟΝΑΣ 1963 = X. I. ΜΑΚΑΡΟΝΑΣ, «Τάφοι παρὰ τὸ Δερβένι Θεσσαλονίκης», *Deltion* 18, B2, chron. 1963, p. 193-196.

MAKARONAS 1968 = X. I. ΜΑΚΑΡΟΝΑΣ, «Χρονολογικὰ ζητήματα τῆς Πέλλης», *Ancient Macedonia* I 1968 (1970), p. 162-167.

MAKARONAS, MILLER 1974 = Ch. I. MAKARO-NAS, Stella G. MILLER, «The Tomb of Lyson and Kallikles. A Painted Hellenistic Tomb», *Archaeology* 27, 1974, p. 249-259.

MAKARONAS, GIOURI 1989 = X. ΜΑΚΑΡΟΝΑΣ, E. ΓΙΟΥΡΗ, *Οἱ οἰκίες Ἁρπαγῆς τῆς Ἑλένης καὶ Διονύσου τῆς Πέλλας*. Athens 1989.

Μακεδονία καὶ Θράκη 1987, 1988, 1989 = Τὸ ἀρχαιολογικό Ἔργο στὴ Μακεδονία καὶ Θράκη. Thessalonike, 1, 1987 (1988); 2, 1988 (1991); 3, 1989 (1992).

MANSEL 1943 = A. M. MANSEL, *Die Kuppelgräber von Kirklareli in Thrakien*. Ankara 1943.

MARTIN 1947 = R. MARTIN, «Les enceintes de Gortys d'Arcadie», *BCH* 71-72, 1947-1948, p. 81-147.

MARTIN 1959 = R. MARTIN, *Etudes thasiennes VI. L'agora I*. Paris 1959.

MARTIN 1968 = R. MARTIN, «Sculpture et peinture dans les façades monumentales au IVᵉ siècle av. J.-C.», *RA* 1968, p. 171-184.

MARTIN 1974 = R. MARTIN, *L'Urbanisme dans la Grèce antique*, 2nd ed. Paris 1974.

MARTIN 1985 = T. R. MARTIN, *Sovereignty and Coinage in Classical Greece*. Princeton 1985.

McCREDIE 1968 = J. R. McCREDIE, «Samothrace. Preliminary Report on the Campaign of 1965-1967», *Hesperia* 37, 1968, p. 200-234.

McCREDIE 1974 = J. R. McCREDIE, «The Lantern of Demosthenes and Lysikrates, Son of Lysitheides, of Kikynna», in *Studies Presented to Sterling Dow*, 1974, p. 181-183.

McCREDIE 1976 = J. R. McCREDIE, «Recent Investigations in Samothrace», in *Neue Forschungen in griechischen Heiligtümern*, U. Jansen (ed.). Tübingen 1976.

McCREDIE, ROUX, SHAW, KURTICH 1992 = J. R. McCREDIE, G. ROUX, St. M. SHAW, J. KURTICH, *Samothrace 7. The Rotunda of Arsinoe*. Princeton 1992.

MERTENS 1982 = D. MERTENS, «Per l'urbanistica e l'architettura della Magna Grecia», in *Megale Hellas, nome e immagine*, Taranto, p. 97-141.

MILLER 1971 = Stella G. MILLER, *Hellenistic Macedonian Architecture. Its Style and Painted Ornamentation*. Bryn Mawr 1971.

MILLER 1973 = Stella G. MILLER, «The Philippeion and Macedonian Hellenistic Architecture», *AM* 88, 1973, p. 189-218.

MILLER 1982 = Stella G. MILLER, «Macedonian Tombs: Their Architecture and Architectural Decoration», in *Macedonia and Greece*, p. 153-171.

MILLER 1993 = Stella G. MILLER, *The Tomb of Lyson and Kallikles*. Mainz 1993.

MILLER 1972 = Stephen G. MILLER, «Round Pegs in Square Holes», *AJA* 76, 1972, p. 78-79.

MILLER 1979 = Stephen G. MILLER, «Excavations at Nemea», *Hesperia* 48, 1979, p. 96-103.

MILLER 1980 = Stephen G. MILLER, «Excavations at Nemea», *Hesperia* 49, 1980, p. 198-200.

Μνήμη Λαζαρίδη 1986 = MNHMH Δ. ΛΑΖΑΡΙΔΗ. *Πόλις καὶ χώρα στὴν ἀρχαία Μακεδονία καὶ Θράκη*. Thessalonike 1986 (1990).

MOOREN 1983 = L. MOOREN, «The Nature of the Hellenistic Monarchy», in *Egypt and the Hellenistic World, Proceedings of the International Colloquium, Leuven, 24-26 May 1982. Louvain 1983, p. 205-240.

MORENO 1965 = P. MORENO, «Il realismo nella pittura greca del 4 secolo a.C.», RIA 13-14, 1964-5, p. 27-98.

NEWELL 1927 = E. T. NEWELL, The Coinages of Demetrius Poliorcetes. London 1927.

OIKONOMOS 1914 = Γ. ΟΙΚΟΝΟΜΟΣ, «Πέλλα», Praktika, 1914, p. 127-148.

OIKONOMOS 1915 = Γ. ΟΙΚΟΝΟΜΟΣ, «Πέλλα», Praktika, 1915, p. 237-244.

OIKONOMOS 1926 = G. P. OIKONOMOS, «Bronzen von Pella», AM 51, 1926, p. 75-76.

PANAYOTOU 1990 = A. PANAYOTOU, «Des dialectes à la koinè: l'exemple de la Chalcidique», Ποικίλα (Μελετήματα 10), Athens 1990, p. 191-228.

PANDERMALIS 1972 = Δ. ΠΑΝΤΕΡΜΑΛΗΣ, «Ο νέος Μακεδονικὸς τάφος τῆς Βεργίνας», Makedonika 12, 1972, p. 147-182.

PANDERMALIS 1973 = Δ. ΠΑΝΤΕΡΜΑΛΗΣ, «Λατρεῖες καὶ ἱερὰ τοῦ Δίου Πιερίας», Ancient Macedonia II, 1973 (1977), p. 331-342.

PANDERMALIS 1976 = D. PANDERMALIS, «Beobachtungen zur Fassalenarchitektur und Aussichtsveranda im hellenistischen Makedonien», in P. ZANKER (ed.), Hellenismus in Mittelitalien, Göttingen 1976, p. 387-395.

PANDERMALIS 1987 = D. PANDERMALIS, «Die Dachziegel des Palastes von Vergina» (in Gr.), in Ἀμητός 1987, p. 579-605.

PANDERMALIS 1989 = Δ. ΠΑΝΤΕΡΜΑΛΗΣ, «Δῖον», Ἀρχαιολογία 33, 1989, p. 5-53.

PANDERMALIS 1992 = D. PANDERMALIS, «Le sanctuaire grec de Dion», Archeologia 279, 1992, p. 14-23.

PAPAKONSTANTINOU-DIAMANTOYROУ 1971 = Δ. ΠΑΠΑΚΩΝΣΤΑΝΤΙΝΟΥ-ΔΙΑΜΑΝΤΟΥΡΟΥ, Πέλλα I. Ἱστορικὴ ἐπισκόπησις καὶ μαρτυρίαι. Athens 1971.

PAPAZOGLOU 1977 = F. PAPAZOGLOU, «Structures ethniques et sociales dans les régions centrales des Balkans la lumière des études onomastiques», Actes du VIIᵉ Congrès international d'épigraphie grecque et latine. Constantza Septembre 1977. Bucarest, Paris 1979, p. 153-169.

PAPAZOGLOU 1988 = F. PAPAZOGLOU, «Les villes de Macédoine à l'époque romaine», BCH, Suppl. XVI, 1988, p. 1-11.

Pella 1987 = Πέλλα, πρωτεύουσα τῶν ἀρχαίων Μακεδόνων. 30 χρόνια ἀνασκαφῆς, 1957-1987. Thessalonike 1987.

PETRAKOS 1968 = Β. Χ. ΠΕΤΡΑΚΟΣ. Ὁ Ὠρωπὸς καὶ τὸ ἱερὸν τοῦ Ἀμφιαράου. Athens 1968.

PETSAS 1960 = Ph. M. PETSAS, «Pella. Literary Tradition and Archaeological Reserarch», Balkan Studies I, 1960, p. 113-128.

PETSAS 1964 = Ph. M. PETSAS, «Ten years at Pella», Archaeology 17, 1964, p. 74-84.

PETSAS 1966 = Φ. Μ. ΠΕΤΣΑΣ, Ὁ τάφος τῶν Λυκαδίων, Athens 1966.

PETSAS 1968 = Φ. Μ. ΠΕΤΣΑΣ, «Ἀνασκαφή Ναούσης», Praktika 1968, p. 65-71.

PETSAS 1976 = Ph. M. PETSAS, «Pella», in Princeton Encyclopedia of Classical Sites, Princeton, 1976, p. 685-686.

PETSAS 1978 = Ph. M. PETSAS, Pella, Alexander the Great's Capital. Thessalonike 1978.

PICARD 1963 = Ch. PICARD, Manuel d'archéologie grecque. La sculpture, 4.2. La période classique. IVᵉ siècle, 2ᵉ partie. Paris 1963.

PICARD 1985 = O. PICARD, «Thasos et la Macédoine aux IVᵉ et IIIᵉ siècles», CRAI 1985, p. 760-776.

Pittura ellenistica 1985 = Ricerche di Pittura Ellenistica. Rome 1985.

POLACCO 1986 = L. POLACCO, «In Macedonia, sulle tracce di Euripide», Dioniso 56, 1986, p. 17-30.

POUILLOUX 1954 = J. POUILLOUX, Etudes Thasiennes III. Recherches sur l'histoire et les cultes de Thasos. I. De la fondation de la cité à 196 av. J. C. Paris 1954.

POULSEN, VALLOIS 1914 = G. POULSEN, R. VALLOIS, Exploration Archéologique de Délos II, complément. Nouvelles recherches sur la salle hypostyle. Paris 1914.

PRAG 1990 = A. J. N. W. PRAG, «Reconstructing King Philip II: The "Nice" Version», AJA 94, 1990, p. 237-247.

PRESTIANNI GIALLOMBARDO 1991 = A. M. PRESTIANNI GIALLOMBARDO, «Recenti testimonianze iconografiche sulla kausia in Macedonia e la datazione del fregio della Caccia della II Tomba reale di Vergina». Dialogues d'histoire ancienne 17, 1, 1991, p. 257-304.

PRICE 1974 = M. PRICE, Coins of the Macedonians. London 1974.

PRICE 1991 = M. PRICE, The Coinage in the Name of Alexander the Great and Philip Arrhidaeus. London 1991.

REUER, FABRIZII-REUER 1988 = E. REUER, S. FABRIZII-REUER, «The Pella Burial Ground: A Preliminary Report». Rivista di Antropologia 66, 1988, p. 261-266.

RHOMAIOS 1951 = Κ. Α. ΡΩΜΑΙΟΣ. Ὁ Μακεδονικός τάφος τῆς Βεργίνας. Athens 1951.

RHOMAIOS 1954 = Κ. Α. ΡΩΜΑΙΟΣ, «Τό ανάκτορο τῆς Παλατίτσας», Arch. Eph. 1953-1954, p. 141-150.

RHOMIOPOULOU, TOURATSOGLOY 1971 = Κ. ΡΩΜΙΟΠΟΥΛΟΥ, Ι. ΤΟΥΡΑΤΣΟΓΛΟΥ, «Ὁ μακεδονικός τάφος τῆς Νιάουστας», Arch. Eph. 1971, p. 146-164.

RHOMIOPOULOU 1973 = Κ. RHOMIOPOULOU, «A New Monumental Chamber Tomb with Paintings of the Hellenistic Period Near Lefkadia,

West Macedonia», AAA VI, 1973, p. 87-92.

ROBERTSON 1965 = M. R. ROBERTSON, «Greek Mosaics», JHS 85, 1965, p. 72-89.

ROBERTSON 1967 = M. R. ROBERTSON, «Greek Mosaics. A Postscript», JHS 87, 1967, p. 133-136.

ROBERTSON 1975 = M. R. ROBERTSON, A History of Greek Art. Cambridge 1975.

ROBERTSON 1982 = M. R. ROBERTSON, «Early Greek Mosaics», in Macedonia and Greece, 1982, p. 241-249.

ROBINSON 1930, 1938, 1942, 1946 = D. M. ROBINSON, Excavations at Olynthus II, 1930; VIII, 1938; XI, 1942; XII, 1946. Baltimore, London.

ROGER 1939 = J. ROGER, «Le monument au Lion d'Amphipolis», BCH 63, 1939, p. 4-42.

ROLLEY 1965 = Cl. ROLLEY, «Le sanctuaire des dieux patrôoi et le Thesmophorion de Thasos», BCH 89, 1965, p. 441-483.

ROLLEY 1986 = Cl. ROLLEY, «Le sanctuaire d'Evraiokastro. Mise à jour du dossier», in Μνήμη Λαζαρίδη, 1986, p. 405-408.

ROUVERET 1989 = A. ROUVERET, Histoire et Imaginaire de la peinture ancienne (vᵉ siècle av. J.-C. — Iᵉʳ siècle apr. J.-C.). Rome 1989.

ROUX 1961 = G. ROUX, L'Architecture en Argolide aux IVᵉ et IIIᵉ siècles av. J.-C. Paris 1961.

ROUX 1981-1 = G. ROUX, «Samothrace, le sanctuaire des Grands Dieux et ses mystères», Bull. de l'Association Guillaume-Budé 1, 1981, p. 2-23.

ROUX 1981-2 = G. ROUX, «Problèmes déliens: le Néôrion», BCH 105, 1981, p. 61-71.

ROUX 1989 = G. ROUX, «L'inventaire ID 1403 du Néôrion délien», BCH 113, 1989, p. 261-275.

SAATSOGLOU-PALIADELI 1984 = Χ. ΣΑΑΤΣΟΓΛΟΥ-ΠΑΛΙΑΔΕΛΗ. Τὰ ἐπιτάφια μνημεῖα ἀπό τῆ Μεγάλη Τούμπα τῆς Βεργίνας. Thessalonike 1984.

SAATSOGLOU-PALIADELI 1987 = Chr. SAATSOGLOU-PALIADELI, «A Dedication of Eurydice, Daughter of Sirras, to Eukleia at Vergina» (in Gr.), in Ἀμητός 1987, p. 733-744.

SAATSOGLOU-PALIADELI 1989 = Chr. SAATSOGLOU-PALIADELI, «Vergina 1989, The Sanctuary of Eukleia», Μακεδονία καὶ Θράκη 3, 1989, p. 25-35.

SAKELLARIOU 1982 = M. B. SAKELLARIOU (ed.), Macedonia, 4000 years of Greek History and Civilization. Athens 1982.

SALZMANN 1982 = D. S. SALZMANN, Untersuchungen zu den Antiken Kieselmosaiken. Berlin 1982.

SALVIAT 1960 = F. SALVIAT, «Le bâtiment de scène du théâtre de Thasos», BCH 84, 1960, p. 300-316.

SMARTZIDOU 1987 = S. SAMARTZIDOU, «Recent Finds from the Cemeteries of Ancient Amphipolis» (in Gr.), Μακεδονία καὶ Θράκη 1, 1987, p. 327-341.

SCHEFOLD, AUBERSON 1972 = K. SCHEFOLD, P. AUBERSON, *Führer durch Eretria*. Berne 1972.

SCHEFOLD 1975 = K. SCHEFOLD, «Der zweite Stil als Zeugnis alexandrinischer Architektur», in B. ANDRAE, H. KYRIELEIS (ed.), *Neue forschungen in Pompeji*, Becklinghausen 1975.

SCHLEIF, ZSCHIETZSCHMANN 1944 = H. SCHLEIF, W. ZSCHIETZSCHMANN, «Das Philippeion», in KUNZE, SCHLEIF 1944, p. 1-52.

SCHULLER, HOEPFNER, SCHWANDNER 1989 = W. SCHULLER, W. HOEPFNER, E. L. SCHWANDNER (ed.), *Demokratie und Architektur, Der hippodamische Städtebau und die Enstehung des Demokratie*. Munich 1989.

Search for Alexander 1980 = *The Search for Alexander*. Exhibition. Toronto 1980.

SEYRIG 1965 = H. SEYRIG, «Un édifice et un rite de Samothrace», *CRAI* 1965, p. 105-109.

SIGANIDOU 1982 = Μ. ΣΙΓΑΝΙΔΟΥ, «Ἡ ἰδιωτικὴ κατοικία στὴν ἀρχαία Πέλλα», *Ἀρχαιολογία* 2, 1982, p. 31-36.

SIGANIDOU 1983 = Μ. ΣΙΓΑΝΙΔΟΥ, «Πέλλα. Πορίσματα ἀνασκαφῶν τριετίας 1981-1983», *Ancient Macedonia IV*, 1983 (1986), p. 553-558.

SIGANIDOU 1986 = M. SIGANIDOU, «Problèmes d'urbanisme à Pella» (in Gr.), in *Μνήμη Λαζαρίδη* 1986, p. 167-174.

SIGANIDOU 1987-1 = M. SIGANIDOU, «Pella Fortifications» (in Gr.), in *Ἀμητός* 1987, p. 765-779.

SIGANIDOU 1987-2 = M. SIGANIDOU, «The Palace of Pella» (in Gr.), *Μακεδονία καὶ Θράκη* 1, 1987, p. 119-124.

SIGANIDOU 1987-3 = Μ. ΣΙΓΑΝΙΔΟΥ, «Τὸ ἀνάκτορο τῆς Πέλλας», in *Pella* 1987, p. 24-26.

SIGANIDOU, 1989 = M. SIGANIDOU, «The Monumental Propylon of the Palace of Pella», *Μακεδονία καί Θράκη* 3, 1989, p. 59-66.

Sindos 1985 = Σίνδος. Κατάλογος τῆς ἔκθεσης στό Ἀρχαιολογικό Μουσεῖο Θεσσαλονίκης, 1985.

SINN 1979 = V. SINN, *Die homerischen Becher. Hellenistische Reliefkeramik aus Makedonien (AM Beih. 7)*. Berlin 1979.

SISMONDO RIDGWAY 1990 = B. SISMONDO RIDGWAY, *Hellenistic Sculpture* I. Madison, Wisconsin 1990.

SIVIGNON 1983 = M. SIVIGNON, «The Geographical Setting of Macedonia», in *Macedonia* 1983, p. 12-26.

SIX 1925 = J. SIX, «Nikomachos et la peinture d'un hypogée macédonien de Niausta», *BCH* 49, 1925, p. 263-280.

SOTERIADIS 1932 = Γ. ΣΩΤΗΡΙΑΔΗΣ, «Ἀνασκαφαὶ ἐν Δίῳ. Ὁ καμαρωτὸς τάφος», *Ἐπετ. φιλ. Πανεπιστ. Θεσσ.*, 2, 1932, p. 5-19.

STEFANIDOU 1975 = Θ. ΣΤΕΦΑΝΙΔΟΥ, «Ἐπιτύμβια στήλη ἀπὸ τὸ Δίον Πιερίας», *Deltion* 30, 1975, p. 35-43.

STEFANIDOU-TIVERIOU 1987 = Th. STEFANIDOU-TIVERIOU, «Research of the Northern Wall of Dion» (in Gr.), *Μακεδονία καὶ Θράκη* 1, 1987, p. 189-199.

STEFANIDOU-TIVERIOU 1988 = Th. STEFANIDOU-TIVERIOU, «Probleme der hellenistischen Stadtbefestigung von Dion» (in Gr.), *Μακεδονία καὶ Θράκη* 2, 1989, p. 153-160.

STEVENS 1949 = G. P. STEVENS, «Model of the Monument of the Lion of Amphipolis», in *Mélanges Charles Picard*. Paris 1949, p. 993-995.

TAPIE 1972 = V. L. TAPIE, *Baroque et Classicisme*. Paris 1972.

TARDITI 1990 = C. TARDITI, «Architettura come propaganda. Esame dell'attività edilizia degli Antigonidi in Grecia e nuove proposte di attibuzione», *Aevum Ant.*, 3, 1990, p. 43-74.

THOMAS 1989 = E. THOMAS, «Nikomachos in Vergina?», *AA* 1989, p. 219-226.

THOMPSON 1982 = H. A. THOMPSON, «Architecture as a Medium of Public Relations among the Successors of Alexander», in *Macedonia and Greece*, 1982, p. 173-189.

TIVERIOS 1986-1 = M. TIVERIOS, «Archaische Keramik aus Sindos», *Makedonika* 25, 1985-6, p. 70-87.

TIVERIOS 1986-2 = M. TIVERIOS, «Restes d'un sanctuaire préhellénistique au bord du golfe Thermaïque», in *Μνήμη Λαζαρίδη* 1986, p. 71-88.

TIVERIOS 1988 = M. TIVERIOS, «Local Pottery of the 6th and 5th Centuries B. C. from Sindos» *Μακεδονία καὶ Θράκη* 2, 1988, p. 297-302.

TOMLINSON 1968 = R. A. TOMLINSON, «Ancient Macedonian Symposia», *Ancient Macedonia* I, 1968 (1970), p. 308-315.

TOMLINSON 1973 = R. A. TOMLINSON, «Vaulting Techniques of the Macedonian Tombs», *Ancient Macedonia* II, 1973 (1977) p. 473-479.

TOMLINSON 1974 = R. A. TOMLINSON. «Thracian and Macedonian Tombs Compared», in *Thracia*, Symposium III, Sofia, p. 247-250.

TOMLINSON 1983 = R. A. TOMLINSON, «The Ceiling Painting of the Tomb of Lyson and Kallikl[id]es at Lefkadia», *Ancient Macedonia* IV, 1983 (1986) p. 607-610.

TOMLINSON 1987 = R. A. TOMLINSON, «The Architectural Context of the Macedonian Vaulted Tombs», *ABSA* 82, 1987, p. 305-312.

TOMLINSON 1990 = R. A. TOMLINSON, «The Chronology of the Perachora Hestiatorion and its Significance», in O. MURRAY (ed.), *Sympotica*, Oxford 1990, p. 95-101.

TOUCHAIS 1987, 1988, 1989 = G. TOUCHAIS, *BCH, Chronique des fouilles*, 111, 1987, p. 557; 112, 1988, p. 668; 113, 1989, p. 663.

TOURATSOGLOU 1973 = I. ΤΟΥΡΑΤΣΟΓΛΟΥ, *Λευκάδια*, Keramos Guides. Athens 1973.

TOURATSOGLOU 1975 = I. ΤΟΥΡΑΤΣΟΓΛΟΥ, «Μεταλεξάνδρεια Πέλλα», *Deltion* 30, *Melet.*, 1975, p. 165-184.

TRAKOSSOPOULOU-SALAKIDOU 1987 = E. TRAKOSSOPOULOU-SALAKIDOU, «Ancient Akanthos: the City and the Cemetery», *Μακεδονία καί Θράκη* 1, 1987, p. 295-304.

Treasures 1979 = *Treasures of Ancient Macedonia*, Arch. Museum of Thessalonike. Athens 1979.

TREHEUX 1987 = J. TREHEUX, «Sur le Néôrion à Délos», *CRAI* 1987, p. 168-184.

TRIPODI 1991 = Br. TRIPODI, «Il fregio della *Caccia* della II Tomba reale di Vergina e le cacce funerarie d'Oriente». *Dialogues d'histoire ancienne,* 17,1,1991, p. 143-209.

TSIMBIDOU-AULONITE 1987 = M. TSIMBIDOU-AULONITE, «Burial Mounds in the Provinces of Thessaloniki and Chalcidice», *Μακεδονία καὶ Θράκη* 1, 1987, p. 261-268.

TZOUVARA-SOULI 1979 = Χρ. ΤΖΟΥΒΑΡΑ-ΣΟΥΛΗ, Ἡ λατρεία τῶν γυναικείων θεοτήτων εἰς τὴν ἀρχαίαν Ἤπειρον, 1979.

VALLOIS 1923 = R. VALLOIS, *Exploration archéologique de Délos VII. Le portique de Philippe*. Paris 1923.

VALLOIS 1944 = R. VALLOIS, *L'Architecture hellénique et hellénistique à Délos I. Les monuments*. Paris 1944.

VASIC 1979 = R. VASIC, «Das Weihgeschenk des Krateros in Delphi und die Löwenjagd in Pella», *Ant. K.* 22, 1979, p. 106-109.

VAVRITSAS 1973 = A. ΒΑΒΡΙΤΣΑΣ, «Ἐπιγραφὴ ἐξ Ἀραβησσοῦ Πέλλης», *Ancient Macedonia* II, 1973 (1977), p. 7-11.

VAVRITSAS 1983 = A. ΒΑΒΡΙΤΣΑΣ, «Ἐπιγραφές ἀπὸ τήν ἀρχαία Ἔδεσσα», *Ancient Macedonia* IV, 1983 (1986), p. 53-69.

VELENIS 1987 = G. VELENIS, «Recent Research of the Hellenistic Houses of Petres» (in Gr.), *Μακεδονία καὶ Θράκη* 1, 1987, p. 9-18.

VELENIS, ADAM-VELENI 1988 = G. VELENIS, P. ADAM-VELENI, «Excavational Evidence of the Hellenistic City of Petres» (in Gr.), *Μακεδονία καί Θράκη* 2, 1988, p. 5-17.

VICKERS 1972 = M. VICKERS, «Hellenistic Thessaloniki», *JHS* 92, 1972, p. 156-170.

VOKOTOPOULOU, KOUKOULI-CHRYSANTHAKI 1988 = I. VOKOTOPOULOU, C. KOUKOULI-CHRYSANTHAKI, «The Early Iron Age», *Ancient Macedonia* 1988, p. 79-83.

VOKOTOPOULOU 1990 = I. ΒΟΚΟΤΟΠΟΥΛΟΥ, «Οἱ ταφικοί τύμβοι τῆς Αἴνειας». Athens 1990.

VOLLMOELLER 1901 = K. G. VOLLMOELLER, «Über zwei euböische Kammergräber mit Totenbetten», *AM* 26, 1901, p. 333-376.

WÖLFFLIN 1888 = H. WÖLFFLIN, *Renaissance und Barok*. Munich 1888.

WÖLFFLIN 1915 = H. WÖLFFLIN, *Kunstgeschichtliche Grundbegriffe*. Munich 1915.

INDEX OF GEOGRAPHICAL NAMES AND NAMES OF PEOPLES

INDEX OF PERSONS, HEROES, DEITIES

Achilles: 116.
Aeropos: 40, 41.
Aeschines: 20, 53.
Agathodaimon: 113.
Agathon: 40.
Agelaos: 222.
Aiakos: 180.
Aleuadai (family): 40, 42.
Alexander I: 19, 21, 22, 26, 27, 28, 40.
Alexander II of Epirus, son of Pyrrhos: 68.
Alexander III, the Great (often referred to by name alone, without further qualification): 13, 14, 49, 53, 55, 56, 57, 60, 62-66, 74, 75, 79, 80, 91, 94, 101, 104, 108, 109, 114, 121, 136, 161, 162, 166, 202, 211, 214, 228, 229.
Alexander IV: 64, 65, 101, 117.
Alexander, son of Krateros, nephew of Antigonos Gonatas: 68.
Amazon: 116, 121.
Amyntas I: 26.
Amyntas II ('the Small'): 41.
Amyntas III: 41, 42, 43, 89, 106, 148.
Amyntas, brother of Perdikkas II: 41.
Amyntas, Macedonian of the 4th century: 196.
Anaxagoras: 188.
Andriskos: 226.
Antigonos Doson: 67, 70, 71, 73, 75, 76, 223.
Antigonos Gonatas, son of Demetrios Poliorketes: 67, 68, 70, 73, 74, 75, 87, 201, 213.
   Stoa of Antigonos Gonatas: 196, 197, 202.
Antigonos (Monophthalmos): 64, 65, 66.
Antiochos III: 223, 224.
Antiope: 116.
Antipatros: 60, 64, 76.
Anubis: 116.
Apelles: 132.
Aphrodite: 96, 106, 113.
   Aphrodite Epitragia: 113.
   Aphrodite Hypolympidia: 106, 116.

Apollo: 52, 75, 108.
   Apollo Dekadryos: 108.
Aratos: 73.
Archelaos: 40, 41, 43, 91.
Argaios: 41.
Ariadne: 114, 175, 188.
Aristotle: 46, 91.
Arrhidaios, father of Amyntas III: 41.
Arrhidaios: see Philip III - Arrhidaios.
Arsinoe II: 206.
   Rotunda of Arsinoe: 206.
Artemis
   Artemis Digaia Blaganitis: 113.
   Artemis Eileithyia: 98, 106, 116.
   Artemis Eukleia: 106, 110.
   Artemis Tauropolos: 108.
Asklepiadai: 116.
Asklepios: 108, 114, 116.
Astion: 188.
Atargatis: 116.
Athena: 75, 108, 109, 196.
Athena Alkidemos: 75, 113.
Attalos I: 222, 223.
Attis: 103.
Augustus: 46.
Auloneitis: 116.

Bacchylides: 27.
Bardylis: 41, 42.

Cassander, son of Antipatros: 65, 66, 67, 73, 74, 75, 79, 91, 99, 101.
Centauress: 121, 133.
Centaurs: 121, 134.
Choirilos: 40.
Cleomenes III: 73.
Cybele: 96, 103.
Darius: 26, 62, 63, 162.
Deianeira: 116, 117, 118.
Demeter: 29, 97, 106, 108, 184.
Demetrios I Poliorketes, son of Antigonos: 65-68, 75, 76, 84, 201, 215.
Demetrios II: 67, 70, 75, 76.
Demetrios of Pharos: 222.

Demetrios, son of Philip V: 224.
Demosthenes: 13, 20, 46, 50, 52, 53.
Diodorus Siculus: 46, 108, 151.
Dionysos: 95, 98, 106, 108, 117, 121, 127, 132, 133, 134, 175, 187, 188.
Doson: see Antigonos Doson.

Eleusis Painter: 160.
Eros: 103, 110, 113, 114.
Erotes hunting: 136.
Eukleia: 79, 106.
Eumenes II of Pergamon: 224, 225, 226.
Euphraios: 42.
Euripides: 40, 114, 142, 153.
Eurydice, wife of Amyntas: 41, 42, 106, 161, 196.
   Tomb of Eurydice: 57, 148, 150, 154, 161, 187.
Eurydice, wife of Philip Arrhidaios: 65, 79, 166.

Fates: 184.
Flamininus: see Quinctius Flamininus.

Gnosis: 95, 121, 129, 132.
Gonatas: see Antigonos Gonatas.
Great Gods: 202, 206.

Hades: 114, 150, 160, 188.
Hecuba: 154.
Helen: 94, 95, 116, 117, 118, 127, 129.
Hellanikos: 27.
Hephaistion: 151.
Hera: 160, 194.
Herakles: 75, 106, 116, 188, 194.
   Herakles Kynagidas: 108, 116.
   Herakles Patroos: 86.
Hermaphrodite: 114.
Hermes: 180, 181.
Herodotus: 26, 27, 60.
Hippodamos of Miletus: 43.
Hippokrates: 40.
Hygeia: 104, 108, 116.

GLOSSARY

ACROTERION: carved ornament set over the peak and the corners of a pediment.

AGORA: public area with a variety of functions, especially religious, civic, commercial and craft.

AGORANOMOS: magistrate in charge of regulating the markets that might be held in the Agora.

ALABASTRON: small vase (frequently imitating Egyptian vases made of alabaster) intended to contain perfumed oil.

ALEXANDRIAN: coin with an image of Alexander the Great.

AMPHICTYONY: association of cities around a common sanctuary.

AMPHORA: vase basically intended for the transportation of liquids, equipped with two vertical handles. The panathenaic amphora was awarded as a prize to the victor in the games in honour of Athena.

ANDRON: reception room in the Greek house reserved for male banquets.

ANTA: treatment of the end of a wall as a vertical pillar. Walls with antae stood on either side of a room, and were connected by a colonnade, said to be in antis

ANTEFIX: ornament of various types adorning the upper line of the gutter and thus marking the base of the roof; also ornament adorning the sides of a pediment.

ANTHEMION: floral decoration, often with a row of alternating palmettes and lotus flowers.

ARCHITRAVE: architectural element forming the lower part of the Greek entablature; this beam, running directly above the columns, below the frieze, is also called an epistyle.

ARCHON: leader, of a confederation for example; also, a magistrate in a city, who might discharge a wide variety of functions.

BASILEIA, pl. BASILEIAI: office of 'king', which evolved at Athens and elsewhere into a kind of magistracy, filled by election and held for a limited period.

BUCRANIUM: representation of an ox-skull.

CELLA: main room of a temple.

CHILIARCH: commander of an army corps of about 1,000 men.

CHITON: item of clothing for men or women, a kind of close-fitting dress; often worn with the himation

CHLAMYS: light cloak, worn mainly by young men.

CHRYSELEPHANTINE (technique): combination of the use of gold and ivory in a sculpture.

CHTHONIC: relating to the Earth, as opposed to Heaven.

CIST: form of grave with walls faced with slabs or perhaps bordered with low brick walls.

CORNICE: see FRIEZE, MUTULE

CYMATION: ornamental moulding, consisting of egg-and-dart pattern, if it is Ionic and leaf-and-dart pattern, if it is Lesbian.

DEMOCRAT: member of a political regime in which power was in the hands of the 'people' (demos), as opposed to the oligarchs.

DIADOCHI: the first generation of the successors of Alexander the Great, who disputed his legacy in wars that resulted, about 280 BC, in its division into independent kingdoms.

DIAGRAMMA, pl. DIAGRAMMATA: circular letter issued by a king.

DIKASTES: citizen serving as a juror in a court (at Athens, this was the Heliaia, which was competent to try most cases).

DITHYRAMBIC: connected with dithyramb, a circular dance in honour of Dionysos.

DRACHMA: coin with a weight of one hundredth part of a mina. See also tetradrachm, octodrachm.

DROMOS: race-track; passageway giving access to a subterranean tomb.

ECHINUS: lower part of a Doric capital, treated as a curve with varying degrees of elongation.

ENKOIMETERION: annex of the sanctuary of Asklepios in which the sick person spent the night while waiting for the god to appear in a dream.

ENTABLATURE: the group of elements in Greek architecture above the columns; it normally consisted of the architrave, frieze and cornice.

EPHEBIC: relating to the young men who were completing their military service (applied, for example, to a law).

EPISTATES: 'placed in charge', a magistrate with a variety of functions, depending on the period and the place.

EPISTYLE: synonym for architrave.

EPONYMOUS: with reference to a priest, for example, one who gives his name to the year.

ETHNOS: social group occupying a fixed space and thus forming a political base unit. It is therefore a 'people', though the word can also sometimes be translated by 'region' or 'territory of the people'.

EUERGETES: title accorded to the 'benefactor' of a social group.

EXETASTES: magistrate responsible for checking.

FASCIA: moulding with a flat, slightly projecting profile.

FRIEZE: element of the entablature between the architrave and the cornice; it had a series of metopes and triglyphs in the Doric order, but was plain in the Ionic.

GORGONEION: representation of a Gorgon's head with prophylactic power.

GUTTA: see MUTULE

GYMNASIUM: educational establishment devoted as much to sport as to study. Its heart was the palaestra, and it also had a xystos, paradromis, etc.

GYMNASIARCH: magistrate in charge of running the gymnasium.

HAWKSBEAK: moulding with a profile recalling a bird's beak. The upper part may be treated as either an ovolo or an ogee curve.

HEGEMON: 'leader', especially military leader.

HELIAIA (court of the -): popular court consisting of a large number of jurors which, at Athens, was competent over all cases except those involving murder.

HEROON: building erected in honour of a hero, at which his cult was practised.

HETAIROS: 'companion', title given to those close to the kings of Macedonia.

HEXASTYLE: having a colonnade with six columns.

HIMATION: cloak made of a simple piece of cloth, like a shawl, and worn equally by women and men.

HYDRIA: vase for carrying and pouring liquid (water, according to its etymology), with two horizontal handles and a vertical handle on the same axis as the spout.

ISODOMIC: applied to masonry constructed of blocks usually of equal lengths, laid in courses of equal height.

KANTHAROS: drinking vessel with two vertical handles rising above the sides.

KOINE: word, meaning 'common', indicating the language formed on the basis of the ancient dialects that established itself throughout Greece in the Hellenistic period.

KORE: statue of a young woman, often richly dressed, rendered in a conventional pose.

KOUROS: statue of a young man, often completely naked, rendered in a conventional pose.

KYNEGOS: adjective meaning 'the hunter', applied to a patron deity of hunting.

LANTERN: normally the central part of a roof raised above a building complex for lighting purposes.

MEGARON: the most important room in the palaces of the pre-Hellenic world, rectangular in shape with an axial opening on one of the short sides and a hearth in the centre; often preceded by an antechamber of the same width. This scheme was the origin of the Greek temple.

METOPE: slab of stone, often decorated, alternating with the triglyphs to form the frieze in the Doric order.

MINA: weight regarded as the standard for coins, varying from city to city (it was 436 grammes in Attica and 628 in the Peloponnese).

MUTULE: ornament in the form of a plaque, carved in relief on the lower part of the cornice. It was itself decorated with small cylinders, the guttae.

NEORION: place for storing a boat, and gallery for displaying a ship of exceptional interest.

NOMOPHYLAX: 'guardian of the law', title of a magistrate responsible for ensuring the implementation of the law.

NYMPHAION: building designed for the cult of the Nymphs, deities of water and also of inspiration, like the Muses; and, like the museum in which the latter were honoured, the nymphaion could be an educational building.

OCTODRACHM: coin with a value of 8 drachmas.

OLIGARCH: member of a political regime in which power is restricted to 'a small number', in opposition to democrat.

OPUS SECTILE: kind of pavement in which the elements are slabs of stone cut into geometric shapes.

OPUS SEGMENTATUM: mosaic technique in which small, irregularly shaped plaques are set in a layer of plaster.

OPUS TESSELATUM: see tessera

ORTHOSTATE: block placed vertically in a row to form the lower part of walls constructed in an advanced masonry style.

OVOLO: moulding with an egg-shaped profile, and which was also often decorated with egg-and-dart pattern.

PALAESTRA: part of a gymnasium with rooms, normally around a courtyard, devoted to all the exercises associated with sport, to conferences and to bathing.

PARADROMIS: uncovered track which, in the gymnasium, was used for training in running events, or simply to stroll.

PARASKENION: structure projecting at either side of the theatre proscenium.

PASTAS: kind of portico in the Greek house that ran along a series of rooms normally located on the north side of the courtyard.

PATERA: kind of cup, often used for libations.

PELTAST: soldier armed with a small round shield, belonging to the light infantry.

PERIBOLOS: perimeter wall normally enclosing a sanctuary.

PERIPTERAL: describes a building surrounded by columns.

PETASOS: wide-brimmed hat.

PEZHETAIROS: soldier in the Macedonian army regarded to be a 'foot companion' of the king and, therefore, a body-guard of a lesser grade than the cavalryman, who was of noble family.

PHALANX: Macedonian military organisation 'in a line'.

PHIALE: bowl without a base, often used for libations.

POLIS pl. POLEIS: the 'city', that is, the unit comprising the city and the territory dependent on it; this was the basic political unit in the Greek world, often also called 'city-state'.

POLITARCH: civic magistrate.

POROS: soft limestone with a granular structure.

PROPYLON: monumental entrance (also PROPYLAEA)

PROSKENION: dais in front of the wall of the stage in the theatre, on which the actors appeared.

PROSKYNESIS: act of prostration in front of an important person.

PROSTYLE: describes a building with a colonnade not in antis in front of a room.

PROTOME: representation of the upper part of the human body or the front part of an animal.

PROXENOS: title accorded to a person recognised as a 'guest', who also cared for the interests of the awarding city and its citizens in his home city.

PSEUDO-ISODOMIC: masonry in which the blocks, normally of equal length, are laid in alternating high and low courses.

REGULA: flat, narrow moulding underneath each triglyph.

RHYTON: vase from which a stream of liquid could be poured, sometimes modelled in the form of an animal, or part of an animal.

SATRAPY: division of the Persian empire, governed by a satrap.

SCOTIA: moulding with a characteristic profile consisting of a convex curve beneath a concave one.

SKOIDOS: title of a magistrate in Macedonia, administrator or treasurer.

SOFA: form of pilaster capital, bordered at either end by a vertical surmounted by a volute, resembling a sofa.

STADE: unit of length equal to roughly 180 m, the length of the 'stadium' where the athletes ran.

STATER: coin with a weight twice that of the drachma. The double stater is also known.

STRATEGOS: general of an army, and also governor of a region.

STRIGIL: metal instrument with a handle, used by athletes to scrape their skin clean.

STYLOBATE: row of stone blocks on which the columns rested.

SYMPOSIUM: gathering of men to 'drink together'.

SYNEDRION: council of people 'sitting together', and the place in which their meetings were held.

TAENIA: moulding forming a flat, narrow band.

TAGOS: head of the Thessalian League; more generally, commander-in-chief.

TALENT: unit of weight and coinage, equal to 60 minae (see DRACHMA)

TEMENID: name of the first Macedonian dynasty, which was traditionally thought to be a branch of the royal house of the Temenids of Argos; it ruled from the middle of the seventh century to the end of the fourth century BC.

TESSERA: small, roughly square piece of stone or terracotta used for the mosaic technique called opus tessellatum.

TETRADRACHM: coin with a value of 4 drachmas.

THEARODOKOS: person responsible for en-

TRIGLYPH: slab with three vertical grooves (in reality, two and two halves), alternating with metopes in the Doric frieze.

TUMULUS: mound of earth accumulated above a tomb.

UNGUENTARIUM: vase for ointment.

XYSTE: the word, which means 'shaven, polished', designates a covered gallery in the gymnasium, the floor of which was perfectly levelled for training in bad weather.

tertaining envoys from another city or sanctuary who have come to announce the date of the next holding of a festival and sacred contest.

THEOROS: sacred envoy.

THOLOS: rotunda.

THYRSOS: wand of Dionysos, often covered with ivy leaves and ending in a pine cone.

TORUS: moulding characterised by its convex profile.

LIST OF FIGURES

This table gives, for each figure, the information not contained in the caption — the place where the object is kept (if there is such a place), and the source of the visual document or photograph. The expression 'Source EKDOTIKE' refers to EKDO-TIKE ATHENON S.A., Athens, the co-publisher of this book.

Cover: Vergina, Tomb of Eurydice. The back of the throne, detail: two of Hades' horses. Source M. Andronicos.

Fig. 1. Vergina, Tomb of Eurydice. The burial chamber. Source M. Andronicos.

Fig. 2. Dionysiac group in ivory. Vergina, Tomb of the Prince. Thessalonike Archaeological Museum. Source EKDOTIKE.

Fig. 3. Pella, Mosaic of the Stag Hunt, central panel. Source EKDOTIKE.

Fig. 4. Macedonian helmet. Wall-painting. Lefkadia, Tomb of Lyson and Kallikles. Source EKDO-TIKE.

Fig. 5. Figure of Victory, bronze cheekpiece. Tymphaia. Thessalonike Archaeological Museum, Source EKDOTIKE.

Fig. 6. Scenery of Mount Olympos. The forest. Source R. Ginouvès.

Fig. 7. The excavation of Aiane, acropolis. Upper terraces. Source G. Karamitrou-Mentessidi.

Fig. 8. Physical map of Macedonia. M. Hatzopoulos EDKOTIKE.

Fig. 9. The Haliakmon near its mouth. Source R. Ginouvès.

Fig. 10. The site of Edessa. Source M. Hatzopoulos.

Fig. 11. A Macedonian lake. Source M. Hatzopoulos.

Fig. 12. Female figurine from Nea Nikomedia. Clay. Beroia Museum. Source EKDOTIKE.

Fig. 13. 'Mycenaean' style amphora, from Ano Komi, Kozani Archaeological Collection. Source G. Karamitrou-Mentessidi.

Fig. 14. Head of a 'Mycenaean' figurine in clay, from Ano Komi. Kozani Archaeological Collection. Source G. Karamitrou-Mentessidi.

Fig. 15. The kingdom of the Argeadai towards the end of the sixth century BC, with the acquisitions of Alexander I (479-442 BC). M. Hatzopoulos EKDOTIKE.

Fig. 16. Coin: Thraco-Macedonian stater with Satyr and Nymph. Paris, Cabinet des médailles. Source Bibliothèque nationale.

Fig. 17. Silver Thraco-Macedonian octodrachm. Paris, Cabinet des médilles. Source Bibliothèque nationale.

Fig. 18. Silver octodrachmn of Alexander I. Paris, Cabinet des médailles. Source Bibliothèque nationale.

Fig. 19. Ionic capital found at Aiane. Source G. Karamitrou-Mentessidi.

Fig. 20. Terracotta head found at Aiane. Source G. Karamitrou-Mentessidi.

Fig. 21. Aiane, acropolis. The terrace with the stoa. Source G. Karamitrou-Mentessidi.

Fig. 22. Aiane, cemetery. Source G. Karamitrou-Mentessidi.

Fig. 23. Miniature iron cart, found in a tomb at Sindos. Thessalonike Archaeological Museum. Source Thessalonike Archaeological Museum.

Fig. 24. Plaque on the shape of a lozenge, found in a tomb at Sindos. Thessalonike Archaeological Museum. Source Thessalonike Archaeological Museum.

Fig. 25. Gold funerary mask and bronze helmet, found in a tomb at Sindos. Thessalonike Archaeological Museum. Source Thessalonike Archaeological Museum.

Fig. 26. Silver sandal-soles. Vergina, fourth Archaic tomb. Thessalonike Archaeological Museum. Source M. Andronicos.

Fig. 27. Gold earrings. Vergina, second Archaic tomb. Thessalonike Archaeological Museum. Source M. Andronicos.

Fig. 28. Gold pin-heads. Vergina, same provenance. Thessalonike Archaeological Museum. Source M. Andronicos.

Fig. 29. Gold fibulae. Vergina, same provenance. Thessalonike Archaeological Museum. Source M. Andronicos.

Fig. 30. Gold necklace. Vergina, same provenance. Thessalonike Archaeological Museum. Source M. Andronicos.

Fig. 31. Head of a woman. Vergina, same provenance. Thessalonike Archaeological Museum. Source M. Andronicos.

Fig. 32. Female terracotta head. Vergina, fourth Archaic tomb. Thessalonike Archaeological Museum. Source M. Andronicos.

Fig. 33. Female terracotta head. Vergina, same provenance. Thessalonike Archaeological Museum. Source M. Andronicos.

Fig. 34. Male terracotta head. Vergina, same provenance. Thessalonike Archaeological Museum. Source M. Andronicos.

Fig. 35. Male terracotta head. Vergina, same provenance. Thessalonike Archaeological Museum. Source M. Andronicos.

Fig. 36. Silver diobol of Archelaos I. Paris, Cabinet des médailles. Source Bibliothèque nationale.

Fig. 37. Silver tetradrachm of Amyntas III. Paris, Cabinet des médailles. Source Bibliothèque nationale.

Fig. 38. The Lion of Chaironeia. Source R. Ginouvès.

Fig. 39. Arrow-head with the name of Philip, bronze, found at Olynthos. Thessalonike Archaeological Museum. Source EKDOTIKE.

Fig. 40. Portrait of Philip, ivory. Thessalonike Archaeological Museum. Source EKDOTIKE.

Fig. 41. Macedonia and Greece at the death of Philip II. M. Hatzopoulos EKDOTIKE.

Fig. 42. The site of Philippoi. Source R. Ginouvès.

Fig. 43. Thessalian horseman. Stele from Pelinna. Paris, Louvre Museum. Source EKDOTIKE.

Fig. 44-45. Coin of the Amphictyony. Paris, Cabinet des médailles. Source Bibliothéque nationale.

Fig. 46. The site of Corinth. Source R. Ginouvès.

Fig. 47-48. Gold stater of Philip II. Paris, Cabinet des médailles. Source Bibliothèque nationale.

Fig. 49-50. Silver tetradrachm of Philip II. Paris, Cabinet des médailles. Source Bibliothèque nationale.

Fig. 51. The Alexander sarcophagus, from Sidon. Istanbul Museum. Source EKDOTIKE.

Fig. 52. Portrait of Alexander, ivory. Thessalonike Archaeological Museum. Source EKDOTIKE.

Fig. 53-54. Silver tetradrachm, known as an 'Alexandrian'. Paris, Cabinet des médailles. Source Bibliothèque nationale.

Fig. 55-56. Silver tetradrachm of Demetrios Poliorketes. Paris, Cabinet des médailles. Source Bibliothèque nationale.

Fig. 57. Head of a Gaul. Rome, National Museum. Source Giraudon.

Fig. 58. Boscoreale, villa of Fannius Sinistor: wall-painting. Source EKDOTIKE.

Fig. 59. The Acrocorinth. Source R. Ginouvès.

Fig. 60. The plain of Sparta. Source R. Ginouvès.

Fig. 61. Scenery in Arkadia, the gorge of Gortynios near Gortys. Source R. Ginouvès.

Fig. 62. Silver tetradrachm of Demetrios Poliorketes. Paris, Cabinet des médailles. Source Bibliothèque nationale.

Fig. 63-64. Antigonos Doson. Paris, Cabinet des médailles. Source Bibliothèque nationale.

Fig. 65. Iron cuirass with applied gold decoration. Found at Vergina in the Tomb of Philip. Thessalonike Archaeological Museum. Source EKDOTIKE.

Fig. 66. Helmet of Macedonian type. Thessalonike Archaeological Museum. Source EKDOTIKE.

Fig. 67. Inscription from Dion. Dion Museum. Source D. Pandermalis.

Fig. 68. Vergina, Palace. Room A and south-east corner of the courtyard. Source R. Ginouvès.

Fig. 69. Vergina, palace, aerial photograph. Source EKDOTIKE.

Fig. 70. Vergina. Reconstruction of palace, plan. Source EKDOTIKE.

Fig. 71. Vergina, palace. View of the complex looking south-west. Source R. Ginouvès.

Fig. 72. Vergina, palace. Entrance to the anteroom F. Source R. Ginouvès.

Fig. 73. Vergina, palace. Threshold of room E. Source R. Ginouvès.

Fig. 74. Pella, palace. General plan. Source I. Akamatis.

Fig. 75. Pella, palace. Base of engaged half-column. Source I. Akamatis.

Fig. 76. Pella, palace. Ionic capital. Source I. Akamatis.

Fig. 77. Pella, palace. Sofa capital. Source I. Akamatis.

Fig. 78. Pella, the city. Plan of the building insulae. Source I. Akamatis.

Fig. 79. Pella, the city. Aerial view. Source EKDOTIKE.

Fig. 80. Pella, the House of Dionysos. Source I. Akamatis.

Fig. 81. Pella, the Agora. Plan. Source I. Akamatis.

Fig. 82. Pella, the Agora. The buildings on the east side. Source I. Akamatis.

Fig. 83. Dion, the Sanctuary of Demeter. Source R. Ginouvès.

Fig. 84. Dion, the Greek theatre, aerial view. Source D. Pandermalis.

Fig. 85. Dion, the city. Plan. Source D. Pandermalis.

Fig. 86. Dion, the city. The fortification wall. Source D. Pandermalis.

Fig. 87. Dion, the city. The Monument of the Shields. Source R. Ginouvès.

Fig. 88. Dion, cemetery. A 'Macedonian Tomb'. Source D. Pandermalis.

Fig. 89. Amphipolis, fortifications. Source D. Lazaridou.

Fig. 90. Amphipolis, the gymnasium. Source D. Lazaridou.

Fig. 91. Amphipolis, the gymnasium. The baths. Source D. Lazaridou.

Fig. 92. Amphipolis, the city. Another mural decoration. Source D. Lazaridou.

Fig. 93. Amphipolis, the city. Mural decoration. Source D. Lazaridou.

Fig. 94. Amphipolis, the lion. Source R. Ginouvès.

Fig. 95. Head of Demeter. Found at Dion. Dion Museum. Source D. Pandermalis.

Fig. 96. Poseidon, bronze statuette. Found at Pella. Pella Museum. Source I. Akamatis.

Fig. 97. Athena with bull's horns, terracotta statuette. Pella Museum. Source I. Akamatis.

Fig. 98. Aphrodite seated, holding a winged Eros, terracotta statuette. Found at Beroia. Beroia Museum. Source I. Akamatis.

Fig. 99. Aphrodite with a mask of Silenos, terracotta statuette. Found at Beroia. Beroia Museum. Source I. Akamatis.

Fig. 100. Alexander with horns of Pan. Marble statue. Pella Museum. Source I. Akamatis.

Fig. 101. Herakles dressed as Omphale. Bronze from the decoration of a bed. Dion Museum. Source D. Pandermalis.

Fig. 102. Cult statue of Aphrodite Hypolympidia. Dion Museum. Source D. Pandermalis.

Fig. 103. Vergina, palace. Mosaic in room E, overall view. Source EKDOTIKE.

Fig. 104. Vergina, palace. Mosaic in room E, detail. Source EKDOTIKE.

Fig. 105. Pella, Mosaic of the Abduction of Helen. Overall view, drawing. After MAKARONAS, GIOURI 1989, plan 3.

Fig. 106. Pella. Mosaic of the Stag Hunt. Overall view, drawing. After MAKARONAS, GIOURI 1989, plan 3.

Fig. 107. Pella, Mosaic of the Amazonomachy. Overall view, drawing. After MAKARONAS, GIOURI 1989, plan 3.

Fig. 108. Mosaic of the Amazonomachy, central panel. Source EKDOTIKE.

Fig. 109. Pella, threshold mosaic: the Centauress. Source M. Lilimbakis-Akamatis.

Fig. 110. Pella. Mosaic of Dionysos, threshold. Griffin attacking a stag. Source EKDOTIKE.

Fig. 111. Pella. Mosaic of Dionysos. Central panel. Source EKDOTIKE.

Fig. 112. Pella. Mosaic of the Lion Hunt. Source EKDOTIKE.

Fig. 113. Pella, House of Dionysos. Aerial view. Source EKDOTIKE.

Fig. 114. Pella, House of Dionysos. Room A: mosaic with inscribed squares. Detail. Source A.-M. Guimier-Sorbets.

Fig. 115. Vergina, palace. Mosaic in room E. Detail of the centre. Source A.-M. Guimier-Sorbets.

Fig. 116. Pella, Tholos Building. Mosaic of the tholos. Drawing. After MAKARONAS, GIOURI 1989, pl. 26

Fig. 117. Pella, South House. Mosaic in the andron, overall view, drawing. Source M. Lilimbakis-Akamatis.

Fig. 118. Pella, House of Dionysos. Room D, mosaic with the chequer board pattern of lozenges. Source A. Guimier-Sorbets

Fig. 119. Pella, Mosaic of the Abduction of Helen. Detail, head of Phorbas. After MAKARONAS, GIOURI 1989, pl. 16.

Fig. 120. Pella, Mosaic of Dionysos. Detail: head of the god. Source A. Guimier-Sorbets.

Fig. 121. Pella, Mosaic of the Stag Hunt. Detail, head of the hunter at the left. Source EKDOTIKE.

Fig. 122. Lefkadia, Great Tomb. Burial Chamber. Source Archaeological Society at Athens.

Fig. 123. Two black-glaze bowls. Pella Museum. Source I. Akamatis.

Fig. 124. Black-glaze kantharos with 'West Slope' decoration. Pella Museum. Source I. Akamatis.

Fig. 125. Pyxis lid with 'West Slope' decoration. Pella Museum. Source I. Akamatis.

Fig. 126. 'Megarian' relief bowl with floral and figure decoration. Pella Museum. Source I. Akamatis.

Fig. 127. 'Megarian' bowl with a scene of the Sack of Troy. Pella Museum. Source I. Akamatis.

Fig. 128. Vergina, Tomb of Philip. The façade. Source EKDOTIKE.

Fig. 129. Vergina, Tomb of Philip. Model. Source EKDOTIKE.

Fig. 130. Door of a tomb. Thessalonike Archaeological Museum. Source R. Ginouvès.

Fig. 131. Funerary couch. Vergina, tomb in the Bella tumulus. Stone. Source EKDOTIKE.

Fig. 132. Silver cup. Vergina, Tomb of Philip. Source EKDOTIKE.

Fig. 133. Gilded silver strainer. Vergina, Tomb of Philip. Source EKDOTIKE.

Fig. 134. Silver oinochoe. Vergina, Tomb of Philip. Source EKDOTIKE.

Fig. 135. Vergina, Tomb of Eurydice. The throne, seen from the side. Source M. Andronicos.

Fig. 136. Vergina, Tomb of Eurydice. The throne, seen from the front. Source M. Andronicos.

Fig. 137. Vergina, Tomb of Eurydice. The back of the throne. Source M. Andronicos.

Fig. 138. Vergina, Tomb of Philip. Fresco of the Hunt. Detail. Source EKDOTIKE.

Fig. 139. Vergina, Tomb of Philip. Gold funerary chest. Source EKDOTIKE.

Fig. 140. Vergina, Tomb of Philip. Funerary cloth. Source EKDOTIKE.

Fig. 141. Vergina, Tomb of Philip. Myrtle wreath. Source EKDOTIKE.

Fig. 142. Vergina, Tomb of Philip. Gold oak wreath. Source EKDOTIKE.

LIST OF AUTHORS

This list gives the names of the authors and references to the texts for which they are responsible.

Ioannis Akamatis

The cities: Pella 91-96

Manolis Andronicos

From the Archaic period to the middle of the fifth century:
The tombs of Vergina 35-38
The 'Macedonian Tombs' 147-190

Aikaterini Despinis

From the Archaic period to the middle of the fifth century:
The tombs of Sindos 33-35

Stella Drougou

The Pottery 138-143

René Ginouvès

Preface 9-10
Introduction 16
From the Archaic period to the middle of the fifth century Artistic life 28-29
From the middle of the fifth century to Philip II: Artistic life 42-43
The Macedonia of Philip II: Aristic life 57
Alexander and the Diadochi: Artistic life 180
The palace at Vergina 84-88
The palace at Pella 88-91
Macedonian dedications outside Macedonia 192-221
Macedonia in Greek history 229

Anne-Marie Guimier-Sorbets

Mosaic 117-136
Parietal art 136-138

Miltiades Hatzopoulos

The rediscovery of Macedonia 14-15
The natural and human resources 19-22
The rise of Macedonia 23-27, 40-41
The Macedonia of Philip II: the political institutions 55-57
The language: the origins of the *koine* 79-80
The sanctuaries 106-109

Lilly Kahil

Iconography of gods and myths 109-117

Georgia Karamitrou-Mendessidi

Aiane 29-32

Kalliopi D. Lazaridou

The cities: Amphipolis 101-106

Dimitris Pandermalis

The cities: Dion 97-101

Olivier Picard

From the Archaic period to the middle of the fifth century: the coinage 27-28
The Macedonia of Philip II 46-55
Alexander and the Diadochi: the coinage 74-76

Michael Sakellariou

Alexander and the Diadochi 60-74, 76-79
The end of the Macedonian kingdom 220-226

TABLE OF CONTENTS

Library of Congress Cataloging-in-Publication Data

Ginouvès, René.
  [Macédoine, English]
  Macedonia: from Philip II to the Roman conquest / René Ginouvès
[with the collaboration of] Iannis Akamatis... [et al.] ;
translated by David Hardy.
      p.   cm.
  Includes bibliographical references and index.
  ISBN 0-691-03635-7 (CL)
  1. Macedonia--Civilization. 2. Greece--History--Macedonian
Expansion, 359-323 B.C. 3. Macedonia--History--To 168 B.C.
4. Philip II. King of Macedonia, 382-336 B.C. 5. Alexander, the
Great, 356-323 B.C. 6. Macedonia--Antiquities. I. Akamatēs,
Giannēs M. II. Title.
DF233, G5613   1994   93-38156
938 . 1--dc20   CIP

Produced in Greece by Ekdotike Athenon S.A.
Printed by Ekdotike Hellados S.A.
Phototypesetting: F. Panagopoulos & Co